Cognitive Psychology
and Its Implications

Cognitive Psychology
and Its Implications.

Second Edition

John R. Anderson

CARNEGIE-MELLON UNIVERSITY

W. H. Freeman and Company
New York

Library of Congress Cataloging in Publication Data

Anderson, John Robert 1947–
    Cognitive psychology and its implications.

    (A series of books in psychology)
    Bibliography: p.
    Includes index.
    1. Cognition. I. Title. II. Series. [DNLM:
1. Cognition. BF 311 A547c]
BF311.A5895 1985   153   84-18687
ISBN 0-7167-1686-0

Printed in the United States of America

2 3 4 5 6 7 8 9 0 MP 3 2 1 0 8 9 8 7 6 5

This book is dedicated to

Gordon H. Bower

who has inspired me in countless discussions and
from whom I have learned the most
about cognitive psychology

Contents

4. Perception-Based Knowledge Representations

7. Memory Elaboration and Reconstruction

8. Problem Solving

11. Language: An Overview

12. Language Comprehension   335

13. Language Generation

14. Cognitive Development 400

Preface

To the Student

This is an exciting time to be a cognitive psychologist. Although the status of cognitive psychology is not yet that of a mature science, we can bring into focus the emerging outline of its permanent scope. Using new and sophisticated techniques, researchers are generating a body of knowledge that when adequately developed will have enormous implications for understanding the structure of human experience. For many of you, the very concept of cognitive psychology will be a little unclear as you begin this book. I have attempted to explain as clearly as possible the theoretical and experimental foundations for our current understanding of higher mental processes. Of equal importance are the many illustrations where the findings of the field are already being applied. I have tried to identify areas of current investigation that show promise for application to our daily lives.

Although experimental results and concepts are analyzed and discussed, it has been necessary to impose some organization on the field, reflecting to some extent my own theoretical biases. At all times, particular attention has been paid to bridging the gap between the world of the laboratory and our experience in everyday living.

To the Instructor

This is a revision of my 1980 book. While it maintains the same style and much of the same content, there have been some substantial changes. Some of these changes have been in response to the rich set of comments I have received over the years from colleagues. I have also introduced three new chapters. Two, on the neural basis of cognition and expert problem solving, were motivated by recent developments in the field. The third, on cognitive development, repairs a serious omission in the original book. Throughout I have tried to update the book with the significant developments of the past five years. To make room, I have tightened the presentation, focusing more on the most important research. In doing this I was particularly helped by the comments of my colleagues on the topics they thought should be discussed.

The text is intended to be covered in a single-semester course. The chapters develop the field in a fairly systematic manner, and although later chapters do build on earlier ones, instructors can resequence the chapters if they choose. The only two obstacles to reordering are the materials on semantic networks (Chapter 5) and production systems (Chapter 8). These formalisms do reappear in later chapters, and if the later chapters are covered before Chapters 5 and 8, the instructor should provide students with advice about how to understand these formalisms. Experience with the first edition indicates that if this is done there is no difficulty in assigning the chapters out of order.

Numerous people have commented on this second edition, and it is much better for their efforts. Lynn Hasher and Tom Trabasso read the entire manuscript. Those who read parts of the manuscript include James Anderson, Bill Chase, Robert Crowder, Michael Gazzaniga, Geoff Hinton, David Klahr, Alan Lesgold, Brian MacWhinney, Alan Paivio, Jim Pomerantz, Lynne Reder, Lance Rips, and Bob Siegler. I also acknowledge the many people who read the first edition: Elizabeth Bjork, Lyle Bourne, John Bransford, Bill Chase, Charles Clifton, Lynne Cooper, Robert Crowder, Susan Fiske, Ellen Gagne, Lynn Hasher, Lynne Hyah, Marcel Just, Stephen Keele, Stephen Kosslyn, Clayton Lewis, Elizabeth Loftus, Allen Newell, Donald Norman, Gary Olson, Allan Paivio, Jane Perlmutter, Peter Polson, Lynne Reder, Stephen Reed, Russell Revlin, Lance Rips, Miriam Schustack, Ed Smith, Kathryn Spoehr, Charles Tatum, David Tieman, Tom Trabasso, and Henry Wall. Their influence still shows strongly in the book.

The students in the classes I have taught over the years at Carnegie-Mellon University have also provided valuable input. Peggy Galdi and Janet Mazurek have worked on all stages of the manuscript preparation. I owe them a considerable debt of gratitude.

Cognitive Psychology
and Its Implications

Chapter 1

The Science of Cognition

Summary

1. Cognitive psychology attempts to understand the nature of human intelligence and how people think.

2. The study of cognitive psychology is motivated by scientific curiosity, by the desire for practical applications, and by the need to provide a foundation for other fields of social science.

3. People have written about human cognition for over 2000 years. Only in the last 100 years, however, has cognition been studied scientifically. In the last 30 years knowledge about human cognition has greatly increased.

4. Cognitive psychology is dominated by the *information-processing approach*, which analyzes cognitive processes into a sequence of ordered *stages*. Each stage reflects an important step in the processing of cognitive information.

Our species is referred to as *homo sapiens*, or "man, the intelligent." This term reflects the general belief that intelligence is what distinguishes us from other animals. The goal of cognitive psychology is to understand the nature of human intelligence and how it works. Subsequent chapters in this book discuss what cognitive psychologists have discovered about various aspects of human intelligence. This chapter attempts to answer the following preliminary questions:

Why do people study cognitive psychology?

Where and when did cognitive psychology originate?

What are the methods of cognitive psychology as a science?

Motivations

Intellectual Curiosity

One reason for studying cognitive psychology motivates any scientific inquiry—the desire to know. In this respect, the cognitive psychologist is like the tinkerer who wants to know how a clock works. The human mind is a particularly interesting device that displays remarkable adaptiveness and intelligence. We are often unaware of the extraordinary aspects of human cognition. Just as we can easily overlook the enormous accumulation of technology that permits a sports event on television to be broadcast live from Europe, so we can forget how sophisticated our mental processes must be to enable us to understand and enjoy that sportscast. One would like to understand the mechanisms that make such intellectual sophistication possible.

The inner workings of the human mind are far more intricate than the most complicated systems of modern technology. Researchers in the field of artificial intelligence (AI) are attempting to develop programs that will enable computers to display intelligent behavior. Although this field has been an active one for more than 25 years, AI researchers still have no idea how to

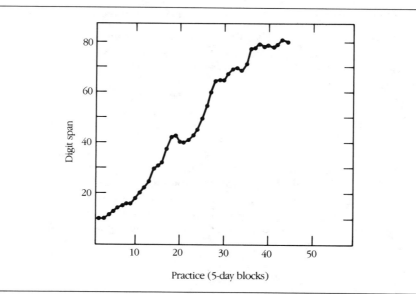

Figure 1-1   The growth in the memory span of the subject SF with practice. Notice how the number of digits he can recall increases gradually but continually with the number of practice sessions. (From Chase & Ericsson, 1983.)

create a truly intelligent computer. No existing programs can recall facts, solve problems, reason, learn, or process language with anything approximating human facility. This lack of success has occurred not because computers are inferior to human brains but because we do not yet know how human intelligence is organized.

Consider the performance of the subject SF, who was studied by Chase and Ericsson (1982) on what is called the memory-span task. On Saturday, December 15, 1979, he was presented with 81 random digits at the rate of 1 digit per second. He then proceeded to reel off the 81 digits perfectly. The average human can recall from 7 to 9 digits with great effort, and almost no one can recall more than 10. Was SF superhuman? Not at all; he was an ordinary undergraduate who trained his memory span according to the principles of cognitive psychology. Figure 1-1 illustrates how his memory span grew over 264 training sessions.

When we look at what gives rise to extraordinary mental feats like SF's, we find that the people involved use abilities that we all have, but that they have developed these abilities in special ways. This book will try to identify what these mental processes are and how they develop with experience.

Practical Applications

The desire to understand is an important motivation to the study of cognitive psychology, as it is in any science, but the practical implications of the field constitute an important secondary motivation. If we really understand how people acquire knowledge and intellectual skills and how they perform feats of intelligence, then we will be able to improve their intellectual training and performance accordingly.

It seems inevitable that cognitive psychology will prove beneficial to both individuals and society. Many of our problems derive from an inability to deal with the cognitive demands made on us. These problems are being exacerbated by the "information explosion" and the technological revolution we are presently experiencing. Cognitive psychology is just beginning to make headway on these issues, but some clear and positive insights with direct application to everyday life have already emerged. For instance, in their recent book, Card, Moran, and Newell (1983) discuss how cognitive psychology can be used to design computer systems.

At many points in this book, research in cognitive psychology will be shown to have implications for study skills. Students who read this text and learn the lessons it has to offer will improve the capacity of their intellects, at least modestly. And, on a larger scale, by the turn of the century the lessons of cognitive psychology will have momentous consequences for intellectual performance. So one reason for studying cognitive psychology and for encouraging its development as a field is to enable people to be more effective in their intellectual pursuits.

Implications for Other Fields

Students and researchers interested in other areas of psychology or social science have another reason for following developments in cognitive psychology. Cognitive psychology attempts to understand the basic mechanisms governing human thought, and these basic mechanisms are important in understanding the types of behavior studied by other social science fields. For example, understanding how humans think is important to understanding why certain thought malfunctions occur (clinical psychology), how people behave with other individuals or in groups (social psychology), how persuasion works (political science), how economic decisions are made (economics), why certain ways of organizing groups are more effective and stable than others (sociology), or why natural languages have certain constraints (linguistics). Cognitive psychology studies the foundation on which all other social sciences stand.

It is certainly true, nonetheless, that much social science has developed without a grounding in cognitive psychology. Two facts account for this situation. First, cognitive psychology is not very advanced. Second, other areas of social science have managed to find higher order principles unrelated to cognitive mechanisms to explain the phenomena in which they are interested. However, much is unknown or poorly understood in these other fields. If we knew how these higher order principles were explained in terms of cognitive mechanisms and how to apply cognitive mechanisms directly to higher order phenomena, we might have a firmer grasp on the phenomena in question. Thus, throughout this text, the implications of cognitive psychology for other areas of social science are cited.

The History of Cognitive Psychology
Early History

In Western civilization, interest in human cognition can be traced to the ancient Greeks. Plato and Aristotle, in their discussions of the nature and origin of knowledge, speculated on memory and thought. These early discussions, which were essentially philosophical in nature, eventually developed into a centuries-long debate. The antagonists were the empiricists, who believed that all knowledge comes from experience, and the nativists, or rationalists, who argued that children come into the world with a great deal of innate knowledge. The debate intensified in the seventeenth, eighteenth, and nineteenth centuries, with such British philosophers as Locke, Hume, and Mill arguing for the empiricist view and such Continental philosophers as Descartes and Kant propounding the nativist view. Though these arguments were at their core philosophical, they frequently slipped into psychological speculations about human cognition. It will be clear throughout this book, but particularly in Chapter 11, on language, and in Chapter 14, on cognitive development, that this debate is still with us.

During this long period of philosophical debate, such sciences as astronomy, physics, chemistry, and biology developed markedly. Curiously, no concomitant attempt was made to apply the scientific method to the understanding of human cognition; this undertaking did not take place until the end of the nineteenth century. Certainly, no technical or conceptual barriers existed to studying cognitive psychology earlier. In fact, many of the experiments performed in cognitive psychology could have been performed and understood in the time of the Greeks. But cognitive psychology, like many other sciences, suffered because of our egocentric, mystical, and confused attitude about ourselves and our own nature. It had seemed inconceivable before the nineteenth century that the workings of the human mind could be susceptible to scientific analysis. As a consequence, cognitive psychology as a science is only 100 years old and lags far behind many other sciences in sophistication. We have spent much of the first 100 years freeing ourselves of the pernicious misconceptions that can arise when people engage in such an introverted enterprise as a scientific study of human cognition. It is the case of the mind studying itself.

Psychology in Germany

The date usually cited as marking the beginning of psychology as a science is 1879, when Wilhelm Wundt established the first psychology laboratory in Leipzig, Germany. Wundt's psychology was cognitive psychology (in contrast to other major divisions of psychology, such as physiological, comparative, clinical, or social), although he had far-ranging views on many subjects. The method of inquiry used by Wundt, his students, and a large portion of the early psychologists was *introspection*. In this method, highly trained observers reported the contents of their consciousness under carefully controlled conditions. The basic belief was that the workings of the mind should be open to self-observation. Thus, to develop a theory of cognition, a psychologist had only to develop a theory that accounted for the contents of introspective reports.

Let us consider a sample introspective experiment. Mayer and Orth (1901) had their subjects perform a free-association task. The experimenters spoke a word to the subjects and then measured the amount of time the subjects took to generate responses to this word. Subjects then reported all their conscious experiences from the moment of stimulus presentation until the response was generated. To get a feeling for this method, try to generate an associate to each of the following words; after each association try to introspect on the contents of your consciousness during the period between reading the word and making your association:

coat

book

dot

bowl

In Mayer and Orth's experiment, many reports were given of rather non-describable conscious experiences. Whatever was in consciousness, it did not seem to involve sensations, images, or other things that subjects in these laboratories were accustomed to reporting. This result started a debate on the issues of *imageless thought*—whether conscious experience could really be devoid of concrete content. As we will see in Chapter 5, this issue is still very much with us.

Psychology in America

Introspective psychology was not well accepted in America. Psychology in America at the turn of the century was largely an armchair avocation, in which the only self-inspection was casual and reflective rather than intense and analytic. William James's (1890) *Principles of Psychology* reflects the best of this tradition, and many of its proposals are still relevant and cogent today. The mood of America was determined by the philosophical doctrines of pragmatism and functionalism. Many of the psychologists of the time were involved in education, and the demand was for an "action-oriented" psychology that would be capable of practical application. The intellectual climate in America was not receptive to a psychology focused on such questions as whether or not the contents of consciousness were sensory.

One of the important figures of early American scientific psychology was Edward Thorndike, who developed a theory of learning that was directly applicable to school situations. Thorndike was interested in such basic questions as the effects of reward and punishment on rate of learning. To him, conscious experience was just excess baggage that could be largely ignored. As often as not, his experiments were done on infrahuman animals such as cats. Animals involved fewer ethical constraints than humans with regard to experimenting, and Thorndike was probably just as happy that such subjects could not introspect.

While introspection was being ignored at the turn of the century in America, it was getting into trouble on the Continent. Different laboratories were reporting different types of introspections—each type matching the theory of the particular laboratory form which it emanated. It was becoming clear that introspection did not give one a clear window onto the workings of the mind. Much that was important in cognitive functioning was not open to conscious experience.

These two factors, the "irrelevance" of the introspective method and its apparent contradictions, set the groundwork for the great behaviorist revolution in American psychology, which occurred around 1920. John Watson and other behaviorists led a fierce attack, not only on introspectionism, but also on any attempt to develop a theory of mental operations. Psychology, according to the behaviorists, was to be entirely concerned with external behavior and was not to try to analyze the workings of the mind that underlay this behavior:

> Behaviorism claims that consciousness is neither a definite nor a usable concept. The Behaviorist, who has been trained always as an experimentalist, holds further that belief in the existence of consciousness goes back to the ancient days of superstition and magic. (Watson, 1930, p. 2)

> ... The Behaviorist began his own formulation of the problem of psychology by sweeping aside all medieval conceptions. He dropped from his scientific vocabulary all subjective terms such as sensation, perception, image, desire, purpose, and even thinking and emotion as they were subjectively defined. (Watson, 1930, p. 5)

The behaviorist program and the issues it spawned all but eliminated any serious research in cognitive psychology for 40 years. The rat supplanted the human as the principal laboratory subject, and psychology turned to finding out what could be learned by studying animal learning and motivation. Quite a bit was discovered, but little was of direct relevance to cognitive psychology.

In retrospect, it is hard to understand how behaviorists could have taken an antimental stand and clung to it so long. Just because introspection proved to be unreliable did not mean that it was impossible to develop a theory of internal structure and process. It only meant that other methods were required. In physics, a theory of atomic structure was developed, although that structure could not be directly observed but only inferred. But behaviorists argued that a theory of internal structure was not necessary to an understanding of human behavior, and in a sense they may have been right (see Anderson & Bower, 1973, pp. 30–37). However, a theory of internal structure makes understanding human beings much easier. The success of cognitive psychology during the past 30 years in analyzing complex intellectual processes testifies to the utility of such concepts as mental structures and processes.

In both the introspectionist and the behaviorist programs, we see the human mind struggling with the effort to understand itself. The introspectionists held a naive belief in the power of self-observation. The behaviorists were so afraid of falling prey to subjective fallacies that they refused to let themselves think about mental processes. Modern cognitive psychologists seem to be much more at ease with their subject matter. They have a relatively detached attitude toward human cognition and approach it much as they would any other complex system.

The Reemergence of Cognitive Psychology

Three main influences account for the modern development of cognitive psychology. The first was the development of what has been called the information-processing approach, which grew out of human-factors work and information theory. Human factors refers to research on human skills and performance. This field was given a great boost during World War II, when practical information on these topics was badly needed. Information theory is a branch of communication sciences that provides an abstract way of analyzing the processing of knowledge. The work of the British psychologist Donald Broadbent at the Applied Psychology Research Unit in Cambridge was probably most influential in integrating ideas from these two fields and developing the information-processing approach. He developed these ideas most directly with regard to perception and attention, but the analyses now pervade all of cognitive psychology. The characteristics of the information-processing approach are discussed later in this chapter. Although other types of analysis in cognitive psychology exist, information-processing is the dominant viewpoint and the main one presented in this book.

Closely related to the development of the information-processing approach were developments in computer science, particularly artificial intelligence, which tries to get computers to behave intelligently. Allen Newell and Herbert Simon (at Carnegie-Mellon University) have spent 30 years educating cognitive psychologists in the implications of artificial intelligence (and educating workers in artificial intelligence about the implications of cognitive psychology). The direct influence of computer-based theories on cognitive psychology has always been minimal. The indirect influence, however, has been enormous. A host of concepts has been taken from computer science and used in psychological theories. Probably more important, observing how we could analyze the intelligent behavior of a machine has largely liberated us from our inhibitions and misconceptions about analyzing our own intelligence.

The third field of influence on cognitive psychology is linguistics. In the 1950s, Noam Chomsky, a linguist at the Massachusetts Institute of Technology, began to develop a mode of analyzing the structure of language. His work showed that language was much more complex than had previously been believed and that many of the prevailing behavioristic formulations were incapable of explaining these complexities. Chomsky's linguistic analyses proved critical in enabling cognitive psychologists to fight off the prevailing behavioristic conceptions. George Miller, at Harvard University in the 1950s and early 1960s, was instrumental in bringing these linguistic analyses to the attention of psychologists and in identifying new ways of studying language.

Cognitive psychology has grown rapidly since the 1950s. A very important event was the publication of Ulric Neisser's book *Cognitive Psychology* in 1967. This book gave a new legitimacy to the field. The book consisted of six chapters on perception and attention and four chapters on language, memory, and thought. Note that this chapter division contrasts sharply with that of this book, which has one chapter on perception and eleven on language, memory, and thought. The chapter division in my book reflects the growing emphasis on higher mental processes. Following Neisser's work, another important event was the beginning of the journal *Cognitive Psychology* in 1970. This journal has done much to give definition to the field.

More recently there has emerged a new field, called *cognitive science*, which attempts to integrate research efforts from psychology, philosophy, linguistics, and artificial intelligence. This field can be dated from the appearance of the journal *Cognitive Science* in 1976. The fields of cognitive psychology and cognitive science overlap. It is not profitable to try to define precisely the differences, but cognitive science makes greater use of methods such as computer simulation of cognitive processes and logical analysis, which are not dominant methods in the rest of psychology. This book draws from both cognitive science and cognitive psychology.

The Methods of Cognitive Psychology

The Need for an Abstract Analysis

How do we go about studying human cognitive functioning? An obvious but naive answer is that we study the physiological mechanisms that underlie the behavior. For example, in this context, to understand how people do mathematics, why not simply inspect their brains and determine what goes on there when they are solving mathematics problems? Serious technical obstacles must be overcome, however, before the physiological basis of behavior can be studied in this way. But even assuming that these obstacles could be properly overcome, the level of analysis required is simply too detailed to be useful. The brain is composed of more than 10 billion nerve cells. Millions are probably involved in solving a mathematics problem. Suppose we had a listing that explained the role of each cell in solving the problem. Since this listing would have to describe the behavior of millions of individual cells, it would not offer a very satisfactory explanation for how the problem was solved. A neural explanation is too complex and detailed to adequately describe sophisticated human behavior. We need a level of analysis that is more abstract.

Computers offer an interesting analogy to help us understand the need for an abstract analysis. Like the brain, a computer consists of millions of components. For any interesting computer task—for example, solving a problem in mathematics such as integration—trying to understand the overall behavior of the machine by studying the behavior of each of its physical components is hopeless. However, high-level programming languages exist for specifying the behavior of the computer. The computer has an *interpreter* for converting each statement in the higher level language into a large number of low-level statements that specify what the physical components of the computer should do. These high-level programming languages can be quite abstract and thus obviate the need to consider many of the physical details of the computer. A person can often obtain a good understanding of the behavior of the computer by studying the high-level computer program. A cognitive theory should be like a computer program. That is, it should be a precise specification of the behavior, but offered in terms sufficiently abstract to provide a conceptually tractable framework for understanding the phenomenon.

As an example of an abstract term in a high-level programming language, consider the LISP programming language, used in creating artificial-intelligence programs, in which there is an associative-retrieval function called GET. This function can be used to retrieve concepts related to other concepts. For instance, to retrieve the capital of the United States, a person might evoke the function GET, giving it the terms USA and CAPITAL (called arguments). The function will return WASHINGTON (called a value). The person need not specify the detailed machine operations that underlie this act. The GET function identifies that portion of the computer's memory that stores information about the United States, searches that portion for the name of the capital, and then returns the answer Washington. This GET function is the sort of concept that would be useful in a cognitive theory. To a large degree, cognitive psychology has been engaged in a search for the right set of higher level concepts with which to describe human intelligence.

What, then, is the relationship between cognitive psychology and physiological psychology? Certainly, cognitive psychologists believe their concepts can be explained in physiological terms, even as computer scientists believe that their programming constructs can be explained in terms of the machine's components. Cognitive psychology is to physiological psychology much as computer science is to electrical engineering. The results from physiological experiments can set constraints on the form of cognitive theories but they do not prescribe these theories. For instance, knowledge about the amount of information the brain can store could serve to rule out certain theories of memory as impossible. Chapter 2 will consider some of the ways knowledge of neural functioning can influence cognitive theorizing.

Information-Processing Analysis

In this chapter the phrase *information processing* has already been bandied about, and you may well have encountered it elsewhere in psychology. What does it really mean? Again, let us begin to answer the question with an analogy. Suppose we followed a letter in a successful passage through the postal system. First, the letter would be put in a mailbox; the mailbox would be emptied and contents brought to a central station. The letter would be sorted according to region, and the letters for a particular region shipped off to their destination. There they would be sorted again as to area within the postal district. Letters having the same destination would be given to a carrier, and the carrier would deliver the letter to the correct address.

Now, just as we traced the letter through the postal system, let us follow this question as it is processed through the human mind:

Where does your grandmother live?

First, you must identify each word and retrieve its meaning. Then you must determine the meaning of this configuration of words, that is, understand the question being asked. Next, you must search your memory for the correct answer. Upon finding the answer in memory, you have to formulate a plan for generating the answer in words, and then transform the plan into the actual answer:

She lives in San Francisco.[1]

What we did in this example was to trace the flow of information through the mind. We use the term *information* to refer to the various mental objects operated on—the question, the representation of its meaning, the memory of where your grandmother lives, the plan for generating an answer, and so on. These objects, although mental and abstract, are analogous to the letter in the postal example. An important aspect of the analogy is that there is a clear *sequence* or *serial ordering* to the mental operations just as there is to the postal operations. The important characteristic of an information-processing analysis, then, is that it involves a tracing of a sequence of mental

---

[1]The fact that your grandmother probably does not live in San Francisco may not be the only inaccurate part of this example. The serial stages described would be somewhat controversial. This example is meant to illustrate the process of information processing, not specific stages.

operations and their products (information) in the performance of a particular cognitive task.

Such analyses are often given in flowchart form. A flowchart is a sequence of boxes, each of which reflects a stage of processing. Arrows from one box to another indicate the temporal sequencing (flow) of the stages. Figure 1-2 is a sample flowchart specifying how students should process the information in a chapter in this text. Each chapter begins with a short summary of the information found there. The first box in the figure specifies the process of studying this summary. In box 2, readers ask themselves if they are interested in learning more about these points. If they are not, an arrow goes from the box to the instruction to quit (in many class situations students will not have this option). If interested, they go on. Note the decision boxes (diamonds in this figure), where students must decide between a number of different paths for further processing. The existence of decision boxes indicates that a fixed sequence of steps will not always be taken.

In the third box, students are to make up a set of questions from the summary to keep in mind while reading the chapter. For instance, one of the summary points for this chapter is

> The study of cognitive psychology is motivated by scientific curiosity, by the desire for practical applications, and by the need to provide a foundation for other fields of social science.

In box 3, students might ask

> What are the practical applications of cognitive psychology?

In box 4, students are to skim the chapter to identify the major sections. Then to each section, they apply steps 5 through 9. They make up specific questions for the section to be read (box 5)—for example, a question for this section on the information-processing approach might be

> How do I interpret a flowchart such as Figure 1-2?

Next, students read the section fairly carefully (box 6) and determine whether the section questions can be answered (box 7). If not, students review the section (box 8) until the questions can be answered. If all the section questions can be answered, students go on, making up more questions if more sections remain to be read (box 9).

The final portion of the flowchart (boxes 10 through 13) involves an end-of-chapter review. Students check to see whether they can answer the questions written for the chapter (boxes 10 and 11). If they cannot, they go back and skim the sections containing the information relevant to the unanswered questions (boxes 12 and 13). Thus, this flowchart provides at a rather global level (in contrast to specifying how to read each sentence) a prescription for sequencing the processing of information in a chapter.

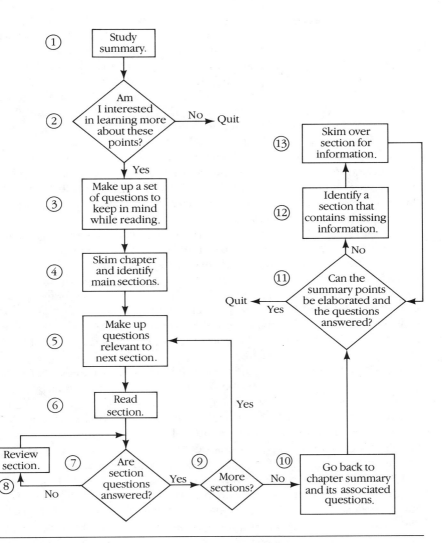

Figure 1-2 A flowchart of the procedure for studying this text.

How To Use This Book

We turn now to the substance of Figure 1-2 as a guide to study rather than as an example of information processing. Obviously, you will be the final judge of how best to study this book, but I recommend that you seriously consider following the scheme outlined in the figure. The chapter summaries are extremely important in this approach. Students have a natural tendency to skip over summaries and get to the "meat" of a text right away. However, research in our laboratory (Reder & Anderson, 1980) suggests that memory for a text is facilitated by initial study of a summary. The summaries are written in a deliberately terse style. Each point is central to the material, and each one is numbered. Take time to consider each point in the summary fully before starting the chapter text.

The summaries represent the most important points covered in the text. If you do not acquire and retain the information in the summary, there has been a serious failure of learning. Of course, I hope you will learn more than this from the chapters. However, what more you should learn should depend, in part, on your purposes.

The summaries serve three functions. First, they reflect the overall structure in each chapter. If you have learned a summary, you will know how the more specific points in the chapter relate to one another. Second, they serve to identify and define the most important new concepts and principles. The first stages of Figure 1-2 are intended to enable you to fix in memory these summary points and to prepare yourself for how the text will relate to the summary. Third, the summaries provide criteria against which you can test your learning of the material. The last stages (11, 12, and 13) of Figure 1-2 are concerned with this function.

To use these summaries to the greatest advantage, you are advised to make up a set of questions, based on the summaries, to keep in mind as you read the text. When you finish a chapter, you should be able to answer these questions and be capable of elaborating each sentence of the summary with at least three or four sentences of additional detail. This question-generation process will encourage you to think deeply about the text and to be aware of your goals in reading it. Another function of the process is to introduce some spacing into your study of the text. You are encouraged first to study the main points, then to skim the chapter, next to read each section carefully and to review each section, and finally to review the chapter. This pattern will allow you to review major points throughout your study of the chapter. In Chapters 7 and 12, where reading is covered in detail, the importance of question making and spaced study will be discussed more fully.

Remarks and Suggested Readings

Boring's (1950) book is a classic review of the early history of psychology. A broad up-to-date survey of current theory and research in cognitive psychology is the six-volume *Handbook of Learning and Cognitive Processes* edited by Estes (1975–1979). This work is designed for a knowledgeable scientist not particularly familiar with cognitive psychology.

There are a great many journals containing research relevant to cognitive psychology, but particularly important are the journals *Cognition*; *Cognitive Psychology*; *Cognitive Science*; *Journal of Verbal Learning and Verbal Behavior*; and *Memory and Cognition*. A recent popular review of cognitive science is Morton Hunt's book *The Universe Within*.

Chapter 2

The Neural Basis of Cognition

Summary

1. Neurons are the most important cells in the brain for neural information processing. They receive electrochemical messages on their dendrites and send messages to other neurons along their axons. The connection from one axon to a dendrite is called a *synapse*.

2. Information is represented in terms of continuously varying electrochemical activity of neurons. Neurons can increase the activity of other neurons on which they synapse (excitation), or decrease the activity (inhibition).

3. Cognition is achieved by patterns of neural activation in large sets of neurons. Permanent memories are encoded by changing the synaptic connections among neurons so that a pattern of activation in one set of neurons will produce a pattern in another set.

4. The cortex is the most evolutionarily advanced part of the brain. The left half of the cortex receives sensory input about the right side of the world and is specialized for symbolic processing. The right half of the cortex receives sensory input about the left side of the world and is specialized for spatial and other forms of perceptual processing.

5. Light falls on the retina of the eye and is converted into neural energy by a photochemical process. This information is sent by various neural paths to the visual cortex of the brain.

6. Low-level cells in the visual system detect simple patterns of spots of light and darkness in the visual field. These are combined at higher levels of the visual system to form bar and edge detectors.

7. David Marr has shown with a computer system that similar edges and bars in an image can be combined to identify the boundaries of objects.

A broad band of fibers, called the *corpus callosum*, connects the right and left halves of the brain. The corpus callosum has been surgically severed in some patients to prevent epileptic seizures. The operation is typically successful and patients seem to function as well as people who have not had such operations. However, careful psychological research has found differences between such patients and subjects who have not had this surgery. In one experiment, the word *key* was flashed on the left side of a screen the subject was looking at. When asked what was presented on the screen the subject was not able to say. However, the subject's left hand (but not the right) was able to pick out a key from a set of objects hidden from view.

This experiment, the background of which we will discuss in more detail later, illustrates the obvious point that the brain underlies cognition and that physical operations on the brain affect cognition. Perhaps more interesting than the problems these patients experienced is the fact that they did not have more serious cognitive deficits after such a major surgical procedure.

We are just beginning to understand the role of the brain in cognition. Usually, the more primitive the cognitive function, the more we understand about how the nervous system achieves it. We have a much greater degree of understanding of the role of the nervous system in simple sensation, motor control, and autonomic regulation than of its role in memory, problem solving, and language. However, we are slowly acquiring understanding in all areas of cognition. In some cases, this understanding takes the form of basic descriptive statements (for instance, such-and-such an area of the brain is involved in language). In other cases, this understanding takes the form of quite speculative proposals; for instance, we will discuss some of the neural mechanisms that may underly learning.

A great deal of research has been done on neural information processing, and this chapter will not attempt anything like an exhaustive review. Rather, the goal of this chapter is to sketch a few of the connections between neural processing and cognition so that you can get an idea of how cognition may actually be physically implemented in the human brain. At this stage in the development of the science, we cannot expect to fully understand the neural basis of cognition; however, even a fragmentary understanding provides an important perspective on the nature of cognition.

The Nervous System

The nervous system refers to more than just the brain. It refers to the various sensory systems that gather information from parts of the body and the motor system that controls movement. In some cases, the information processing that takes place outside the brain is considerable. From an information-processing point of view, the most important components of the nervous system are the neurons.[1] The human brain itself contains roughly 100 billion neurons, each of which may have roughly the processing capability of a medium-sized computer.[2] A considerable fraction of the 100 billion neurons are active simultaneously and do much of their information processing through interactions with one another. Imagine the information-processing power in 100 billion interacting computers! According to this view of the brain, there is more computational power in one 3-lb brain than in all the computers in the world. Lest you become overwhelmed by the brain, we note that it is not good at doing some things the computer does well. There are many tasks, like finding square roots, at which a hand calculator can outperform all 100 billion neurons. Understanding the strengths and weaknesses of the human nervous system is a major goal in understanding the nature of human cognition.

The Neuron

Neurons come in all shapes and sizes, depending on their exact location and function. (Figure 2-1 illustrates some of the variety.) There is, however, a generally accepted notion of what the prototypical neuron is like, and individual neurons match up with this prototype to greater or lesser degrees. This prototype is illustrated in Figure 2-2. The main body of the neuron is called the *soma*. Typically, the soma is 5–100 microns (μm, millionths of a meter) in diameter. Extending from the soma are a set of short branches called *dendrites*. Also attached to the soma is a long tube called the *axon*. The axon can vary in length from a few millimeters to a meter.

Axons provide the fixed paths by which neurons communicate with each other. The axon of one neuron extends toward the dendrites of others. At its end, the axon branches into a large number of terminal *arborizations*. Each arborization ends in terminal *buttons* that almost make contact with the dendrite of the other neuron. The gap separating the terminal button and the dendrite is typically in the range of .00001–.00005 millimeters (mm). This near contact between axon and dendrite is called a *synapse*. The most typical means of communication between neurons is that the axon terminal on one side of the synapse releases chemicals, called *neurotransmitters*, that act on

---

[1]Neurons are by no means the majority of cells in the nervous system; there are many others, such as glial cells, whose main function is thought to be supportive of the neurons.

[2]For instance, according to one view, each neuron computes on the order of 1000 multiplications and additions of real numbers every 10 msec.

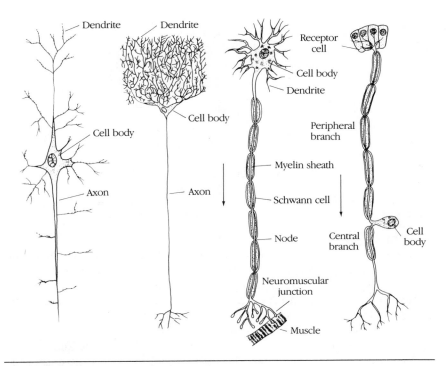

Figure 2-1   Some of the variety of neurons. (From Keeton, 1980.)

the membrane of the receptor dendrite to change its polarization, or electrical potential. The inside of the membrane covering the entire neuron tends to be 70 millivolts (mV; a millivolt is one one-thousandth of a volt, or .001 V) more negative than the outside due to the greater concentration of negative chloride ions inside and positive sodium and potassium ions outside. Depending on the nature of the neurotransmitter, the potential difference can decrease or increase. Synaptic connections that decrease the potential difference are called *excitatory* and synapses that increase the difference are called *inhibitory*.

In a mature adult the synaptic connections among neurons have all grown in, and new synapses are not formed among neurons. The average soma and dendrite have about 1000 synapses from other neurons and the average axon synapses to about 1000 neurons. The change in electrical potential due to any one synapse is rather small, but the individual excitatory and inhibitory effects can sum (the excitatory effects positive in the summation and the inhibitory effects negative). If there is enough net excitatory input, the potential difference in the soma can drop sharply. If the reduction in potential

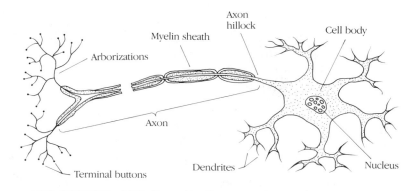

Figure 2-2 A schematic representation of a typical neuron. (From Katz, 1952.)

is large enough, a depolarization will occur at the *axon hillock*, where the axon joins the soma (see Figure 2-2). The inside of the neuron momentarily (for a millisecond) becomes more positive than the outside. This sudden change, referred to as an *action potential* (or *spike*), will propagate down the axon. That is, the potential difference will suddenly and momentarily change down the axon. The rate at which this change travels down the neuron can vary from .5 meter per second (m/sec) to 130 m/sec, depending on the characteristics of the axon. When the nerve impulse reaches the end of the axon, it will cause neurotransmitters to be released from the terminal buttons, thus completing the cycle.

To review, potential changes accumulate on a cell body, reach threshold, and cause an action potential to propagate down an axon. This pulse in turn causes neurotransmitters to be transmitted from the axon terminal to the body of a new neuron, causing changes in its membrane potential. It should be emphasized that this sequence is almost all there is to neural information processing, yet intelligence arises from this simple system of interactions. A major challenge to cognitive science is to understand how.

The time for this neural communication to complete the path from one neuron to another is roughly 10 msec—definitely more than 1 msec, and definitely less than 100; the exact speed depends on the characteristics of the neurons involved. This is much slower than the millions of operations that can be performed in 1 sec by a computer. There are, however, billions of these activities occurring simultaneously throughout the brain.

Neural Representation of Information

Information in the brain is represented in terms of continously varying quantities. There are two such quantities. First, the membrane potential can range more or less negative. Second, the axon can vary in terms of the number of nerve impulses it transmits per second. This is referred to as its *rate of firing*. It is the number, not the pattern, of impulses along a single axon that is important. There can be hundreds of nerve impulses per second. The greater the rate of firing, the more effect the axon will have on the cells to which it synapses. Information representation in the brain is to be contrasted with information representation in a computer, where individual memory cells or "bits" can have just one of two values—off and on, or 0 and 1. There is not a continuous variation in a typical computer cell as there is in a typical neural cell.

There is a general way to conceptualize the interactions among neurons that captures the many specific variations on information transfer in the nervous system. This is to think of a neuron as having an "activation level" that corresponds roughly to its firing rate on the axon or to the degree of depolarization on the dendrite and soma. Neurons interact by driving up the activation level of other neurons (excitation) or driving down their activation level (inhibition). All neural information processing takes place in terms of these excitatory and inhibitory effects; they are what underlies human cognition.

There are serious problems in understanding how these basic processes really produce cognitive phenomena. How can such processes represent our concept of baseball; how can they result in our solution of an algebra problem; how can they result in our feeling of frustration? Similar questions can be asked of computer systems, which have been shown to be capable of answering questions about baseball, solving algebra problems, and displaying frustration. Where in the millions of off-and-on bits in a computer does the concept of baseball lie; how does a change in a bit result in the solution of an algebra problem or in a feeling of frustration? The answer in every case is that these questions are failing to see the forest for the trees. The concepts of baseball, problem solution, and emotion occur in large patterns of bit changes. Cognition resides in patterns of the primitive elements of computers. Similarly, we can be sure that human cognition is achieved through large patterns of neural activity.

We do not really know how the brain encodes cognition in neural patterns, but the evidence is strong that it does. There are computational arguments that this is the only way to achieve cognitive function (see Hinton & Anderson, 1981). There is also a fair amount of evidence suggesting that human knowledge is not localized in any single neuron, but is distributed over the brain in large patterns of neurons. Damage to any small area of the brain generally does not result in the loss of specific memories. On the other hand, massive damage to large areas of the brain will result in temporary or permanent loss of a large set of memories.

It is informative to consider how the computer stores information. Consider a simple case: the spelling of a word. Most computers have codes by which individual patterns of binary values (1's and 0's) represent letters. Table

Table 2-1 *Coding of cognitive psychology in Ascii*

1	1	1	1	1	1	1	1	1
0	0	0	0	0	0	0	0	0
0	0	0	0	0	1	0	1	0
0	1	0	1	1	0	1	0	0
0	1	1	1	0	1	0	1	1
1	1	1	1	0	0	0	1	0
1	1	1	0	1	0	1	0	1
1	1	0	0	1	1	1	0	1

1	1	1	1	1	1	1	1	1	1
0	0	0	0	0	0	0	0	0	0
1	1	1	0	0	0	0	0	0	1
0	0	1	0	1	1	1	1	0	1
0	0	0	0	0	1	1	1	1	0
0	1	0	1	0	1	0	1	1	0
0	1	1	1	0	1	0	1	1	1
0	0	0	1	0	1	1	1	0	0

2-1 illustrates the use of one coding scheme, called *Ascii*; it contains a pattern of 0's and 1's that codes the words "cognitive psychology."

Similarly, information in the brain can be represented in terms of patterns of neural activity rather than simply as cells firing. The code in Table 2-1 includes certain redundant bits that allow the computer to correct errors should certain bits be lost (note that each column has an even number of 1's). Like the computer case, it seems that the brain codes information redundantly so that even if certain cells are missing, it can still determine what the pattern is encoding. It is generally thought that the brain uses very different schemes for encoding information and achieving redundancy than the computer. It also seems that the brain utilizes a much more redundant code than the computer. This is because individual neurons are not particularly reliable in their behavior.

Coding of Permanent Memories

So far we have talked only about patterns of neural activation. However, such patterns are transitory. The brain does not maintain the same pattern for minutes, let alone days. This means that these patterns cannot encode our permanent knowledge about the world. The frequent belief, for which there is some evidence (Eccles, 1979), is that memories are encoded by changes in the synaptic connections among neurons. There is little evidence for growth of new synapses in the adult, but synapses can change in their effectiveness in response to experience. That is, neuron A can become more effective in exciting or inhibiting neuron B. If neuron A must stimulate neuron B to retrieve some memory pattern, this can be achieved by making the synaptic connection between A and B more effective. The next time A is activated, it will activate B and the memory pattern will be retrieved.

Organization of the Brain

Having reviewed some of the basic principles of neural information processing, we will look at the overall structure of the central nervous system and then focus on the nature of information processing in the visual system. The central nervous system consists of the brain and the spinal cord. The major function of the spinal cord is to carry neural messages from the brain to the muscles and sensory messages from the body back to the brain.

Figure 2-3 shows a cross section of the brain with some of the more prominent neural structures labeled. The lower parts of the brain are evolutionarily more primitive. The higher portions of the brain are only well developed in the higher species. Correspondingly, it appears that the lower portions of the brain are responsible for more basic functions. The medulla controls breathing, swallowing, digestion, and heartbeat. The cerebellum plays an important role in motor coordination and voluntary movement. The thalamus serves primarily as a relay station for motor and sensory information from lower areas to the cortex. The hypothalamus regulates expression of basic drives.

The cerebral cortex, or neocortex, is the most recently evolved portion of the brain. Although it is quite primitive in many mammals, it accounts for three-fourths of the neurons in the human brain. In the human, this cerebral cortex can be thought of as a rather thin neural sheet about 1 m square. To fit this neural sheet into the skull, it has to be highly convoluted. The amount of folds and wrinkles on the cortex is one of the striking physical differences between the human brain and those of lower mammals.

Left and Right Hemispheres

The neocortex is divided into left and right hemispheres. One of the interesting curiosities of anatomy is that the right part of the body tends to be connected to the left hemisphere and the left part of the body tends to be connected to the right hemisphere. Thus, motor control and sensation in the right hand is controlled by the left hemisphere. The right ear is most strongly connected to the left hemisphere. The neural receptors in either eye that

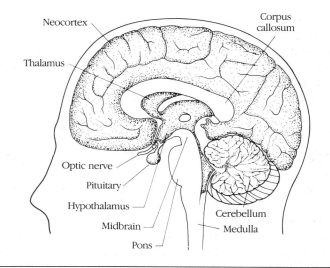

Figure 2-3 Some of the major components of the brain. (From Keeton, 1980.)

receive input from the left part of the visual world are connected to the right hemisphere. The left and right hemispheres communicate by several pathways, the most prominent of which is the *corpus callosum*.

Each hemisphere can be divided into four lobes: frontal, parietal, occipital, and temporal (see Figure 2-4). Major folds on the cortex or fissures separate the areas. The frontal lobe is primarily involved with motor functions and contains an area, called the *prefrontal association cortex*, that is thought to be involved in higher level processes like planning. The occipital lobe contains the primary visual areas, while the temporal lobe has the primary auditory areas. The parietal lobe is concerned with some sensory functions.

In general, we do not have a good understanding of where higher level cognitive functions occur in the brain, let alone how they are achieved. We do know that a number of cortical areas are important as regards language. There are areas in the left frontal lobe, called *Broca's area* and *Wernicke's area*, that seem critical for speech, since damage to them results in severe impairment to speech. They may not be the only neural areas involved in speech, but they certainly are important.

It also appears that the two hemispheres are somewhat specialized for different types of processing. As we already noted, the so-called language areas are localized in the left hemisphere. In general, the left hemisphere seems associated with symbolic and analytic processing, while the right hemisphere is more associated with perceptual and spatial processing. Much of the evidence for the difference between the hemispheres comes from split-brain patients, such as the ones discussed in the introduction to this chapter.

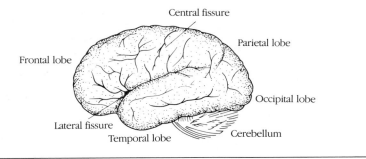

Figure 2-4 Major components of the cortex. (From Gray, 1948.)

By severing the connections between the left and right hemispheres in epileptic patients, physicians have created a situation in which psychologists can study the separate functions of the right and left hemispheres. Commands can be presented to the patients in their right ears (and hence to their left brains) or in their left ears (and hence to their right brains). The right hemisphere can comprehend only the simplest linguistic commands, whereas the left hemisphere displays full comprehension to produce spatial patterns. A quite different result is obtained when the ability of the right hand (hence left hemisphere) is compared with that of the left hand (hence right hemisphere). In this situation, the right hemisphere clearly outperforms the left hemisphere.

Evidence for such cortical localization of function is regarded as important in cognitive psychology. It is argued that distinct localization of various functions means that distinct cognitive principles underlie the functions. Thus, we will see in Chapter 11 that evidence for special localization of language function is used to support the position that language is distinct in its processing from that of other higher level cognitive functions. Such evidence is certainly suggestive, but we can argue against the inference from distinct cortical localization to distinct principles of operation. To return to the computer metaphor, we know that different programs operating *according to the same principles* can occupy distinct areas of the computer's memory. What is really required is evidence concerning how language processes are performed, not evidence concerning where they are localized.

The Visual System

In contrast to our uncertainty about the neural underpinnings of higher level systems like language, we have some grasp of the neural information processing underlying low-level vision. This knowledge is worth reviewing as a

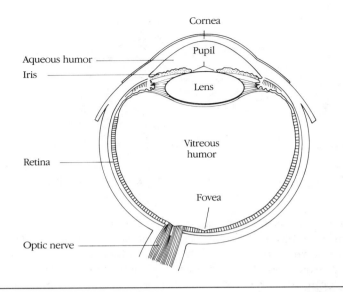

Figure 2-5   The eye. Light enters through the cornea, passes through the aqueous humor, pupil, lens, and vitreous humor to strike the retina, which is stimulated by the light. (From Lindsay & Norman, 1977.)

model of what neural information processing is like. It is also an area where artificial intelligence and psychological research have recently made major advances.

Figure 2-5 is a schematic representation of the eye. Light passes through the lens and the vitreous humor and falls on the retina at the back of the eye. The retina contains the light-sensitive cells that actually respond to the light. It should be pointed out that light is scattered slightly in passing through the vitreous humor, so the image falling on the back of the retina is not perfectly sharp. One of the important functions of early visual processing is, as we will see, to sharpen that image.

Light is converted into neural energy by a photochemical process. There are two distinct types of photoreceptors in the eye—rods and cones. Cones are involved in color vision and show high resolution and acuity. Less light energy is required to trigger a response in the rods, but they are associated with poorer resolution. As a consequence, they are principally responsible for the less acute, black-and-white vision we experience at night. Cones are especially concentrated in a particular area called the *fovea*. When we fixate on an object, we move our eyes so that the object falls on the fovea. This enables us to maximize the high resolution of the cones in perceiving the object. The fovea covers just a small region of the retina. Foveal vision is

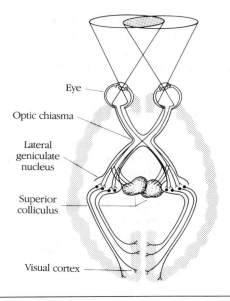

Figure 2-6   Neural paths from the eye to the brain. (From Keeton, 1980.)

concerned with detection of fine details. The rest of the visual field, the *periphery*, is responsible for detection of more global information, including movement.

The receptor cells synapse onto bipolar cells and these onto ganglion cells, whose axons leave the eye and form the optic nerve, which goes to the brain. Altogether there are about 800,000 ganglion cells in the optic nerve from each eye. Each ganglion cell encodes information from a small region of the retina. The amount of neural firing on a ganglion axon will typically encode the amount of light stimulation in that region of the retina.

Figure 2-6 illustrates the neural paths from the eye to the brain. The optic nerves from both eyes meet at the optic chiasma, and the nerves from the nasal side of the retina cross over and go to the other side of the brain, while the nerves from the outside of the retina continue to the same side of the brain as the eye. This means that the right halves of both eyes are connected to the right brain. Since the left part of the visual field falls on the right half of each eye, information about the left part of the visual field goes to the right brain; similarly, information about the right side of the visual field goes to the left brain. We have already discussed this in considering research with split brain patients.

The fibers from the ganglion cells synapse to cells in either the lateral geniculate nucleus or the superior colliculus. Both of these are areas below the cortex in the brain. It is thought that the lateral geniculate nucleus is important in perceiving details and recognizing objects whereas the superior colliculus is involved in the localization of objects in space. Both of these neural structures are connected to the visual cortex.

Information Coding in Visual Cells

The research of Kuffler (1953) is important for an understanding of how information is encoded by the ganglion cells. These cells generally have a spontaneous rate of firing. For some ganglion cells, if light falls on a small region of the retina, there will be an increase from these spontaneous rates of firing. If light is presented in the region just around this sensitive center, however, the spontaneous rate of firing will go down. Light farther from the center elicits no response at all. These are known as on–off cells. There are also off–on ganglion cells, where light at the center suppresses the spontaneous rate of firing and light in the surround increases the rate of firing. Figure 2-7 illustrates the receptive fields of these cells. Cells in the lateral geniculate nucleus respond in the same way.

Hubel and Wiesel (1962), in their study of the visual cortex in the cat, found that visual cortical cells responded in a more complex manner than these lower cells. Figure 2-8 illustrates four of the patterns that have been observed in cortical cells. As can be seen, all of these receptive fields have an elongated shape, in contrast to the on–off cells. Types (a) and (b) are edge detectors. They respond positively to light on one side of a line and negatively to light on the other side. They will respond maximally if there is an edge of light lined up so as to fall at the boundary point. Types (c) and (d) are bar detectors. They respond positively to light in the center and negatively to light at the periphery, or vice versa. Thus, a bar with a positive center will respond maximally if there is a bar of light just covering its center.

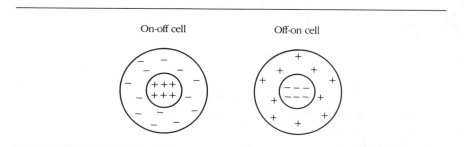

Figure 2-7 On–off and off–on receptive fields of ganglion cells and the cells in the lateral geniculate nucleus.

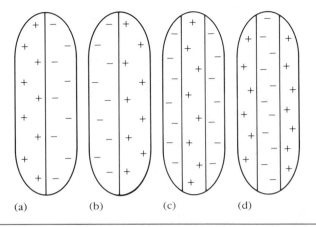

Figure 2-8 Response patterns of cortical cells.

Both edge and bar detectors are specific with respect to position, orientation, and width. That is, they respond only to stimulation in a certain part of the visual field, to bars and edges of certain orientations, and to bars and edges of certain widths. Thus, a striped pattern like the one in Figure 2-9 will excite a particular bar detector only if the stripes are of the appropriate orientation and width for that detector. However, different detectors seemed tuned to different widths and orientations, so some subset of bar detectors would be stimulated by this pattern.

Figure 2-9 A pattern that excites detectors of a particular width and orientation.

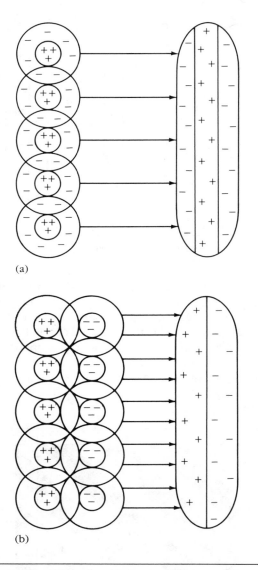

(a)

(b)

Figure 2-10 Hypothetical combinations of on–off and off–on cells to form (a) bar detectors and (b) edge detectors.

One of the interesting features of edge and bar detectors is that they respond if stimulation is presented to the corresponding visual region of either eye. Thus, visual information from corresponding points in either eye must converge on the same detector.

Figure 2-10 illustrates how a number of on–off and off–on cells might combine to form bar or edge detectors. Note that no single on–off cell is sufficient to stimulate a detector. Rather, the detector is responding to *patterns* of the on–off cells, so even at this low level we see the nervous system processing information in terms of patterns of neural activation.

David Marr's Work

The late David Marr developed a computer model of how information from the on-and-off cells could be used to yield a useful analysis of the visual image. Figure 2-11 shows a typical image that a computer might be asked to process. It is an image of the end of a bar. This image is a 128 × 128 grid where the lightness of each dot represents the intensity of light information at that point. However, it is not particularly easy to circumscribe the boundaries of the image. There are similar problems with the image that falls on the human retina. A major information-processing problem, then, is to identify the boundaries of an object in an image.

Marr and Hildreth (1980) combined the output of off–on detectors to calculate bars and edges of various widths and orientations. Wherever an edge or bar was detected, a symbolic description was created. Thus, the following descriptions might be created:

> There is an edge with coordinates (184,23), orientation 128°, contrast 25, length 32, and width 4.

> There is a bar with coordinates (118,134), orientation 105°, contrast 76, length 16, and width 6.

Where the coordinates are the horizonal and vertical position of the object, orientation measures the degree of rotation from the horizontal, contrast the intensity of brightness change, length the length of the bar, and width the width of the detectors.

Figure 2-12 illustrates the application of Marr's procedure to a figure (Figure 2-12a). Figure 2-12b shows the output of the on–off detectors adjusted to a particular width; each dark point is an on–off detector of that width. The output of the edge detectors is shown in Figure 2-12c; each line reflects a particular edge. Finally, Figure 2-12d shows the bars detected in the image. The information in parts (c) and (d) of the figure is still quite low level, and the representation of this information Marr calls the *raw primal sketch*. To recognize an image, Marr must put the various edges and bars together. His system does this on the basis of similarity. so, suppose Marr's system has formed the following symbolic descriptions:

> (a) There is an edge with coordinates (112,39), orientation 128°, contrast 82, and width 4.

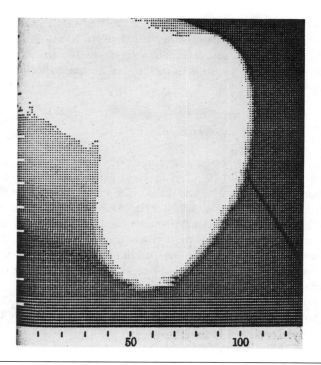

Figure 2-11 A typical visual image that is processed in computer vision. Problems in processing these images are typical of problems in processing an image on the retina of the eye. (From Marr, 1976.)

(b) There is an edge with coordinates (111,38), orientation 119°, contrast 79, and width 5.

(c) There is an edge with coordinates (109,37), orientation 117°, contrast 81, and width 4.

It would assume that these descriptions were all part of one edge, and would put them together. Figure 2-13 illustrates various stages of the analysis of the rod in Figure 2-11. The dots in Figure 2-13a reflect various symbolic statements. The connected points in Figure 2-13b reflect statements his system has put together because of similarity. We still have not identified the contour. A second-order analysis is required to put together similar lines to come up with a contour representation like that in Figure 2-13c.

Marr's system has proven quite successful at identifying the boundaries of objects in real images, a difficult problem in computer vision. There is some evidence that the visual system does an analysis somewhat like Marr's. There

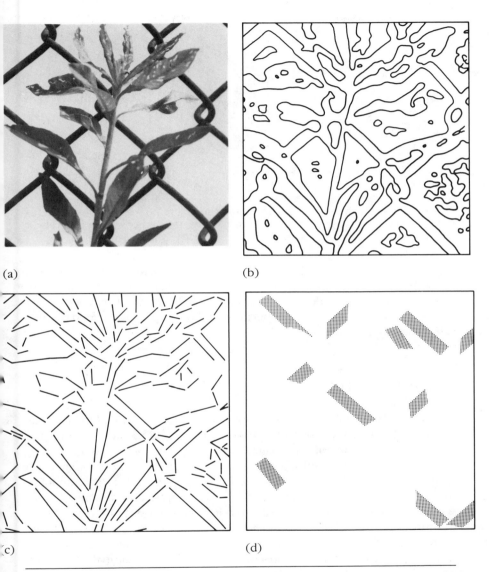

(a)

(b)

(c)

(d)

Figure 2-12 (a) The original image processed by Marr and Hildreth (1980); (b) the output of the on–off detectors; (c) the output of the edge detectors; (d) the output of the bar detectors.

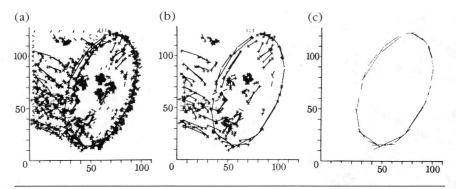

Figure 2-13 Analysis of the image of a bar in Figure 2-11 by Marr's system. (a) The symbolic description in the raw primal sketch; (b) and (c) different levels of aggregation into larger segments.

are so-called complex and hypercomplex cells in the visual cortex that seem to combine the output of the simple bar and edge cells, just as Marr's system combines the symbolic description to identify the contour of an object. However, the exact character and connections of the complex and hypercomplex cells remain a little obscure.

Conclusions

We have surveyed some of what is known about the structure of the nervous system and how it processes information. An interesting question concerns what implications neural information processing has for the issues of cognitive psychology that will occupy us in subsequent chapters. Some have argued that there are no implications. These people point to the computer, where the actual hardware has relatively little implication for the kinds of programs that run on it. Recent research in cognitive psychology has shown that this negative position is too strong. Time and time again, our knowledge of the neural processes has affected theorizing at levels more abstract than neural. We will see a number of instances of neural arguments in the following chapters.

Remarks and Suggested Readings

There are numerous books concerned with neuropsychology, including those by Bennett (1977), Brown (1980), Gazzaniga, Steen, and Volpe (1979), and

Thompson (1972, 1976). A recent paper by Gazzaniga (1983) discusses the different character of the left and right hemispheres of the brain.

There has been surge of interest in the computational character of neural processing. A recent series of papers edited by Hinton and Anderson (1981) provides a good discussion of this material. Fodor (1975) should be read for a critique of neural considerations in cognitive psychology. There is a great deal of work on computer vision, some of it based on human models and some of it not. This work tends to be published in the journal *Artifical Intelligence* and in proceedings of meetings such as the International Joint Conference on Artificial Intelligence, the American Association for Artificial Intelligence, and the International Conference on Pattern Recognition. Marr's recent (1982) book gives a good discussion of his research on vision.

Chapter 3

Perception and Attention

Summary

1. When information first enters the human system, it is registered in sensory memories. These sensory memories include an iconic memory for visual information and an echoic memory for auditory information. Sensory memories can store a great deal of information, but only for brief periods of time.

2. Attention is a very limited mental resource that can only be allocated to at most a few cognitive processes at a time. The more frequently that processes have been practiced, the less attention they require; eventually they can be performed without interfering with other cognitive processes. Processes that are highly practiced and require little or no attention are referred to as *automatic*. Processes that require attention are called *controlled*.

3. Two types of models have been proposed to describe how perceptual patterns are recognized. One, template matching, involves matching a whole pattern at once. The other involves feature analysis, in which components of a pattern are first recognized and then combined. The evidence appears to favor feature analysis.

4. A set of Gestalt principles organizes perceptual features into units for perception. We can sometimes recognize large organized units before we can recognize the components that make up these units.

5. Combining features in order to recognize a pattern requires attention. The amount of attention required decreases with the familiarity of the pattern.

6. Pattern recognition involves an integration of bottom-up processing and top-down processing. Bottom-up processing is the use of sensory information in pattern recognition. Top-down processing is the use of the context of the pattern as well as general knowledge in recognition.

In the preceding chapter we discussed how information is processed by the visual system. We noted how information works its way through the visual system to the point where lines are detected and contours of objects are identified. However, a great deal more information processing than this is required before we can recognize objects. An interesting demonstration for this fact concerns a soldier who suffered brain damage due to accidental carbon monoxide poisoning. He could recognize objects through their feel, smell, or sound, but was unable to distinguish a circle from a square or recognize faces or letters (Benson & Greenberg, 1969). On the other hand, he was able to discriminate light intensities and colors and tell in what direction an object was moving. Thus, his system was able to register visual information, but somehow his brain damage resulted in a loss of the ability to combine visual information into perceptual experience. This case shows that perception is much more than simply the registering of sensory information. In this chapter we will review what is known about the ways sensory information is processed and patterns are recognized, as well as the role of attention in guiding these information-processing activities.

Thus, this chapter is concerned with how information is initially structured as it comes into the perceptual system. In addition to examining visual pattern recognition, we will discuss speech recognition. Subsequent chapters will be concerned with how information is processed after its initial analysis by the perceptual system; that is, they will be concerned with the processing of knowledge by higher level systems such as those of memory, reasoning, problem solving, and language.

Sensory Memory

Visual Sensory Memory

Many studies of visual information processing have involved determining what a subject can extract from a brief visual presentation. A typical trial in such an experiment begins with the subject's fixating on a dot in a blank white field. By having the subject so fixate, the experimenter can control where the subject is focusing during stimulus presentation. The stimulus, perhaps a set of letters, is visually projected where the subject is looking. After a brief exposure (e.g., 50 msec), the stimulus is removed.

A number of studies have been concerned with the capacity of the memory that first registers this sensory information. In such experiments, displays of letters such as that in Figure 3-1 are presented briefly and subjects are then

X	M	R	J
C	N	K	P
V	F	L	B

Figure 3-1 An example of the kind of display used in a visual-report experiment. This display is presented briefly to subjects, who are then asked to report the letters it contains.

asked to report as many items as they can recall from such displays. Usually, subjects are able to report three, four, five, or at most six items. Many subjects report that they saw more items but that the items faded away before they could be reported.

An important methodological variation on this task was performed by Sperling in 1960. He presented an array consisting of three rows of four letters, as shown in Figure 3-1. Immediately after this stimulus was turned off, the subject was cued to report just one row of the display. The cues were in the form of differential tones (high tone for top row, medium for middle, and low for bottom). Sperling's method was called the *partial-report procedure* in contrast with the *whole-report procedure*, which had been used until then.

By using the number of letters that the subject was able to report from a particular row, Sperling was able to estimate the number of letters the subject had available the instant the display was turned off. Subjects were able to recall a little over three items from a row of four. Because subjects did not know beforehand which row would be cued, they had to have more than three items available from each of the three rows. The total number of items available, then, would be three rows times more than three items per row, which is more than nine items. This result contrasts sharply with the four or five items subjects typically recall in the whole-report procedure. So, subjects were correct in their claims that they could see more items than they could report before the items faded from the image of the display. Indeed, they probably could see all 12 letters. Sperling's estimate was less than 12 however, probably due to subjects' failures to use the partial-report procedure perfectly.

In the procedure just described, the tone cue was presented immediately after offset of the display. Sperling also varied the length of the delay between the offset of the display and the tone. The results he obtained in terms of numbers of letters available out of 12 are presented in Figure 3-2. (Recall our estimate that the number of letters available is three times the number reported from a row.) As the delay increases to 1 sec, subjects' performance decays back to the original whole-report level of four or five items. Thus, it

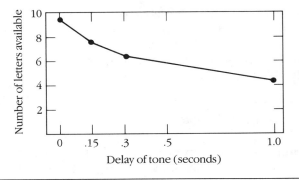

Figure 3-2 Results from Sperling's experiment. As the tone that signals the row to report is delayed, number of items reported decreases. (Adapted from Sperling, 1960.)

appears that the memory for the actual display decays very rapidly and is essentially gone by the end of 1 sec. All that is left after a second is what the subject has had time to more permanently encode.

Sperling's experiments indicate the existence of a brief *visual sensory store*—a memory that can effectively hold all the information in the visual display. While information is being held in this store, it can be processed by higher level mental routines such as those involved in making a report of the display's content. This sensory store appears to be particularly visual in character. In one experiment showing the visual character of sensory store, Sperling (1967) varied the postexposure field (the visual field after the display). He found that when the postexposure field was light the sensory information remained for only a second, but when the field was dark it remained for a full 5 sec. Thus, a bright postexposure field tends to "wash out" memory for the display. Further, following the display with another display of characters effectively "overwrites" the first display and so destroys the memory for the letters. The brief visual memory revealed in these experiments is called an *icon* by Neisser (1967). Without such a visual icon, perception would be much more difficult. Many stimuli are of very brief duration. In order to recognize them, the system needs some means of holding on to them for a short while until they can be analyzed.

The brevity of the sensory register contrasts sharply with the duration of some of the higher level memories that we will discuss in later chapters. For instance, in Chapter 6 we will discuss *short-term memory* which can, in some circumstances, hold information such as telephone numbers almost indefinitely. In the Sperling experiment information is being recoded from the sensory memory into some more permanent form—such as this short-term memory. Presumably, subjects are able to report four or five letters even minutes after the display has disappeared because the visual information has been recoded. Subjects recode as many letters as they can into a more permanent form before the display disappears from the sensory register, and they are then able to retain the recoded items for relatively long periods.

Auditory Sensory Memory

Evidence for an auditory sensory memory similar to the visual memory comes from experiments by Moray, Bates, and Barnett (1965) and by Darwin, Turvey, and Crowder (1972). The setup of the Darwin, Turvey, and Crowder study is illustrated in Figure 3-3. The subject listened to a recording over stereo headphones, hearing three lists of three items read simultaneously. Because of stereophonic mixing, one list seemed to come from the left side of the subject's head, one from the middle, and one from the right side. The investigators compared results derived from a whole-report procedure, in which subjects were instructed to report all nine items, with a partial-report procedure, in which they were cued visually after the presentation of the lists as to whether they should report the items coming from the left, middle, or right locations.

A greater percentage of the letters were reported in the partial-report procedure than in the whole-report procedure. Thus, as with iconic memory, it appears that more information is immediately available in auditory memory that can be reported. Neisser has called this auditory memory the *echoic memory*. It is clear that we need such a memory to process many aspects of speech information. Neisser (1967, p. 201) gives the example of a foreigner who is told, "No, not zeal, seal." Foreigners would not be able to benefit from this information if they could not retain the "z" long enough to compare it with the "s".

Attention and Sensory Information Processing

A Model of Attention

The types of studies described above on sensory memory show that a large amount of information gets into sensory memory, but that it is quickly lost if not attended to. Thus, attention plays an important role in selecting sensory information for further processing.

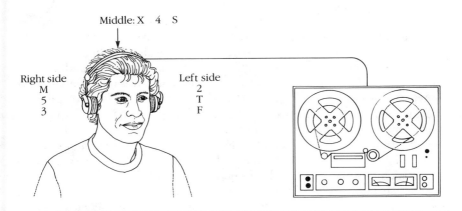

Figure 3-3 The experimental situation in the Darwin, Turvey, and Crowder experiment. By stereophonic mixings, lists of digits and letters are simultaneously presented to the left, middle, and right of the subject's head. (From Loftus & Loftus, 1976.)

A great many theories of attention have been developed in cognitive psychology. In this section we describe a recent kind of theory that has been quite successful in accounting for a wide range of attentional phenomena (Kahneman, 1973; LaBerge & Samuels, 1974; Norman & Bobrow, 1975; Posner & Snyder, 1975; Shiffrin & Schneider, 1977; Schneider & Shiffrin, 1977). Attention is conceived of as being a very limited mental resource. Numerous metaphors can help us think about the limited-resource characteristic of attention. One is energy—imagine an energy limitation, as if attention were powered by a fixed electrical current. Given the fixed energy supply, attention would be allocable to only so many tasks. (If allocated to more, the performance would degrade or a fuse would blow.) A second metaphor is spatial: think of attention as a workspace in which only so many tasks can be performed. A third metaphor is animate: think of attention as a small set of agents, often called *demons*, that can perform tasks, but only one at a time; thus, attention cannot be assigned to more tasks than there are demons.

Attention is sometimes thought of as being single minded. In terms of the metaphors just cited, this single-mindedness would mean that only enough energy, only enough workspace, or only a single attention demon was available for one task or process. Evidence for this single-minded character of attention is the fact that performing two attention-demanding tasks at once is difficult. For instance, it is difficult if not impossible to simultaneously do two addition problems, or to hold two conversations, or to hold a conservation and do an addition problem. Rather than thinking of attention as single-minded, however, it is probably more accurate to think of it as not having the capacity to perform two *demanding* tasks simultaneously. Tasks that are practiced to the point at which they do not make excessive demands can be performed simultaneously. For instance, we can walk and talk at the same time. Perhaps the reason we cannot simultaneously do mental addition and carry on a conversation is that each activity in itself involves multiple attention-demanding subcomponents. For instance, addition may involve reading, retrieving addition facts from memory, and writing—all three activities that make separate demands on attention. In any case, it is clear that whether or not attention is truly single minded, its capacity is severely limited.

The limited capacity of attention is the root cause of the reporting limitations demonstrated in visual and auditory reporting tasks. All the information gets into sensory memory, but to be retained, each unit of information must be attended to and transformed into some more permanent form. Given that attention has a limited capacity, all the elements in sensory memory cannot be attended to before they are lost. If subjects are immediately cued to report only a subset, they can attend to these items before they fade from memory. However, if the cue is delayed until the terms have faded from memory, subjects will be able to report only those elements of the subset they were able to attend to and transform into a more permanent form.

Divided-Attention Studies

Considerable research has been done on how subjects select what sensory input they attend to. Most of this research has involved a dichotic listening task. In a typical dichotic listening experiment, illustrated in Figure 3-4, subjects wear a set of headphones. Subjects hear two messages, one entering each ear, and are asked to "shadow" one of the two messages (i.e., report the words from one message as they hear them). Most subjects are able to attend to one message and tune out the other.

Psychologists have discovered that very little about the unattended message is processed in a shadowing task (e.g., Cherry, 1953; Moray, 1959). Subjects can tell if the unattended message was a human voice or a noise; if human, whether male or female; and whether the sex of the speaker changed. However, this information is about all they can report. They cannot tell what language was spoken or report any of the words spoken, even if the same word was repeated over and over again. An analogy is often made between performing this task and being at a cocktail party, where a guest tunes in to one message (a conversation) and filters out others.

We might think that the subject simply "turns one ear off," but a number of experiments have shown that this is not always the case. A couple of undergraduates at Oxford, Gray and Wedderburn (1960), demonstrated that subjects were quite successful in following a message that jumped back and

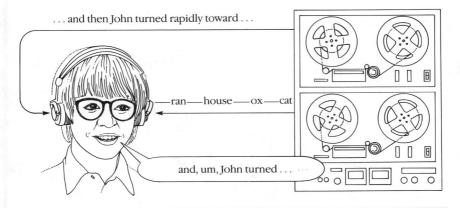

Figure 3-4 A typical shadowing task. Messages are presented to the left and right ears and the subject attempts to shadow one ear. (From Lindsay & Norman, 1977.)

forth between ears. Figure 3-5 illustrates the subjects' task in their experiment. Suppose that part of the meaningful message that subjects were to shadow was "dogs scratch fleas." The message to one ear might be "dogs six fleas," while the message to the other might be "eight scratch two." Instructed to shadow the meaningful message, subjects will report "dogs scratch fleas."

Figure 3-5 An illustration of the shadowing task in the Gray and Wedderburn experiment. The subject follows the meaningful message as it moves from ear to ear. (Adapted from R. L. Klatzky, *Human Memory,* 1st ed., W. H. Freeman and Company, copyright 1975.)

Figure 3-6 An illustration of the Treisman experiment. The meaningful message moves to the other ear, and the subject sometimes continues to shadow it against instructions. (Adapted from R. L. Klatzky, *Human Memory,* 1st ed., W. H. Freeman and Company, copyright 1975.)

Thus, subjects are capable of shadowing a message on the basis of meaning rather than physical ear.

Treisman (1960) looked at a situation in which subjects were instructed to shadow a particular ear. The result is illustrated in Figure 3-6. The message in the to-be-shadowed ear was meaningful until a certain point, at which it turned into a random sequence of words. Simultaneously, the meaningful message switched to the other ear—the one to which the subject had not been attending. Some subjects switched ears, against instructions, and continued to follow the meaningful message. Thus, it seems that messages from both ears get into sensory memory, and that subjects choose certain features for selecting what to attend to in sensory memory. If subjects use meaning as the criterion (either according to or in contradiction to instructions), they will switch ears to follow the message. If subjects use ear of origin in deciding what to attend to, they will shadow the proper ear. The conclusion is that a lot of information gets into sensory memory, but that only a small portion of it is attended to and only that portion is later remembered.

Automaticity

Recall that the capacity of attention for separate tasks is limited and must be divided up among competing processes. The amount of attention required by a process depends on how practiced that process is. The more a process has been practiced, the less attention it requires, and there is speculation that highly practiced processes require no attention at all. Such highly practiced processes that require little attention are referred to as *automatic*. Although it is probably more correct to think of automaticity as a matter of degree rather than as a well-defined category, it is useful to classify cognitive processes into two distinct types—*automatic processes*, which do not require attention, and *controlled processes*, which do (LaBerge & Samuels, 1974; Shiffrin & Schneider, 1977). Automatic processes complete themselves without conscious control by the subject. In the visual- and auditory-report tasks reviewed earlier, the registering of the stimuli in sensory memory is an automatic process. Many aspects of driving a car and comprehending language appear to be automatic. Controlled processing seems to require conscious control. In the report studies, reporting a row of items in the visual task or a spatial location in the auditory task is a controlled process. Many higher cognitive processes, such as performing mental arithmetic, are controlled.

A nice demonstration of the way practice affects attentional limitations is the study reported by Underwood (1974) on the psychologist Neville Moray, who has spent many years studying shadowing. In that time, Moray practiced shadowing a great deal. Unlike most subjects, he has a good ability to report what is contained in the nonattended channel. Through a great deal of practice, the process of shadowing has become partially automated, and Moray now has capacity left over to attend to the nonshadowed channel.

Schneider and Fisk (1982), Schneider and Shiffrin (1977), Shiffrin and Dumais (1981), and Shiffrin and Schneider (1977) have been engaged in a series of studies contrasting controlled processing with automatic processing. They have addressed this issue in an experimental paradigm that requires subjects to scan visual arrays. Figure 3-7 illustrates the Schneider and Shiffrin paradigm. Subjects are given a target letter or number and are instructed to scan a series of visual displays for the target. The displays consist of 20 different frames flashed on a screen; subjects are to report if the target occurred in one of these frames. Two factors are varied. First, each frame has one, two, or four characters on it. This factor is referred to as *frame size*. The other important variable is the relationship between the target item and the items on the frames. In the same-category condition the target is a letter, as were all items on the frames. In the different-category condition the target is always a number and all nontargets on the frames are letters. Thus, in the different-category condition, either one number appears on 1 of the 20 frames, in which case it is the target and the subject is to respond *yes*, or no number occurs on any of the frames, in which case the subject is to respond *no*.

As reported in Schneider and Shiffrin (1977), performance was strikingly different between the different- and the same-category conditions. In the different-category condition subjects required an exposure of only 80 msec per frame to achieve 95 percent accuracy, but in the same-category condition

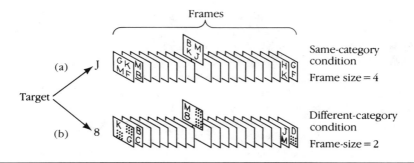

Figure 3-7 Two examples of positive trials in the Schneider and Shiffrin experiment. (a) The same-category condition, in which the target is a letter (J), as are the distractors; (b) the different-category condition, in which the target is a digit (8) and the distractors are letters. (Adapted from Schneider & Shiffrin, 1977. Copyright 1977 by the American Psychological Association. Reprinted by permission.)

they needed 400 msec per frame to achieve the same degree of accuracy. In the different-category condition the number of items per frame had little effect on performance, but in the same-category condition subjects' performance deteriorated dramatically as the number of items per frame increased.

Schneider and Shiffrin argue that before coming into the laboratory, subjects were so well practiced at detecting a number among letters that this process was automatic. In contrast, when subjects had to identify a letter among letters, controlled processing was needed. In this situation, subjects had to attend separately to each letter in each frame and compare it with the target. All these steps took time, and thus, subjects were able to inspect each frame properly and achieve respectable levels of performance only when the slides were presented slowly. Also, the more letters that were in a frame, the more slowly the frames had to be presented, since subjects had to check each letter in the frame separately. In contrast, subjects could check all items simultaneously in the different-category situation to see if any were numbers. They were able to perform this processing simultaneously because the detection process was automatic.

Schneider and Shiffrin's results in the same-category condition are similar to Sperling's study reviewed earlier. Just as Sperling found limitations on ability to report, so Schneider and Shiffrin found limitations on ability to detect letters among other letters. However, when the task was a letter–number discrimination, subjects were able to revert to an automatic process that was not limited as to capacity.

Shiffrin and Schneider (1977) ran another experiment similar to the one just described but in which the target always came from one set of letters (B, C, D, F, G, H, J, K, L) and the distractors always came from another set

(Q, R, S, T, V, W, X, Y, Z). After 2100 trials, subjects were at the same levels of performance as in the different-category condition of the previous experiment. Thus, subjects need 2100 trials of practice before discriminating numbers from letters. This result demonstrates that processes can become automatic with enough practice. When they do, devoting attention to them is no longer necessary and performance is no longer affected by the number of processes being performed simultaneously.

Pattern Recognition

Thus far we have considered how sensory information is first recorded and selected for processing by attentional mechanisms. We are now in a position to answer the critical question for a theory of perception: How is this information recognized for what it is? To a large extent, we will focus on a more specific, deceptively simple question: How do we recognize a presentation of the letter *A* as an instance of the pattern *A*?

Template-Matching Models

Perhaps the most obvious way to recognize a pattern is by means of template matching. The template-matching theory of perception assumes that a retinal image of an object is faithfully transmitted to the brain, and that an attempt is made to compare it directly to various stored patterns. These patterns are called *templates*. The basic idea is that the perceptual system tries to compare the letter to templates it has for each letter and reports the template that gives the best match. Figure 3-8 illustrates various attempts to make template matching work. In each case, an attempt is made to achieve a correspondence between the retinal cells stimulated by the *A* and the retinal cells specified for a template pattern. The first diagram in the figure, (a), shows a case in which a correspondence is achieved and an *A* is recognized. The second diagram, (b), shows that no correspondence is reached between the input of an *L* and the template pattern for an *A*. But *L* is matched in the third diagram, (c), by the *L* template. However, things can go wrong very easily with a template. The fourth diagram, (d), shows a mismatch that occurs when the image falls on the wrong part of the retina, and diagram (e) shows the problem when the image is a wrong size. Diagram (f) shows what happens when the image is in a wrong orientation, and diagrams (g) and (h) show the difficulty when the images are nonstandard *A*'s. There is no known way to correct templates for all these problems.

A common example of template matching involves the account numbers

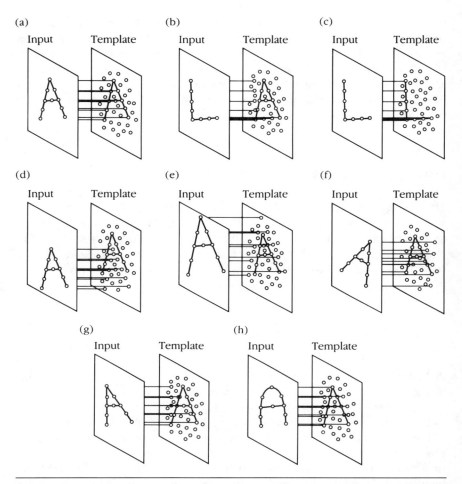

Figure 3-8 Examples of template-matching attempts. (a) and (c) Successful template-matching attempts; (b) and (d)–(h) failed attempts. (Adapted from Neisser, 1967.)

printed on checks, which are read by check-sorting machines used by bank computers. Figure 3-9 shows my check blank (actually from a former account). The account number is the bottom line. A great deal of effort has gone into making the characters in this number maximally discernible. To assure standardization of size and position, they must be printed by machine; a check-sorter would not recognize hand-printed numbers. The very fact that a standardized system is needed for template matching to work reduces the credibility of this process as a model for human pattern recognition. In humans,

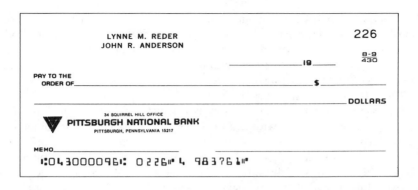

LYNNE M. REDER
JOHN R. ANDERSON

226

8-9
430

PAY TO THE
ORDER OF_____

$_____

_____ DOLLARS

34 SQUIRREL HILL OFFICE
PITTSBURGH NATIONAL BANK
PITTSBURGH, PENNSYLVANIA 15217

MEMO_____

⑆043000096⑆ 0226⑈ 4 98376⑆

Figure 3-9 A typical blank check, with specially designed account numbers to permit successful template matching.

pattern recognition is very flexible; we can recognize LARGE characters and small characters; characters in the wrong place; in strange o^r_ie^{n}t$_a$t^i_ons; in unusual SHaPes; **blurred** or broken characters, and even, with some effort, -əpısdn uʍop characters.

Feature Analysis

Partly because of the difficulties posed by template matching, psychologists have proposed that pattern recognition occurs through feature analysis. In this model, stimuli are thought of as combinations of elemental features. The features for the alphabet might consist of horizontal lines, vertical lines, lines at approximately 45° angles, and curves. Thus, the capital letter *A* can be seen as consisting of two lines at 45° angles (∧) and a horizontal line (−). The pattern for the letter *A* consists of these lines plus a specification as to how they should be combined. These features are very much like the output of edge and bar detectors in the visual cortex (discussed in Chapter 2).

You might wonder how feature analysis represents an advance beyond the template model. After all, what are the features but minitemplates? However, the feature model has a number of advantages over the template model. First, since the features are simpler, it is easier to see how the system might try to correct for the kinds of difficulties caused by template models. A second advantage of the feature-combination scheme is that it is possible to specify those relationships among the features that are most critical to the pattern. Thus, for *A*, the critical point is that the two approximately 45° lines intersect (or almost intersect) at the top and that the cross bar intersects both of these. Many other details are unimportant. Thus, all the following patterns are *A*s:

A, *A*, *A*, *A*, ⋏. A final advantage is that use of features rather than larger patterns will reduce the number of templates needed. In the feature model, we would not need a template for each possible pattern but only for each feature. Since the same features tend to occur in many patterns, this would mean a considerable savings.

There is a fair amount of behavioral evidence for the existence of features as components in pattern recognition. For instance, where letters have many features in common—as with *C* and *G*—evidence suggests that subjects are particularly prone to confuse them (Kinney, Marsetta, & Showman, 1966). When such letters are presented for very brief intervals, subjects often misclassify one stimulus as the other. So, for instance, subjects in the Kinney et al. experiment made 29 errors when presented with the letter *G*. Of these errors, 21 involved misclassification as *C*, 6 misclassification as *O*, 1 misclassification as *B*, and 1 misclassification as *9*. No other errors occurred. It is clear that subjects were choosing items with similar feature sets as their responses. Such a response pattern is what we would expect if a feature-analysis model were used. If subjects could extract only some of the features in the brief presentation, they would not be able to decide among stimuli that shared these features.

Speech Recognition

Up to this point we have considered only the recognition of written characters. Recognition of a spoken message poses some new problems. One major problem is segmentation. Speech is not broken up into discrete units the way printed text is. Well-defined gaps seem to exist between words in speech, but often this is an illusion. If we examine the actual physical speech signal, we often find undiminished sound energy at word boundaries. Indeed, a cessation of speech energy is as likely to occur within a word as between words. This property of speech becomes clear when we listen to a foreign language that we do not know. The speech appears to be a continuous stream of sounds with no obvious word boundaries. It is our familiarity with our own language that leads to the illusion of word boundaries.

Even within a single word, segmentation problems exist. These intraword problems involve the identification of *phonemes*. Phonemes are the basic vocabulary of speech sounds; it is in terms of them that we recognize words. A phoneme is defined as the minimal unit of speech that can result in a difference in the spoken message. To illustrate, consider the word *bat*. This word is analyzed into three phonemes: [b], [a], and [t]. Replacing [b] by the phoneme [p], we get *pat*; replacing [a] by [i], we get *bit*; replacing [t] by [n], we get *ban*. Obviously, a one-to-one correspondence does not always exist between letters and phonemes. For example, the word *one* consists of the phonemes [w], [ə], and [n]; *school* consists of the phonemes [s], [k], [ú], and [l]; and *night* consists of [n], [ī], and [t]. It is the lack of perfect letter-to-sound correspondence that makes English spelling so difficult.

A segmentation problem arises when the phonemes composing a spoken word are to be identified. The difficulty is that speech is continuous, and phonemes are not discrete the way letters are on a printed page. Segmentation at this level is like recognizing a written (not printed) message, where one letter runs into another. Also, as in the case of writing, different speakers vary in the way they produce the same phonemes. The variation among speakers is dramatically clear, for instance, when a person first tries to understand a speaker with a strong and unfamiliar dialect—as when an American listener tries to understand an Australian speaker. However, examination of the speech signal will reveal that even among speakers with the same accent considerable variation exists. For instance, the voices of women and children normally have a much higher pitch than those of men.

It is fair to say that we do not yet understand how the human speech-perception system deals with problems of phoneme segmentation or phoneme identification. Attempts have been made in artificial intelligence to build speech-recognition systems that can take a spoken message and put out a printed version (e.g., Reddy, 1978). Some progress has been made in this direction, and perhaps in 5 more years we will have systems whose perception approaches human quality. When that happens, we may also gain a better understanding of how speech perception is accomplished in humans.

Even now, however, some things are clear about speech perception. Feature-analysis and feature-combination processes seem to underlie speech perception much as they do visual recognition. As with individual letters, individual phonemes can be analyzed as consisting of a number of features. It turns out that these features refer to aspects of how the phoneme is generated. Among the features for phonemes are the consonantal feature, voicing, and the place of articulation (Chomsky & Halle, 1968). *Consonantal* is the quality in the phoneme of having a consonantlike property (in contrast to vowels). *Voicing* is the sound of a phoneme produced by the vibration of the vocal cords. For example, compare the ways you produce *sip* and *zip*. The [s] in *sip* is voiceless but the [z] in *zip* is voiced. You can detect this difference by placing your fingers on your larynx as you generate these sounds. The larynx will vibrate for a voiced consonant.

Place of articulation refers to the place at which the vocal track is closed or constricted in the production of a phoneme. (It is closed at some point in the utterance of most consonants.) For instance [p], [m], and [w], are considered *bilabial* because the lips are closed during their generation. The phonemes [f] and [v] are considered *labiodental* because the bottom lip is pressed against the front teeth. Two different phonemes are represented by [th]—one in *thy* and the other in *thigh*. Both are *dental* because the tongue

Table 3-1 *The classification of [b], [p], [d], and [t] according to voicing and place of articulation*

| | Voicing | |
Place of articulation	Voiced	Voiceless
Bilabial	[b]	[p]
Alveolar	[d]	[t]

presses against the teeth. The phonemes [t], [d], [s], [z], [n], [l], and [r] are all *alveolar* because the tongue presses against the alveolar ridge of the gums just behind the upper front teeth. The phonemes [sh], [ch], [j], and [y] are all *palatal* because the tongue presses against the roof of the mouth just behind the alveolar ridge. The phonemes [k] and [g] are *velar* because the tongue presses against the soft palate, or velum, in the rear roof of the mouth.

Consider the phonemes [p], [b], [t], and [d]. All four share the feature of being consonants. However, the four can be distinguished according to voicing and place of articulation. Table 3-1 classifies these four consonants according to these two features.

Considerable evidence exists for the role of such features in speech perception. For instance, in 1955, Miller and Nicely had subjects try to recognize consonants such as [b], [d], [p], and [t] when presented in noise. Subjects exhibited confusion, thinking they had heard one sound in the noise when actually another sound had been presented. Miller and Nicely were interested in what sounds subjects would confuse with what. It seemed likely that subjects would most often confuse consonants that were distinguished by just a single feature, and this prediction was confirmed. To illustrate, when presented with [p], subjects more often thought that they heard [t] than that they heard [d]. The phoneme [t] differs from [p] only in terms of place of articulation, whereas [d] differs in both place of articulation and voicing. Similarly, subjects presented with [b] more often thought they heard [p] than [t].

This experiment is an earlier demonstration of the kind of logic we saw in the Kinney, Marsetta, and Showman study on letter recognition. When the subject can identify only a subset of the features underlying a pattern (in this case the pattern is a phoneme), the subject's responses will reflect confusion among the phonemes sharing the same subset of features.

Voice-Onset Time

The features of phonemes refer to properties by which they are articulated. What are the properties of the acoustic stimulus that encode these articulatory features? This issue has been particularly well researched in the case of voicing. In the pronunciation of such consonants as [b] and [p], two things happen: The closed lips are opened, releasing air, and the vocal cords begin vibrating (voicing). In the case of the voiced consonant [b], the release and the vibration of the vocal cords are nearly simultaneous. In the case of the unvoiced consonant [p], the release occurs 60 msec before the vibration begins. What we are detecting when we perceive a voiced versus an unvoiced consonant is the presence or absence of a 60-msec interval between release and voicing. This period of time is referred to as *voice-onset time*. The difference between [p] and [b] is illustrated in Figure 3-10. Similar differences exist in other such voiced–unvoiced pairs, such as [d] and [t]. Again, the factor controlling the perception of a phoneme is the delay between the release of closure and vibration of the vocal cords.

Lisker and Abramson (1970) performed experiments with artificial (computer-generated) stimuli in which the delay between release of closure and voicing was varied from − 150 msec (voicing 150 msec before release) to + 150 msec (voicing 150 msec after release). The task was to identify which sounds were [b]'s and which were [p]'s. Figure 3-11 plots the percentage of [b] identifications and [p] identifications. Throughout most of the continuum, subjects agreed 100 percent on what they heard, but there is a sharp switch from [b] to [p] at about 25msec. At a 10-msec voice onset, subjects are in nearly unanimous agreement that the sound is a [b]; at 40 msec they are in nearly unanimous agreement that the sound is a [p]. Because of this sharp boundary between the voiced and unvoiced phoneme, perception of this feature is referred to as *categorical.*

Other evidence for categorical perception of speech comes from discrimination studies (see Studdert-Kennedy, 1976, for a review). Subjects are very poor at discriminating between a pair of [b]'s or a pair of [p]'s that differ in voice-onset time. However, they are good at discriminating pairs that have the same difference in voice-onset time but where one is identified as a [b] and the other is identified as a [p]. It seems that subjects can only identify the phonemic category of a sound and are not able to make acoustic dis-

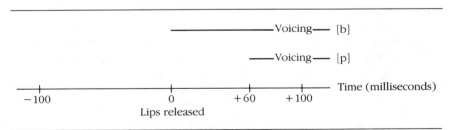

Figure 3-10   The difference between [b] and [p], the delay between the release of the lips and voicing in the case of [p]. (From *Psychology and Language* by Herbert H. Clark and Eve E. Clark. Copyright 1977 by Harcourt Brace Jovanovich. Reproduced by permission of the publisher.)

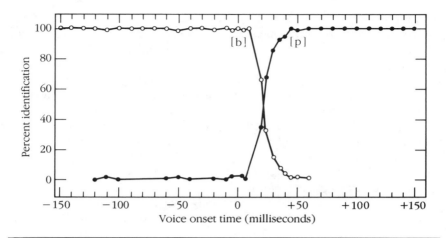

Figure 3-11   Percentage identification of [b] versus [p] as a function of voice-onset time. A sharp shift in these identification functions occurs at about 25 msec. (From Lisker & Abramson, 1970.)

criminations within that phonemic category. Thus, subjects are able to discriminate two sounds only if they fall on different sides of a phonemic boundary.

Another line of research showing evidence for such features in speech recognition involves an *adaptation paradigm*. Eimas and Corbit (1973) had their subjects listen to repeated presentations of *da*. This sound involves a voiced consonant, [d]. The experimenters reasoned that this constant repetition of the voiced consonant might fatigue, or *adapt*, the feature detector that responded to the presence of voicing. They then presented subjects with a series of artificial sounds that spanned the acoustic continuum—such as that between *ba* and *pa* (as in the Lisker and Abramson study mentioned earlier). Subjects had to indicate whether each of these artificial stimuli sounded more like *ba* or more like *pa*. (Remember, the only feature difference between *ba* and *pa* is voicing.) Eimas and Corbit found that some of the artificial stimuli that subjects would normally have called the voiced *ba* they now called the voiceless *pa*. Thus, the repeated presentation of *da* had fatigued the *voiced* feature detector and raised the threshold for detecting voicing in *ba*, making many former *ba* stimuli sound like *pa*.

Gestalt Principles of Organization

The preceding discussion of pattern recognition left open an important issue: When we recognize an *E* as made up of various vertical and horizontal bars,

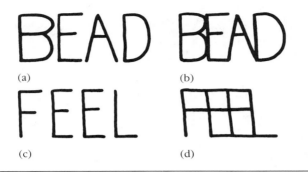

(a)   (b)

(c)   (d)

Figure 3-12 Illustrations of where Gestalt principles facilitate perceptual segmentation of letters and where they do not.

how did we decide to put those features together to recognize the pattern? Consider the four stimuli in Figure 3-12. Stimuli (a) and (c) are very easy to recognize because the letters are segmented by spaces. However, consider what happens when we run the letters together, as in (b) and (d). *Bead* in (b) is still quite recognizable, whereas *feel* in (d) is extremely difficult to perceive. Various principles determine how we segment an object into components. Only after the segmentation does perceptual pattern matching come into play. In Chapter 2 we discussed Marr's ideas for aggregating various lines and images into segments. Principles such as those he used for segmentation are very similar to what have been referred to as *Gestalt principles of perceptual organization*, after the Gestalt psychologists who documented many of them. Consider the various parts of Figure 3-13. In Figure 3-13a we perceive four pairs of lines rather than eight separate lines. This picture illustrates the principles of *proximity*: Elements close together tend to organize into units. Figure 3-13b illustrates the principle of *similarity*. Even though elements in a column are closer, we tend to see this array as five rows of alternating O's and X's. Objects that look alike tend to be grouped together. Figure 3-13c illustrates the principle of *good continuation*. We perceive part c as two lines, one from *A* to *B* and the other from *C* to *D*, although there is no reason why this sketch could not represent another pair of lines, one from *A* to *D* and the other from *C* to *B*. However, the line from *A* to *B* displays better continuation than the line from *A* to *D*, which has a sharp turn. Figure 3-13d illustrates the principles of *closure* and *good form*. We see the drawing as one circle occluded by another, although the occluded object could have many other possible shapes.

These principles will tend to organize even completely novel stimuli into units. Palmer (1977) studied subjects' recognition of figures such as the ones in Figure 3-14. He first showed subjects stimuli such as (a) in the figure and then asked them to decide whether fragments like (b)–(e) were part of the

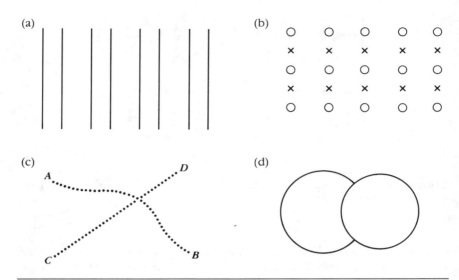

Figure 3-13 Illustrations of the Gestalt principles of organization. (a) The principle of proximity; (b) the principle of similarity; (c) the principle of good continuation; (d) the principle of closure.

original figure. Figure 3-14a tends to organize itself into a triangle (closure) and a bent letter *n* (good continuation). Palmer found that subjects could recognize the parts most rapidly when they were the segments predicted by the Gestalt principles. So, stimuli (b) and (c) were recognized more rapidly than (d) and (e). Thus, we see that recognition depends critically on the initial segmentation of the figure. Recognition can be impaired when this Gestalt-based segmentation contradicts the actual pattern structure. FoRi-NsTaNcEtHiSsEnTeNcEiShArDtOrEaD. The reasons for the difficulty are that the Gestalt principle of similarity is influencing you to perceive nonadjacent letters together, and that the proximity cues have been eliminated by removing the spaces between words.

One of the important Gestalt claims is that the whole is more than the sum of its parts. The rows, columns, lines, and circles seen in Figure 3-13 are more than just the sum of the parts that compose them. These whole units are emergent properties of the perception. There is some evidence that we actually perceive these larger configurations faster and more accurately than we perceive their components. An experiment by Pomerantz, Sager, and Stoever (1977) illustrated one situation in which subjects recognized a configuration faster than its components.

They wanted to demonstrate that people could recognize a whole pattern faster than they could recognize part of it. To do so, they had subjects try to

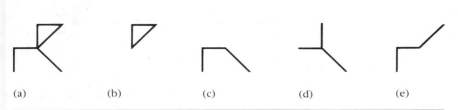

(a) (b) (c) (d) (e)

Figure 3-14 Examples of stimuli used by Palmer (1977) for studying segmentation of novel figures. (a) The original stimulus that subjects saw; (b)–(e) subparts presented for recognition. Stimuli (b) and (c) are good subparts; (d) and (e) are bad subparts.

discriminate between ( ) and ((in the configural condition, or between) and (in the part condition. In both the configural and the part condition, the difference between the test stimuli was always the same single element. That is, the configural-test patterns differed in the same way as the part-test patterns. Nevertheless, subjects in the configural condition made their choices more quickly. Clearly, then, since a configuration can be recognized more quickly than its parts, perception of the configuration must be something other than the separate perception of the elements.

Attention and Pattern Recognition

There is also evidence that attention is required in order to combine the features to perceive the pattern. Treisman and Gelade (1980) had subjects try to detect a *T* in an array of 30 *I*'s and *Y*'s. They reasoned that subjects could do this by simply looking for the cross-bar feature of the *T* that distinguishes it from all *I*'s and *Y*'s. Subjects took about 800 msec to make this decision. In a second condition, Treisman and Gelade required subjects to detect a *T* in an array of *I*'s and *Z*'s. In this condition, they could not use just the vertical bar or just the horizontal bar of the *T*; they would have to look for the conjunction of these features. It took subjects over 1200 msec to make their decision. Thus, a condition requiring them to recognize the conjunction of features took subjects about 400 msec longer than one in which perception of a single feature was sufficient. Moreover, when Treisman and Gelade varied the size of the display they found that subjects were much more affected by display size in the condition that required recognition of the conjunction of features. Figure 3-15 shows these results. Subjects showed no difference between the single-feature and the conjunction condition for displays containing fewer than five letters. Only with displays presenting more distractors did subjects attention become overloaded.

It might seem surprising that attention is required to detect patterns of

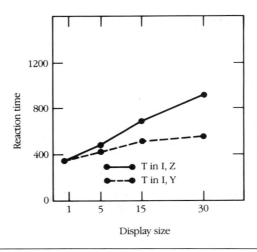

Figure 3-15   Results from Treisman and Gelade: Reaction time to detect a target as a function of number of distractors and whether the distractors contain separately all the features of the target. (Adapted from Treisman and Gelade, 1980.)

features. We have the experience of automatically recognizing letters. It should be noted, however, that for familiar letters the deficit in perception of feature conjunction occurs only in large displays. Only then does the processing load get large enough to expose attention deficits.

Pattern Familiarity

There is evidence that subjects will suffer attentional deficits in much simpler conditions than those used by Treisman and Gelade, for this to happen the use of unfamiliar patterns seems necessary. Experiments by LaBerge confirm that the recognition of unfamiliar patterns makes high demands on attention. LaBerge wanted to compare recognition of a familiar set of characters *(p,q,b,d)* with that of an unfamiliar set (ʔ,ʇ,ʃ,ɭ). In his paradigm, subjects were presented with a *prime stimulus*, which lasted 1 sec. The prime stimulus was then removed and a *test stimulus* was presented. Table 3-2 lists the various kinds of trials presented to subjects. The prime stimulus was always a single character, such as *p*. The test stimulus was usually a single character too; thus, subjects simply had to judge whether the two stimuli were the same. Occasionally, however, the test stimulus consisted of two characters and subjects had to judge whether the two characters were identical—a judgment that did

Table 3-2 *The different types of trials in LaBerge's experiment*

Types of stimuli	Condition			
	Familiar, expected, positive	Unfamiliar, expected, positive	Familiar, unexpected, positive	Unfamiliar, unexpected, positive
Prime	p	↑	a	a
Test	p	↑	qq	↑↑
	Condition			
	Familiar, expected, negative	Unfamiliar, expected, negative	Familiar, unexpected, negative	Unfamiliar, unexpected, negative
Prime	p	↑	a	a
Test	q	↑	bq	↓↑

not depend on the prime stimulus. Usually (75 percent of the time) subjects were tested with a single letter.

To illustrate the paradigm, let us consider a couple of the conditions in Table 3-2. In the familiar, expected, and positive condition, subjects might first see a *p* as a prime. After 1 sec during which subjects could study the *p*, the stimulus would be removed and another *p* would be presented. Subjects were to respond *yes*, since the prime and the test were the same. This condition is called *familiar* because *p* is a familiar letter; it is called *expected* because the subject expected to see the single letter *p*; and it is called *positive* because a match occurred and a *yes* response was given. Now consider the unfamiliar, unexpected, and positive condition. Here subjects initially see the prime *a*. They expect the test stimulus to be either an *a* or some other single stimulus, since they usually see single stimuli. However, after the prime the subjects actually see ↑↑. Because subjects see a pair, they know they must decide whether the two stimuli are identical. The stimuli are identical in this case, so the correct response is *yes*. The condition is called *unfamiliar* because the test judgment involves unfamiliar stimuli, *unexpected* because the subject did not expect two characters in the test, and *positive* because both of the test characters matched and a *yes* response was given.

We will consider just those trials where the response was positive. When the stimulus was expected, whether it was familiar or unfamiliar did not make any difference. Subjects made their positive judgments equally fast. They focused their attention on the test pattern and were ready to recognize it. When the stimulus was unexpected, however, a considerable difference in judgment speed was exhibited between familiar letters (530 msec) and unfamilar letters (580 msec). Presented with unexpected familiar stimuli, subjects seemed to recognize the items automatically and were able to compare their encoding of the two characters. With unfamiliar stimuli, however, it seemed that attention had to be shifted from the expected pattern to the presented patterns, and this shift took time. However, after 1 hour's practice for each of 5 days, subjects came to recognize the new characters when unexpected as quickly as they recognized the familiar characters when unexpected. Thus, this amount of practice made recognition nearly automatic. In conclusion, although experiments like those of Treisman and Gelade indicate that there is some attentional cost with feature combination in familiar patterns, there is much more attentional cost with unfamiliar patterns.

Context and Pattern Recognition

Our discussion of the Gestalt principles indicates one way in which context influences pattern recognition. These Gestalt principles are typically viewed as innate, reflecting factors wired into the perceptual system at birth. However, there is also evidence that pattern recognition is influenced by acquired knowledge about the structure of the world and the structure of stimuli.

Consider the example in Figure 3-16. We perceive these symbols as *THE CAT* even though the *H* and the *A* are identical. The general context provided by the words forces the appropriate interpretation. When context or general world knowledge guides perception, we refer to the processing as *top-down* processing, because high-level general knowledge determines the interpretation of the low-level perceptual units.

One important line of research on top-down, or contextual, effects comes from a series of experiments on letter identification, starting with the experiments of Reicher (1969) and Wheeler (1970). Subjects in these experiments were given a very brief presentation of either a letter (such as *D*) or a word (such as *WORD*). Immediately afterward they were given a pair of alternatives and instructed to report which they had seen. (The initial presentation was sufficiently brief that subjects made a good many errors in this identification task.) If they had been shown *D*, subjects might be presented with *D* or *K* as alternatives. If they had been shown *WORD*, they might be given *WORD* or *WORK* as alternatives. Note that the two word choices differ only in the *D* or *K* letter. Subjects were about 10 percent more accurate in the word condition. Thus, they more accurately discriminated between *D* and *K* in the context of a word than as letters alone, even though, in a sense, they had to process four times as many letters in the word context. This phenomenon is known as the *word superiority effect*.

THE CAT

Figure 3-16 A demonstration of context. The same stimulus is perceived as an *H* or an *A*, depending on the context. (From Selfridge, 1955.)

Rumelhart and Siple (1974) have provided one explanation for how this feat might have been accomplished. Suppose subjects are able to identify the first three letters as *WOR*. Now consider how many four-letter words are consistent with a *WOR* beginning: *WORD, WORK, WORM, WORN, WORT*. Suppose subjects only detect the bottom curve ($\cup$) in the fourth letter. In the *WOR* context, they know the stimulus must have been *WORD*. However, when the letter is presented alone and subjects detect the curve, they will not know whether the letter was *B, D, C, O,* or *Q*, since each of these letters is consistent with the curve feature. Thus, in the *WOR* context subjects need only detect one feature (e.g., the $\cup$) in order to perceive the fourth letter, but when the letter is presented alone they must identify a number of features. Note that the Rumelhart and Siple analysis implies that perception is a highly inferential process. In the context of *WOR*, it is not that the subject sees the *D* better; rather the subject is better able to infer that *D* is the fourth letter. However, the subject is not conscious of these inferences; rather the subject is said to make *unconscious inferences* in the act of perception.

This example illustrates the *redundancy* of many complex stimuli such as words. These stimuli consist of many more features than are required for recognition. Thus, perception can proceed successfully when only some of the features are recognized, with context filling in the remaining features. In language, this redundancy exists on many levels besides the feature level. For instance, redundancy occurs at the letter level. We do not need to perceive every letter in a string of words to be able to read it. To xllxstxatx. I cxn rxplxce xvexy txirx lextex of x sextexce xitx an x, anx yox stxll xan xanxge xo rxad xt—ix wixh sxme xifxicxltx. (This example is adapted from Lindsay & Norman, 1977.)

Figure 3-17 illustrates just a part of a pattern-recognition network that McClelland and Rumelhart (1981) have implemented to model our use of word structure to facilitate recognition of individual letters. In this model, individual features are combined to form letters and individual letters are combined to form words. The model depends heavily on excitatory and inhibitory activation processes such as those discussed in Chapter 2. Activation spreads from the features to excite the letters and from the letters to excite the words. Alternative letters and words inhibit each other. Activation can

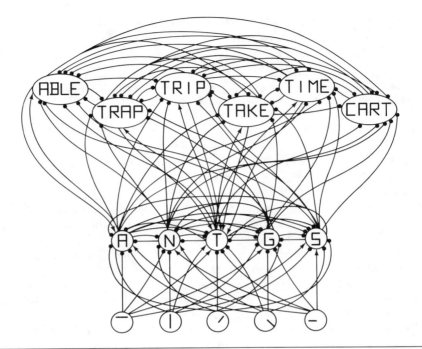

Figure 3-17 The pattern-recognition network proposed by McClelland and Rumelhart (1981) to perform word recognition by performing calculations on neural activation values. Connections with arrowheads (→) indicate excitatory connections from the source to the head. Connections with rounded heads (—•) indicate inhibitory connections from the source to the head.

also spread down from the words to excite the component letters. In this way a word can support the activation of a letter and hence promote its recognition.

In such a system, activation will tend to accumulate at one word and it will repress the activations of other words through inhibition. The dominant word will support the activation of its component letters, and these letters will repress activation of alternative letters. The word superiority effect is due to the support a word gives to its component letters. The computation proposed by McClelland and Rumelhart's interactive activation model is extremely complex, as is the computation of any model that simulates neural processing. However, they are able to reproduce many of the results on word recognition in their system. Their success encourages us in the belief that we are beginning to make some headway in understanding how neural processing underlies pattern recognition.

Effects of Sentence Context

Effects similar to the Reicher–Wheeler effect have been shown at the multiword level in an experiment by Tulving, Mandler, and Baumal (1964). The following are examples of the material they used:

Countries in the United Nations form a military *alliance.*

The political leader was challenged by a dangerous *opponent.*

A voter in municipal elections must be a local *resident.*

The huge slum was filled with dirt and *disorder.*

Each sentence provides an eight-word context preceding a critical word. Subjects were given either none, four, or eight of the context words and then shown the target word for a brief period. So, in the various conditions subjects would see the following:

0 context	disorder
4 context	*Filled with dirt and* disorder
8 context	*The huge slum was filled with dirt and* disorder,

where the italicized words constitute the context first studied and *disorder* the critical word, presented after the context for a very brief period. The experimenters manipulated the duration of this critical word from 0 to 140 msec. They were interested in how bottom-up information (manipulated by exposure duration) interacted with context (manipulated by number of words).

Figure 3-18 presents the results of the experiment. It can be seen that the probability of a correct identification increases both as the amount of context increases and as the exposure duration increases. Note that subjects benefit from context even in the 0-msec exposure conditon, where they are clearly guessing. In this exposure condition, subjects are performing 16 percent better with an eight-word context than with a zero-word context. Note, however, that this benefit of context is larger with longer exposures—more than 40 percent at a 60-msec exposure and about 30 percent at the longest, the 140-msec, exposure. (The effect diminishes somewhat between 60 and 140 msec because subjects in the eight-word context condition are performing almost perfectly and show little benefit of further exposure, whereas subjects in the zero-word condition continue to benefit from the longer exposure.) These results indicate that subjects can take advantage of the context to improve their identification of the words. As was the case in the Reicher–Wheeler letter-identification paradigm, subjects are using the context to reduce the amount of perceptual information they need in order to identify the word.

The experiment by Tulving et al. shows that we can use sentence context

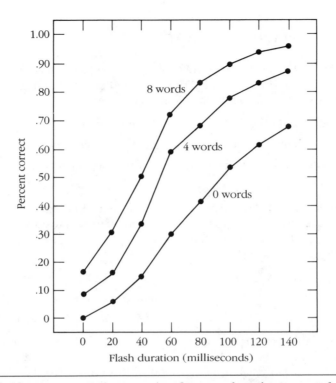

Figure 3-18   Percentage of correct identifications of word strings as a function of the duration of a string's exposure and the number of preceding context words. (From Tulving et al., 1964. Copyright 1964 by the Canadian Psychological Association. Reprinted by permission.)

to help identify words. With context we need to extract less information the word itself in order to identify it. In fact, we can use context to fill in words that did not even occur in the sentence, as the previous sentence illustrates. Presumably, you were able to fill in the missing *from* as your read the sentence, and perhaps you did not even notice that it was missing. (This example was also adapted from Lindsay & Norman, 1977.)

Context and Speech

Equally good evidence exists for the role of context in the perception of speech. A nice illustration is the *phoneme-restoration effect*, demonstrated in an experiment by Warren (1970). He had subjects listen to the sentence, "The state governors met with their respective legislatures convening in the capital city," with a 120-msec pure tone replacing the middle *s* in legislatures. However, only 1 in 20 subjects reported hearing the pure tone, and that subject was not able to locate it correctly.

A nice extension of this first study is an experiment by Warren and Warren (1970). They presented subjects with sentences such as the following:

It was found that the *eel was on the axle.

It was found that the *eel was on the shoe.

It was found that the *eel was on the orange.

It was found that the *eel was on the table.

In each case, the * denotes a phoneme replaced by nonspeech. For the four sentences above, subjects reported hearing *wheel*, *heel*, *peel*, and *meal*, depending on context. The important feature to note about each of these sentences is that the sentences are identical through the critical word. The identification of the critical word is determined by what occurs after it. Thus, the identification of words is often not instantaneous but can depend on the perception of subsequent words.

These two experiments on speech perception illustrate how context can cause us to hear what is not there. We found instances of such illusory perception when we considered visual perception, but we also found clear instances (e.g., Reicher 1969; Wheeler 1970) in which context appeared to facilitate the identificaton of what was actually presented. Facilitation has been similarly demonstrated in the domain of speech perception. For example, Miller and Isard (1963) presented sentences to subjects in noise; subjects were to listen to the sentences and report them back. Some sentences were perfectly normal:

A witness signed the official document.

Sloppy fielding loses baseball games.

Other sentences were what the experimenters called *anomalous*:

A witness appraised the shocking company dragon.

Sloppy poetry leaves nuclear minutes.

These sentences obey the rules of English grammar; they just do not make any sense. The third category of sentences was called *ungrammatical*:

A legal glittering the exposed picnic knight.

Loses poetry spots total wasted.

These "sentences" are just random strings of words.

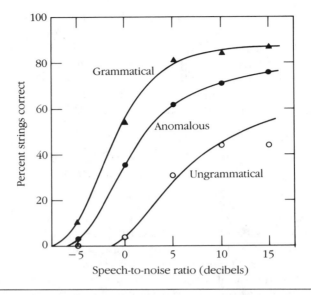

Figure 3-19 Percentage of correct identifications of word strings as a function of the type of string and the speech-to-noise ratio. (From Miller & Isard, 1963.)

Figure 3-19 shows the percentage of correct perceptions of these three kinds of sentences. The data are plotted as a function of the speech-to-noise ratio—naturally, subjects perceived less when there was more noise. However, what is critical in the figure is that at all levels of speech-to-noise ratio the normal (grammatical) is clearly superior to the anomalous and the anomalous is superior to the ungrammatical. These results show that subjects were able to improve their speech perception through the use of both meaning constraints (differences between normal and anomalous) and grammar constraints (differences between anomalous and ungrammatical).

Context and the Recognition of Faces and Scenes

So far, our discussion has focused almost entirely on the role of context in the perception of printed and spoken material. However, some work has been done on how more complex visual stimuli are perceived. In dealing with linguistic material, we are processing very highly overlearned patterns. When we process other highly overlearned patterns, such as faces, the same kind of interaction seems to take place between features and context that

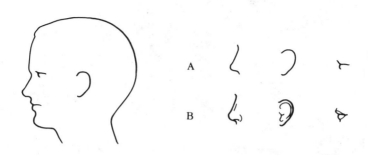

Figure 3-20 Facial features in the context of a face and out of context. Minimal information is necessary in context, but the same minimal features are not easily recognized in row A. More of the features' internal structure must be provided to permit recognition, as in row B. (Adapted from Palmer, 1975.)

occurs with linguistic stimuli. Consider Figure 3-20, which is derived from work by Palmer (1975). He pointed out that in the context of a face, very little feature information is required for recognition of the individual parts, such as nose, eye, ear, or lips. In contrast, when these parts are presented in isolation, considerably more visual detail is required to permit their recognition.

Context also appears to be important for visual stimuli that are not highly overlearned patterns. Biederman, Glass and Stacy (1973) have looked at perception of objects in novel scenes. Figure 3-21 illustrates the two kinds of scenes presented to their subjects. Part (a) of the figure is a normal scene, whereas in part (b) the same scene is jumbled. The scene was briefly presented to subjects on a screen, and immediately after the presentation an arrow was shown that pointed to a position on the screen where an object had been. Subjects were asked to identify the object that had been in that position in the scene. So, in the example scene, the object pointed to might have been the fire hydrant. Subjects were considerably more accurate in their identificaton with the coherent than with the jumbled pictures. Thus, as with their processing of written text or speech, subjects are able to recruit context in a visual scene to help their identification of an object.

More recently, Biederman, Mezzanotte, and Rabinowitz (1982) did a series of studies to determine the constraints that subjects are sensitive to in a picture. They list five such constraints that pictures tend to satisfy. (1) There is the interposition constraint, which is that objects tend to occlude their background. Figure 3-22a illustrates a violation of this constraint. (2) The support constraint specifies that objects tend to rest on surfaces; a sofa floating in the air would violate this constraint. (3) The probability constraint states

(a)

(b)

Figure 3-21 Scenes used in the study by Biederman et al. (1973). (a) A coherent scene. (b) A jumbled scene. It is harder to recognize the fire hydrant in the jumbled scene. (From Biederman et al., 1973. Copyright 1973 by the American Psychological Association. Reprinted by permission.)

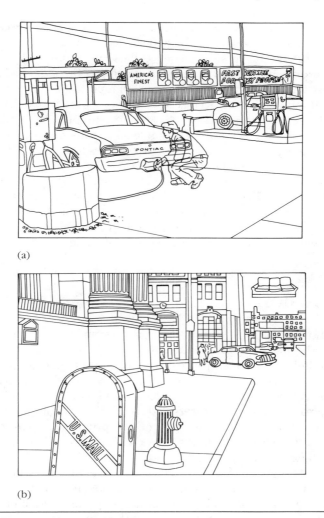

(a)

(b)

Figure 3-22 Two examples of stimuli from Biederman et al. (1982). Part (a) violates the interposition constraint; part (b) violates the probability, size, and support constraints.

that objects are found only in certain contexts; a fire hydrant in a living room would be a violation of this constraint. (4) The position constraint states that even if an object is probable for a certain context, it is found there only in certain positions; a fire hydrant on a mailbox would be a violation of this constraint. (5) The familiar-size constraint specifies that objects are found only in certain sizes.

Figure 3-22b illustrates an object, the sofa, that simultaneously violates three constraints—probability, size, and support. The subjects of Biederman et al. were briefly shown such scenes as those in Figure 3-22 and asked to identify various objects such as the sofa. When an object violated any of the constraints, there was an increase in reaction time and error rate. The effect of violation was cumulative, so that two violations were worse than one, and three violations was the worst of all. An interesting result concerned what Biederman et al. called "innocent bystanders." For instance, consider the fire hydrant in Figure 3-22b. Although the sofa violates three constraints, the fire hydrant is an innocent bystander that violates none. Biederman et al. looked at recognition of such innocent bystanders and found that recognition of these objects was not affected by the number of constraints violated by some other object. Thus, it appears that constraint violations interfere only with the perception of the specific object violating the constraints; they do not interfere with the perception of the scene as a whole.

Conclusions

An enormous amount of sensory information comes into our system every moment. The major problem facing the perceptual system is that it must, with only limited resources, process this great load of information in such a way that the environment makes sense. Unless sensory information is encoded quickly, it is very rapidly lost from iconic and echoic stores. The system utilizes various pattern recognizers and some basic Gestalt principles of organization to structure this sensory input. The pattern recognizers appear to combine both sensory features and contextual information in identifying familiar configurations.

Figure 3-23 is an attempt to sketch out this overall flow of information in an abstract way, combining ideas from this chapter and Chapter 2. Perception begins with energy, such as light or sound, from the external environment. Receptors, such as those on the retina, transform this energy to neural information. Early sensory processing is concerned with making initial sense of the information. Last chapter we looked at this aspect of the visual system in some detail. The output of this system is a feature description of the stimulus and some segmentation of the stimulus into units or bundles. The Gestalt principles have already operated in producing this initial segmentation. This representation of the stimulus as bundles of features is what resides in the sensory memories like the iconic and echoic memories. The various pattern recognizers attempt to identify these feature bundles. This process of pattern recognition is attention demanding, especially when the patterns are unfamiliar. We also saw that context has a strong impact on this recognition

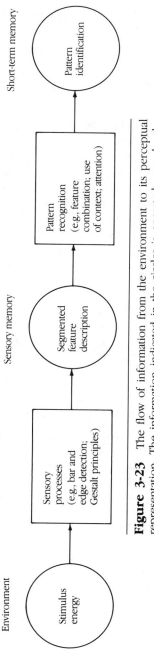

Environment   Sensory memory   Short-term memory

Stimulus energy

Sensory processes (e.g., bar and edge detection; Gestalt principles)

Segmented feature description

Pattern recognition (e.g., feature combination; use of context; attention)

Pattern identification

Figure 3-23 The flow of information from the environment to its perceptual representation. The information indicated in the circles is operated upon by the sensory and perceptual processes indicated in the boxes.

process. The output of this recognition process is object recognition. Subsequent chapters will discuss the further cognitive processes that apply to the objects once they have been recognized.

Remarks and Suggested Readings

The topics covered in this chapter are easily expanded into a full course; most colleges offer at least one course on this material. Such courses focus particularly on what is known about the elemental sensory processes. A fair amount of physiological evidence is available about these processes, and direct connections can be made between physiology and psychological experience. (We reviewed a small amount of that physiological evidence in Chapter 2.) Among the standard texts providing extensive surveys of the research on sensation and perception are those of Rock (1975) and Kaufman (1974).

James Gibson (e.g., 1950, 1966, 1979) has developed a very influential theory of perception, quite different from the one presented here. Ideas from this theory are beginning to appear in analyses of other higher level cognitive phenomena. For instance, Turvey and Shaw (1977), in their analysis of human memory, have been strongly influenced by Gibson. Neisser (1976) presents a view of perception, attention, and cognition that also shows the influence of Gibson.

A number of texts dealing with human information processing provide somewhat different, and also often more extensive, discussions of perception and attention. You should not think that the model of attention presented here is the only one in cognitive psychology. For discussions of a number of alternative attention models, read Massaro (1975) and Norman (1976). Other texts on attention and perception include those of Klatzky (1979), Lindsay and Norman (1977), Rumelhart (1977), and Wickelgren (1979).

The book by Spoehr and Lehmkuhle (1982) is a good discussion of many aspects of visual information processing. That by Clark and Clark (1977) contains good discussions of speech generation and perception. Two books edited by Solso (1973, 1975) contain papers on attention and perception. Very current research can be found in an annual series titled *Attention and Performance*. For information on attempts at making computers see, read the book edited by Winston and Brown (1980), and on attempts at making computers recognize speech, read Reddy (1978).

Chapter 4

Perception-Based Knowledge Representations

Summary

1. Knowledge can be represented in terms of images that encode the spatial structure of items or in terms of linear orderings that encode the sequence of items.

2. When asked to perform a mental transformation on an image, such as rotating it 180°, subjects imagine the image moving through the intermediate states in the transformation. The greater the transformation that must be performed, the longer subjects take to perform it.

3. When subjects are asked to compare two mental objects with regard to dimension such as magnitude, they engage in a process similar to that of discriminating between the size of two physically presented objects.

4. Although many people report experiences of visualizing objects in tasks, a mental image does not seem to be a "picture in the head." It differs from a picture in that it is not precise, it can be distorted, and it is segmented into meaningful pieces.

5. Both spatial images and linear orderings have a hierarchical organization in which subimages or sublists can occur as elements in larger images or lists.

6. Subjects have more rapid access to the first and last elements of a linear ordering, and they tend to search from beginning to end. They can more rapidly judge the order of elements in a linear ordering the farther the elements are apart.

This chapter and the next will be concerned with the different ways in which information is represented in memory. Chapter 3 discussed the evidence for sensory memories—repositories that can store sensory representations for a few seconds at most. Beyond the first few seconds, information must be transformed, or encoded, into more permanent representations. Some of these permanent representations tend to preserve much of the structure of the original perceptual experience. Others, however, are quite abstracted from the perceptual details and encode the meaning of the experience. This chapter will focus on perception-based representations, whereas the next one will focus on meaning-based representations.

In this chapter we will consider two types of knowledge representation— spatial images and linear orderings—that partially preserve the structure of perceptions. Spatial images preserve information about the position of objects in space. Images are often described in visual terms, but it is questionable whether spatial images are tied to the visual modality. Linear orderings preserve information about the sequence of events, such as the order of words in a sentence. A linear ordering represents events by organizing them sequentially, like beads on a string.

A famous theory in cognitive psychology, called the *dual-code theory* (Bower, 1972; Paivio, 1971), is concerned with a spatial and a linear knowledge representation. The dual-code theory ties the spatial code to the visual modality and the linear code to the verbal modality. The dual-code theory has proven to be quite controversial in the connections it makes between these two representations and two modalities. The other hypothesis, equally controversial, is that these representations are not tied to any particular modality.

Spatial versus Linear Representations

An experiment by Santa (1977) nicely illustrates the difference between spatial and linear representations. The two conditions of Santa's experiment are illustrated in Figure 4-1. In the geometric condition, subjects studied a spatial array of three geometric objects, two geometric objects above and one below. As the figure shows, this array had a facelike property—without much effort we can see eyes and a mouth. After subjects studied it, this array was removed and subjects were immediately presented with one of a number of test arrays. The subjects' task was to verify that the test array contained the same elements, although not necessarily in the same spatial configuration, as the study array. Thus, subjects should respond positively to the first two arrays in the figure and negatively to the other two arrays. Interest was focused on the contrast

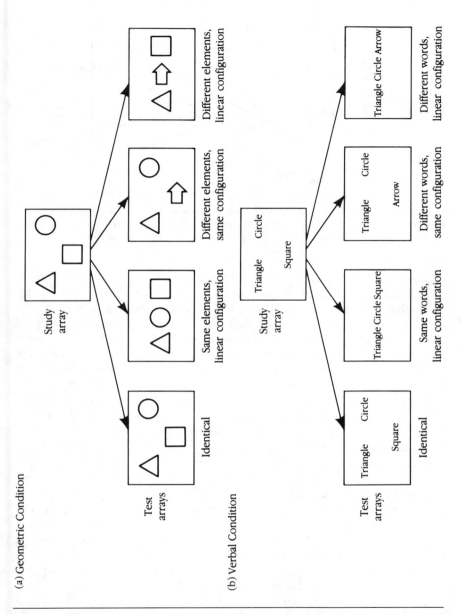

Figure 4-1 Procedure in Santa's experiment (1977). Subjects studied an initial array and then had to decide whether a test array contained the same elements.

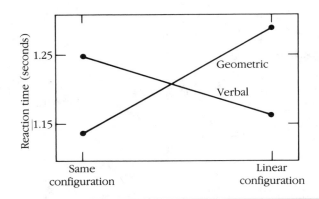

Figure 4-2   Reaction times for Santa's experiment (1977), showing an interaction between type of material and test configuration.

between the two positive test arrays. The first array is identical to the study array, but in the second array the elements are arrayed linearly. Santa predicted that subjects would make a positive judgment more quickly in the first case, where the configuration was identical, since, he hypothesized, the visual memory for the study stimulus would preserve spatial information. The results for the geometric condition are displayed in Figure 4-2. As can be seen, Santa's predictions were confirmed. Subjects were faster when the geometric test array preserved the configuration information in the study array.

The results from the geometric condition are more impressive when they are contrasted with the results from the verbal condition, illustrated in Figure 4-1b. Here subjects studied words arranged in spatial configurations identical with geometric objects in the geometric condition. However, because it involved words, the study stimulus did not suggest a face or have any pictorial properties. Santa speculated that subjects would encode the word array according to normal reading order—that is, left to right and top to bottom. So, given the study array in Figure 4-1b, subjects would encode it "triangle, circle, square." Following the study stimulus, one of the test stimuli was presented. Subjects had to judge whether the words in the test stimulus were identical with those in the study stimulus. All the test stimuli involved words, but otherwise they presented the same possibilities as the tests in the geometric condition. In particular, the two positive stimuli exhibited the same configuration and a linear configuration, respectively. Note that the configuration of linear array is the same as that in which Santa predicted subjects would encode the study stimulus. Santa predicted that, since subjects had encoded the words linearly from the study array, they would be fastest when the test array was linear. As Figure 4-2 illustrates, his predictions were again confirmed. The verbal and the geometric conditions display a sharp interaction.

In conclusion, Santa's experiment indicates that some information, such as geometric objects, tends to be stored according to spatial position, whereas other information, such as words, tends to be stored according to linear order.

Mental Imagery

There has been a great deal of research during the last 20 years on the nature of spatial knowledge representations. These representations are typically referred to as *spatial images*, or *mental images*. Much of this research has been concerned with the types of mental processes that can be performed on spatial images. *Spatial imagery*, or *mental imagery*, is the term used to refer to these processes. Study of these imagery processes has done much to define our conception of a spatial image.

Mental Rotation

Among the most influential research on spatial images is the long series of experiments on mental rotation performed by Roger Shepard and his colleagues. The first experiment was that of Shepard and Metzler (1971). Subjects were presented with pairs of two-dimensional representations of three-dimensional objects like those in Figure 4-3. Their task was to determine if the objects were identical except for orientation. The two figures in Figure 4-3a and 4-3b are identical; they are just presented at different orientations. Subjects report that to match the two shapes they rotated one of the objects in each pair mentally until it was congruent with the other object. Figure 4-3c is a foil pair: There is no way of rotating one object so that it is identical with the other.

The graphs in Figure 4-4 show the time required for subjects to decide that the members of pairs such as those in Figure 4-3a and 4-3b were identical. The reaction times are plotted as a function of the angular disparity between the two objects presented to the subject. This angular disparity represents the amount one object would have to be rotated in order to match the other object in orientation. Note that the relationship is linear—for every equal increment in amount of rotation, an equal increment in reaction time is required. Reaction time is plotted for two different kinds of rotation. One is for two-dimensional rotations (Figure 4-3a), which can be performed in the picture plane (i.e., by rotating the page). The other is for depth rotations (Figure 4-3b), which require the subject to rotate the object *into* the page.

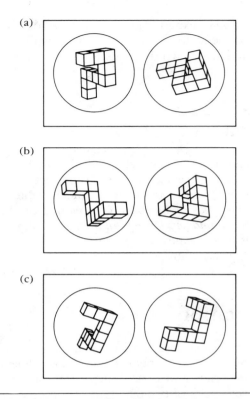

Figure 4-3 Stimuli in the Shepard and Metzler study on mental rotation (1971). (a) The objects differ by an 80° rotation in the picture plane. (b) The objects differ by an 80° rotation in depth. (c) The pair cannot be rotated into congruence. (From Metzler & Shepard, 1974.)

Note that the two functions are very similar. Processing an object in depth (in three dimensions) does not appear to take longer than processing in the picture plane. Hence, subjects must be operating on three-dimensional representations of the objects in both the picture-plane condition and the depth condition.

These data might seem to indicate that subjects rotate the object in a three-dimensional space within their heads. The greater the angle of disparity between the two objects, the longer subjects take to complete the rotation. Of course, subjects are not actually rotating an object in their heads. However, whatever the actual mental process is, it appears to be an *analog* of a physical rotation.

Mental rotation has also been studied in a series of experiments by Cooper and Shepard (1973), who used letter stimuli such as those in Figure 4-5. The

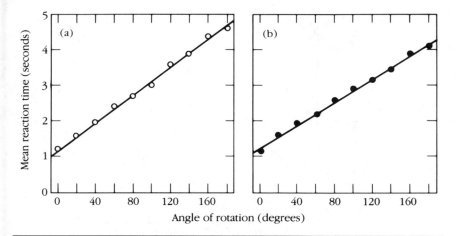

Figure 4-4 Mean time to determine that two objects have the same three-dimensional shape as a function of the angular difference in their portrayed orientations. (a) Plot for pairs differing by a rotation in the picture plane. (b) Plot for pairs differing by a rotation in depth. (From Metzler & Shepard, 1974.)

six items on the left are well-formed *R*'s that have been rotated varying numbers of degrees from the vertical. The six items to the right are backward *R*'s, which have also been rotated varying numbers of degrees. The subjects were presented with one of the 12 stimuli in Figure 4-5 and had to decide whether the stimulus was a normal or a backward *R*. Figure 4-6 presents the

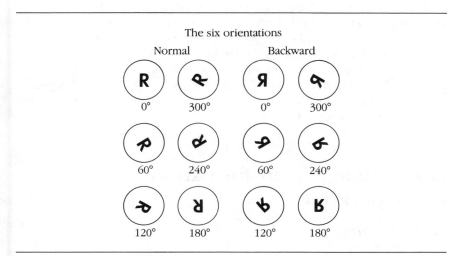

Figure 4-5 Normal and backward versions of one of the stimuli in the mental-rotation study by Cooper and Shepard (1973).

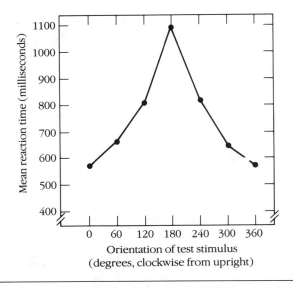

Figure 4-6   Mean reaction time for judging the normality of a letter as a function of orientation in Cooper and Shepard (1973).

times subjects took to judge that a letter was normal as a function of its deviation in orientation from upright. Subjects' judgment times increase with deviation from the upright up to 180°. This result suggests that a mental-rotation process took place in which the stimulus was rotated in the plane until it was upright and then judged as normal or backward. That subjects are slowest at 180° indicates that they will rotate clockwise or counterclockwise—whichever way is shorter. Note that the rotation times for this experiment are much faster than those in the Shepard and Metzler study. Subjects seem to be rotating at a rate of more than 300°/sec (as opposed to only 50°/sec in Shepard and Metzler). Although the exact reason for this difference in rotation rates is somewhat in dispute, it is probably related to the greater complexity of the Shepard and Metzler figures.

Other Image Transformations and Operations

Paper Folding

Researchers have looked at a number of other tasks that seem to show that when subjects are performing certain mental computations they are operating

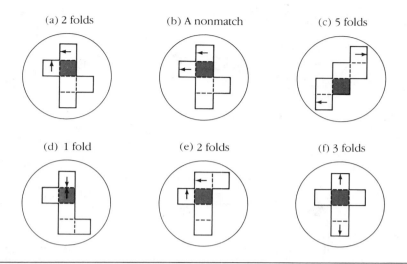

(a) 2 folds   (b) A nonmatch   (c) 5 folds

(d) 1 fold   (e) 2 folds   (f) 3 folds

Figure 4-7 Six illustrative problems adapted from Shepard and Feng (1972). The overall task was to determine whether the heads of arrows would meet when the patterns were folded into cubes.

on a visual image the way a person might perform continuous operations on a physical object. Shepard and Feng (1972) looked at a task in which subjects were required to make judgments about paper cubes that had been unfolded into patterns of six squares. Figure 4-7 illustrates some of their problems. Subjects were asked to determine from a two-dimensional pattern whether the heads of the two arrows marked on the pattern would or would not meet if the squares were folded into a cube. The time subjects took to answer the questions were recorded. Subjects reported going through the mental process of refolding the squares in order to answer these questions. Moreover, their reaction-time data were consistent with these reports. Figure 4-8 plots decision times as a function of the number of folds required to bring the arrows into correspondence. These data approximate a linear function of the number of folds. Thus, it seems that processing time is a function of the amount that the image must be transformed.

Image Scanning

An experiment by Kosslyn, Ball, and Reiser (1978) shows that it takes time to scan between two locations on a mental image. These investigators presented subjects with a map of a fictitious island (see Figure 4-9) containing a hut, a tree, a rock, a well, a lake, sand, and grass. Subjects were trained on this map

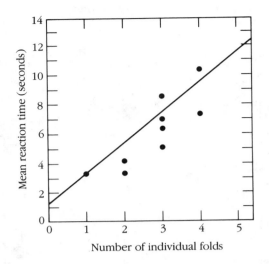

Figure 4-8 Time of correct "match" responses in the mental-folding experiment as a function of the number of individual folds that would be needed to bring the two arrows into 90° coincidence with each other. The subjects had to fold these patterns along the dotted lines to see if the arrows would meet. (From Shepard & Feng, 1972.)

Figure 4-9 The fictitious map used by Kosslyn et al. (1978) to determine differences in processing time relative to the distance between images to be recalled. Subjects had to commit this map to memory and then mentally scan from point to point in the map. (Copyright 1978 by the American Psychological Association. Reprinted by permission.)

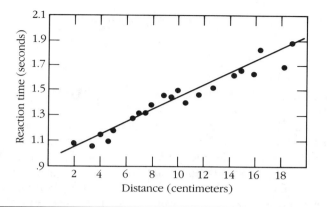

Figure 4-10   Time to scan between two points in Figure 4-9 as a function of the distance between the points. (From Kosslyn et al., 1978. Copyright 1978 by the American Psychological Association. Reprinted by permission.)

until they could draw it with great accuracy. Then an object was named aloud and subjects were asked to picture the map mentally and focus on the object named. Five seconds later, a second object was named. Subjects were instructed to scan the map for this second object and to press a button when they had mentally focused on it.

Figure 4-10 presents the times subjects needed to perform this mental operation as a function of the distance between the two objects in the original map. There are 21 possible pairs of points, and each point is represented in Figure 4-10. The abscissa gives the distance between each pair. The farther apart the two objects were, the greater was the reaction time. Clearly, subjects did not have the actual map in their heads and therefore were not moving from one location in their heads to a second location. However, they were going through a process analogous to this physical operation.

Summary

We have now reviewed a variety of experiments that all make the same point: When people operate on mental images they appear to go through a process analogous to actually operating on a physical object. In the case of rotation, folding, and scanning, we saw that time needed to perform the mental operation increased with the amount of time needed to perform the analogous physical operation. These findings leave open the issue of how close the similarity is between a mental image and a physical object. Many believe a mental image is like the visual perception of the object. The next set of studies that we will review is concerned with whether mental images are tied to the visual modality.

Interference and Image Scanning

Brooks performed an important series of experiments in 1968 on the scanning of visual images. He had subjects scan imagined diagrams such as the one in Figure 4-11. For example, the subject was to scan around an imagined block *F* from a prescribed starting point and in a prescribed direction, categorizing each corner as a point in the extreme top or bottom (assigned a yes response) or as a point in between (assigned a no response). In the example, the correct sequence of responses is yes, yes, yes, no, no, no, no, no, no, yes. For a nonvisual contrast task, Brooks also gave subjects sentences such as *A bird in the hand is not in the bush*. Subjects had to scan through such a sentence while holding it in memory, classifying each word as a noun or not. A second experimental variable was how subjects made their responses. Subjects either (1) said yes and no; (2) tapped with the left hand for yes and the right hand for no; or (3) pointed to successive *Y*'s or *N*'s on a sheet such as that in Figure 4-12. The two variables of stimulus material (diagram or sentence) and output mode were crossed to yield six conditions.

Table 4-1 gives the results of Brook's experiment in terms of the mean

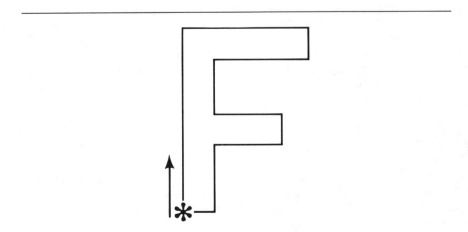

Figure 4-11   An example of a simple block diagram used by Brooks (1968) to study the scanning of mental images. The asterisk and arrow showed the subject the starting point and the direction for scanning the image. (Copyright 1968 by the Canadian Psychological Association. Reprinted by permission.)

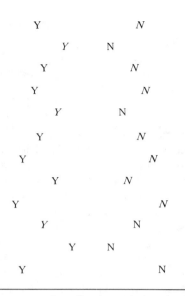

Figure 4-12 A sample output sheet for the pointing condition in Brooks (1968) for mental-image scanning. The letters are staggered to force careful visual monitoring of pointing. (Copyright 1968 by the Canadian Psychological Association. Reprinted by permission.)

time spent in classifying the sentences or diagrams in each output condition. The important result for our purposes is that subjects took much longer for diagrams in the pointing condition than in any other condition. This was not the case for sentences. Apparently, scanning a sheet like the one in Figure 4-12 conflicted with scanning a mental array. Thus, this result strongly reinforces the conclusion that when subjects are scanning a mental array, they are scanning a representation that is an analog of a physical array. Requiring the subject to simultaneously engage in a conflicting scanning action on an external physical array causes great interference to the mental scan.

It is sometimes thought that Brooks's result was due to the conflict between engaging in a visual pointing task and scanning a visual image. However,

Table 4-1 *Mean classification times in Brooks, 1968 (seconds)*

Stimulus Material	Output		
	Pointing	Tapping	Vocal
Diagrams	28.2	14.1	11.3
Sentences	9.8	7.8	13.8

subsequent results make it clear that the interference is not due to the visual character of the task. Rather, the problem is more abstract, arising from the conflicting directions in which subjects had to scan the physical array versus the mental image. For instance, in another experiment, Brooks found evidence of similar interference when subjects had their eyes closed and indicated yes and no by scanning an array of raised *Y*'s and *N*'s, as in Figure 4-12, with their fingers. In this case the actual stimuli were tactile, not visual. Thus, the conflict is *spatial*, not visual per se.

Baddeley and Lieberman (reported in Baddeley, 1976) performed an experiment that strongly supports the view that the nature of the interference in the Brooks task is spatial rather than visual. Subjects were required to perform two tasks simultaneously. All subjects performed the Brooks letter-image task. However, subjects in one group simultaneously monitored a series of stimuli of two possible brightnesses. Subjects had to press a key whenever the brighter stimulus appeared. This task involved the processing of visual but not spatial information. Subjects in the other condition were blindfolded and seated in front of a swinging pendulum. The pendulum emitted a tone and contained a photocell. Subjects were instructed to try to keep the beam of a flashlight on the swinging pendulum. Whenever they were on target, the photocell caused the tone to change frequency, thus providing auditory feedback. This test involved the processing of spatial but not visual information. The spatial-auditory tracking task produced far greater impairment in the image-scanning task than did the brightness-judgment task. This result also indicates that the nature of the impairment in the Brooks task was spatial, not visual. These results reinforce the conclusion that an image is an abstract analog of a spatial structure.

Comparisons of Analog Quantities

Judgments of Remembered Quantities

Processes performed on images tend to vary continuously with the properties of the images—for instance, with angular disparity in the rotation studies or with distance in the scanning studies. At an abstract level, we can summarize these results as follows: When subjects transform a mental object spatially, processing time increases continuously with the amount of the spatial transformation. However, another set of imagery results in the literature shows mental distance exerting the reverse effect: When subjects try to discriminate between two objects, their time to make this discrimination decreases continuously with the amount of difference between the two objects.

One experiment illustrating this result was performed by Moyer (1973). He was interested in the speed with which subjects could judge the relative

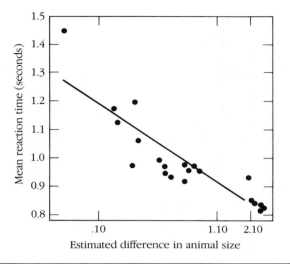

Figure 4-13 Results from Moyer (1973). Mean time to judge which of two animals is larger as a function of the estimated difference in size of the two animals. The difference measure is plotted on the abscissa in a logarithmic scale.

size of two animals from memory. For example, *Which is larger, moose or roach?* and *Which is larger, wolf or lion?* Many people report that in making these judgments, particularly for the items that are similar in size, they experience images of the two objects and seem to compare the size of the objects in their image.

In Moyer's experiment, he also asked subjects to estimate the absolute size of these animals. He plotted the reaction time for making a mental-size-comparison judgment between two animals as a function of the difference between the two animals' estimated sizes. Figure 4-13 reproduces these data. The individual points in the figure represent comparisons between pairs of items. In general, the judgment times decrease as the difference in estimated size increases. The graph shows that a fairly linear relation exists between the scale on the abscissa and the scale on the ordinate. Note, however, that on the abscissa of Figure 4-13 the differences have been plotted logarithmically. (A log-difference scale makes variations among small differences large relative to the same variations among large differences.) Thus, the linear relationship in Figure 4-13 means that increasing the size difference has a diminishing effect on reaction time.

Significantly, very similar results are obtained when subjects make comparisons of actual physical magnitudes. For instance, Johnson (1939) had subjects judge which of two simultaneously presented lines were longer. Figure 4-14 plots subject judgment time as a function of the log difference

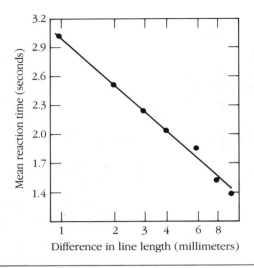

Figure 4-14 Results from Johnson (1939). Mean time to judge which of two lines is longer as a function of the difference in line length. The difference measure is plotted on the abscissa in a logarithmic scale.

in line length. Again a linear relation is obtained. It is reasonable to expect perceptual judgments to take longer the more similar the quantities being compared are, since discriminating accurately is more difficult in such circumstances. The fact that similar functions are obtained when mental objects are compared indicates that making mental comparisons involves difficulties of discrimination similar to those involved in perceptual comparisons.

Many other studies have shown that the time required to determine the difference between two objects is a function of the magnitude of their difference. Paivio (1975) showed that Moyer's result extended to mental-size judgments for all kinds of objects besides animals (e.g., *Is a drum larger than a chair?*). Holyoak and Walker (1976) showed similar effects for mental judgments of time (e.g., *Which is longer, a minute or year?*), temperature, and quality. Another experiment, by Moyer and Landauer (1967), showed this same effect for judgments about the larger of two digits from the set of 1 through 9. Again judgment time was a function of the logarithm of the difference between the two digits. In an important follow-up to this study, Buckley and Gillman (1974) replicated the finding of a logarithmic function of difference for number judgments. They found the same logarithmic function whether subjects were comparing numeric symbols (i.e., the digits 1 through 9) or clusters of one to nine dots. Again, it seems that whatever comparison process is being evoked in the symbolic situation, there is a similar comparison process evoked in the perceptual situation.

Judgments of Abstract Qualities

A number of experiments have required that subjects make quantitative comparisons of qualities with no obvious physical representation. For instance, Banks and Flora (1977) had one group of subjects rate animals on a 1-to-10 scale as to intelligence. The mean ratings of the eight animals rated were ape (9.20), dog (7.36), cat (6.57), horse (5.57), cow (3.58), sheep (3.42), chicken (3.36), and fish (1.68). A second, independent, group of subjects was then presented with pairs of these animals and asked to judge which member of the pair was the more intelligent. Banks and Flora found that judgment time decreased as the distance in rated intelligence between the two animals increased. Similar distance effects are found when subjects make judgments as to ferocity of animals (Kerst & Howard, 1977) or pleasantness of words (Paivio, 1978). Even though such judgments do not involve picturable quantities, Paivio (1978) has argued that the imagery system is involved in making these judgments just as it is in making judgments about concrete quantities. The implication again is that mental imagery is not tied to the visual modality but involves a more general ability for processing analog information.

Thus, similar inverse distance functions are found at three levels, varying from the perceptual to the abstract:

1. when the objects being compared are physically presented to subjects, as when two lines are being compared with respect to length;

2. when the physical attributes of mental objects are being compared—for instance, size of animals;

3. when quantities that cannot be visualized are being compared—for instance, pleasantness of objects.

This array of results points to the conclusion that the process for mentally making comparison between qualities is abstract in that it is not tied to a perceptual modality. This conclusion corresponds to our earlier conclusion that the processes for performing continuous transformations on an imagined object are abstract.

Images versus Mental Pictures

We have reviewed the ample evidence showing that images are analogs that vary continuously with properties of the objects they represent. People have a natural tendency to think of images as "pictures in the head." Most theorists in the area resist this temptation, and for good reason. Let us review their reasons for distinguishing between images and mental pictures.

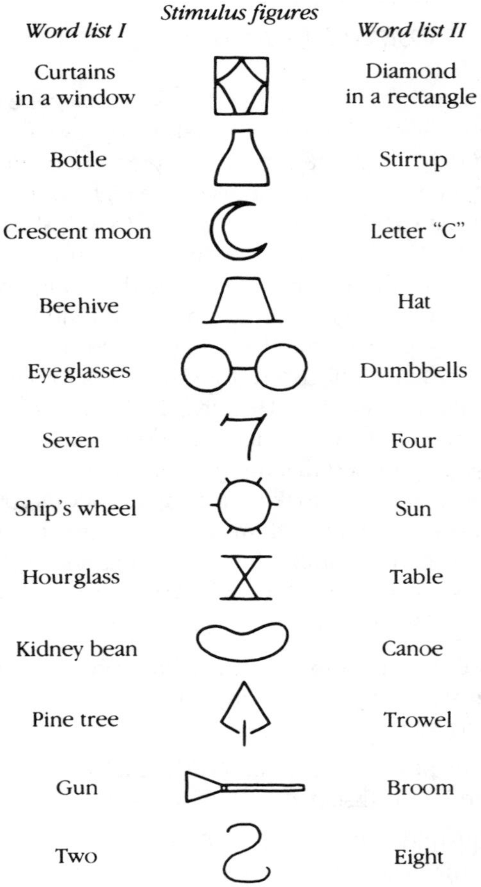

Word list I	Stimulus figures	Word list II
Curtains in a window		Diamond in a rectangle
Bottle		Stirrup
Crescent moon		Letter "C"
Beehive		Hat
Eyeglasses		Dumbbells
Seven		Four
Ship's wheel		Sun
Hourglass		Table
Kidney bean		Canoe
Pine tree		Trowel
Gun		Broom
Two		Eight

Figure 4-15   Materials used in the Carmichael et al. (1932) experiment in which subjects were shown figures accompanied by cue words and were then asked to reproduce the figures. Subjects studied the stimulus figures with one of the two verbal labels.

First, as we have emphasized, images are abstract and not tied to visual properties. Properties associated with visual images can derive from tactile as well as visual experience (Brooks). Also, we can process in imagelike manner such quantities as intelligence.

Some operations are easy to perform on a picture but hard to perform on an image. Consider the following example (adapted from Simon, 1978b):

Imagine but do not draw a rectangle 2 inches wide and 1 inch high, with a vertical line cutting it into two 1-inch squares. Imagine a diagonal from the upper left-hand corner to the lower right-hand corner of the 2 × 1-inch rectangle. We will call this line diagonal A. Imagine a second diagonal from the upper right-hand corner to the lower left-hand corner of the right *square*. Call this line diagonal B. Consider where diagonal A cuts diagonal B. What is the relationship of the length of B above the cut to the length of B below the cut?

This is a very difficult imaginal task. To the extent that we can answer the question accurately, we have to call on abstract knowledge about geometry. However, if presented with a physical picture of the figure described, we could quickly and fairly accurately report the length relation between the two segments of line B. This example shows that an image cannot always be inspected like a picture.

A third point of distinction is that images can be distorted by general knowledge. Consider the classic study by Carmichael, Hogan, and Walter (1932). Subjects were exposed to the shapes in Figure 4-15 along with one of the two verbal descriptions. Thus, the fifth object might be described to the subject as *eyeglasses* or *dumbbells*. In either case, subjects were to remember the exact drawing. When asked to draw the objects from memory, however, subjects' drawings were distorted in the direction of the named category. For instance, given *eyeglasses*, a subject might put a bend in the shaft; but given *dumbbells*, a subject might put a double shaft between the two circles. Thus, subjects' memory for the physical properties of the drawings was distorted by general knowledge about a category. A true picture would not be distorted by knowledge of the object pictured. Thus, images seem to be more malleable than pictures.

Hierarchical Structure of Images

A fourth property that distinguishes images from physical pictures is that images consist of parts, whereas pictures do not. Consider Figure 4-16a. Reed presented subjects with such forms and asked them to hold images of the forms in their minds (Reed, 1974; Reed & Johnsen, 1975). The form was removed and subjects were presented with parts of the form, such as Figures 4-16b–d. Subjects were able to identify forms (b) and (c) as parts of form (a) 65 percent of the time but were successful with form (d) only 10 percent of the time. The reason for the difference was that subjects' image of Figure 4-16a consisted of parts such as forms (b) and (c) but not form (d). A picture would not show this property. All parts of Figure 4-16a would be equally represented in a physical picture. A physical picture is just ink on paper; the ink does not know which portions go together; that segmentation is in the

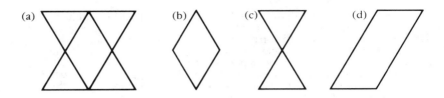

Figure 4-16 Forms used by Reed in his studies concerning the components of images. Forms (b), (c), and (d) are all contained in form (a). However, subjects appear to see forms (b) and (c) as part of form (a) more easily than they can see form (d) as part of form (a). (From Reed, 1974.)

mind of the perceiver. The human perceiver creates a mental image that is segmented. One of the serious problems in artificial-intelligence efforts to get computers to see is similarly going from raw pictures to such segmented images.

Complex images appear to admit of a hierarchy of units. For instance, consider an image of a house such as the one illustrated in Figure 4-17. At one level, it consists of a square and a triangle. However, the images of the squares and angles themselves consist of units, namely, lines. The term *chunk* is frequently used in cognitive psychology to refer to a unit like the triangle (e.g., Miller, 1956; Simon, 1974). At one level a chunk combines a number of primitive units. At another level it is a basic unit in a larger structure.

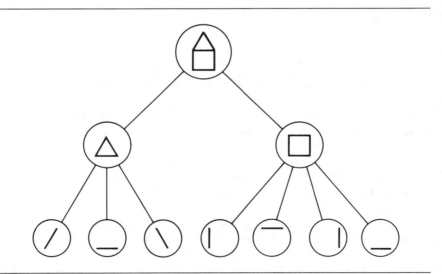

Figure 4-17 The house figure has a hierarchical representation.

Mental Maps

Subjects' memory for maps appears to have the hierarchical structure associated with spatial images. Consider your mental map of the map of the United States. It is probably divided into regions, and these regions into states, and cities are presumably pinpointed within the states. It turns out that certain systematic distortions arise because of the hierarchical structure of these mental maps. Stevens and Coupe (1978) documented a set of misconceptions people have about North American geography. Consider the following questions taken from their research:

> Which is farther east: San Diego or Reno?
>
> Which is farther north: Seattle or Montreal?
>
> Which is farther west: The Atlantic or the Pacific entrance to the Panama Canal?

The first choice is the correct answer in each case, but most people hold the wrong opinion. Reno seems to be farther east because Nevada is east of California, but this reasoning does not account for the curve in California's coastline. Montreal seems to be north of Seattle, since Canada is north of the United States, but the border dips in the east. And the Atlantic is certainly east of the Pacific, but consult a map if you need to be convinced about the Panama Canal. The geography of North America is quite complex, and subjects resort to abstract facts about relative locations of large physical bodies (e.g., California and Nevada) to make judgments about smaller locations (e.g., San Diego and Reno). These outcomes are similar to results of Carmichael et al. (1932) that we reviewed earlier, and demonstrate again the close connection between imaginal information and more general knowledge.

Stevens and Coupe were able to demonstrate such confusions with experimenter-created maps. Figure 4-18 illustrates the maps that different groups of subjects learned. The important feature of the incongruent maps is that the relative location of the Alpha and Beta counties is inconsistent with the X and Y cities. After learning the maps, subjects were asked a series of questions about the locations of cities, including *Is* X *east or west of* Y? for the left-hand maps, and *Is* X *north or south of* Y? for the right-hand maps.

Subjects were in error 18 percent of the time on the X–Y question for the congruent maps and 15 percent for the homogeneous maps, but they were in error 45 percent of the time for the incongruent maps. Subjects were using information about the location of the counties to help them remember the city locations. This reliance on "higher order" information led them to make errors, just as similar reasoning can lead to errors in questions about North American geography.

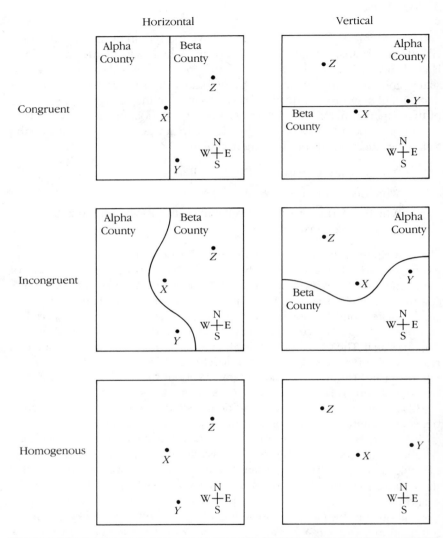

Figure 4-18   Maps studied by subjects in the experiments of Stevens and Coupe (1978), which demonstrated the effects of "higher order" information (location of county lines) on subjects' recall of city locations.

General Properties of Images

If an image is not a picture, what is it? Based on evidence reviewed in this chapter, we can specify some of the properties of images:

1. They are capable of representing continuously varying information.

2. They are capable of having operations performed on them that are analogs of spatial operations.

3. They are not tied to the visual modality, but seem to be part of a more general system for representing spatial and continuously varying information.

4. Quantities, such as size, are harder to discriminate in images the more similar the quantities are.

5. Images are more malleable and less crisp than pictures.

6. Images of complex objects are segmented into pieces.

Linear Orderings

Another kind of representational structure encodes the linear order of a set of elements. Most of the research on linear representations has used a memory paradigm of one sort or another. Subjects commit or try to commit to memory elements in a fixed order. By looking at subjects' ability to access this information, it is possible to make inferences about the structure of that information in memory. Consider an experiment from my laboratory: We had subjects learn sequences of four consonants. So, subjects might learn the consonant string *K R T B*. They also learned to associate a digit to the consonant string. Thus, they might learn that 7 is the digit associated to *K R T B*. After this learning phase, they were presented with four consonants, and they had to recall the digit associated to the consonants. We were interested in how fast they could make their recall, which we interpreted as a measure of how long it took to recognize the consonant string. The major experimental manipulation involved the order in which the four consonants were presented. The consonants were not always presented in the order in which they had been studied. For instance, subjects had to recognize *R T K B* as a variation of the string *K R T B* that they had studied. Below are some of the orders that were tested and reaction times for these orders:

(a) identical: *K R T B*	1.55 sec
(b) same first two letters: *K R B T*	1.55 sec
(c) same first letter: *K T B R*	1.59 sec
(d) same last two letters: *R K T B*	1.59 sec
(e) same last letter: *T K R B*	1.64 sec
(f) totally different: *T K B R*	1.74 sec

As can be seen, reaction time are quickest when the first two letters of the string are in the same order as in the study string. There is little difference between the conditions when all letters match, case (a), and when just the first two match, case (b). The next fastest condition is when just the first letter matches, case (c). Reaction times are as fast when just the first letter matches, case (c), as when the last two letters match, case (d), but slower when only the last letter matches, case (e). Reaction times are a good bit slower when there is no match at the beginning or end, case (f). These data show two major effects governing access to ordinal structure. The first, called *front anchoring*, concerns the fact that subjects have better access to the structure

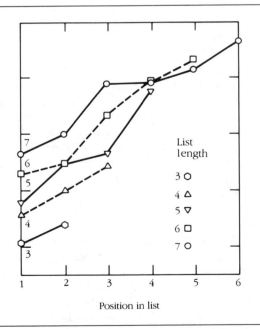

Position in list

Figure 4-19 Time to generate the next digit in a string of digits as a function of the ordinal position in the string and the length of the list. From Sternberg (1969).

from the beginning of the string. The second, called *end anchoring*, is less pronounced, but there is some advantage when the end of the string matches. Angiolillo-Bent and Rips (1982) report similar reaction-time data from the recognition of three consonant strings. They report data to indicate that the memory for these strings is not like a visual image. For instance, there is little effect of whether the case of the letters at study matches the case of the letters at test. That is, if subjects study *A R B*, they can quickly recognize *a r b*.

An experiment by Sternberg (1969) also shows the importance of front anchoring in a linear ordering. He had subjects memorize strings of up to seven digits and asked them to generate the next item in the string after a probe digit. Thus, a subject might be given 3 8 9 2 6 and be asked for the digit after 9, in which case the answer would be 2. Figure 4-19 illustrates the results from his experiment as a function of the position of the probe digit in the sequence of digits for lists of varying lengths. Note that subjects are fastest to access the first digit and get progressively slower to the end of the string. It has been suggested that subjects answer such questions by starting at the beginning of the string, searching forward until they find the probe, and then generating the next digit.

Hierarchical Encoding of Orderings

So far we have discussed the representation of rather short sequences of elements. What happens with longer sequences? There is considerable evidence that subjects store these hierarchically, with subsequences as units in larger sequences. So, for instance, consider how people might represent the order of the 26 letters in the alphabet. A possible hierarchical representation, based on the "Alphabet Song," is illustrated in Figure 4-20. This song is in turn based on the rhythm and melody of "Twinkle, Twinkle Little Star," and this correspondence is also illustrated in Figure 4-20. Thus, the alphabet is a hierarchical structure whose major constituents are ABCD, EFG, HIJK, LMNOP, QRS, TUV, WXYZ. In the "Alphabet Song" there are pauses, as indicated here by the spacing, between the sublists.

Klahr, Chase, and Lovelace (1983) did an experiment to look for effects of this hierarchical structure on time to generate the next letter in the alphabet. Thus, the subject might be given *K* and asked to generate the next letter (i.e., *L*). Figure 4-21 shows the generation times for each letter in the alphabet. Note that generation times are fastest at the beginning of a major constituent and get progressively slower toward the end of the constituent. Thus, within a constituent, subjects' judgment times show the same front-anchoring effect found by Sternberg in Figure 4-19. Klahr et al. theorize that subjects have access to the beginning of a sublist and search forward for the target letter.

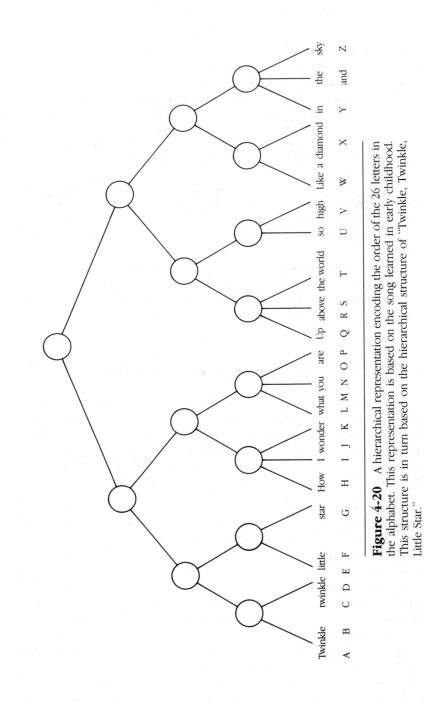

Figure 4-20 A hierarchical representation encoding the order of the 26 letters in the alphabet. This representation is based on the song learned in early childhood. This structure is in turn based on the hierarchical structure of "Twinkle, Twinkle, Little Star."

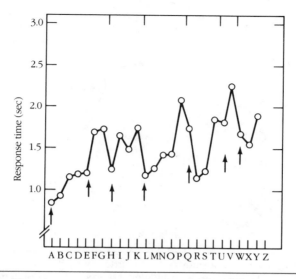

Figure 4-21 Time to generate the next letter in the alphabet. Arrows indicate beginning of new major constituents in the hierarchical encoding.

The research of Johnson (1970) provides more evidence for the reality of the hierarchical structure of long lists. He had subjects commit to memory random strings of letters, but used spacing to encourage a particular hierarchical organization. So, he might present his subjects with the following string to memorize:

D Y   J H Q   G W

He assumed subjects would set up hierarchies in which the individual phrases would be strings like *J H Q*, as dictated by the spacing. He looked at subjects' later recall of these strings and found that subjects tended to recall these substrings as units. If they recalled the first letter of a substring, there was a 90 percent probability of recalling the next letter. For instance, if they recalled the *J*, they would be very likely to recall the *H*. There was not the same tendency across unit barriers. For instance, if the subjects recalled *Y* in the foregoing string, there was only a 70 percent probability of recalling the *J* that follows.

Judgments of Linear Order

Another issue that has been explored concerns how people judge the relative order of items in a list of items. For instance, which comes first in the alphabet,

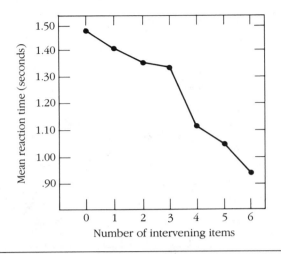

Figure 4-22 Data from a study of linear ordering by Woocher et al. (1978). The graph shows mean reaction times for judging the order of pairs of items as a function of the number of intervening items in the linear ordering.

J, or *L*? This issue is usually studied experimentally by having subjects commit to memory a set of facts specifying the order of various pairs of items. For instance, subjects are asked to learn such information as the following:

> John is taller than Fred.
>
> Fred is taller than Bill.
>
> Bill is taller than Herb.
>
> Herb is taller than Dave.
>
> Dave is taller than Alex.

After having committed these pairs to memory, subjects are able to recite the order of all of the items.

> John, Fred, Bill, Herb, Dave, and Alex

Thus, they commit this information to memory as a list of items. Subjects are then asked to answer questions such as *Who is taller, Dave or Fred?*— that is, they are asked to make judgments about which item is more extreme in the linear ordering. Many such experiments have been performed using linear orderings, such as those of Potts (1972, 1975) and Trabasso and Riley (1975). In this section, we consider a recent experiment by Woocher, Glass, and Holyoak (1978) in which subjects were to learn quite long linearly ordered lists. The results of this experiment are typical. Subjects learned about the linear ordering on the dimension of height of 16 people, referred to by name, and were asked to judge the relative heights of various pairs of items in the list. Interest focused on the amount of time subjects took to answer these questions as a function of the distance between the two items in the list. The latter varied from a distance of no intervening items (members of the pair were adjacent in the ordering) to a distance of six intervening items. Figure 4-22 plots the subjects' reaction times as a function of this distance. Note that a decreasing function was obtained, similar to that obtained when subjects make magnitude estimates of natural categories. A particularly striking feature of these data concerns the results for pairs with no intervening items. These are the pairs subjects were trained on to learn the linear orderings. Although subjects were directly trained on only these pairs, they were slowest in judging these pairs.

This distance effect for linear orderings is like the distance effect for sizes of images (p. 87). In that case we found that subjects found it easier to judge the relative size of two objects the greater the difference in the actual size of the objects.

Summary: Spatial Images and Linear Orderings

Although they represent different things, spatial images and linear orderings do have a number of features in common. First, both are abstracted from the original stimulus and preserve only some of the structure of the original stimulus. The spatial image preserves the position of objects in space; it does not preserve the modality. The linear ordering preserves the sequence of objects, but does not preserve whether the sequential information was encoded from hearing the order spoken or from reading the order.

It is possible to encode both spatial images and linear orderings into hierarchical structures in which smaller units appear as chunks within larger units. We will also see similar hierarchical encodings for memory representations for meaningful material. It seems that human memory tries to encode the world in terms of small, easy-to-process packets, and when there are too many items, memory creates packets within packets. It is frequently speculated (e.g., Broadbent, 1975) that this is because the human information processor is limited in terms of the amount of information that it can process at once.

Remarks and Suggested Readings

Paivio (1971) and Yuille (1983) should be consulted for Paivio's dual-code theory and particularly his theory on imagery. Shepard and Podgorny (1978) provide a good overview of the research on mental imagery and some discussion of this controversy. The research on imagery has suffered from a lack of explicit theories regarding the exact processes and representations involved. One attempt to remedy this deficit is the computer simulation program of Kosslyn and Shwartz (1977).

Kosslyn (1980) should be consulted for a thorough exposition of his views on imagery. Another recent book on imagery is that of Shepard and Cooper (1983). For papers critical of this research, consult Pylyshyn (1973, 1981).

A fair amount of recent research has been concerned with how mental images are used to encode maps of our environment. For two representative papers, read those of Hintzman, O'Dell and Arndt (1981) and Thorndyke and Stasz (1980). An interesting book is *Maps and Minds* by Downs and Stea (1977).

Lee and Estes (1981), Ratcliff (1981), and Wickelgren (1967) have been concerned about how we represent linear orders. Recently, I (Anderson, 1983; Chapter 2) have written about the relation between spatial and ordinal representations and the meaning-based representations to be discussed in the next chapter.

Chapter 5

Meaning-Based Knowledge Representations

Summary

1. Evidence for the importance of meaning-based representations comes from experiments showing that memory for a verbal communication retains not the exact wording but just the meaning of the communication, and from experiments showing that memory for a picture retains not the visual details but rather a meaningful interpretation of the picture.

2. Initial memory for an event contains both verbal and visual details. However, information about these details tends to be rapidly forgotten within the first minute following the stimulus, leaving only memory for the meaning of the event.

3. Because memory for meaning is longer lasting than memory for physical details, individuals can improve their memories by converting meaningless to-be-remembered information into a more meaningful form.

4. The meaning of a sentence or picture can be represented as a network of propositions. Often propositions enter into hierarchical relationships in which one proposition occurs as part of another proposition. Propositional networks reveal in graphical form the associative connections between concepts.

5. The closer together the concepts in a propositional network are, the better cues they are for each other's recall.

6. Schemas are large, complex units of knowledge that encode the typical properties of instances of general categories.

7. Schemas are organized according to a set of slots, or attributes. One slot specifies schemas more general than the current schema. Other slots specify schemas that define parts of the current schema. An important function of schemas is to enable a person to infer unseen information from what is seen.

8. Individual instances of natural categories, such as birds or fruits, vary in how well they match the schema for their category.

9. Schemas can represent stereotypic sequences of actions, such as going to a restaurant. Such event schemas are referred to as scripts. Scripts play an important role in the understanding of stories.

At the time of the writing of this book, the motion picture *ET* is the most attended film in history. Therefore, many of you should be able to recall the scene where the boy gets drunk and rescues the frogs. If you can recall the scene at all, you probably can recall many of the events involved in it. But reflect on your memory for the events. Can you remember what the boy wore? Can you remember any of the exact words that were said? Can you remember how many frogs he held? What exact physical details can you remember? In contrast, you can probably remember how the boy got drunk and why the frogs were in danger. It seems that we have an ability to remember the gist of an event without recalling any of its exact details. A fair amount of research in cognitive psychology has been devoted to documenting the importance of such meaning-based memories and establishing that they are different from the perception-based memories discussed in Chapter 4. We will review that research. Next we will review the nature of the propositional units that encode this information. Finally, we will consider how these units are combined in larger units, called *schemas*, to provide meaningful encodings of the properties of events and objects.

Memory for Verbal Information

In the last chapter we discussed the linear orderings that store information about the exact order of elements. There is no doubt that we use such a representation to encode some verbal information—that is, sometimes we can remember verbatim lines from poems, songs, plays, and speeches. However, considerable doubt exists as to whether all or even most of our memory for verbal communication can be accounted for in terms of memory for the verbatim (auditory or written) message.

An experiment by Wanner (1968) illustrates circumstances in which people do and do not remember information about exact wording. Wanner had subjects come into the laboratory and listen to tape-recorded instructions. For one group of subjects, "the warned group," the tape began this way:

> The materials for this test, including the instructions, have been recorded on tape. Listen very carefully to the instructions because you will be tested on your ability to recall particular sentences which occur in the *instructions*.

The second group received no such warning and so had no idea that they would be responsible for the verbatim instructions. After this point, the instructions were the same for both groups. At a later point in the instructions, one of four possible critical sentences occurred:

1. When you score your results, do nothing to correct your answers but mark carefully those answers which are wrong.

2. When you score your results, do nothing to correct your answers but carefully mark those answers which are wrong.

3. When you score your results, do nothing to your correct answers but mark carefully those answers which are wrong.

4. When you score your results, do nothing to your correct answers but carefully mark those answers which are wrong.

Immediately after presentation of this sentence, all subjects (warned or not) heard the following conclusion to the instructions:

> To begin the test, please turn to page 2 of the answer booklet and judge which of the sentences printed there occurred in the instructions you just heard.

On page 2 they found the critical sentence they had just heard plus a similar alternative. Suppose they had heard sentence 1. They might have to choose between 1 and 2 or between 1 and 3. Both pairs differ in the ordering of two words. However, the difference between 1 and 2 does not contribute critically to the meaning of the sentences; the difference is just stylistic. On the other hand, sentences 1 and 3 clearly do differ in meaning. Thus, by looking at subjects' ability to discriminate between different pairs of sentences, Wanner was able to measure their ability to remember the meaning versus the style of the sentence and to determine how this ability interacted with whether or not they were warned. The relevant data are displayed in Figure 5-1.

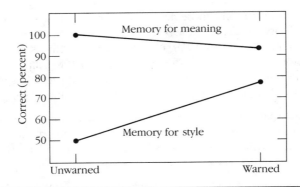

Figure 5-1   Ability of warned versus unwarned subjects to remember a wording difference that affected meaning versus style. (Adapted from Wanner, 1968.)

In this display, the percentage of correct identifications of sentences heard before is a function of whether subjects had been warned. The percentages correct for subjects who were asked to discriminate a meaningful difference in wording and for subjects who were asked to discriminate a stylistic difference are plotted separately. If subjects were just guessing, they would have scored 50 percent correct by chance; thus, we would not expect any values below 50 percent.

The implications of Figure 5-1 are clear. First, memory is better for changes in wording that result in changes of meaning than for changes in wording that result just in changes of style. The superiority of memory for meaning indicates that people normally extract the meaning from a linguistic message and do not remember its exact wording. Moreover, memory for meaning is equally good whether subjects are warned or not. (The slight advantage for unwarned subjects does not approach statistical significance.) Thus, subjects retain the meaning of a message as a normal part of their comprehension process. They do not have to be especially cued to memorize the sentence. In Chapter 7 we will see more evidence showing that intention to learn is often irrelevant to good memory.

The second implication of these results is that the warning did have an effect on memory for the stylistic change. Subjects were almost at chance in remembering stylistic change when unwarned, but they were fairly good at remembering when warned. This result indicates that we do not naturally retain much information about exact wording, but that we can do so when we are especially cued to pay attention to such information. Even with such a warning, however, memory for stylistic information is much poorer than memory for meaning.

Memory for Visual Information

On many occasions, our memory capacity seems much greater for visual information than for verbal information. A representative experiment was reported by Shepard (1967) in which he had subjects study a set of magazine pictures one picture at a time. After studying the pictures, subjects were presented with pairs of pictures consisting of one they had studied and one they had not studied. The subjects' task was to recognize which of each pair was the studied picture. This task was contrasted with a verbal situation in which subjects studied sentences and were similarly tested on their ability to recognize studied sentences when presented with pairs containing one new and one studied sentence. Subjects exhibited 11.8 percent errors in the sentence condition but only 1.5 percent errors in the picture condition. Recognition memory was fairly high in the sentence condition, but it was virtually perfect in the picture condition. There have been a number of experiments like Shepard's. Shepard's experiment involved 600 pictures. Perhaps the most impressive demonstration of visual memory is the experiment by Standing (1973), who showed that subjects could remember 73 percent of 10,000 pictures!

You might think that such high memory for pictures means people show very high retention of spatial images such as those discussed in Chapter 4. However, the evidence is that subjects are not likely to remember the exact visual details or spatial relations in a picture. Instead, they are remembering some rather abstract representation that captures the picture's meaning. That is, it proves useful to distinguish between the meaning of a picture and the physical picture, just as it proves important to distinguish between the meaning of a sentence and the physical sentence. A number of experiments point to the utility of this distinction with respect to picture memory and to the fact that we tend to remember the picture's meaning, not the physical picture. For example, subjects show poor memory for pictures that they are unable to interpret meaningfully. Consider the picture in Figure 5-2, which appears to be a random collection of ink blobs. The picture seems to have no meaning, and subjects show poor memory for it. However, if you look carefully, you will see a dog hidden in the picture. If people are able to detect the hidden figure in pictures like these, they will show much better memory for the picture (Wiseman & Neisser, 1974).

Figure 5-3 contains some of the material from the experiment of Bower, Karlin, and Dueck (1975), which makes the same point as Wiseman and Neisser's experiment. These investigators had subjects study such pictures, called *droodles*, with or without an explanation of their meaning. After subjects had studied the pictures, they were given a memory test in which they had to redraw the pictures. Subjects who had been given labels with which

Figure 5-2 A picture that at first appears to consist only of meaningless blobs. Subjects show better memory for this picture when they can recognize the dog. (From Ronald James.)

to study the pictures showed better recall of these pictures (70 percent correctly reconstructed) than subjects who were not given the verbal labels (51 percent).

It seems that people normally extract and remember the meaning from a picture just as they do with sentences. A recent experiment by Mandler and Ritchey (1977) made this point in yet another way. The experimenters had subjects study pictures of scenes, such as the classroom scene in Figure 5-4a. After studying eight such pictures for 10 sec each, subjects were tested for their recognition memory of the pictures. In the test, subjects were presented with a series of pictures and instructed to identify which pictures they had studied in the series. The series contained the exact pictures they had studied as well as distractor pictures such as Figure 5-4b and 5-4c. A distractor such as Figure 5-4b was called a *token distractor*. It differs from the target only with respect to the pattern on the teacher's dress, a visual detail relatively unimportant to the meaning of the picture. In contrast, the distractor in Figure

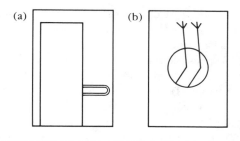

Figure 5-3 Droodles used by Bower et al. (1975). (a) A midget playing a trombone in a telephone booth. (b) An early bird who caught a very strong worm.

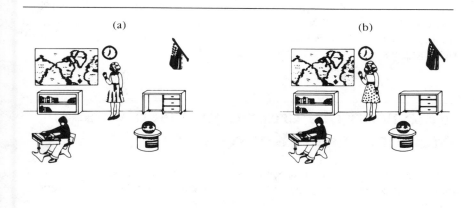

Figure 5-4 Pictures similar to those used in Mandler and Ritchey (1977). (a) Subjects studied this target picture. Later they were tested with a series of pictures that included the target (a) along with token distractors such as (b) and type distractors such as (c). (Copyright 1977 by the American Psychological Association. Reprinted by permission.)

5-4c involves a *type change*—from a world map to an art picture used by the teacher. This visual detail is relatively more important to the meaning of the picture, since it indicates the subject being taught. All eight pictures shown to subjects contained possible token changes and type changes. In each case, the type change involved a more important change to the picture's meaning than did the token change. There was no systematic difference in the amount of physical change involved in a type versus a token change. Subjects were able to recognize the original pictures 77 percent of the time, reject the token distractors only 60 percent of the time, but reject the type distractors 94 percent of the time. Chance guessing performance would have been 50 percent.

The conclusion in this study is very similar to that in the Wanner experiment reviewed earlier. Just as Wanner found that subjects were much more sensitive to meaning-significant changes in a sentence, so Mandler and Ritchey have found that subjects are sensitive to meaning-significant changes in a picture. It may be that subjects have better memory for the meanings of pictures than for the meanings of sentences, but that they have poor memory for the physical details of both.

Retention of Perception-Based versus Meaning-Based Knowledge

There is some evidence that subjects initially encode verbatim information about a sentence and spatial information about a picture, but they tend to rapidly forget this information. Once the exact information is forgotten, subjects retain only information about the meaning.

A classic experiment making this point was performed by Posner (1969). He presented subjects with two letters, with the presentations separated by varying intervals of time (called *interstimulus intervals*). The subjects' task was to decide as quickly as possible if the second letter—the *probe*—was the same as the first. The letters could be upper- or lowercase, but this did not matter for their judgment; an *A* followed by an *a* required a *same* response. The first letter was always uppercase, but the second letter was either upper- or lowercase. Thus, there were two *same* possibilities—*AA* and *Aa*—and two *different* possibilities—*AB* and *Ab*. (Of course, more letters than *A* and *B* were used.) Of principal interest was the difference between *AA*, called an *identity match*, and *Aa*, called a *name match*. We would expect subjects to be faster at making an identity match if they had exact visual information available. Figure 5-5 presents the subjects' reaction times in making their judgements as a function of the interstimulus interval. Note that initially there

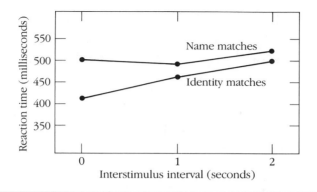

Figure 5-5 Reaction times for matching successively presented letters as a function of the interstimulus interval. Functions for identity matches and name matches are shown. (Adapted from Posner, 1969.)

is a large advantage for the identity match but that after 2 sec this advantage has almost completely disappeared. This alteration indicates that memory for the initial stimulus is rapidly transformed into an abstract code that does not retain specific visual information.

An experiment by Anderson (1974b) made the same point in the verbal domain. Subjects listened to a story that contained various critical sentences that would be tested, for instance:

1. The missionary shot the painter.

Later, subjects were asked to judge whether any of the following sentences followed logically from the story they had heard:

2. The missionary shot the painter.

3. The painter was shot by the missionary.

4. The painter shot the missionary.

5. The missionary was shot by the painter.

The first two sentences require a positive response and the last two require a negative response. Sentence 2 is analogous to Posner's identity match, whereas sentence 3, the passive transform, is analogous to Posner's name match. Here these sentences were called *same voice* (sentence 2) and *different voice* (sentence 3). As in Posner's test, the delay between the initial stimulus and the test probe was manipulated: Subjects were tested either immediately after hearing the sentences or a delay of about 2 min. The delay was filled with a presentation of more of the story. The manipulated delay of 2 min in

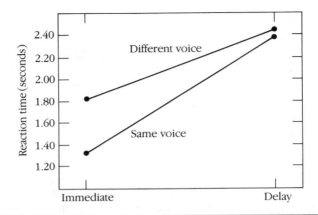

Figure 5-6 Time to judge that a test sentence has the same meaning as a studied sentence. Times are shown as a function of delay in testing and as a function of whether study and test sentences have the same voice.

this design is much longer than Posner's 2-sec delay, since longer delay manipulations seemed necessary with verbal material.

The results of this experiment are reported in Figure 5-6. As in the Posner experiment, same-voice probes exhibit a large reaction-time advantage immediately but little advantage with delay. So, it seems that verbal information, like visual information, tends to be short-lived and that after delays we mainly remember abstract information.

However, you should not conclude from these findings that people have no memory for physical features after long delays. With effort, we can remember verbatim passages and exact visual details. In a series of clever experiments, Kolers (1979) has shown that under the appropriate conditions we can retain visual details about the typography of a page of print for months! It does seem, however, that after long delays most exact physical information is lost, and that we are mainly left with a general characterization of the meaning of the stimulus.

Implications of Good Memory for Meaning

It has been shown over and over again that meaningful information is better remembered than meaningless information. If people have a choice about whether to commit information to memory meaningfully or nonmeaningfully, they are well advised to go the meaningful route. Unfortunately, there are many people who are unaware of this fact, and their memory performance suffers as a consequence.

I can still remember the traumatic experience I had in my first paired-associate experiment. It was part of a sophomore class on experimental psychology. For reasons I have long since forgotten, we had designed a class experiment that involved learning 16 memorable pairs such as DAX–GIB. That is, our task was to be able to recall GIB when prompted with the cue DAX. I was determined to outperform other members of my class. My personal theory of memory at that time, which I intended to apply, was basically that if you try hard and intensely you will remember well. In the impending experimental situation, this meant that during the learning period I would say (as loud as was seemly) the paired associates over and over again, as fast as I could. My theory was that by this method the paired associates would be forever burned into my mind. To my chagrin, I wound up with the worst score in the class.

My theory of "loud and fast" was directly opposed to the true means of improving memory. I was trying to commit a meaningless auditory pair to memory. But the material in this chapter suggests that we have best memory for meaningful information, not meaningless verbal information. I should have been trying to convert my memory task into something more meaningful. For instance, DAX is like *dad* and GIB is the first part of *gibberish*. So I might have created an image of my father speaking some gibberish to me. This would have been a simple *mnemonic* (memory-assisting) *technique* and would have worked quite well as a means of associating the two.

We do not often have the need to learn pairs of nonsense syllables outside the laboratory situation. However, in many situations we have to associate various combinations of terms that do not have much inherent meaning. We have to learn shopping lists, names for faces, telephone numbers, rote facts in a college class, vocabulary items in a foreign language, and so on. In all cases, we can improve memory if we transform the task into one of associating the items meaningfully. Transforming meaningless information into meaningful information is a prime trick of the memory experts who perform in nightclubs.

Recall from the introductory chapter the subject SF, who was able to recall 81 digits in a memory span (Chase & Ericsson, 1982). He was a long-distance runner, and part of his technique was to convert digits into running times. So, he would take four digits, like 3492, and convert them into "Three minutes, 49.2 seconds—near world-record mile time." Such descriptions were very meaningful for him, and he found them much easier to remember than the original digits. His is one example among many of the importance of meaningful encoding to good memory.

One mnemonic technique that can help in the classroom is the *key-word method* for learning vocabulary items. Consider, for instance, the Italian *for-*

maggio (pronounced FOR MODGE JO), which means "cheese." No inherently meaningful connection exists between the Italian and English equivalents, but the key-word method forces one. The first step is to transform the foreign word into some English sound-alike phrase—for example, FOR MODGE JO sounds like "for much dough." The second step is to invent a meaningful connection between the two. In this case, we might imagine an expensive cheese that sold for much money, or "for much dough." Or consider *carciofi* (pronounced CAR CHOH FEE), which means "artichokes." We might transform CAR CHOH FEE into "car trophy" and imagine a winning car at an auto show with a trophy shaped like an artichoke. Atkinson and Raugh (1975) studied such a key-word technique in language learning and showed it to be very effective. They claimed that as students become familiar with a foreign language, their consciousness of the key words drops out. Thus, it appears that the key word provides a helpful crutch for getting started but does not stay around to clutter up memory.

Summary of Research on Memory for Meaning

The mainstay of long-term memory is a representation that does not preserve the exact structure of the event remembered. Rather, it preserves the meaning. There remains the question of how to represent that meaning. *Propositional representations* are often used for this purpose.

Propositional Representations
Analysis into Propositions

The idea that information is represented in terms of propositions is currently the most popular concept of how meaning is represented in memory. In a propositional analysis, only the meaning of an event is represented. The unimportant details—details that humans tend not to remember—are not represented. This idea has been incorporated into such contemporary theories as Anderson (1976), Anderson and Bower (1973), Clark (1974), Frederiksen (1975), Kintsch (1974), and Norman and Rumelhart (1975). The concept of a *proposition*, borrowed from logic and linguistics, is central to this analysis. A proposition is the smallest unit of knowledge that can stand as a separate assertion, that is, the smallest unit about which it makes sense to make the judgment true or false. Propositional analysis most clearly applies to linguistic information, and it is with respect to this information that the topic is developed here.

Consider the following sentence:

1. Nixon gave a beautiful Cadillac to Brezhnev, who is leader of the USSR.

This sentence can be seen to be composed from the following simpler sentences:

2. Nixon gave a Cadillac to Brezhnev.

3. The Cadillac was beautiful.

4. Brezhnev is leader of the USSR.

If any of these simple sentences were false, the complex sentence would not be true. These sentences closely correspond to the propositions that underlie the meaning of sentence 1. Each simple sentence expresses a primitive unit of meaning. One condition that our meaning representations must satisfy is that each separate unit in them correspond to a unit of meaning.

However, the propositional-representation theory does not claim that a person remembers in exact sentences such as 2 through 4. Past research indicates that subjects do not remember the exact wording of such underlying sentences any more than they remember the exact wording of the original sentences. For instance, Anderson (1972) showed that subjects would demonstrate poor ability to remember whether they heard sentence 2 or another sentence, labeled 5:

5. Brezhnev was given a Cadillac by Nixon.

Thus, it seems that information is represented in memory in a way that expresses the meaning of the primitive assertions but does not preserve exact wording. A number of propositional notations represent information in this abstract way. One, used by Kintsch (1974), represents each proposition as a list containing a *relation* followed by an ordered list of *arguments*. The relations correspond to the verbs (in this case, *give*), adjectives (*beautiful*), or other relational terms (*is leader of*) in the sentences, while the arguments correspond to the nouns (*Nixon, a Cadillac, Brezhnev,* and *USSR*). The relations assert connections among the entities referred to by these nouns. As an example, sentences 2 through 4 would be represented by these lists:

6. (*Give*, Nixon, Cadillac, Brezhnev, *Past*)

7. (*Beautiful*, Cadillac)

8. (*Leader-of*, Brezhnev, USSR)

Kintsch standardly embeds a list of relations plus arguments in parentheses, as above. Whether the subject had heard sentence 1 or sentence 9,

9. The leader of the USSR, Brezhnev, was given a Cadillac by Nixon and it was beautiful.

the meaning of the message would be represented by lists 6 through 8. Note that various relations take different numbers of arguments. For instance, the relation *give* is assumed to take four arguments—the agent of the giving, the object of the giving, the recipient of the giving, and the time of the giving.

Propositional Networks

There is another way to represent the meaning of the sentence labeled 1 in the preceding subsection—by means of a *propositional network*.[1] Figure 5-7 illustrates the structure of a propositional network. In such a network, each proposition is represented by an ellipse, which is connected by labeled arrows to its relation and arguments. The propositions, the relations, and the arguments are called the *nodes* of the network, and the arrows are called the *links* because they connect nodes. For instance, the ellipse labeled 6 in Figure 5-7a represents proposition 6. This ellipse is connected to the relation *give* by a link labeled *relation*, to indicate that it is pointing to the relation node to *Nixon* by an *agent* link, to *Cadillac* by an *object* link, to *Brezhnev* by a *recipient* link, and to *past* by a *time* link. The three network structures in Figures 5-7a–c represent the individual propositions 6 through 8 listed in the preceding subsection. Note that these different networks contain the same nodes; for example, part (a) and part (b) both contain *Cadillac*. This overlap indicates that these networks are really interconnected parts of a larger network. This larger network is illustrated in Figure 5-7d.

The spatial location of elements in a network is totally irrelevant to the interpretation of the network. A network can be thought of as a tangle of marbles connected by strings. The marbles represent the nodes, and the strings represent the links between the nodes. The network represented on a two-dimensional page is that tangle of marbles laid out in a certain way. We try to lay the network out in a way that facilitates its interpretation, but any order is possible. Thus, Figure 5-7 is another way of representing the network shown in Figure 5-7. All that matters is which elements are connected to which, not where the components lie.

We now have two ways of representing the same propositional information:

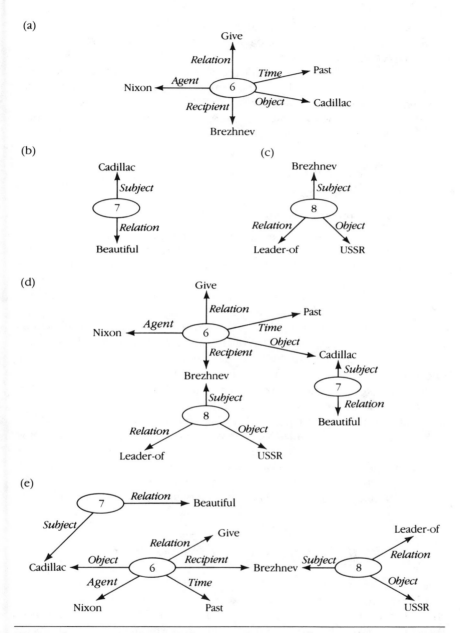

Figure 5-7 Examples of propositional-network representations. Parts (a)–(c) represent propositions 6–8. Part (d) illustrates the combined networks (a)–(c). Part (e) is another way of displaying the network in part (d).

with a set of linear propositions, as in propositions 6 through 8, or with a network, as in Figure 5-7. Since the information represented is abstract, either notational convention will work. The linear representation is somewhat neater and more compact, but the network representation reveals the connections among elements. As we will see, this connectivity proves useful for understanding certain memory phenomena.

Besides the basic propositional structure, some other structures are needed to create adequate meaning representations. Suppose we wanted to represent the following three sentences:

10. Nixon gave Brezhnev a Cadillac.

11. Fred owns a Cadillac.

12. Fred shouted "Nixon."

(We will assume that Fred is the same person in sentences 11 and 12.) Given the representational concepts discussed so far, we would represent this information with the network in Figure 5-8a. However, this network exhibits a number of inadequacies. First, it is not the case that the object of Fred's shouting in sentence 12 is the same as the agent of the giving in sentence 10. In one case we are dealing with the person, and in the other case we are dealing with his name. Therefore, we need to distinguish between words and the concepts they refer to. This distinction is made in Figure 5-8b, where words and concepts have different nodes. In this network (and as a general rule) words are written within quotation marks, whereas concepts are represented by words without quotation marks. A link labeled *word* indicates the connection between the concept and the word.

Another problem with Figure 5-8a is that only one node exists for Cadillac, which implies that the Cadillac Nixon gave is the one Fred owns. This example illustrates the need for a distinction between specific objects, such as the particular Cadillacs, and general classes, such as the category *Cadillac*. In Figure 5-8b, the distinction is made: Two instance nodes, X and Y, stand for the two Cadillacs. Links labeled *isa* indicate that each node is a Cadillac.

Hierarchical Organization of Propositions

One of the important features about propositions is that, like spatial images and linear orderings, they are capable of entering into hierarchical relationships where one proposition occurs as a unit within another proposition. Parts (a) and (b) of Figure 5-9 illustrate the propositional representations for the following two sentences:

John bought some candy because he was hungry.

John believed Russia would invade Poland.

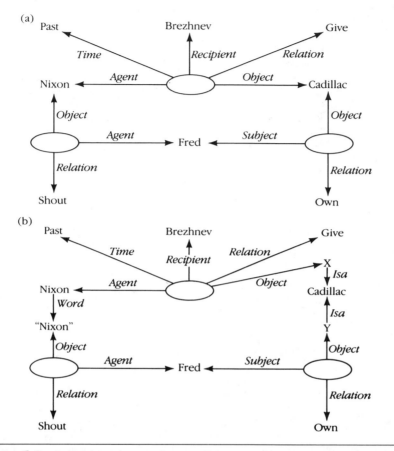

Figure 5-8 Propositional-network representations of sentences 10–12. Part (a) is inadequate; part (b) is more adequate because it distinguishes between words and concepts and between classes and instances.

Note in Figure 5-9 that both the proposition *John bought some candy* and the proposition *John was hungry* occur as arguments within a larger proposition that asserts that the first proposition is caused by the second. Similarly, the proposition *Russia would invade Poland* occurs as the object of the proposition about John's believing.

Propositional Networks as Associative Structures

It is useful to think of the nodes in a semantic network as ideas and to think of the links between the nodes as associations between the ideas, as a number

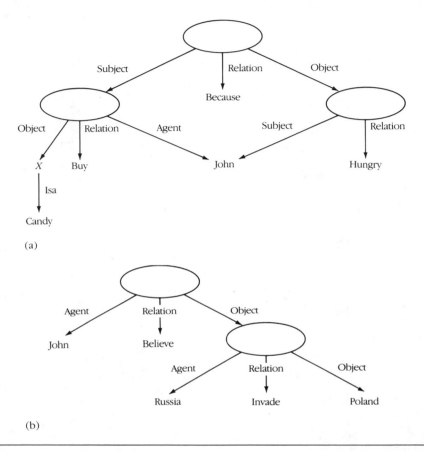

(a)

(b)

Figure 5-9 Propositional representations for (a) *John bought some candy because he was hungry* and (b) *John believed Russia would invade Poland*.

of experiments suggest. Consider an experiment by Weisberg (1969). He had subjects study and commit to memory such sentences as *Children who are slow eat bread that is cold*. The propositional-network representation for this sentence is illustrated in Figure 5-10. After learning a sentence, subjects were administered free-association tasks in which they were given a word from the sentence and asked to respond with the first word from the sentence that came to mind. Subjects cued with *slow* almost always free associated *children* and almost never *bread*, although *bread* is closer to *slow* in the sentence than *children*. However, Figure 5-10 shows that *slow* and *children* are nearer each other (three links) than *slow* and *bread* (five links). Similarly, subjects cued with *bread* almost always recalled *cold* rather than *slow*, although in

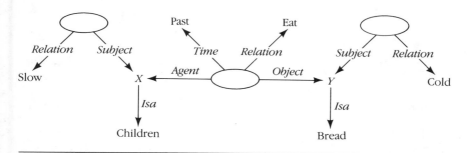

Figure 5-10 A propositional-network representation of the sentence *Children who are slow eat bread that is cold.*

the sentence *bread* and *slow* are closer than *bread* and *cold*. This is because *bread* and *cold* are closer to each other (three links) in the network than are *bread* and *slow* (five links). (A similar point has been made in an experiment by Ratcliff & McKoon, 1978.)

Retrieval from Propositional Networks

This associative analysis of propositional structures has proven to be very useful in understanding variations in the times subjects take to retrieve information from memory. Collins and Quillian (1969) had subjects judge the truth of assertions about concepts such as the following:

1. Robins eat worms.
2. Robins have feathers.
3. Robins have skin.

Subjects were shown facts such as these as well as false assertions, such as *Apples have feathers*. They were asked to judge whether a statement was true or false by pressing one of two buttons. The time from presentation of the statement to the button press was measured.

Figure 5-11 illustrates the kind of network structure that Collins and Quillian assumed represented the information in subjects' memories. Sentence 1 is directly stored with *robin*. However, sentence 2 is not directly stored at the *robin* node. Rather, the *have feathers* property is stored with *bird*, and sentence 2 can be inferred from the directly stored facts that *a robin is a bird* and *birds have feathers*. Again, sentence 3 is not directly stored with *robin*; rather, the *have skin* predicate is stored with *animal*. Thus, sentence 3 can be inferred from the facts *a robin is a bird* and *a bird is an animal* and *animals have skin*. Thus, with sentence 1, all the requisite information

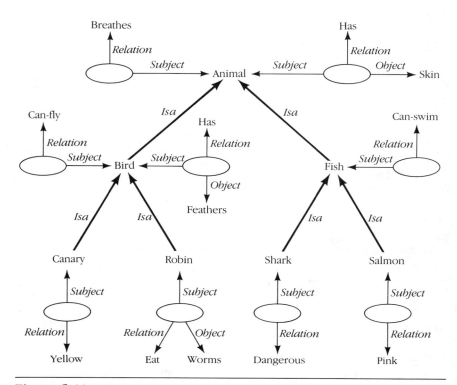

Figure 5-11 The network of concepts assumed by Collins and Quillian (1969) in their experiment to compare reaction times in making true-or-false judgments about statements. A hierarchy of concepts and associated properties can be seen in the figure.

for its verification is stored with *robin*; in the case of sentence 2, subjects must traverse one link from *robin* to *bird* to retrieve the requisite information, and in sentence 3, subjects would have to traverse two links from *robin* to *animal*.

If our memories were structured like Figure 5-11, we would expect statement 1 to be verified more quickly than statement 2, which would be verified more quickly than statement 3. This is just what Collins and Quillian found. Subjects required 1310 msec to make judgments about statements like statement 1, 1380 msec for questions like 2, and 1470 msec for statements like 3. Subsequent research on the retrieval of information from memory has somewhat complicated the conclusions drawn from the initial Collins and Quillian experiment. The frequency with which facts are experienced has been observed to have strong effects on retrieval time (e.g., Conrad, 1972). Some facts, such as *Apples are eaten*, for which the predicate could be stored with an intermediate concept such as food, but that are experienced quite frequently, are verified as fast as or faster than facts such as *Apples have dark seeds*, which must be stored more directly with the *apple* concept. It seems that if a fact about a concept is frequently encountered, it will be stored with that concept even if it is also stored with a more general concept. The following statements about the organization of facts in propositional memory and their retrieval times seem to be valid conclusions from the research:

1. If a fact about a concept is frequently encountered, it will be stored with that concept even if it could be inferred from a more distant (in the network) concept.

2. The more frequently encountered a fact about a concept is, the more strongly that fact will be associated with the concept. And the more strongly associated with concepts facts are, the more rapidly they are verified.

3. Verifying facts that are not directly stored with a concept but that must be inferred takes a relatively long time.

Thus, both the strength of the connections between facts and concepts (determined by frequency of experience) and the distance between them propositionally have effects on retrieval time. We will have much more to say about the strength factor in Chapter 6, which discusses memory retrieval.

We can use the following facts (still all true in 1984) to illustrate the conclusions listed above:

1. Ronald Reagan was a movie star.

2. Ronald Reagan lives in the White House.

3. Ronald Reagan was president of the actor's union.

4. Ronald Reagan is immune from criminal prosecution.

We would expect fact 1 to be verified very rapidly because it is stored directly with the concept *Ronald Reagan* and is frequently encountered. Fact 2 would be quickly verifiable, even though it could be retrieved from the facts *Ronald Reagan is president* and *The president lives in the White House*. However, because fact 2 is frequently associated with Reagan, it should be directly associated to *Reagan*. Verifying fact 3 should take longer, even though this fact is directly stored with *Ronald Reagan*, since it is not often encountered (in fact, some people may not know it is true). Fact 4 should also take a long time to verify since it is probably not stored with *Reagan* but must be inferred from the fact that he is president.

Schemas

Propositions are fine for representing small units of meaning, but they fail when it comes to representing the large sets of organized information that we know about particular concepts. Consider, for instance, our knowledge of what a house is like. We know many propositions about a house, such as the following:

> Houses have rooms.
>
> Houses can be built of wood.
>
> Houses have roofs.
>
> Houses have walls.
>
> Houses have windows.
>
> People live in houses.

Just to list such facts, however, does not capture their interrelational structure. The basic insight is that concepts like *house* are defined by a configuration of features, and each of these features involves specifying a value the object has on some attribute. The schema representation is the way to capture this basic insight. Schemas represent the structure of an object according to a *slot* structure, where slots specify values that the object has on various attributes. So, we have the following partial schema representation of a house.

> *House*
>
> superset: building
>
> material: wood, brick
>
> contains: rooms
>
> function: human dwelling
>
> shape: rectilinear
>
> size: 500–5000 ft^2
>
> location: on ground

In this list, terms like *material* or *shape* are the *attributes*, or *slots*, and terms like *wood*, *brick*, or *rectilinear* are the *values*. Each pair of a slot and a value amounts to a proposition about a house. In some cases the values specify typical categories. The fact that houses are typically built of material like wood and brick does not exclude such possibilities as cardboard.

A special slot in each schema is its superset. Basically, unless contradicted, a concept inherits the features of its superset. Thus, stored with *building*, the superset of *house*, we would have features such as that it has a roof and walls.

These supersets are basically the *isa hierarchies* that we saw with semantic networks. In the case of schemas, they are sometimes called *generalization hierarchies*.

Schemas have another type of hierarchy, called a *part hierarchy*. Thus, parts of houses such as walls and rooms, have their own schema definitions. Stored with schemas for *walls* and *rooms* we would find that these have windows and ceilings. Thus, using the part relationships, we would be able to infer that houses have windows and ceilings.

Schemas are designed to facilitate making inferences about the concepts. If we know something is a house, we can use the schema definition to infer that it is probably made of wood or brick, and that it has walls, windows, and the like. However, the inferential processes for schemas must be able to deal with exceptions. So, we can still understand what a house without a roof is. Also, it is necessary to understand the constraints between slots of a schema. So, if we hear of a house that is underground, we can infer that it will not have windows.

Psychological Reality of Schemas

Brewer and Treyens (1981) provided an interesting demonstration of the effects of schemas in memory inferences. Thirty subjects were brought individually to the room shown in Figure 5-12. They were told that this was the office of the experimenter, and they were asked to wait there until the experimenter went to the laboratory to see if the previous subject had finished. After 35 sec the experimenter returned and took the waiting subject to a nearby seminar room. Here the subject was asked to write down everything he or she could remember about the experimental room. What would you be able to recall?

Brewer and Treyens argued that their subjects' recall would be strongly influenced by their schema of what an office contains. Subjects would do very well recalling items that are part of that schema; they should do much less well at recalling office items that are not part of the schema; they should falsely recall things that are part of the typical office but not of this one. This is just the pattern of results that Brewer and Treyens found. For instance, 29 of the 30 subjects recalled that the office had a chair, a desk, and walls. However, only eight subjects recalled that it had a bulletin board or a skull. On the other hand, nine subjects recalled that it had books, which it did not. Thus, we see that a subject's memory for location is strongly influenced by that person's schema for the location.

Schemas as a formalism for representing knowledge were developed in the field of artificial intelligence, where they have proven very useful for organizing and reasoning about large and complex knowledge bases (Bobrow

Figure 5-12   The experimental room used in the memory experiment of Brewer and Treyens (1981).

& Winograd, 1977; Minsky, 1975; Schank & Abelson, 1977). Winston (1977) provides a readable discussion of their use in artificial intelligence. We are still in the process of trying to understand the psychological significance of this representational construct (see discussions by Abelson, 1981, and Rumelhart & Ortony, 1977). Although experiments such as those of Brewer and Treyens indicate that humans have knowledge representations like schemas, it is not clear that human schemas have all and only the properties associated with schemas as they are used in artificial intelligence.

Schemas Represent Natural Categories

One of the important features of schemas is that they allow variation in the objects that might fit a particular schema. There are constraints on what typically occupies various slots of a schema, but there are few absolute prohibitions. This suggests that if schemas encode our knowledge about various object categories, we ought to see a shading from less typical to more typical members of the category as the features of the members better satisfy the schema contraints. There is now considerable evidence that natural categories like *birds* have the kind of structure that would be expected of a schema.

Much of the research documenting such variation in category membership has been done by Rosch. In one experiment (1973), Rosch had subjects rate the typicality of various members of a category on a 1-to-7 scale, where 1 meant very typical and 7 meant very atypical. Subjects were extremely consistent in their responses. In the bird category, *robin* got an average rating of 1.1 and *chicken* a rating of 3.8. In reference to sports, *football* was thought to be very typical (1.2), whereas *weightlifting* was not (4.7). *Murder* was rated a very typical crime (1.0), whereas *vagrancy* was not (5.3). *Carrot* was a very typical vegetable (1.1); *parsley* was not (3.8).

Rosch (1975) asked subjects to judge actual pictures of objects rather than to judge words. Subjects are faster to judge a picture as an instance of a category when it presents a typical member of the category. For instance, apples are more rapidly seen as fruits than are watermelons, and robins are more rapidly seen as birds than are chickens. Thus, typical members of a category appear also to have an advantage in perceptual recognition.

Rosch (1977) demonstrated another way in which central members of a category are more typical. She had subjects compose sentences for category names. For *bird*, subjects generated sentences such as these:

I heard a bird twittering outside my window.

Three birds sat on the branch of a tree.

A bird flew down and began eating.

Rosch replaced the category name in these sentences with a central member (robin), a less central member (eagle), or a peripheral member (chicken) and asked subjects to rate the sensibleness of the resulting sentences. Sentences involving central members got high ratings, sentences with less central members got lower ratings, and sentences with peripheral members got the lowest ratings. So, the evidence is that when people think of a category member, they generally think of typical instances of that category.

A prediction that derives from the schematic structure of categories is that they do not have fixed boundaries. People should have great difficulty and should be quite inconsistent in judging whether items at the periphery of a category are actually members of that category. McCloskey and Glucksberg (1978) looked at people's judgments as to what were or were not members of various categories. They found that although subjects did agree on some items, they disagreed on many. For instance, whereas all 30 subjects agreed that *cancer* was a disease and *happiness* was not, 16 thought *stroke* was a disease and 14 did not. Again, all 30 subjects agreed that *apple* was a fruit and *chicken* was not, but 16 thought *pumpkin* was and 14 disagreed. Once again, all subjects agreed that a *fly* was an insect and a *dog* was not, but 13 subjects thought a *leech* was and 17 disagreed. Thus, it appears that subjects do not always agree among themselves. McCloskey and Glucksberg tested the same subjects a month later and found that many had changed their mind

Figure 5-13 The various cuplike objects used in the experiment by Labov studying the boundaries of the *cup* category (1973). (Reprinted with permission from W. Labov. "The Boundaries of Words and Their Meanings." In *New Ways of Analyzing Variation in English*. Edited by C.-J. N. Bailey and R. W. Shuy. Washington, DC: Georgetown University Press. Pages 354 and 356. Copyright 1973 by Georgetown University.)

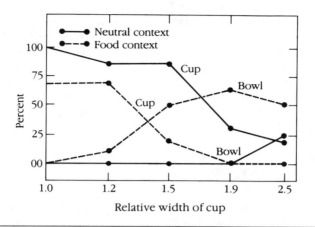

Relative width of cup

Figure 5-14 The percentage of subjects who used the terms *cup* or *bowl* to describe the objects shown in Figure 5-13 as a function of the ratio of cup width to cup depth imagined. The solid lines are for the neutral-context condition; the dotted lines are for the food-context condition. (Reprinted with permission from W. Labov. "The Boundaries of Words and Their Meanings." In *New Ways of Analyzing Variation in English*. Edited by C.-J. N. Bailey and R. W. Shuy. Washington, DC: Georgetown University Press. Pages 354 and 356. Copyright 1973 by Georgetown University.)

about the disputed items. For instance, 11 out of 30 reversed themselves on *stroke*, 8 reversed themselves on *pumpkin*, and 3 reversed themselves on *leech*. Thus, disagreement as to category boundaries does not just occur *among* subjects. Subjects are very uncertain *within* themselves exactly where the boundaries of a category should be drawn.

Figure 5-13 illustrates a set of material used by Labov (1973). He was interested in which items subjects would call cups and which they would not. Which do you consider to be cups? The interesting point is that these concepts do not appear to have clear-cut boundaries. In one experiment, Labov used the series of items 1 through 4. These items reflect an increasing ratio of width of the cup to depth. For the first item the ratio is 1, while for item 4 it is 1.9. Labov also used an item (not shown) where the ratio was 2.5 to 1. Figure 5-14 shows the percentage of subjects calling each of the five objects a cup and the percentage calling it a bowl. The solid lines indicate the classifications when subjects were simply presented with pictures of the objects (the neutral context). As can be seen, the percentages of *cup* responses gradually decreased with increasing width, but there is no clear-cut point where subjects stopped using *cup*. At the extreme 2.5-width ratio, about 25 percent of the subjects still used the *cup* response, while another 25 percent used *bowl*. (The remaining 50 percent used other responses.) The dotted lines give classifications when subjects were asked to imagine the object filled with mashed potatoes and placed on a table. In this context, fewer *cup* responses and more *bowl* responses were given, but the data show the same gradual shift from *cup* to *bowl*. Thus, it appears that subjects' classification behavior varies continuously not only with the properties of an object but also with the context in which the object is imagined or presented.

Event Schemas

It is not just objects and concepts that can be encoded by schemas. It is also possible to represent events as schemas. That is, we can encode our knowledge about stereotypic events, such as going to a movie, according to their parts—for instance, going to the theater, buying the ticket, buying refreshments, seeing the movie, and returning from the theater. Each of these can be divided into its parts. So, as with object schemas, we have part hierarchies. We also can have generalization hierarchies—going to a drive-in theater is a special case of going to a movie, which is a special case of an entertainment event. The slots associated with a story schema also include typical participants (ticket-takers in movies) and typical objects (e.g., a movie screen). As with objects, slots of event schemas have typical values or constraints. For instance, the typical choice for refreshments is popcorn and soda, whereas the means of going is typically the same as the means of leaving and typically involves a vehicle (e.g., car, bus).

Roger Schank and Robert Abelson (1977) at Yale University have worked extensively on event schemas that they call scripts. They pointed out that many circumstances involve stereotypic sequences of actions. For instance, the list below shows their hunch as to what stereotypic aspects of dining at a restaurant might be, and represents the components of a script for such an occasion.

> *Scene 1: Entering*
> Customer enters restaurant.
> Customer looks for table.
> Customer decides where to sit.
> Customer goes to table.
> Customer sits down.
>
> *Scene 2: Ordering*
> Customer picks up menu.
> Customer looks at menu.
> Customer decides on food.

Customer signals waitress.
Waitress comes to table.
Customer orders food.
Waitress goes to cook.
Waitress gives food order to cook.
Cook prepares food.

Scene 3: Eating
Cook gives food to waitress.
Waitress brings food to customer.
Customer eats food.

Scene 4: Exiting
Waitress writes bill.
Waitress goes over to customer.
Waitress gives bill to customer.
Customer gives tip to waitress.
Customer goes to cashier.
Customer gives money to cashier.
Customer leaves restaurant.

Bower, Black, and Turner (1979) report a series of experiments in which the psychological reality of the script notion was tested. They had subjects name what they considered the 20 most important events in an episode such as going to a restaurant. With 32 subjects, they failed to get complete agreement on what these events were. No action was listed as part of the episode by all of the subjects. However, considerable consensus was reported. Table 5-1 lists the events named. The items in roman were listed by at least 25 percent of the subjects. The italicized items were named by at least 48 percent of the subjects, and the items in capitals were given by at least 73 percent. Using the 73 percent as a criterion, we find the stereotypic sequence was *sit down, look at menu, order, eat, pay bill,* and *leave.*

Bower et al. went on to show a number of effects of such action scripts on memory for stories. They had subjects study stories that included some but not all of the typical events from a story. Subjects were then asked to recall the stories (in one experiment) or to recognize (in another experiment) whether various statements came from the story. When recalling these stories, subjects tended to report statements that were part of the script but that had not been presented as part of the stories. Similarly, in the recognition test, subjects thought they had studied script items that had not actually been in the stories. However, subjects showed a greater tendency to recall actual items from the stories or to recognize actual items than to falsely recognize foils not in the stories, despite the distortion in the direction of the general schema.

Table 5-1   *Empirical script norms at three agreement levels*

Going to a restaurant

Open door.
Enter.
Give reservation name.
Wait to be seated.
Go to table.
BE SEATED.
Order drinks.
Put napkins on lap.
LOOK AT MENU.
Discuss menu.
ORDER MEAL.
Talk.
Drink water.
Eat salad or soup.
Meal arrives.
EAT FOOD.
Finish meal.
Order dessert.
Eat dessert.
Ask for bill.
Bill arrives.
PAY BILL.
Leave tip.
Get coats.
LEAVE.

Adapted from Bower et al. (1979).

Note. The items in capitals were mentioned by the most subjects (73 percent), items in italic by fewer subjects (48 percent), and items in lowercase roman by still fewer subjects (25 percent).

In another experiment, these investigators read to subjects stories composed of 12 prototypical actions in an episode. Eight of the actions occurred in their standard temporal position, but four were rearranged. Thus, in the restaurant story the bill might be paid at the beginning and the menu read at the end. In recalling these stories, subjects showed a strong tendency to put the events back in their normal order. In fact, about half of the statements were put back. This experiment serves as another demonstration of the powerful effect of general schemas on memory for stories.

These experiments indicate that new events are encoded with respect to these general schemas and that subsequent recall is influenced by the schemas. We have talked about these effects as if they were "bad"; that is, as if subjects were misrecalling the stories. However, it is not clear that these results should be classified as acts of misrecall. Normally, if a certain standard event such as paying a check is omitted in a story, we are supposed to assume it occurred. Similarly, if the storyteller says the check was paid at the beginning of the restaurant episode, we have some reason to doubt the storyteller. Scripts or schemas exist because they encode the predominant sequence of events in a particular kind of situation. Thus, they can serve as valuable bases for predicting missing information and for correcting errors in information.

This research on scripts has served as a stimulus for a great deal of recent research on cognitive science concerned with how people organize their knowledge of events. For more recent ideas read Schank (1982).

Conclusions

We have reviewed meaning-based representations at two levels. Propositions represent the atomic units of meaning and can be used to represent the meaning of sentences and pictures. The interconnections among propositions define a network that can be profitably used to understand memory phenomena. In this chapter we discussed a few examples of how these networks can be used to understand memory phenomena (e.g., Weisberg's constrained association task). The next two chapters on memory will make extensive use of this network representation.

However, there are features of our knowledge that cannot be represented simply by the network structures defined by propositions. Certain sets of propositions cohere together in larger order units called schemas. For instance, part of our knowledge about restaurants is not just that certain events happen there, but that they tend to occur together in certain sequences. Thus, schemas represent our knowledge about how features tend to go together to define objects or how events tend to go together to define episodes. This knowledge about what tends to occur with what is very important to our ability to predict what we will encounter in our environment. The meaning encoded by schemas are these co-occurrence relations.

A natural inference from the structure of this chapter is that the units that make up schemas are propositions. However, this is not always the case. For instance, some of the components that make up a house include spatial information about object shape as well as propositional information about the function of a house. Similarly, a major part of an event schema is information about the order of subevents. Spatial information is encoded by images and order information by linear orderings, as discussed in the Chapter 4. Thus, we see that schemas encode the co-occurrence relations among propositions, spatial images, and linear orderings.

Remarks and Suggested Readings

The exact details of the propositional network given in this chapter differ from those described in any of the specific proposals in the literature. See Anderson (1976), Anderson and Bower (1973), Kintsch (1974), and Norman and Rumelhart (1975) for some of these specific proposals about how propositional information is represented. Lindsay and Norman (1977) provide another introductory exposition of propositional networks.

In the 1970s there was a debate between dual-code theorists, who believed only in spatial and verbal codes, and propositional theorists. Key papers in this debate include those of Pylyshyn (1973), Kosslyn and Pomerantz (1977), Palmer (1978), Paivio (1975), and Anderson (1978a). Researchers are now moving to a more catholic viewpoint, which allows all representations. In this assessment I may be biased because I have strongly argued for a multiple representations (Anderson, 1983). That book can also be consulted for proposals about how these representational types should be combined into schemas.

Any number of popular books on mnemonic techniques are available. Perhaps the best is the book by Harry Lorayne and Jerry Lucas (1974), but be warned that the techniques detailed there are at times difficult to acquire and that some of the recommendations might be simply incorrect. For a historical perspective on mnemonic techniques, read Yates (1966). For examples of the scientific study of mnemonic techniques see Bower (1970a) or Atkinson and Raugh (1975).

A great many of the ideas about schemas have come from artificial intelligence, where they have proven very useful. For artificial-intelligence research on schemas and related concepts, consult Bobrow and Winograd (1977), Minsky (1975); Schank and Abelson (1977), and Schank (1982). For more psychologically oriented research on schemas, read Bower et al. (1979), Rumelhart and Norman (1978, 1981), and Rumelhart and Ortony (1977). Alba and Hasher (1983) provide a thorough review of the psychological evidence for a schematic theory of memory.

Chapter 6

Human Memory: Basic Concepts and Principles

Summary

1. Short-term memory refers to a capacity for keeping a limited amount of information in a special active state. Information can be used only when it is in this active state.

2. The speed with which information can be processed in short-term memory is a function of its level of activation. Activation refers to finite mental capacity for processing information.

3. To be recalled or retrieved from long-term memory, information must be activated. Activation spreads along paths through a long-term network of associations from the currently active portion of memory to the to-be-retrieved portion.

4. The level, or amount, of activation spread to information in long-term memory determines how rapidly that information can be inspected and used.

5. The level of activation spread to a knowledge structure depends directly on the strength of the path along which the activation spreads and inversely on the number of competing paths. The detrimental effect of competing paths on the amount of activation spread down a path is referred to as associative interference.

6. The strength of a knowledge structure increases with practice of the structure, but there is diminishing benefit from practice. The form of this practice effect conforms to a power function.

7. If the level of activation of a knowledge structure is low, because of either low strength or associative interference, there will be failure of recall.

8. Performance is usually better on recognition tests than on recall tests. This fact illustrates that information can be in long-term memory but not available for recall. A recognition question is easier than a recall question because it offers more ways (network paths) in which memory can be searched for the queried information.

9. The strength of a knowledge structure decreases with the retention interval, but the rate of decrease slows down with time. The form of this forgetting process conforms to a power function.

The First Memory Experiment

Hermann Ebbinghaus, an early experimental investigator of human memory, published a significant research monograph in 1885. The research reported in this monograph was probably the first rigorous experimental investigation of human memory. No pools of subjects were available when Ebbinghaus was doing his research. Therefore, he used himself as his sole subject. He taught himself series of nonsense syllables, consonant-vowel-consonant trigrams such as DAX, BUP, and LOC. In one of his many experiments, Ebbinghaus required himself to learn lists of 13 syllables to the point of being able to repeat the lists twice in order without error. Then he tested his retention for these lists at various delays. He counted the amount of time he took to relearn the lists, using the same criterion of two perfect recitations. Of interest was how much faster the second learning was than the first. Suppose it took him 1156 sec to learn the list initially and only 467 sec to relearn the list. This meant he had saved 1156 − 467 = 689 sec in the relearning. This savings can be expressed as a percentage of the original learning: 689/1156 = 64.3 percent. Ebbinghaus used percent-savings scores as the standard measure of his retention. Figure 6-1 plots these percent-savings scores as a function of retention intervals. As this figure clearly shows, rapid forgetting occurs initially, but some forgetting still occurs up to 30 days following the learning of the material.

Using a 24-hour retention interval. Ebbinghaus considered what would happen if, after learning the list to the criterion of two perfect recitals, he rehearsed it 30 additional times. Without this overlearning, Ebbinghaus achieved a savings score of 33.8 percent, but with this amount of overlearning, his savings on a subsequent 24-hour retention test was 64.1 percent. So, the additional study trials resulted in increased savings on a subsequent retention test.

Over the decades, the basic experimental results of Ebbinghaus have been reproduced by many other researchers using a large variety of techniques

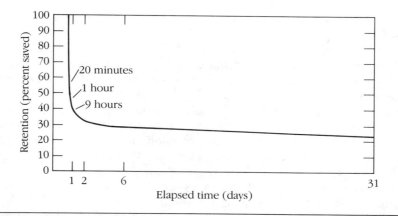

Figure 6-1 Ebbinghaus's forgetting function. Retention of nonsense syllables is measured by savings in relearning. Retention decreases as the retention interval (the time between initial learning and the retention time) increases, but the rate of forgetting slows down.

and measures. In all cases, subjects show rapid initial forgetting of the material they have learned. The effect of extra study time is to protect the memory against the process of forgetting.

Although Ebbinghaus was correct in identifying delay and amount of study as two important determinants of recall, his research left many important factors undiscovered. Also, Ebbinghaus was not very successful at identifying the mechanisms underlying the effects of study time and retention interval. In this chapter, we will review the more recent research and theories that serve to broaden the picture of the mechanisms underlying the retention of information in memory.

Short-Term Memory

In his experiments, Ebbinghaus studied a list many times before he achieved the criterion of one perfect recital. However, he discovered that if the list was short enough—say, had fewer than five items—he could achieve the criterion of a perfect recital in a single study. We have all had the experience of holding a seven-digit phone number in memory long enough to dial it. There appears to be a transient memory that can temporarily encode information perfectly after a single study. This transient memory is to be contrasted with the more permanent *long-term memory* (LTM), which holds information for hours, days, and years. Ebbinghaus's research basically addressed long-term memory. The transient memory is referred to as *short-term memory* (STM).

Now classical experiments by Brown (1958) and by Peterson and Peterson (1959) illustrate the transient character of short-term memory. Peterson and Peterson had subjects study three letters and then asked for recall of the letters after various intervals of time up to 18 sec. Normally, subjects would have no difficulty performing this task perfectly. However, to prevent the subjects from rehearsing the material, Peterson and Peterson had subjects count backward by threes during the retention interval. Thus, following presentation of the letters, subjects might be asked to count backward by threes as fast as possible from 418: 415, 412, and so on. Figure 6-2 illustrates recall at various retention intervals up to 18 sec from a similar experiment by Murdock (1961). At 18 sec, subjects are only recalling less than 20 percent of the three letters—or an average of less than 1 letter. The decay in recall to this level is rapid, largely complete after only 9 sec. After this point the recall level appears to approach an asymptote; that is, it does not decrease much more. We can conclude from these results that when subjects are distracted from rehearsing, they will lose information very rapidly. People are only able to keep a telephone number in short-term memory when they can rehearse it to themselves. The very low levels of performance after a delay, such as those in the Peterson and Peterson task, occur only when the stimuli are presented over and over (see Keppel & Underwood, 1962.) This suggests that the problem may lie in retrieving the items after a delay. That is, the subject may not be able to find the to-be-recalled stimuli mixed in among the old stimuli from the previous trails.

It is useful to think of short-term memory as a *working memory* holding only knowledge currently in use. The amount of information that we can hold in short-term memory represents a fundamental limitation on our mental capacity. A mental process cannot properly function unless we can keep in working memory the knowledge required by the process. For instance, if we lose track of the telephone number, we are unable to dial it.

Numerous attempts have been made to determine the number of items that short-term memory can hold. For instance, it has been found that people can hold in immediate memory seven or eight digits (a convenient fact, given the length of phone numbers!). However, reasoning from such facts to the exact capacity of short-term memory is difficult. Suppose I hold in memory that Mary's phone number is 436-8071. How many items am I holding in short-term memory? There are reasons to suspect that I am holding fewer than seven items. I may encode "80" as "eighty," in which case it is perhaps one item. I may not encode 43 at all, since I know that this is the prefix for all Yale numbers and that Mary is at Yale. On the other hand, there is also reason to wonder if I have not encoded more than seven items. I have also encoded the knowledge that *this is Mary's telephone number*—how many

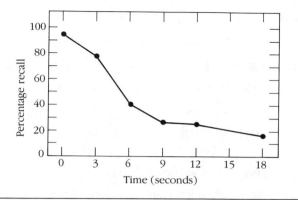

Figure 6-2   Decrease in recall as a function of duration of interpolated activity. This graph shows the rapid loss of information from short-term memory. (From Murdock, 1961.)

items does this fact represent? I may also be holding other information in short-term memory simultaneously, such as the location of the telephone on which I am dialing the number and my reason for dialing the number. Thus, although it is clear that the capacity of short-term memory is limited, how to measure that capacity is not at all clear. Cognitive psychology is still working at developing adequate measures of the capacity of short-term memory.

Chunking

A fundamental question is whether the information in short-term memory is in a different mental location than that in long-term memory, or whether it is in the same location as the knowledge in long-term memory, but just in a special state. The evidence favors the latter conclusion. Particularly compelling here is the fact that the capacity of short-term memory varies with the meaningfulness of the material. Thus, subjects are usually able to successfully repeat back four nonsense syllables:

DAX   JIR   GOP   BIF

but not six:

PID   LOM   FIK   GAN   WUT   TIB

They are able to repeat back six one-syllable words:

TILE   GATE   ROAD   JUMP   BALL   LIME

but not nine one-syllable words:

HAT   SAINT   FAN   RUN   GAIN   LIKE   NAIL   RICE   LAKE

And they can repeat three four-syllable words (which equal 12 syllables):

AMERICAN   DICTIONARY   GEOLOGY

but not six four-syllable words:

CONSTITUTION   MAJORITY   OPTIMISTIC   TERMINALLY
DOMESTICATE   CANADIAN

Finally, they are able to repeat back a 19-word sentence:

Richard Milhous Nixon, former president of the United States,
wrote a book about his career in the White House.

The way to make sense of what seems to be an extreme variability in the size of short-term memory is to realize that the units remembered are different in each case. In the case of nonsense syllables, the units are individual letters or letter pairs. In the case of words, they are words or meaningful parts of words. And in the case of sentences, they are the meaningful phrases. George Miller (1956) introduced the term *chunk* to describe these units of memory. He argued that memory was limited not by the number of physical units (letters, syllables, words) in the stimulus but rather by the number of meaningful chunks. Miller contended that subjects remembered approximately seven chunks. But where are these chunks (letters, words, meaningful phrases) stored as units? The answer is that they are defined as units in long-term memory. Therefore, it is assumed that when subjects remember a stimulus like those displayed earlier, they are placing these long-term memory units in a special state in which they are immediately accessible. This state is referred to as *active*, and the process of bringing nodes into the active states is called *activation*.

We now have three terms for referring to different aspects of the same phenomena. The empirical term short-term memory connotes the transient character of the memory. The term working memory conveys the fact that information is being held for use by mental procedures. Finally, the technical phrase *active memory* implies that the units of this memory are in a special active state.

Retrieval from Short-Term Memory

It is natural to believe that we have immediate access to the contents of short-term memory, but this proves not to be the case. A classic series of experiments by Saul Sternberg (1969) at Bell Laboratories demonstrated an

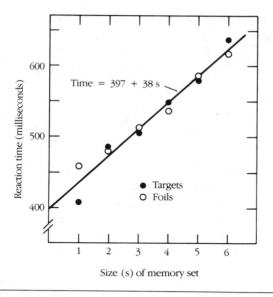

Figure 6-3 Time to recognize a digit increases with the number of items in the memory set (from Sternberg, 1969). The straight line represents the linear function that fits the data best.

important factor controlling the rate of access to information in short-term memory. He presented subjects with a *memory set* of digits (e.g., 3, 4, 8, 1) to hold in short-term memory. He then presented a test digit, and the subjects were required to determine whether it was in the memory set. Sternberg varied the size of the memory set from one digit to six. Figure 6-3 displays the results of his manipulation in terms of the time it took to recognize targets (digits in the memory set) and to reject foils (digits not in the memory set). As can be seen, there is a nearly linear relationship between memory-set size and judgment time. With each additional digit in the memory set, judgment time increases by about 38 msec. Thus, increasing the number of items that a subject must keep in memory increases the time to access any item. This is one of the most robust and well-studied phenomena in cognitive psychology. The same effect of memory-set size on judgment time has been found when the items are letters, words, colors, and so on, with all kinds of subject populations, in all kinds of mental states.

These results have attracted a wide range of theoretical interpretations. An early and dominant theory is the one proposed by Sternberg himself: Subjects had to search through their short-term memories to see if the test digit was there. He theorized that subjects serially considered one digit after another, and that it required about 38 msec to consider each digit in short-term memory. Of course, a search of 38 msec per item is much too rapid to be open to conscious inspection; but by assuming this search of short-term memory, Sternberg was able to explain why reaction time increased 38 msec with each additional item the subject was holding in short-term memory.

Sternberg's theory has been criticized on many grounds, although none of the criticisms have proven definitive. J. A. Anderson (1973) argued that it was implausible to suppose that our brains worked fast enough to perform a comparison in every 38 msec. Recall the earlier evidence that our brains are parallel devices, quite unlike the serial computer, and that they compute many relatively slow operations simultaneously.

An alternative to Sternberg's *serial theory* would be a *parallel theory* that held that each item in the memory set was simultaneously being compared to the test item. Numerous parallel theories have been proposed, but a common one (e.g., Baddeley & Ecob, 1973) holds that the rate at which these comparisons can be performed is a function of how active the items are. Further, it is assumed that there is a limitation of the amount of activation available to items in short-term memory. When there are more items in the memory set, the activation must be divided among these items, and the activation given to any one item is less. Consequently, it will be compared less rapidly to the test item. Thus, these parallel theories agree with Sternberg that access to information in short-term memory is not immediate. However, parallel theories argue that the time is spent inspecting all items at once rather than in serial searching through the items. The speed of inspection decreases with number of items because a finite amount of mental energy must be divided among the items. This energy, or activation, construct is similar to attention (discussed in Chapter 3), which is also thought of as a finite resource that has to be divided among competing processes.

Long-Term Memory

The activation concept can be extended to retrieval from long-term memory. Information in long-term memory is normally in an inactive state. To use that information it is necessary to activate that knowledge. The process of retrieving information from long-term memory can be thought of as the process of activating that information. Once the information is activated, it is regarded as part of short-term memory. The process of activation takes time, and, hence, recall of information already in the STM state should be faster than recall of information that starts out in the LTM state. That this is true is illustrated by an experiment from my laboratory.

In the experiment, subjects studied two paired associates such as *dog–3* and *vanilla–8*. After studying such a pair for 2 sec, subjects were either immediately tested for their memory or were given 48 sec of arithmetic tasks and then tested. In either case, a test consisted of presenting *dog* or *vanilla* and requiring the subject to recall the second item in the pair. Subjects were 98 percent correct immediately and only 48 percent correct after the 48-sec delay. This result is quite similar to the result from Murdock shown in Figure 6-2. Again, it illustrates that information is lost rapidly from short-term memory if the subject is distracted from rehearsing the information. After a 48-sec delay in which other activities intervene, the information is very unlikely to be active in short-term memory. Therefore, the 48 percent correct recall at this delay reflects information that can be retrieved from long-term memory.

The point of interest in this experiment was the amount of time subjects took to recall, when they could do so, in the immediate condition versus the 48-sec delay condition. Subjects took 1.31 sec in the immediate condition but 1.96 sec in the delayed condition, the difference being almost two-thirds of a second. This extra time reflects the amount of time needed to return the information from long-term memory to the STM state. The recall of information is dependent on the reactivation of the information.

Retrieving Well-Known Information

We have been focusing on changes in memory for information subjects have learned in the minute prior to testing. What about memory for information that is well established in long-term memory? Are large temporal fluctuations demonstrated in its availability as well? An experiment by Loftus (1974) nicely answers this question. She looked at the time subjects required to retrieve well-learned information about categories such as fruit. She had subjects retrieve instances of a category that began with a certain initial letter. For instance, subjects might have to retrieve a fruit beginning with *p*. She found that subjects took an average of 1.53 sec to perform this task the first time they were asked about a category. Then after varying delays she asked subjects to retrieve from the same category another member beginning with a different letter. Thus, she might ask subjects to retrieve a fruit beginning with *b*. She manipulated delay by inserting tests on other unrelated categories between the two tests on a category. For instance, during a two-item delay, subjects might be asked to retrieve a breed of dog that begin with *c* and a country that began with *r*. Looking at zero, one, and two intervening items, she found retrieval times of 1.21 sec, 1.28 sec, and 1.33 sec, respectively. The first time they were tested, subjects took 1.53 sec to generate an associate. So, relative to this initial retrieval time, we see strong facilitation if the category is tested again immediately, when the memory about the category is still in an active short-term state. With increasing delay, however, the activation in this portion of memory decays, producing longer and longer retrieval times.

Degree of Learning

From the Loftus experiment we can estimate the time required to activate knowledge from long-term memory by subtracting the zero-delay question (1.21 sec) from the time to answer the first question about the category (1.53 sec). The difference of .32 sec is much smaller than the estimate of .65 obtained in the paired-associate experiment previously discussed. The material in the paired-associate experiment was considerably less well learned than the category information in the Loftus study. There is evidence that material can be more rapidly activated if it is better learned and hence more strongly encoded.

Another experiment from my laboratory (Anderson, 1976) illustrates how speed of retrieval varies with strength of the memory trace.[1] In the first phase of this experiment, subjects committed to memory facts about locations of various people. For instance, the subject might learn the following sentences:

The sailor is in the park.

The lawyer is in the church.

Subjects were drilled over and over again on these sentences until they knew them by heart. Later, subjects were presented with sentences and asked to say whether each sentence was among the sentences they had studied. Thus, subjects might see

The sailor is in the park,

which would require a positive response. Negative items were created by recombining people and locations in ways that had not been studied. For example, the subject might be presented with the following negative test item:

The sailor is in the church.

Subjects had not studied this sentence and therefore were required to give a negative response. Since subjects knew the material well enough to be correct almost all the time, we were interested only in the speed with which subjects made their correct recognition judgments.

We were interested in two variables. One was differences in the amount of study applied to different sentences before testing. Some sentences were studied twice as frequently as others. We would expect frequency to be related to the strength of the encoding of a sentence, and hence that more frequently encountered information would be retrieved more quickly from long-term

---

[1]A *memory trace* is the encoding of a memory. For instance, a network representation of a remembered event would be a memory trace.

Table 6-1 *Effects of delay of repetition and frequency of exposure on recognition time for second presentation of a sentence*

	Delay	
Degree of study	Short (0 to 2 intervening items)	Long (3 or more intervening items)
Less study	1.11 seconds	1.53 seconds
More study	1.10 seconds	1.38 seconds

From Anderson, 1976.

memory. The second variable was the delay between any two presentations of a particular sentence. We compared the situation in which zero to two items intervened between repetitions and the sentence was still likely to be in the active short-term memory with the situation in which three or more items intervened and the sentence probably had to be reactivated. We were interested in the effect of this delay between tests on recognition time for the second presentation of a sentence. The difference between the short delay and the long delay is a measure of the amount of time that activation of the information takes.

Table 6-1 displays judgment times for the second sentence in a repetition classified according to these two variables. After short test delays, frequency of study had very little effect on recognition time. On the other hand, following a long delay between repetitions, subjects were considerably faster on the more frequently studied sentence. Time to activate a sentence in long-term memory can be estimated as the difference between three or more intervening items and zero to two intervening items. Using this estimate, it takes 1.53 − 1.11 = .42 sec to activate the less frequently studied items from long-term memory, but only 1.38 − 1.10 = .28 sec to activate the more frequently studied items. Thus, as expected, it takes longer to reactivate the weaker memories.

The effects of practice on memory retrieval are extremely regular and very large. In one study, Anderson (1983) had subjects practice sentences like the ones displayed earlier for 25 days and looked at the effects of this practice on time to recognize a sentence. Figure 6-4 illustrates the result of this manipulation. As can be seen, subjects sped up from about 1.6 sec to .7 sec, cutting their retrieval time by more than 50 percent. Figure 6-4 also shows that the rate of improvement decreases with more practice. The data in Figure 6-4 are nicely fit by a power function[2] of the form

$$RT = .36 + .96(D - \tfrac{1}{2})^{-.36}$$

---

[2] Power functions define the dependent variable (in this case, RT) by raising the independent variable (in this case, D) to an exponent. The simplest form of a power function is $y = ax^b$.

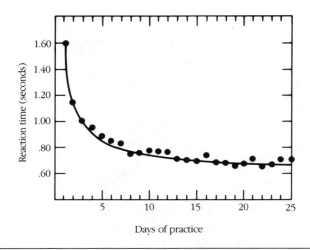

Figure 6-4 Time to recognize a sentence as a function of the number of trials of practice.

where *RT* is the reaction time and *D* is the number of days of practice. We will have more to say about such practice functions in Chapter 9, where the development of expertise is discussed.

At the beginning of this chapter we saw in Ebbinghaus's research that frequency of exposure affected probability of recall. The data in Table 6-1 and Figure 6-4 show that frequency also affects retrieval time. These effects on retrieval time and effects on retention are probably manifestations of the same underlying memory mechanisms. One view is that failure to recall is just the result of an extreme retrieval time—that the item is still in memory, but its retrieval is just too slow. We will return to this point later in the chapter.

Spread of Activation

It is informative to think about the activation concept within the network framework developed in Chapter 5. Consider Figure 6-5, which illustrates part of the propositional network surrounding the concept *dog*. Note that *dog* is connected to the concept *bone*. Thus, when the word *dog* is presented to the subject, not only will that concept become active, but activation should spread to the concepts surrounding *dog*, so that terms such as *bone* become active as well. An unpublished experiment by Perlmutter and Anderson nicely

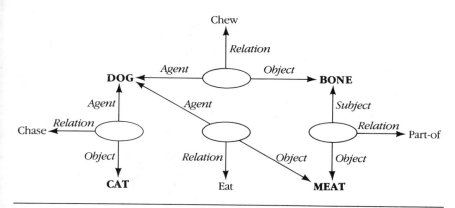

Figure 6-5 A representation of *dog* in memory and some of its associated concepts.

illustrates the kind of evidence that exists for this spreading-activation process. Subjects were presented with a sequence of words and asked to generate associates that began with specific letters. We were interested in contrasting such sequences as the two following:

Priming	*Control*
dog–c	gambler–c
bone–m	bone–m

In the first case, the subject might generate *cat* as the associate to *dog* and then be presented with *bone* and generate *meat* as an associate. In the second case, the control case, the responses might be *card* and *meat*. The important feature of the priming condition is that an already existing associative path leads from *dog* to *bone* and to *meat*. Therefore, activating the network structure to answer the first associate should help activate the structure needed to answer the second. The first associate (dog–c) serves to prime the second (bone–m). In contrast, no priming connection exists in the second case. Therefore, subjects were expected to generate the second associate faster in the priming condition. This expectation was confirmed: Subjects took 1.41 sec to generate an associate in the priming case, as contrasted with 1.53 sec in the control case.

The notion of *spread of activation*, illustrated in this and other experiments, is fundamental to an understanding of recall from long-term memory. Activation spreads through long-term memory from active portions to other portions of memory, and this spread takes time. Consider the results in Table 6-1, drawn from the experiment in which subjects were required to recognize sentences of the form *A sailor is in the park*. Figure 6-6 is the propositional-

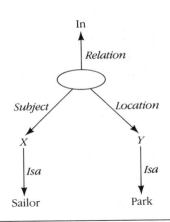

In

Relation

Subject   *Location*

X   *Y*

Isa   *Isa*

Sailor   Park

Figure 6-6   A propositional-network representation for the statement *A sailor is in the park.* This structure must be activated in order for the proposition to be recognized.

network representation of such a sentence. This sentence, presented as a test probe, should activate the words *sailor, in,* and *park.* Activation spreads from link to link through the structure shown in Figure 6-6 like water flowing through irrigation channels. Before the sentence can be recalled, the whole structure in Figure 6-6 must be activated. Thus, the time spent in the retrieval of a memory structure would reflect the time taken for the spread of activation through that structure.

If one concept is activated, a good many associated concepts will become active because of spreading activation. Thus, the amount of active information resulting can be much greater than the "approximately seven" measure that was ascribed to short-term memory earlier in this chapter. We saw that the exact size of short-term memory was difficult to measure. The existence of the spreading-activation phenomenon is one reason for this difficulty. The figure "approximately seven" refers to the amount of information that can be maintained in an active state. However, a great deal more information can be active momentarily. For instance, I can rehearse to myself Mary's phone number—which conforms to the seven-unit approximation—and keep it in short-term memory for minutes while I am finding a phone. However, while I am holding this information in short-term memory, other associations generated through the spreading activation process temporarily enter and leave my short-term memory. In addition to the free-association information, observations of my environment can temporarily enter my short-term memory. Thus, the "approximately seven" figure represents the core focus of my immediate attention, while factors such as spreading activation and external stimulation create wide fluctuations in activation around this core.

Note that the spread-of-activation process is not entirely under an individual's control. For example, when subjects generated an associate to *dog* in the Perlmutter and Anderson experiment described earlier, they had no reason to *want* to activate the *bone–meat* association. Still, some activation spread to this part of the network and helped to prime knowledge of the connection between *bone* and *meat*. Many experiments in cognitive psychology have demonstrated this unconscious priming—called *associative priming*—of knowledge through spreading activation.

Associative Priming

Meyer and Schvaneveldt (1971) performed what has become a classic demonstration of associative priming. They had subjects judge whether or not pairs of items were words. Table 6-2 shows examples of the materials used in their experiments and subjects' judgment times. The items were presented one above the other. If either item in a pair was a nonword, subjects were to respond no. It appears from examining the negative pairs that subjects judged first the top item and then the second. Where the top item was a nonword, subjects were faster to reject the pair than when only the second item was a nonword. Where the top item was not a word, subjects did not have to judge the second item and so could respond sooner.

The major interest in this study was in the positive pairs. There were unrelated items such as *nurse* and *butter*, and pairs with an associative relation such as *bread* and *butter*. Subjects were 85 msec faster on the related pairs. This result indicates that because subjects judged the first item to be a word, activation spread from that word and primed information about the second, associatively related, item. If a subject is to make a judgment about whether an item is a word, the representation of the word has to be active in short-term memory. The implication of this result is that the associative spreading of activation through memory can facilitate the rate at which words are read.

Table 6-2 *Examples of the pairs used to demonstrate associative priming*

Positive pairs		Negative pairs		
Unrelated	Related	Nonword first	Nonword second	Both nonwords
Nurse	Bread	Plame	Wine	Plame
Butter	Butter	Wine	Plame	Reab
940 msec	855 msec	904 msec	1087 msec	884 msec

From Meyer and Schvaneveldt, 1971.

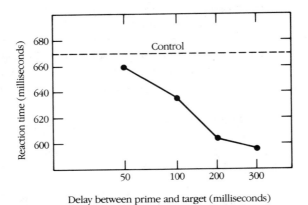

Figure 6-7   Difference between primed and control conditions as a function of the interval between priming word and target word.

Thus, we can read material that has a strong associative coherence more rapidly than incoherent material in which the words are unrelated.

Ratcliff and McKoon (1981) report a rather different priming demonstration of spreading activation. They had subjects commit to memory sentences like *The doctor hated the book*. After committing these sentences to memory, subjects were transferred to a word-recognition paradigm where they saw nouns from the sentences and had to recognize whether the nouns came from the studied sentences. So, if subjects saw a word like *book*, which was in the memorized sentences, they would respond yes.

Sometimes, before presenting the target (e.g., book), Ratcliff and McKoon presented a prime noun that came from the same sentence (i.e., doctor). They found subjects faster in this primed condition compared to a control condition that did not have the prime noun. Subjects took 667 msec in the control condition compared to 624 msec in the primed condition. Thus, Ratcliff and McKoon demonstrated that experimentally learned associates could prime a recognition judgment.

Ratcliff and McKoon varied the delay between the prime (doctor) and the target (book) from 50 to 350 msec. All of these intervals were too short for subjects to develop any conscious expectations. So, we are looking at the effects of automatic spread of activation. The interesting issue is how the priming effect grew over the 350-msec interval. Figure 6-7 shows how reaction times in the priming condition decreased over this interval. This decrease in reaction time reflects the growth in the level of activation.

The priming effect appears very rapidly. Subjects are somewhat faster in the primed condition than in the control condition even when there is just

50 msec between prime and target. The priming essentially reached asymptotic levels in 200 msec. Thus, it appears that activation can spread very rapidly.

Summary: Relation of Activation to Processing Time

For information to be used in a task such as a recognition judgment, it must first be activated and then inspected. When information is in long-term memory but not currently in short-term memory, activation must spread to it, which takes some amount of time, as we saw in the McKoon and Ratcliff study. Once activated, the time to inspect the information will depend on its level of activation, as was illustrated in the Sternberg experiment.

Interference

The Fan Effect

Various factors can affect the amount of activation that is spread to a knowledge structure. From the results reviewed before (Table 6-1 and Figure 6-4), we can infer that strength of encoding has an effect such that more strongly encoded information receives greater activation. Another factor, to be discussed here, is the number of alternative network paths down which activation can spread. In one experiment (Anderson, 1974b) we had subjects memorize 26 facts, again of the form *A person is in a location*. Some persons were paired with only one location and some locations with only one person. Other persons were paired with two locations and other locations were paired with two persons. For instance, suppose that subjects studied these sentences:

1. The doctor is in the bank. (1-1)
2. The fireman is in the park (1-2)
3. The lawyer is in the church. (2-1)
4. The lawyer is in the park. (2-2)

Each statement is followed by two numbers, reflecting the number of facts associated with the subject and the location. For instance, sentence 3 is labeled 2-1 because its subject occurs in two sentences (sentences 3 and 4) and its location occurs in one (sentence 3).

Subjects were drilled on this material until they knew it quite well. Before beginning the reaction-time phase, subjects were able to recall all the locations associated with a particular type of person (e.g., doctor) and all the people associated with a particular location (e.g., park). Then they began a speeded-

Table 6-3 *Mean recognition time for sentences as a function of number of facts learned about person and location*

Number of sentences using a specific location	Number of sentences about a specific person	
	1 sentence	2 sentences
1 sentence	1.11 sec	1.17 sec
2 sentences	1.17 sec	1.22 sec

From Anderson, 1974b.

recognition phase of the experiment, during which they were presented with sentences and had to judge whether they recognized them from the study set. New foil sentences were created by the re-pairing of people and locations from the study set. The reaction times involving sentences such as those listed above are displayed in Table 6-3, which classifies the data as a function of the number of facts associated with a person and a location. As can be seen, recognition time increases as a function of both the number of facts studied about the person and the number of facts studied about the location.

Figure 6-8 shows the network representation for sentences 1 through 4.[3] By applying the activation concept to this representation, we can nicely account for the increase in reaction time. Consider how the subject might recognize such a probe as *A lawyer is in the park*. First, suppose that the presentation of the terms *lawyer, in,* and *park* serves to activate their representations in memory. Then activation will spread from these nodes to activate the target proposition and enable it to be recognized. The critical assumption is that the amount of activation reaching the proposition is inversely related to the number of links leading from it. So, given a structure like Figure 6-8, subjects should be slower to recognize a fact involving *lawyer* and *park* than one connecting *doctor* and *bank* because more paths emanate from the first set of concepts. That is, in the *lawyer* and *park* case two paths point from each of the concepts to the two propositions in which each was studied, whereas only one path leads from each of the *doctor* and *bank* concepts.

This is one experiment among many that point to a *limited-capacity feature* of the spreading-activation process. The nodes, such as *lawyer* and *park*, from

---

[3]For simplicity, we have not represented the distinction between instances and concepts in the figure. As indicated in Chapter 5, this distinction is important. Therefore, the representation in Figure 6-5 is only an approximation of the true underlying representation. However, the figure highlights the features of the propositional network that are significant for an understanding of this experiment.

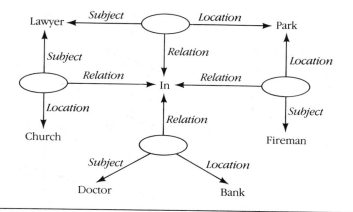

Figure 6-8   Network representations for four sentences used in the experiment of Anderson (1974a). The sentences are *The doctor is in the bank; The fireman is in the park; The lawyer is in the church;* and *The lawyer is in the park.*

which the spread of activation starts can be called *source nodes.* A source node has a certain fixed capacity for emitting activation. This capacity is divided among all the paths emanating from that node. The more paths that exist, the less activation will be assigned to any one path and the slower will be the rate of activation. The *fan effect* is the name given to this increase in reaction time related to an increase in the number of facts associated with a concept. It is so named because the increase in reaction time is related to an increase in the fan of facts emanating from the network representation of the concept.

Interference is the more general term used to refer to such phenomena. The term conveys the fact that additional information about a concept interferes with memory for a particular piece of information. As we will see, such interference affects a wider range of measures than just recognition time. The term fan effect is reserved for interference effects as measured by recognition time.

Interference and Historical Memories

An experiment by Lewis and Anderson (1976) investigated whether the fan effect could be obtained with material the subject knew before the experiment. We had subjects learn fantasy facts about public figures—for example, *Napoleon Bonaparte was from India.* Subjects studied from zero to four such fantasy facts about each public figure. After learning these "facts," they proceeded to a recognition-test phase. In this phase they saw three types of

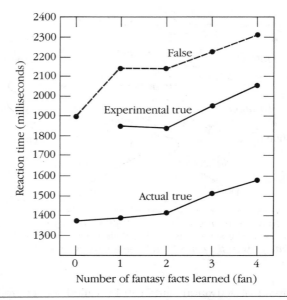

Figure 6-9 Reaction times from Lewis and Anderson (1976). The task was to recognize true and fantasy facts about a public figure and to reject statements that were neither true nor fantasy facts. This figure shows that the time subjects took to make all three judgments increased as subjects learned more fantasy facts about public figures.

sentences: (1) statements they had studied in the experiment, (2) true facts about the public figures (such as *Napoleon Bonaparte was an emperor*), and (3) statements about the public figure that were false both in the experimental fantasy world and in the real world. Subjects had to respond to the first two types of facts as true and to the last type as false.

Figure 6-9 presents subjects' reaction time in making these judgments as a function of the number of fantasy facts (the fan) studied about the person. Note that reaction time increased with fan for all types of facts. Also note that subjects responded much faster to actual truths than to experimental truths. The advantage of actual truths can be explained, because these true facts would be much more strongly encoded in memory than the fantasy facts because of greater prior exposure. The most important result to note in Figure 6-9 is that the more fantasy facts subjects have learned about an individual such as Napoleon Bonaparte, the longer subjects take to recognize a fact that they already know about the individual, for example, *Napoleon Bonaparte was an emperor*. Thus, we can produce interference with preexperimental material. For further research on this topic, see Peterson and Potts (1982).

Interference and Retention

So far, we have considered how interference from other information associated with a concept can slow down the speed with which the fact can be retrieved. The effects have been a matter of a few hundred milliseconds. We will now consider what happens as these interfering effects get more extreme—either because the to-be-recalled fact is very weak or because the interference is very strong. There is evidence that the subject simply fails to remember the information under both conditions. Results showing such failures of memory have traditionally been obtained with paired-associate material, although similar results have been obtained with other material.

In the typical interference experiment, two critical groups are defined: These are illustrated in Table 6-4. The *A–D* experimental group learns two lists of paired associates, the first list designated *A–B* and the second designated *A–D*. The lists are so designated because they share common stimuli (the *A* terms). For example, among the pairs that the subject studies in the *A–B* list might be *cat–43* and *house–61*, and in the *A–D* list *cat–82* and *house–37*. The *C–D* control group also first studies the *A–B* list, but then studies a different second list, designated *C–D*, which does not contain the same stimuli as the first list. For example, in the *C–D* list subjects might study *bone–82* and *cup–37*. After learning their respective second lists, both groups are retested for their memory of their first list, in both cases the *A–B* list. Often this retention test is administered after a considerable delay, such as 24 hours or a week. In general, the *A–D* group does not do as well as the *C–D* group with respect to both rate of learning of the second list and retention of the original *A–B* list.

These results are to be expected given our understanding of interference. Figure 6-10 shows the network representation of the knowledge structures for the two groups. Part (a) illustrates the assumed memory structure for the experimental group. Members of this group have *A* stimuli in both lists and so have learned interfering associations to these stimuli. Part (b) of the figure illustrates the assumed memory structure for the control group. There were different stimuli in the two lists—in list 1 subjects associated *43* to *cat*, while

Table 6-4 *Experimental and control groups used in a typical interference paradigm*

A–D experimental		C–D control	
LEARN	A–B	LEARN	A–B
LEARN	A–D	LEARN	C–D
TEST	A–B	TEST	A–B

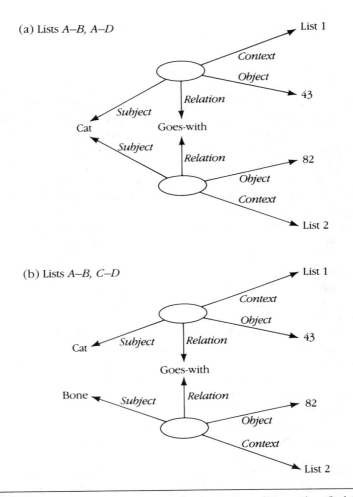

Figure 6-10 Network representations for the two conditions identified in Table 6-4. (a) Network representing the encodings of the *A–B* and *A–D* associations in the experimental condition; (b) network representing the encodings of the *A–B* and *C–D* associations in the control condition.

in list 2 they associated *82* to *bone*. Thus, the experimental group has an extra list 2 association to interfere with the *cat–43* memory while the control group does not. In the reaction-time experiments discussed earlier, such interference (two associations rather than one) resulted in increased reaction time, but not failure to recall. In those experiments, however, the items had been highly overlearned before reaction time was tested. In the interference experiments, subjects are tested as they are learning the paired associates. Here the strengths of associations are much weaker. When the exposure to the pairs has been minimal and their associations barely learned, the interference of associates learned in the second list can result in failure to recall. The implication is that failure to recall is the extreme case of a long retrieval time. Thus, it is not the case that the forgotten information is not in memory, but rather that it is in memory but is too weak to be activated in the face of the interference from other associations. In this view, forgetting is not actual loss of information from memory but rather loss of the ability to activate that information.

Recall versus Recognition

Consistent with the hypothesis that there exists in memory information that we cannot recall is the fact that we can recognize many things we cannot recall.[4] This phenomenon suggests that information can be in memory even though it cannot be activated in the recall-test situation. The memory-network analysis we have been developing makes clear the reason that recognition often works even when recall fails. For example, let us compare the efforts of students trying to answer the following questions:

1. Who was the president after Wilson?

2. Was Harding the president after Wilson?

Figure 6-11 illustrates the memory structure that is being addressed by the questions. The first question, a recall question, provides subjects with Wilson as a probe from which to search memory. The question requires that subjects access memory from *Wilson* and search to *Harding*. To do this the subject must activate the Wilson node and have activation spread to the Harding node. Suppose, however, that the network link between proposition 3 and 2 cannot be sufficiently activated. Then there will be failure of recall. However, when asked the recognition question, that is, question 2, subjects might be able to go from *Harding* to *Wilson* even if they were unable to go from *Wilson* to *Harding*. That is, they might be able to retrieve proposition 3 from proposition 2 even though they were not able to retrieve 2 from 3. A recognition question is easier than a recall question because it offers the subject more ways to search memory.

---

[4]There are, however, situations where performance on a recall test can be better than performance on a recognition test, as we will discuss in the next chapter.

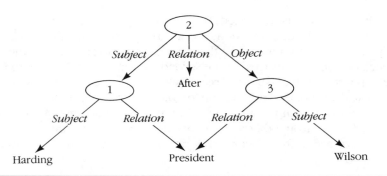

Figure 6-11 A propositional-network representation of the information that Harding was president after Wilson.

Note that in our analysis of Figure 6-11 we assumed that subjects might be able to activate the association between propositions 2 and 3 but not the association between 3 and 2. In distinguishing between recall and recognition, it is useful to think of a link between two nodes as consisting of two separate associations going in opposite directions, with the possibility existing for one association to be available but not the other. The idea of associations different in two directions has played an important role in the paired-associate literature where subjects have to learn pairs such as *house–46*. The connection from *house* to *46* is referred to as *forward association*, and the connection from *46* to *house* is referred to as a *backward association*. Usually the forward association (as indexed by subjects' ability to recall *46* when given a cue of *house*) is stronger than the backward association (as indexed by subjects' ability to recall *house* when given the cue of *46*). However, in line with our analysis earlier, subjects perform best in a recognition test where they are given *house–46* and can use either the forward or backward association.

A Mathematical Analysis

The foregoing analysis of recall versus recognition memory has been nicely confirmed by a series of experiments by Wolford (1971). He had subjects commit to memory noun–number paired associates such as *girl–62*. Subjects were tested in a number of ways. In a *forward-recall condition* they were presented with the word *girl* and asked to recall the response. Responses were correctly recalled 38 percent of the time in this condition. In a *backward-recall condition*, subjects were presented with the number 62 and asked to recall the word. In this condition they gave 21 percent correct recall. Interest focused on a *two-alternative forced-choice recognition condition*, in which subjects were presented with the probe *girl* (*71* or *62*) and had to recognize the correct number. (The number *71* had occurred with another word.) Wolford reasoned that subjects would identify the correct response if the forward association from *girl* was intact (we will call the probability of this association's being intact P_f). Or, if this association was not intact, they would still be able to tell if the backward association from *62* was intact (this probability is P_b). Or, if this association was not intact, subject would still be able to tell if the association from *71* was intact, since they could reject *girl* as its stimulus (the probability of this repsonse is also P_b). Finally, if this association was not intact, the subject would be able to guess and be correct half the time. From these possible responses, we come up with the following formula for probablity correct on the forced-choice list:

$$\text{Probability of a correct recognition} = \text{probability of a forward association}$$

+ probability of no forward association but a backward association from *62*

+ probability of no forward association nor a backward association from *62* but a backward association from *71*

+ probability of no forward association nor a backward association from *62* or *71* but a correct guess. (1)

Substituting probabilities for the components in equation 1, we obtain the following:

$$P_f = \text{probability of a forward association;} \quad (2)$$

$$(1 - P_f)P_b = \text{probability of no forward association but a backward association from } 62. \quad (3)$$

$$(1 - P_f)(1 - P_b)P_b = \text{probability of no forward association nor a backward association from } 62 \text{ but a backward association from } 71 \quad (4)$$

$$(1 - P_f)(1 - P_b)(1 - P_b).50 = \text{probability of no forward association nor a backward association from } 62 \text{ or } 71 \text{ but a correct guess.} \quad (5)$$

Substituting equations 2–5 into 1 we get

Probability of a
correct recognition $= P_f + (1 - P_f)P_b$
$+ (1 - P_f)(1 - P_b)P_b$
$+ (1 - P_f)(1 - P_b)(1 - P_b).50.$ (6)

Wolford was able to use the forward- and backward-recall probabilities to estimate the probability of a forward association, $P_f = .38$, and the probability of a backward association, $P_b = .21$. Substituting these values into equation 6, we get the following results:

$(.38) + (1 - .38)(.21) + (1 - .38)(1 - .21).21$
$+ (1 - .38)(1 - .21)(1 - .21).5 = .806.$

The observed probability of correct recognition was .80! This analysis illustrates beautifully how recognition can be conceived of as a combination of forward and backward associations. Wolford reports a number of other tests that support this view of paired-associate recognition.

Decay Process in Forgetting

Although interference is an important cause of forgetting, it seems unlikely that interference is the only cause of forgetting. Memories appear to decay very systematically with delay, independent of any interference. Much of the research documenting this fading has been done by Wickelgren. In one recognition experiment (Wickelgren, 1975) he presented subjects with a sequence of words to study and then looked at their probability of recognizing the words after delays ranging from 1 min to 14 days. Figure 6-12 shows performance as a function of delay. The performance measure Wickelgren used is called d'; it is derived from probability of recognition and is thought to be a measure of memory strength. In a laboratory experiment of mine (Anderson & Paulson, 1977) I looked at speed of recognizing a sentence for delays ranging from 5 sec to 30 min. Figure 6-13 presents the data from that experiment.

In each of these figures we see that performance systematically deteriorates (the d' measure of recognition goes down, reaction time goes up) with delay. However, these changes are *negatively accelerated*—that is, the rate of change gets smaller and smaller with delay. In each of these figures I have also replotted the data, plotting the logarithm of the performance measure and the logarithm of delay. Marvelously, all these functions become linear. Log performance is a linear function of delay, that is,

$$\log(d') = A - b \log D$$

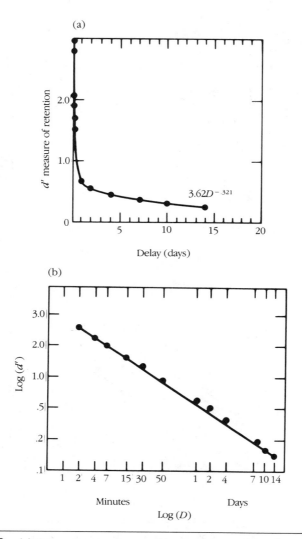

Figure 6-12 (a) Success at word recognition as measured by d' as a function of delay (D); (b) the data in (a) replotted on a log–log scale. (Adapted from Wickelgren, 1975.)

and

$$\log(RT) = C + f \log D$$

where d' is Wickelgren's strength measure derived from probability of recognition, RT is reaction time, and D is delay. These equations can be transformed to become

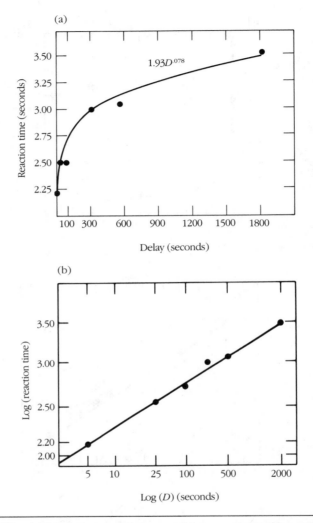

Figure 6-13 (a) Success at sentence recognition as measured by reaction time as a function of delay (D); (b) the data in (a) replotted as a log–log plot. (Adapted from Anderson & Paulson, 1977.)

$$d' = A^*D^{-b}$$

$$RT = C^*D^f$$

where $A^* = 10^A$ and $C^* = 10^C$. That is, these performance measures are power functions of delay. Interestingly, the Ebbinghaus retention function in Figure 6-1 can also be shown to be a power function. These forgetting functions are highly systematic and appear to describe forgetting in the absence of any apparent interference. Their existence argues for a decay component to forgetting in addition to interference. Objections have been raised to decay theories because they do not identify the psychological factors producing the forgetting, but rather assert that forgetting occurs spontaneously with time. It may be possible, however, that there is no explanation of decay at the purely psychological level. The explanation may be physiological. It has been shown that synaptic efficacy deteriorates with delay, and apparently this deterioration also follows a power law (Barnes & McNaughton, 1980). Thus, it seems that the mechanism underlying the very lawful functions in Figures 6-12 and 6-13 may be neural. Just as our muscles will atrophy with lack of use, so will neural connections. This analogy to muscles also suggests that our memories may not be lost because of decay; the memories may still be encoded in our brains but are too weak to be retrieved.

Are Forgotten Memories Truly Lost?

An interesting possibility is that we never do really lose our memories—that forgotten memories are still there but are too weak to be revived. The results reported by Penfield (1959) are consistent with this notion. As part of a neurosurgical procedure, Penfield electrically stimulated portions of patients' brain and asked patients to report what they experienced (patients were conscious during the surgery but the stimulation technique was painless). In this way Penfield was able to determine the function of various portions of the brain. Stimulation of the temporal lobes of the brain led to reports of memories that patients were unable to report in normal recall—for instance, events from their childhood. It was as if Penfield's stimulation activated portions of the memory network that spreading activation could not reach. Unfortunately, it is hard to know whether the patients' memory reports were accurate, since going back in time to check on whether the events reported actually occurred was nearly impossible. Therefore, although suggestive, the Penfield experiments are generally discounted by memory researchers.

A better experiment, conducted by Nelson (1971), also indicates that "forgotten" memories still exist. He had subjects learn 20 number–noun paired associates; they studied the list until they reached a criterion of one errorless trial. Subjects returned for a retest two weeks later, recalling 75 percent of the items on this retention test. However, interest focused on the 25 percent of the items for which the subjects were unable to recall the noun response to the digit stimulus. Subjects were given new learning trials on the 20 paired associates. The paired associates they had missed were either kept the same or changed. In the changed case, a new response was associated to an old stimulus. If subjects had learned 43–dog, but failed to recall the response to

43, they might now be trained on either *43–dog* (unchanged) or *43–house* (changed). They were tested after studying the new list once. If subjects had lost all memory for the forgotten pairs, there should be no difference between changed and unchanged pairs. However, subjects correctly recalled 78 percent of the unchanged items formerly missed but only 43 percent of the changed items. This large advantage for unchanged items indicates that subjects had retained something about the paired associates even though they had been unable to recall them initially. This retained information was reflected in the savings displayed in relearning.

Nelson (1978) also looked at the situation in which the retention test involved recognition. Four weeks after learning, subjects failed to recognize 31 percent of the paired associates they had learned. As in the previous experiment, Nelson had subjects relearn the missing items. For half the stimuli the responses were changed and for the other half they were left unchanged. After one relearning trial, subjects recognized 34 percent of the unchanged items but only 19 percent of the changed items. The recognition-retention test should have been very sensitive to whether the subject has anything in memory. However, even when subjects fail this sensitive test, there appears to be some evidence that a record of the items is still in memory—the evidence that relearning was better for the unchanged than the changed pairs. The implication of the Nelson studies is that if we can come up with a sufficiently sensitive measure, we can show that apparently forgotten memories are still there.

Remarks and Suggested Readings

There are a good many texts on human memory including those of Crowder (1976) and Klatzky (1979). The book by Anderson and Kosslyn (1984) contains a series of essays surveying the current state of literature in the field.

Many different views have been expressed regarding the nature of short-term memory. Melton (1963) put forth the thesis that short-term memory as distinct from long-term memory does not exist. Atkinson and Shiffrin (1968) originated many of the ideas about short-term memory reviewed in this chapter. However, ideas about short-term memory have evolved considerably in the past 15 years. For more recent discussions of the nature of short-term memory, see Bjork (1975), Craik and Jacoby (1975), Shiffrin (1975) and Wickelgren (1973, 1974a). Crowder (1982) presents a good review of the research on short-term memory and argues that there is no such thing as an all-purpose short-term memory such as that proposed by Atkinson and Shiffrin.

The concept of spreading activation became popular in cognitive psychology with work on computer-simulation models by Quillian (1966, 1969) and by Reitman (1965). A comprehensive statement of the application of Quillian's ideas to psychological issues is to be found in Collins and Quillian (1972). A more up-to-date discussion is in Collins and Loftus (1975). I gave a recent review of this topic in Anderson (1984).

The research on interference in long-term memory has had a very long research tradition. Many current issues could not be considered in this chapter. For discussions of the current ideas about forgetting, see the relevant chapters in Anderson and Bower (1973) and Crowder (1976). See also the papers by Postman (1971), Postman and Underwood (1973) and by Wickelgren (1976).

Chapter 7

Memory Elaboration and Reconstruction

Summary

1. When information is committed to memory it is often elaborated with additional redundant information. Those elaborations facilitate recall by providing additional retrieval paths and by permitting recall by inference and reconstruction.

2. Memory for a piece of information can be improved by manipulations that increase the amount of elaboration performed by a subject.

3. Intention to learn is irrelevant to the amount learned. What is relevant is the way in which the information is processed.

4. People often recall by infering what is plausible given what they can remember. Such inferential recall will cause subjects to recall what they did not study but will also help them recall more of what they did study and more rapidly.

5. Schemas are a major mechanism for elaborating material during study, and they are a major mechanism for reconstructing memories at test. Recall will be distorted to fit the schemas that a subject has.

6. Memory performance improves the more closely the context at test matches the context at study. This has been shown to be true with respect to physical context, emotional and internal context, and the context provided by other study materials.

7. Studying material at widely spaced intervals tends to lead to better long-term retention because the material is learned in more different contexts.

8. Methods like the PQ4R method for studying textbooks are effective because they impose a retrieval structure on the text, because they enforce spaced study, and because they promote more elaborate processing of the text.

Elaborations and Their Network Representations

In Chapter 6, we assumed, for simplicity's sake, a rather impoverished conception of the material that is typically committed to memory. Now, consider an experiment where a subject must commit to memory the following sentence.

1. The doctor hated the lawyer.

Figure 7-1a illustrates the kind of memory-network representation that we have been assuming for such a sentence. However, a subject presented with sentence 1 is unlikely to deposit only this structure in memory. Figure 7-1b is a network representation of what a subject might really think while studying the sentence. The difference between this structure and the simplified one is that the subject has elaborated upon the sentence with new thoughts or propositions. Since the subject thinks these propositions upon being presented with the sentence, they might be committed to memory—just as the studied proposition is. In such a case, in addition to the studied proposition, the subject would have stored the following information:

2. The subject studied this sentence in the psychology laboratory one dreary morning.

3. The lawyer had sued the doctor for malpractice.

4. The malpractice suit was the source of the doctor's hatred.

5. This sentence is unpleasant.

Another fact representing some relevant information was probably already in memory:

6. Lawyers sue doctors for malpractice.

Such structures as that in Figure 7-1b—called *elaborated structures*, since they incorporate *elaborations* on the original proposition—can have profound effects on memory. The function of this chapter is to review research that studies these effects.

One effect we would expect is that memory for any event would improve the more it is elaborated. Elaborations can lead to better memory in at least two ways. First, they provide redundant retrieval routes for recall. To see this, contrast figures 7-1a and 7-1b. Suppose the link from node X (the doctor node) to the target proposition (node 1) is too weak to be revived at recall. If this were true and if the subject had only structure (a), he or she would be unable to recall proposition 1 when prompted with *doctor*. On the other hand in representation (b), even if the first link were too weak, there are other ways of retrieving the target proposition. For instance, the subject could

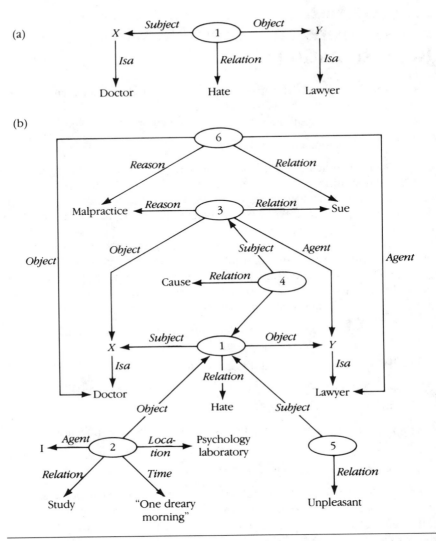

Figure 7-1 A comparison of (a) an unelaborated encoding with (b) an elaborated encoding of the sentence *The doctor hated the lawyer.*

recall from *X* the proposition that the lawyer sued the doctor for malpractice (node 3). From the proposition node 3, the subject could recall the proposition that the malpractice suit led to the doctor's hating the lawyer (node 4). From here the subject would be able to recall node 1, which he or she had been unable to recall directly from *X*. That is, although the subject could not traverse the direct path from X to 1, he or she would be able to go from X to 3 to 4 to 1. Thus, this elaborated structure would help recall by providing the subject with *alternate retrieval routes* through the network to be used should the more direct ones fail.

Now, suppose the subject completely failed to encode the target proposition 1. Then, no matter what the attempts, recall would fail. However, if the subject were able to recall the elaborations on the target proposition, his or her knowledge state would be following.

> I cannot remember the target sentence but I can remember conjecturing that it was caused by the lawyer's suing the doctor for malpractice and I can remember it was a negative sentence.

With this information the subject might infer that the target sentence was *The doctor hated the lawyer*. Thus, a second way in which elaboration aids memory is that it helps individuals to infer what they can no longer actually remember.

Both of these processes can be said to work because elaborations increase the *redundancy* with which information is encoded in memory. *Redundant elaboration* means that additional information is encoded in memory that provides more paths for retrieving and bases for inferring the to-be-remembered information. We would predict that experimental manipulations that increase the amount of redundant elaboration should increase the amount of recall.

The interference manipulations that we studied in Chapter 6 showed that a subject's memory was poorer the more information that was learned about a concept. Here the argument is that memory is being improved by redundant elaborations. The difference is that in the former case the additional information is irrelevant. To illustrate, if we wanted to learn (1) *The doctor hated the lawyer*, learning an irrelevant fact such as (2) *The doctor vacationed in Guadaloupe* would represent an interference. However, it would be facilitating to embellish sentence 1 with relevant fact, such as (3) *The lawyer sued the doctor*. In this case, the relevant fact provides an alternate retrieval path (like those we analyzed with respect to Figure 7-1), which the interfering sentence 2 did not.

Elaborateness of Processing

Representative Studies

A number of experiments have appeared in the literature that can be interpreted as illustrating that more fully elaborated material results in better memory. These experiments have sometimes been viewed as illustrating the principle of *depth of processing*. Fergus Craik at the University of Toronto has promoted the term depth of processing (e.g., see the paper of Craik & Lockhart, 1972), but a great many independent researchers have been involved. They have shown in various ways that manipulations to increase the depth with which information is processed result in better memory. *Depth* here is used as an intuitive term to reflect how fully the subject processes the meaning of the material to be learned. It is probably best interpreted as referring to the number of elaborations that the learner generates. Therefore, we will refer to this factor as *elaborateness of processing*.

A classic demonstration of elaborateness of processing comes from the 1969 experiments of Bobrow and Bower. These investigators had subjects try to commit to memory simple subject-verb-object sentences. There were two conditions of interest. In condition 1 subjects were provided with sentences written by the experimenters. In condition 2 subjects had to generate a sentence to connect the subject noun and object noun. After studying the sentences, subjects were prompted with the first (*subject*) noun and were required to generate the second (*object*) noun. Levels of recall in the two conditions were these: in condition 1 (sentences provided by experimenter), 29 percent; in condition 2 (sentences provided by subject), 58 percent. Presumably, in generating their own sentences subjects had to think more carefully about the meaning of the two nouns and their possible interrelationships. They probably considered a number of tentative connections between the two nouns before they chose one. This extra mental effort or deeper processing would have led to more elaborations of the nouns, and particularly to more elaborations that served to connect the two nouns. Similar demonstrations of the advantage of generation have been provided by Jacoby (1978) and by Slamecka and Graf (1978).

A number of devices are known to improve subjects' memory for sentences provided by an experimenter. One is to ask the subject to generate a logical continuation to the sentence. So, given the sentence *The fireman stabbed the dancer*, a subject might continue *in a lovers' quarrel*. Another technique is simply to ask subjects to develop a vivid visual image of the situation described by the sentence. As with the Bobrow and Bower manipulation, both of these techniques encourage the subject to process the sentence more deeply and more elaborately.

A series of experiments by Stein and Bransford (1979) shows why self-generated elaborations are often better than experimenter-provided elaborations. In one of these experiments, subjects were to remember 10 sentences like *The fat man read the sign*. There were four conditions of study. In the base condition, subjects studied just the sentence. In the self-generate condition, subjects were to generate an elaboration of their own. In the imprecise elaboration condition, subjects were presented with a continuation of the sentence like *that was two feet tall*. In the precise elaboration condition, they were presented with a continuation like *warning about the ice*. After studying the material, subjects in all conditions were presented with sentence frames like *The   man read the sign*, and they had to recall the missing adjective. Subjects recalled 4.2 of the 10 adjectives in the base condition and 5.8 when they generated their own elaboration. Thus, self-generated elaborations helped. They could recall only 2.2 of the adjectives in the imprecise elaboration condition, replicating the typical inferiority found for experimenter-provided elaborations relative to self-generated ones. However, subjects recalled the most—7.8—adjectives in the precise elaboration condition. So, by careful choice of elaboration, experimenter elaborations can be made better than subject elaborations.

Thus it appears that the critical factor is not whether the subject or the experimenter generates the elaborations. Rather, it is whether the elaborations are such that they constrain the to-be-recalled material. Subject-generated elaborations are quite effective because these elaborations reflect the idiosyncratic constraints of the particular subject's knowledge. However, as Stein and Bransford demonstrate, it is possible for the experimenter to construct elaborations that are even more precise in their constraints. Thus, elaborations help to the degree that they are an effective means of redundancy and so provide a means for reconstructing the to-be-remembered information.

These sorts of results are not limited to sentences. One important experiment, reported by Hyde and Jenkins (1973), involved memory for individual words. Subjects saw groups of 24 words presented at the rate of 3 sec per word. One group of subjects was asked to check whether each word had an *e* or a *g*. The other group of subjects was asked to rate the pleasantness of the words. These two tasks were called *orienting tasks*. It is reasonable to assume that the pleasantness rating involved deeper and more elaborate processing that the letter-verification task. Another manipulation in the experiment was whether subjects were told that the true purpose of the experiment was to learn the words. Half the subjects in each group were told the true purpose of the experiment. These subjects were said to be in the intentional-learning condition. The other half in each group, who thought the true purpose was to rate the words or check for letters, were said to be in the incidental-learning condition. Thus there are altogether four conditions: pleasantness intentional, pleasantness incidental, letter-checking intentional, and letter-checking incidental.

After studying the list, all subjects were asked to recall as many words as they could. Table 7-1 presents the results from the Jenkins and Hyde experiment in terms of percentage of the 24 words recalled. Two results are noteworthy. First, subjects' knowledge of the purpose of learning the words (of whether they would be tested for recall) had relatively little effect. Second, a large elaborateness-of-processing effect was demonstrated; subjects showed much higher recall in the pleasantness-rating condition independent of whether

Table 7-1 *Percentage of words recalled as a function of orienting task and whether subjects were aware of learning task*

	Orienting task	
Learning-purpose conditions	Rate pleasantness	Check letters
Incidental	68	39
Intentional	69	43

Adapted from Hyde and Jenkins, 1973.

they believed word learning was part of the experimental task. In rating a word for pleasantness, subjects had to think about its meaning, which gave them an opportunity to elaborate upon the word. For instance, a subject presented with *duck* might think "Duck—oh yes, I used to feed the ducks in the park; that was a pleasant time."

Incidental versus Intentional Learning

The Hyde and Jenkins experiment illustrates an important finding that has been proven over and over again in the research on intentional versus incidental learning: Whether a person intends to learn or not really does not matter (see Postman, 1964, for a reivew). What matters is how the person processes the material during its presentation. If the individual engages in identical mental activities when not intending as when intending to learn, he or she gets identical memory performance in both conditions. People typically show better memory when they intend to learn because they are likely to engage in activities more conducive to good memory, such as rehearsal and elaborative processing. The small advantage of intentional subjects in the Jenkins and Hyde experiment may reflect some small variation in processing. Experiments that take great care to control processing find that intention to learn or amount of motivation to learn has no effect (see Nelson, 1976).

In fact, in some experiments in which processing is not carefully controlled, subjects actually do better in an incidental condition. One such study was a sentence-memory experiment by Anderson and Bower (1972). We had two groups of subjects generate short continuations to sentences. So, a subject might see *The minister hit the landlord* and add *with a cross*. One group of subjects was informed that there would be a memory test, and the other group was not. The intentional group recalled 48.9 percent of the sentences, while the incidental group recalled 56.1 percent. Later, interviews of the subjects revealed that the intentional subjects performed less well because some of them were busy employing poor memorization strategies, such as saying the sentence over and over again to themselves. The incidental subjects simply elaborated on the sentences and were not hampered by poor theories of what makes for good memory. Brown (1979) also reported situations in which children were hampered in an intentional-learning situation by their mistaken ideas about memory.

Nonmeaningful Elaborations

The studies we have discussed to this point have confounded processing material in a more *meaningful* way with processing in a more *elaborate* way. More recent research has indicated that the important variable is really elaborateness of processing. For instance, Slamecka and Graf (1978) found improved memory when subjects had to generate rhymes like *save–cave* rather than to read them. Similarly, Nelson (1979) has shown that phonemic rather than semantic processing will improve memory. Apparently, the process the subject goes through in generating the rhyme leaves traces behind in memory. The traces of rhyme generation are elaborations of the memory just as much as traces of sentence continuation. These process traces provide a redundant means for reconstructing the memory.

Some psychologists, such as Kolers (1979), have argued that the entire depth-of-processing literature is to be accounted in terms of memory for the processes involved in the original study of the material. Kolers has looked at subjects' memory for sentences that are read in normal form versus sentences that are printed upside down, and has found that subjects can remember more about the upside-down sentences. He argues that the extra processing involved in processing the typography of upside-down sentences provides the basis for the improved memory. Again, it is not a case of more meaningful processing but rather of more elaborate processing.

Text Material

Frase (1975) has found evidence for the benefit of elaborative processing with text material. He compared two groups of subjects on their memory for a text: one that had been given topics to think about before reading the text, and a control group that simply studied the text without advance topics. The topics given to the test group were similar to the summaries beginning the chapters in this book. They were sometimes called *advance organizers*, and in the Frase experiment they were in the form of questions that the subjects had to answer.[1] The subjects were to find answers to the advance

---

[1] Ausubel (1968) introduced the term advance organizers to refer to general statements of information such as those in the chapter summaries here.

questions as they read the text. This requirement should have forced them to process the text more carefully and to think about its implications. The advance-organizer group answered 64 percent of the questions correctly in a subsequent test, while the control group answered 57 percent correctly. The questions in the final test could be divided into those relevant to the advance organizers and those not relevant. For instance, if a test question was about an event that precipitated America's entry into World War II, it would be considered relevant if the advance questions directed the subject to learn why America entered the war. Such a test question would be considered not relevant if the advance question directed students to learn about the economic consequences of World War II. The advance-organizer group answered 76 percent of the relevant questions correctly and 52 percent of the irrelevant. Thus, they did only slightly worse than the control group on those topics for which they had not been given advance warning, but much better on topics for which they had been given advance warning.

Summary

The evidence is quite clear that elaborative processing produces better memory for all sorts of material. This conclusion would be expected from the network model described earlier. Thus, students should elaborate on the material that they are learning in a course. This recommendation should please most teachers, because it coincides with the recommendation that students think about the implications of what they are learning.

Inferential Reconstruction in Recall

Let us return to the discussion of a subject's memory for this sentence:

1. The doctor hated the lawyer.

Elaborations improve memory for this sentence by increasing the redundancy of its encodings. Note that redundancy is not created by the subject's simply making multiple mental copies of the sentence. Rather, redundancy is created by the storing of additional propositions that weakly or strongly imply the target sentence, as the following propositions do:

2. The lawyer sued the doctor for malpractice.

3. The doctor cursed the lawyer in court.

4. The doctor glared at the lawyer.

5. The lawyer assailed the doctor with a stream of questions.

Suppose subjects are no longer able to remember the studied sentence at test, but are able to recall two of their elaborations, say:

2. The lawyer sued the doctor for malpractice.

4. The doctor glared at the lawyer.

In this case, the subject might well infer that the doctor hated the lawyer. Note, however, that this inference need not be true. For instance, the doctor and lawyer might be in cahoots, trying to defraud the doctor's malpractice-insurance company. Thus, when people do try to recall by inference, there always is the possibility that their recall will be in error.

Bransford, Barclay, and Franks (1972) reported an experiment that demonstrates how inference can lead to incorrect recall. They had subjects study on of the following sentences:

1. Three turtles rested beside a floating log, and a fish swam beneath them.

2. Three turtles rested on a floating log, and a fish swam beneath them.

Subjects who had studied sentence 1 were later asked whether they had studied this sentence:

3. Three turtles rested beside a floating log, and a fish swam beneath it.

Not many subjects thought they had studied this. Subjects who had studied sentence 2 were tested with

4. Three turtles rested on a floating log, and a fish swam beneath it.

Many more subjects thought they had studied this sentence than thought they had studied sentence 3. Of course, sentence 4 is implied by sentence 2, whereas sentence 3 is not implied by sentence 1. Thus, subjects thought that they had actually studied what was implied by the studied material.

A study by Sulin and Dooling (1974) provides an illustration of how inference can bias subjects' memory for a text. They had subjects read the following passage:

Carol Harris's Need for Professional Help

Carol Harris was a problem child from birth. She was wild, stubborn, and violent. By the time Carol turned eight, she was still unmanageable. Her parents were very concerned about her mental health. There was no good institution for her problem in her state. Her parents finally decided to take some action. They hired a private teacher for Carol.

A second group of subjects read the same passage except that the name *Helen Keller* was substituted for *Carol Harris*. A week after reading the passage, subjects were given a recognition test in which they were presented with a sentence and asked to judge whether it had occurred in the passage. One of the critical sentences was *She was deaf, dumb, and blind*. Only 5 percent of the subjects who read the Carol Harris passage accepted this sentence, but a full 50 percent of the Helen Keller subjects thought they had read the sentence. This is just what we would expect. The second group of subjects had elaborated the story with facts they knew about Helen Keller. Thus, it would seem reasonable to them at test that this sentence had appeared in the studied material, but in this case their inference would have been wrong.

It is interesting to inquire whether such an inference as *She was deaf, dumb, and blind* was made while the subject was studying the passage or only at the time of the test. This is a subtle issue to get at, and subjects certainly do not have reliable intuitions about the matter. However, a couple of techniques are generally considered to yield evidence that inferences are being made at test. One is to determine whether the inferences increase in frequency with delay. With delay, subjects' memory for the studied passage should deteriorate and they will have to do more reconstruction, which will lead to more inferential errors. Both Dooling and Christiaansen (1977) and Spiro (1977) have found evidence for increased inferential intrusions with increased delay of testing.

Dooling and Christiaansen (1977) used another technique with the Carol Harris passage to show that inferences were being made at test. They had the subjects study the passage and told them a week later, just before test, that Carol Harris really was Helen Keller. In this situation, subjects also made many inferential errors, accepting such sentences as *She was deaf, dumb, and blind*. Since they did not know Carol Harris was Helen Keller until test, they must have made such inferences at test. Thus, it seems that subjects do make reconstructive inferences at time of test.

Plausible Retrieval

In the foregoing analysis we spoke of subjects as making errors when they recalled or recognized facts that were not explicitly presented. In real life, however, such acts of recall would often not be regarded as errors, but as intelligent inferences. Reder (1982) has argued that much of recall in real life involves plausible inference rather than exact recall. For instance, in deciding that Darth Vader was evil in *Star Wars* a person does not search memory for the specific proposition that Darth Vader was evil, although the proposition may well have been directly asserted in the movie. The person infers that Darth Vader was evil from memories about his behavior.

Reder has demonstrated that subjects will display very different behavior, depending on whether they are asked to engage in exact retrieval or plausible retrieval. She had subjects study passages such as the following:

> The heir to a large hamburger chain was in trouble. He had married a lovely young woman who had seemed to love him. Now he worried that she had been after his money after all. He sensed that she was not attracted to him. Perhaps he consumed too much beer and french fries. No, he couldn't give up the fries. Not only were they delicious, he got them for free.

Then she had subjects judge sentences such as the following:

1. The heir married a lovely young woman who had seemed to love him.

2. The heir got his french fries from his family's hamburger chain.

3. The heir was very careful to eat only healthy food.

The first sentence was studied; the second was not studied, but is plausible; and the third was neither studied nor plausible. Subjects in the exact condition were asked to make exact recognition judgments, in which case they were to accept the first sentence and reject the second two. Subjects in the plausible condition were to judge if the sentence was plausible given the story, in which case they were to accept the first two and reject the last. Reder tested subjects immediately after studying the story, 20 min later, or 2 days later.

She was interested in judgment time for subjects in the two conditions, exact versus plausible. Figure 7-2 shows the results from Reder's experiment as a function of delay. Plotted in the figure are the average judgment times for sentence types 1 and 2. As might be expected, subjects get slower with delay in the exact condition. However, they get faster in the plausible condition. They start out slower in the plausible than in the exact condition, but this is reversed after 2 days. Reder argues that subjects get worse in the exact condition because the exact traces are getting weak. However, a plausibility judgment is not dependent on any particular trace, and so is not similarly vulnerable to forgetting. Subjects get faster in the plausible condition with delay because they no longer try to use inefficient exact retrieval, but use plausibility, which is faster.

Reder and Ross (1983) compared exact versus plausible judgments in another paradigm. They had subjects study sentences such as the following:

> Alan bought a ticket for the 10:00 A.M. train.

> Alan heard the conductor call "All aboard."

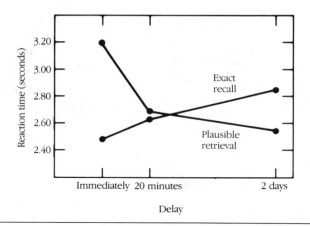

Figure 7-2 Time to make exact versus plausible recognition judgments of sentences as a function of delay since study of a story. (From Reder, 1982.)

Alan read a newspaper on the train.

Alan arrived at Grand Central Station.

They manipulated the number of sentences that subjects had to study about a particular person like Alan. Then they looked at subjects' times to recognize sentences like

1. Alan heard the conductor call "All aboard."

2. Alan watched the approaching train from the platform.

3. Alan sorted his clothes into colors and whites.

In the exact condition subjects had to judge whether the sentence had been studied. So, given the foregoing material, subjects would accept test sentence 1 and reject test sentences 2 and 3. In the plausible condition subjects had to judge whether it was plausible that Alan was involved in the activity, given what they had studied. Thus, subjects would accept sentences 1 and 2 and reject 3.

In the exact condition, Reder and Ross found that subjects took longer the more facts they studied about Alan. This is basically a replication of the fan effect discussed in Chapter 6. In the plausible condition, however, subjects were faster the more facts they had learned about Alan. The more facts they knew about Alan, the more ways there were to judge a particular fact plausible. Thus, plausibility judgment did not have to depend on retrieval of a particular fact.

The Interaction of Elaboration and Inferential Reconstruction

We have discussed inferential processes by which subjects elaborate a memory at study and inferential processes by which they reconstruct the memory at test. We would expect that the more a subject embellished a sentence at study, the more inferential reconstruction would be possible at test. In fact, to use elaborations at study to improve memory performance, subjects often have to go from these elaborations to inferences about what was studied. Thus, we expect elaborative processing to lead to both an improvement in memory for what was studied and an increase in the number of inferences recalled. An experiment by Owens, Bower, and Black (1979) confirms this prediction. Subjects studied a story that followed the principle character, a college student, through a day in her life: making a cup of coffee in the morning, visiting a doctor, attending a lecture, going shopping for groceries, and attending a cocktail party. The following is a passage from the story:

> Nancy went to see the doctor. She arrived at the office and checked in with the receptionist. She went to see the nurse, who went through the usual procedures. Then Nancy stepped on the scale and the nurse recorded her weight. The doctor entered the room and examined the results. He smiled at Nancy and said, "Well, it seems my expectations have been confirmed." When the examination was finished, Nancy left the office.

Two groups of subjects studied the story. The only difference between the groups was that the theme group had read the following additional information at the beginning:

> Nancy woke up feeling sick again and she wondered if she really were pregnant. How would she tell the professor she had been seeing? And the money was another problem.

College students who read this additional passage characterized Nancy as an unmarried student who is afraid she is pregnant as a result of an affair with a college professor. Subjects who had not read this opening passage had no reason to suspect that there is anything special about Nancy. We would expect subjects in the theme condition to make many more theme-related elaborations of the story than subjects in the neutral condition.

Subjects were asked to recall the story 24 hours after studying it. Subjects in the theme condition introduced a great many more inferences that had not actually been studied. For instance, subjects often reported that the doctor told Nancy she was pregnant. Intrusions of this variety are expected if subjects

Table 7-2 *Number of propositions recalled*

	Theme condition	Neutral condition
Studied propositions	29.2	20.2
Inferred propositions	15.2	3.7

Adapted from Owens et al., 1979.

reconstruct the story on the basis of their elaborations. Table 7-2 reports some of the results from the study. Many more inferences are added in recall for the theme condition than for the neutral condition. However, a second important observation is that subjects in the theme condition also remembered more of the propositions they had actually studied. Thus, because of the additional elaborations made by subjects in the theme condition, they may be able to recall more of the story.

We might question whether subjects really benefited from their elaborations, since they also "misrecalled" many things that did not occur in the story. However, it is wrong to characterize the intruded inferences as misrecalls. Given the theme information, subjects were perfectly right to make these inferences and to recall them. In a nonexperimental setting (e.g., recalling information on an exam) we would expect these subjects to treat such inferences as facts that were actually studied.

Advertisers often capitalize on our tendency to embellish what we hear with plausible inferences. Consider the following portion of a Listerine commercial:

> "Wouldn't it be great," asks the mother, "if you could make him coldproof? Well, you can't. Nothing can do that. [Boy sneezes.] But there is something that you can do that may help. Have him gargle with Listerine Antiseptic. Listerine can't promise to keep him coldfree, but it may help him fight off colds. During the cold-catching season, have him gargle twice a day with full-strength Listerine. Watch his diet, see he gets plenty of sleep, and there's a good chance he'll have fewer colds, milder colds this year."

A verbatim text of this commercial, with the only change that of the product name to "Gargoil," was used by Harris (1977). After hearing this commercial, all 15 of his subjects checked that "gargling with Gargoil Antiseptic helps prevent colds," although this assertion was clearly not made in the commercial. The Federal Trade Commission explicitly forbids advertisers from making false claims, but does the Listerine ad make a false claim? In a potential landmark case, the courts have ruled against Warner-Lambert, makers of Listerine, for implying false claims in this commercial.

Use of Schemas

In Chapter 5 we discussed the role of schemas in guiding the interpretation of a story. To review, schemas are organized sets of facts, such as beliefs about what goes on in a restaurant. Subjects use schemas to infer that certain unobserved and unmentioned elements must be present. Thus, a subject who heard, "Fred ordered a duck. He drank red wine with his meal. He left a generous tip," would tend to infer that Fred ate the duck. It seems that schemas are a major mechamism for elaborating material during study, and they are a major mechanism for reconstructing memories at test. Some striking evidence for the role of schemas in memory was obtained by Bartlett (1932) in research with English subjects before World War I. He used a story called "The War of the Ghosts." It has been used in research on many subsequent occasions and is still a popular research item today. The story is reproduced in its entirety here:[2]

The War of the Ghosts

One night two young men from Egulac went down to the river to hunt seals, and while they were there it became foggy and calm. Then they heard war-cries, and they thought: "Maybe this is a war-party." They escaped to the shore, and hid behind a log. Now canoes came up, and they heard the noise of paddles, and saw one canoe coming up to them. There were five men in the canoe, and they said:

"What do you think? We wish to take you along. We are going up the river to make war on the people."

One of the young men said, "I have no arrows."

"Arrows are in the canoe," they said.

"I will not go along. I might be killed. My relatives do not know where I have gone. But you," he said, turning to the other, "may go with them."

So one of the young men went, but the other returned home.

And the warriors went on up the river to a town on the other side of Kalama. The people came down to the water, and they began to fight, and many were killed. But presently the young men heard one of the warriors say: "Quick, let us go home: that Indian has been hit." Now he thought: "Oh, they are ghosts." He did not feel sick, but they said he had been shot.

So the canoes went back to Egulac, and the young man went ashore to his house, and made a fire. And he told everybody and said: "Behold I accompanied the ghosts, and we went to fight. Many of our fellows were killed, and many of those who attacked us were killed. They said I was hit, and I did not feel sick."

He told it all, and then he became quiet. When the sun rose he

[2]Frederic C. Bartlett, *Remembering: A Study in Experimental and Social Psychology* (New York: Cambridge University Press), 1967, p. 65. (Originally published in 1932.)

fell down. Something black came out of his mouth. His face became contorted. The people jumped up and cried.
He was dead.

Presumably, you find this a rather bizarre story. Certainly, it appeared bizarre to Bartlett's subjects, accustomed as they were to the world of upper-class Edwardian England. This story, however, would be perfectly reasonable to the people from which it was taken. It was part of the oral literary tradition of Indians on the West Coast of Canada a century ago. It fit in very well with their schemas for how the world worked. It does not fit in well with our cultural schemas nor with those of Bartlett's subjects.

Bartlett was interested in how subjects would remember a story that fit in so poorly with their cultural schemas. He had his subjects recall the story after various delays, from immediately after study to years later. To get a feeling for their task, you might put this book aside and try to write down all you can remember from this story.

Bartlett's subjects showed clear distortions in their memory for the story, and these distortions appeared to grow with time. Below is a representative recall (Bartlett, 1932, p. 66) given 20 hours after hearing the story:

The War of the Ghosts

Two men from Edulac went fishing. While thus occupied by the river they heard a noise in the distance.

"It sounds like a cry," said one, and presently there appeared some in canoes who invited them to join the party on their adventure. One of the young men refused to go, on the ground of family ties, but the other offered to go.

"But there are no arrows," he said.

"The arrows are in the boat," was the reply.

He thereupon took his place, while his friend returned home. The party paddled up the river to Kaloma, and began to land on the banks of the river. The enemy came rushing upon them, and some sharp fighting ensued. Presently someone was injured, and the cry was raised that the enemy were ghosts.

The party returned down the stream, and the young man arrived home feeling none the worse for his experience. The next morning at dawn he endeavored to recount his adventures. While he was talking something black issued from his mouth. Suddenly he uttered a cry and fell down. His friends gathered around him.

But he was dead.

Subjects omitted much of the story, changed many of the facts, and imported new information. Such inaccuracies in memory are not particularly interesting in and of themselves. The important observation is that these inaccuracies were systematic: The subjects were distorting the story to fit with their own cultural stereotypes. For instance, "something black came from his mouth" in the original story became "he frothed at the mouth" or "he vomited" in some stories. In the recall above, we find "hunting seals" changed to "fishing" and "canoe" changed to "boat." The hard-to-interpret aspects are omitted, including the hiding behind the log and the connection between the Indian's injury and the termination of the battle. Further, this subject has the role of the ghosts completely turned around. Thus, when subjects read a story that does not fit with their own schemas, they will exhibit a powerful tendency to distort the story to make it fit.

Organization and Recall

Hierarchical Structures and Other Organizations

Numerous manipulations have been shown to improve subjects' memory in recalling a long list of items. Many such devices involve organizing the material in such a way that subjects can systematically search their memories for the items. A nice demonstration of this use of organization is an experiment by Bower, Clark, Lesgold, and Winzenz (1969). They had subjects learn all the words in four hierarchies such as the one in Figure 7-3. Two conditions of learning were compared. In the organized condition, the four hierarchies were presented in upside-down trees, as in Figure 7-3. In the random condition subjects saw four trees, but the positions in the trees were filled by random combinations of words from the four categories. Thus, instead of

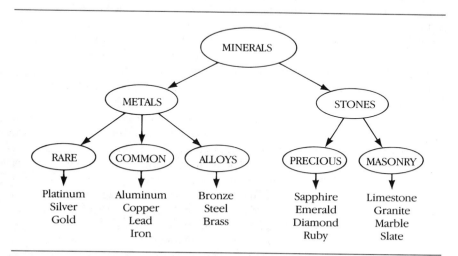

Figure 7-3   A hierarchical tree presented to subjects in the free-recall experiment of Bower et al. The relationships among the items in the tree are categorical. (From Bower et al., 1969.)

Table 7-3 *Average number of words recalled over four trials as a function of organization*

Conditions	Trials			
	1	2	3	4
Organized	73.0	106.1	112.0	112.0
Random	20.6	38.9	52.8	70.1

Adapted from Bower et al., 1969.

seeing separate trees for animals, clothing, transportation, and minerals, subjects saw four trees, each containing some items from each category.

Subjects were given a minute to study each tree, and after studying all four trees they were asked to recall all the words in the four trees in any order. This study–test sequence was repeated four times. The performance of the two groups over the four trials is given in Table 7-3 in terms of number of words recalled. The maximum possible recall was 112. The organized group was shown to have an enormous advantage. Analysis of the order in which the organized group recalled the words indicated that subjects had organized their recall according to the tree hierarchies and recalled the words going down a tree from the top—for example, using Figure 7-3, first they would recall *minerals* and then *metals*.

The associative-network explanation of this result is straightforward: In the organized condition subjects were forming a memory network during the study phase similar to the hierarchy in Figure 7-4. To do this they had only to elaborate on connections already in memory. Thus, to return to the main topic of this chapter, another important function of elaborations can be imposing a hierarchical organization on memory. Such a hierarchical organization allows a person to structure the search of memory and to retrieve information more efficiently.

The implication for study habits of the results in Bower et al. is both important and clear. Course material can often be organized into hierarchies just as word lists can. Table 7-4 is a hierarchical organization for the material up to this point in the chapter. (In actually studying this material, students would be better off deriving their own organizations, since doing this will force deeper processing of the material.) For readability, levels of the hierarchy are represented by levels of indentation. Note that in this hierarchy the connections are often not categorical, unlike those in Figure 7-3. For instance, the relation of *network representation* to *elaborations and reconstructions* is not one of an instance to a category. Rather, *network representation* serves as an explanation of or a mechanism for describing a phenomenon.

Table 7-4 *Chapter outline to this point*

Elaborations and reconstruction
  Network representation
    Inferences and embellishments
    Contextual elements
    Connections to past knowledge
    Alternate retrieval routes
    Inferences at time of test

Elaborateness of processing
  Representative studies
    Bobrow and Bower (self-generation)
    Use of continuations
    Stein and Bransford (precision of elaborations)
  Incidental versus intentional learning
    Hyde and Jenkins (rating of pleasantness)
    Anderson and Bower (continuation generation)
  Non-meaningful elaborations
  Text material (Frase; advance organizers)
    Effect of questions on relevant material
    Effect of questions on irrelevant material

Inference in recall
  Bransford, Barclay, and Franks (three turtles)
  Dooling's studies with the Helen Keller passage
  Plausible retrieval (Reder)
  Interaction between elaboration and reconstruction

Use of schemas
  Bartlett's "War of the Ghosts"

Effects of organization
  Hierarchies
    Bower, Clark, Lesgold, and Winzenz
    This example

Bower et al. have shown that an individual need not utilize a strict categorical organization in order to derive the benefits of hierarchical structure. They investigated hierarchies such as the one in Figure 7-4, where the organization involves a loose associative structure. The presentation of information in such a hierarchy resulted in a considerable advantage over a random presentation.

Another demonstration of the importance of organization to recall was provided by Bower and Clark (1969). They required subjects to commit to memory lists of 10 unrelated nouns. The experimental group was told to study these nouns by constructing a narrative story around them. An example story generated by one subject, with the to-be-recalled words capitalized, is given below.

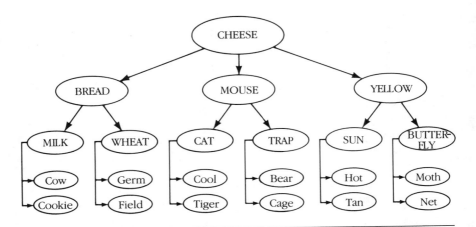

Figure 7-4   A second type of hierarchical tree presented to subjects in the free-recall experiment of Bower et al. Here the relationships among the items are general associative rather than strictly categorical, as in Figure 7-3. (From Bower et al., 1969.)

> A LUMBERJACK DARTed out of a forest, SKATEd around a HEDGE past a COLONY of DUCKs. He tripped on some FURNITURE, tearing his STOCKING while hastening toward the PILLOW where his MISTRESS lay.

A control group was given the same amount of time to study the 10 nouns but no special instructions. Both groups were tested immediately after the list was studied; immediate recall was almost perfect for both groups. However, a final test was given after the two groups had learned 12 lists in this manner. This final test was for all 120 words in all 12 lists. The experimental group recalled 94 percent, whereas the control group recalled 14 percent.

The Method of Loci

A classic mnemonic technique, the *method of loci*, has its effect by promoting good organization in recall situations. This technique, used extensively in ancient times when speeches were given without written notes, is still used today. Cicero (in *De Oratore*) credits the method to a Greek poet, Simonides. Simonides had delivered a lyric poem at a banquet. Following his delivery, he was called from the banquet hall by the gods Castor and Pollux, whom he had praised in this poem. While he was absent the roof fell in, killing all the participants at the banquet. The corpses were so mangled that relatives could not identify them. However, Simonides was able to identify each corpse according to where the person had been sitting in the banquet hall. This feat of total recall convinced Simonides of the usefulness of an orderly arrangement of locations into which a person could place objects to be remembered. This story may be rather fanciful, but whatever the true origin of the method of loci, it is well documented (e.g., Christen & Bjork, 1976; Ross & Lawrence, 1968) as a useful technique for remembering an ordered sequence of items, such as the points a person wants to make in a speech.

Basically, to use the method of loci the individual imagines a fixed path through a familiar area with some fixed locations along the path. For instance, if there were such a path on campus from the bookstore to the library, we might use it. To remember a series of objects, we simply mentally walk along the path, associating the objects with the fixed locations. As an example, consider a grocery list of six items—milk, hot dogs, dog food, tomatoes, bananas, and bread. To associate the milk with the bookstore, we might imagine a puddle of milk in front of the bookstore with books fallen into the milk. To associate hot dogs with the record shop (the next location in the path from the bookstore), we might imagine a package of hot dogs spinning on a record player turntable. The pizza shop is next, and to associate this with dog food we might imagine a pizza with dog food on it (well, some people even like anchovies). Then we come to the intersection; to associate this with tomatoes we can imagine an overturned vegetable truck and tomatoes splattered everywhere. Then we come to the administration building—and an image of the president coming out, wearing only a hula-type skirt made of bananas. Finally, we reach the library and associate it to bread by imagining a huge loaf of bread serving as a canopy under which we must pass to enter. To recreate the list, we need only take an imaginary walk down this path, reviving the associations to each location. This technique works well with very much longer lists; we only need more locations. There is considerable evidence (e.g., Christen & Bjork, 1976) that the same loci can be used over and over again in the learning of different lists.

Two important principles underlie the effectiveness of the method of loci. First, the technique imposes organization on an otherwise unorganized list. We are guaranteed that if we follow the mental path at time of recall, we will pass all the locations for which we created associations. The second principle is that generating connections between the locations and the items forces us to process the material elaboratively.

The Effects of Encoding Context

A clear implication of the network representation in Figure 7-1b is that reviving the experimental context in which items have been studied should aid recall. Note that such concepts as *psychology laboratory, one dreary morning*, and *unpleasant* are associated with the experimental memory. If at test such contextual stimuli and concepts could be revived, the subject would have additional ways to reactivate the target memory. There is ample evidence that context can greatly influence memory. This section will review some of the ways in which context influences memory. These context effects are often referred to as *encoding effects* because the context is affecting what is encoded into the memory trace that records the event.

Smith, Glenberg, and Bjork (1978) performed an experiment that showed the importance of physical context. In their experiment, subjects learned two lists of paired associates on different days and in different physical settings. On day 1, subjects learned the paired associates in a windowless room in a building near the University of Michigan campus. The experimenter was neatly groomed, dressed in a coat and a tie, and the paired associates were shown on slides. On day 2, subjects learned the paired associates in a tiny room with windows on the main campus. The experimenter was dressed sloppily in a flannel shirt and jeans (it was the same experimenter, but some subjects did not recognize him) and presented the paired associates via a tape recorder. A day later, subjects made their recall, half in one setting and half in the other setting. Subjects could recall 59 percent of the list learned in the same setting as tested, but only 46 percent of the list learned in the other setting. Thus, it seems that recall is better if the context at test is the same as the context at study.

A perhaps more extreme version of this experiment was performed by Godden and Baddeley in 1975. They had divers learn a list of 40 unrelated words either on the shore or 20 feet under the sea. The divers were then asked to recall the list in either the same or a different environment. Figure 7-5 displays the results of this study. Subjects clearly showed superior memory when they were asked to recall in the same context in which they studied. So, it seems that contextual elements get associated to memories, and that memory is improved when subjects are provided with these contextual elements again.

Research by Bower, Monteiro, and Gilligan (1978) shows that emotional context can have the same effect as physical context. They also had subjects learn two lists. For one list they hypnotically induced a positive state by having subjects review a pleasant episode in their lives, and for the other list they hypnotically induced a negative state by having subjects review a traumatic event. A later recall test was given under either a positive or a negative emotional state (again hypnotically induced). Better memory was obtained when the emotional state at test matched the emotional state at study.

As an aside it is worth commenting that, despite popular reports, the best evidence is that hypnosis per se does nothing to improve memory (see Hilgard, 1968; Smith, 1982), although it can help memory to the extent that

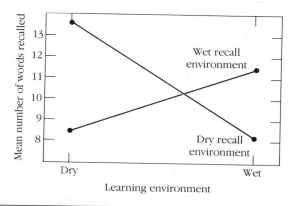

Figure 7-5   Mean number of words recalled as a function of environment in which learning took place. Word lists were recalled better in the same environment in which they were learned than in a different environment. (Data from Godden & Baddeley, 1975.)

it can be used to recreate the contextual factors at the time of test. However, much of a learning context can also be recreated by nonhypnotic means, such as through free association about the circumstances of the to-be-remembered event.

A related phenomenon is referred to as *state-dependent learning*. People find it easier to recall information if they can return to the same emotional and physical state they were in when they learned the information. For instance, it is often casually claimed that heavy drinkers when sober are unable to remember where they hid their alcohol when drunk, and when drunk they are unable to remember where they hid their money when sober. In fact, some experimental evidence does exist for this state dependency of memory with respect to alcohol, but the more important factor seems to be that alcohol has a general debilitating effect on the acquisition of information (Parker, Birnbaum, & Noble, 1976). Marijuana has been shown to have similar state-dependent effects. In one experiment (Eich, Weingartner, Stillman, & Gillin, 1975), subjects learned a free-recall list after smoking either a marijuana cigarette or an ordinary cigarette. Subjects were tested 4 hours later—again after smoking either a marijuana cigarette or a regular cigarette. Subjects who learned in the marijuana condition recalled 12 percent of the items when tested while nonintoxicated and 23 percent when tested while intoxicated. Subjects who learned in the ordinary-cigarette condition recalled 25 percent of the items when tested while nonintoxicated and 20 percent when tested after smoking a marijuana cigarette.

Encoding Specificty

The effects of general environmental and internal context are fairly easy to understand intuitively, but evidence suggests that there can be less obvious effects of the context in experimental situations. For example, there is now good evidence that memory for to-be-learned material can be heavily dependent on the context of other to-be-learned material in which it is embedded. Consider a recognition-memory experiment by Thomson (1972). He had subjects study pairs of words such as *sky blue*. Subjects were told that they were responsible only for the second item of the pair—in this case *blue*; the first word represented context. Later, they were tested by being presented with either *blue* or *sky blue*. In either case, they were asked whether they had originally seen *blue*. In the single-word case they recognized *blue* 76 percent of the time, while in the pair condition their recognition rate was 85 percent. This difference indicates a dependence of memory on the context in which a to-be-recognized item is studied.

A series of experiments (e.g., Tulving & Thomson, 1973; Watkins & Tulving, 1975) has dramatically illustrated how memory for a word can depend on how well the test context matches the original study context. In one experiment (1975), Watkins and Tulving had subjects learn pairs of words such as *train–black* and told them that they were only responsible for the second word, referred to as the *to-be-remembered word* (again, the first word in the pairs served as the context). After this study phase, subjects were given words such as *white* and asked to generate four free associates to the word. So, a subject might generate *snow*, *black*, *wool*, and *pure*. The stimuli for the associate task were chosen to have a high probability of eliciting a to-be-remembered word. For instance, *white* has a high probability of eliciting *black*. Overall, the to-be-remembered word was generated 66 percent of the time as the one of the four associates. After they had generated their associates, subjects were told to indicate which of the four associates was the one they had studied. They were forced to indicate a choice even if they thought they had not studied any of the words. In cases where the to-be-remembered word was generated, subjects correctly chose the word 54 percent of the time. Since subjects were always forced to indicate a choice, some of these correct choices must have been lucky guesses, meaning that true recognition was even lower. Following this test in which subjects free associated and then recognized study words, subjects were presented with the original context words and asked to recall the to-be-recalled words. Subjects recalled 61 percent of the words—higher than their recognition rate without any correction for quessing! Moreover, Tulving and Watkins found that 42 percent of the words recalled had not been recognized earlier when the subjects gave them as free associates.

As we saw in the previous chapter, recognition is generally superior to recall. Conversely, we would expect that if subjects could not recognize a word, they would be unable to recall it. Usually, we expect to do better on a multiple-choice test than on a recall-the-answer test. Experiments such as the one just described have provided some very dramatic reversals of such standard expectations. Their results can be understood in terms of the similarity of the test context to the study context. The context in which the word *white* and its associates were studied was quite different from that in which *black* had originally been studied. In contrast, in the cued-recall task, subjects were given the original context (*train*) with which they had studied the word. Thus, if the contextual factors are sufficiently weighted in favor of recall, as they were in these experiments, recall can be superior to recognition. Tulving offers these results as illustrating what he calls the *encoding-specificity principle*: The probability of recalling an item at test depends on the similarity of its encoding at test and its original encoding at study.

Encoding Variability and the Spacing Effect

When facts are studied on multiple occasions, their encodings will be slightly different on each occasion. An important factor determining the measure of difference among the various encodings is the measure of difference among the learning contexts on each occasion. An obvious factor influencing the differences among learning contexts is the spacing over time of these contexts. The importance of spacing is illustrated in an experiment by Madigan (1969), again on the free recall of single words. Forty-eight words were presented at the rate of 1.5 sec per word. Some words were presented once and others twice. After study, subjects were asked to recall as many words as they could. They recalled 28 percent of the words that appeared once and 47 percent of the words that appeared twice. Figure 7-6 shows an analysis of Madigan's data in the twice-presented condition. The data for the twice-presented condition are plotted as a function of *lag*, or the number of intervening words between the two presentations. Probability of recall increases systematically with lag. There is a very rapid increase over the initial lag, and the benefit increases, if more slowly, to lags of 40 intervening items. To date, no evidence suggests that there is an amount of spacing after which recall will not further improve. Memory improves with the increase in lag between study episodes, although the advantage diminishes as the spacing is increased. This result is known as the *spacing effect*.

The spacing effect is an extremely robust and powerful phenomenon, and it has been repeatedly shown with many kinds of material. Spacing effects have been demonstrated in free recall, in cued recall of paired associates, in the recall of sentences, and in the recall of text material. It is important to

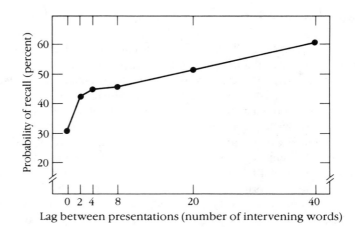

Lag between presentations (number of intervening words)

Figure 7-6 Recall probability of twice-presented words as a function of the lag between the two occurrences of the word in Madigan (1969). Memory improves as the lag between presentations increases.

note that these spacing results do generalize to textbook materials (Reynolds & Glaser, 1964; Rothkopf & Coke, 1963, 1966). Spacing effects are even more potent in skill learning than in fact learning, as we will discuss in Chapter 9.

It is probable that a number of factors combine to produce the spacing effect. For instance, subjects may do poorly at short lags simply because of inattention. That is, they may regard a second study at such a short lag as unnecessary and ignore it. Rundus (1971) asked subjects to rehearse material out loud and found that they spent less rehearsal time on the second presentation of items after short lags. Although other factors are probably involved (e.g., see Hintzman, 1974), an important factor in the lag effect, especially after long lags, is that suggested at the start of this subsection: *encoding variability* due to change of context. Probability of recall depends in the part on the study context matching the test context. At long lags, it is likely that the two study contexts will be quite different from each other. The greater the difference between the two study contexts, the greater is the probability that one of the contexts will overlap with the test context. On the other hand, at short lags the two study contexts will be more similar, and the probability of the study contexts matching the test context will be not much greater than in the single-presentation condition.

The importance of encoding variability to the spacing effect is nicely demonstrated in some of the other analyses reported by Madigan (1969). He presented subjects with pairs of words but told them they were responsible for remembering only the second—the first just provided context (as in the previously described studies of Thomson and of Watkins and Tulving). Some target words were presented twice and some only once. When items were repeated, they occurred each time either with the same context word or with different context words. For example, the target word *chill* might occur twice in a list, separated by a lag of four intervening items. In the different condition it might occur the first time with *fever* and the second time with *snow*. In the same condition it would occur both times with *fever*. Madigan found that subjects performed better in the different condition. Moreover, the different condition did not show as large a spacing effect as the same condition. That is, the advantage of long lags over short lags was smaller in the different condition.

Madigan's results would be expected from the encoding-variability interpretation of the spacing effect. By providing different context words, Madigan forced a change in the encoding context. This change should be particularly important at short lags when large variations in context do not occur naturally. Note that the Madigan experiment demonstrates that it is possible to make repetition at short lags more effective by taking measures to create a change in the context. The implications of these results for study habits are almost too obvious to require comment: We should space our study of particular material over time; and when such spacing is impossible, we should change the context of repetitive study. At a physical level, we can change the location in which we study. At a more abstract level, we can try to change the perspective we take on the to-be-learned material.

The encoding-variability analysis of the spacing effect does not imply that spaced study and variable encoding will always result in superior memory. What is really important is that one of the contexts in which the material is studied overlap with the context in which the material is tested. When students are not sure how the material is to be tested, they should study it in contexts as varied as possible. Spacing study is one way of ensuring a variety of contexts, but, as we have noted, other ways are also effective, such as changing the physical environment or the mental set. However, when students know the context in which they are to be tested, then variable encoding may not be such a good idea. In this case, the ideal study location would be the location in which the test is to be administered. Of course, with respect to college exams this ideal may be hard to achieve. Gaining access to an exam room is often difficult, and in any case, the difference between an empty exam room and one filled with anxious students and a monitor pacing slowly around the room is considerable.

Conclusions

Consider again Figure 7-1, which compares the simplified conception of the information deposited in memory with an elaborated conception. The research reviewed in this chapter indicates that the elaborative conception is more accurate. Subjects elaborate the information they study with the following:

1. connections to prior knowledge;

2. imaginings and inferences about the material;

3. features from the current context.

The evidence we have reviewed indicates that this process of elaboration leads to improved memory in the following ways:

1. It increases the redundancy of interconnections among the to-be-remembered information.

2. It imposes an organization on the information that can be used to guide the retrieval process.

3. It can increase the number of contextual elements that will overlap between study and test.

The PQ4R Method

Many college study-skills departments as well as private firms offer courses designed to improve students' memory for text material. These courses mainly teach study techniques for such texts as those used in the social sciences, not the more dense texts used in the physical sciences and mathematics nor less dense, literary materials such as novels. The study techniques from different programs are fairly similar, and their success has been documented to some extent. Two of the more publicized and publicly accessible techniques are the *SQ3R method* (Robinson, 1961) and the later *PQ4R method* (Thomas & Robinson, 1972). Other techniques are quite similar and are often adaptations of these methods. These methods are strongly supported by the ideas covered in this chapter. We will examine the PQ4R method as an example.

The PQ4R method derives its name from the six phases it advocates for studying a chapter in a textbook:

1. *Preview.* Survey the chapter to determine the general topics being discussed. Identify the sections to be read as units. Apply the next four steps to each section.

2. *Questions.* Make up questions about the section. Often, simply transforming section headings results in adequate questions. For example, a section heading might be *Encoding*

Variability, resulting in such questions as "What is encoding variability?" and "What are the effects of encoding variability?"

3. *Read*. Read the section carefully, trying to answer the questions you have made up about it.

4. *Reflect*. Reflect on the text as you are reading it, trying to understand it, to think of examples, and to relate the material to prior knowledge.

5. *Recite*. After finishing a section, try to recall the information contained in it. Try answering the questions you made up for the section. If you cannot recall enough, reread the portions you had trouble remembering.

6. *Review*. After you have finished the chapter, go through it mentally, recalling its main points. Again try anwering the questions you made up.

A slight variation on this technique for studying this text is detailed in Chapter 1. Clearly, one of the reasons for the success of this kind of technique is that all the passes through the material serve as spaced study of the material. Another probable effect is to make the student aware of the way the material is organized. As we have seen, organization leads to good memory, especially on free-recall-type tests.

The central feature of the PQ4R technique, however, is the question-generation and question-answering characteristics. There is reason to suspect that the most important aspect of this feature is that it encourages (perhaps *forces* would be a better word) deeper or more elaborative processing of the text material. Earlier, we reviewed the experiment by Frase that demonstrated the benefit of reading a text with a set of advance organizers in mind. It seems that the benefit of that activity was specific to test items related to the questions.

The distinction between test items related to the study questions and those not related is important. Suppose that a study question in a text on African economics was "What were the effects of the transition from colonialism on economic growth?" A *related* test question might then be "Did the rate of foreign investment decrease as a result of the transiton from colonialism?" An *unrelated* test question might be "What factors limit the rate of development of the forestry industry in Africa?" Clearly, study questions related to test questions would be expected to aid memory more effectively than unrelated ones. Therefore, creating study questions that tap the most important topics is an important aspect of the study technique.

Another experiment by Frase (1975) compared the effects of making up questions and answering them. He had pairs of subjects study a text that was divided into halves. For one half, one subject in the pair read the passage and made up study questions as he or she went along. These questions were given to the second subject, who then read the text while trying to answer them. The subjects switched roles for the second half of the text. All subjects answered a final set of test questions about the passage. A control group, who just read without doing anything special, answered correctly 50 percent of the set of questions that followed. Experimental subjects, when they read to make up questions, answered correctly 70 percent of the test items that were relevant to their questions and 52 percent of the irrelevant test items. When they read to answer questions, experimental subjects answered correctly 67 percent of the relevant test items and 49 percent of the irrelevant items. Thus, it seems that both question generation and question answering contribute to good memory. If anything, question making contributes the most. T. H. Anderson (1978), in a review of the research literature, finds further evidence for the particular importance of question making.

In another study lending support to the PQ4R techniques, Rickards (1976) looked at the effect of different types of questions as advance organizers for reading. He had subjects study a passage about a fictitious African nation called Mala. The experiment compared the effectiveness of conceptual questions, which required the subjects to process a general issue such as exploitation of the people, and verbatim questions, which required subjects to recall a specific fact. Subjects responding to the conceptual questions showed better recall. Such results are the justification for prefacing each chapter in this book with general statements about the chapter contents. You should be using these statements to form general conceptual questions.

Reviewing the text with the questions in mind is another important component of the PQ4R technique. Rothkopf (1966) compared the benefit of reading a text with questions in mind and the benefit of considering a set of questions after reading the text, which enabled subjects to review the text. Rothkopf had subjects read a long text with questions interspersed every three pages. The questions were relevant to the three pages either following or preceding the questions. In the former condition, subjects were supposed to read the subsequent text with these questions in mind. In the latter condition, they were to review what they had just read and answer the questions. The two experimental groups were compared with a control group, which read the text without any special questions. This control group answered 30 percent of the questions correctly in a final test of the whole text. The experimental group whose questions previewed the text answered correctly 72 percent of the test items relevant to their questions and 29 percent of the irrelevant items—basically the same results as those Frase obtained in comparing the effectiveness of relevant and irrelevant test items. The experimental group whose questions reviewed the text answered correctly 72 percent of the relevant items 42 percent of the irrelevant items. Thus, it seems that reviewing the text with questions in mind is more generally beneficial.

Remarks and Suggested Readings

The topics of this chapter are discussed more fully in a number of sources. The elaboration analysis comes from work by Reder and me (Anderson, 1983, Chapter 5; Anderson & Reder, 1979; Reder, 1979, 1982). An up-to-date survey of research and opinion about depth of processing is found in the book edited by Cermak and Craik (1979). Shaw and Bransford (1977) provide another perspective of the integrative and constructive nature of cognition. Graesser (1981) describes a general model of text comprehension and inference and relates it to memory. Alba and Hasher (1983) discuss evidence for the use of schema in memory research. Johnson and Raye (1981) discuss how people discriminate between what they actually heard and saw and what they inferred. Good reviews of research on organizational factors in memory are to be found in Bower (1970) and Mandler (1967, 1972). Good sources for Endel Tulving's opinions on encoding and memory are the articles by Watkins and Tulving (1975) and Flexser and Tulving (1978) and Tulving's 1983 book. The book edited by Melton and Martin (1972) is a collection of papers on encoding effects, especially effects of encoding variability. Crowder's 1976 and Underwood's 1983 memory texts provide excellent surveys of many of these topics, including the spacing effect.

A number of papers set forth recommendations from memory research for learning and teaching techniques. Among these are Bower (1970), Bjork (1979), Greeno (1974), and Norman (1973). Frase (1975), R. C. Anderson and Biddle (1975), and Rothkopf (1972) provide reviews of a good deal of research that is relevant to evaluating the PQ4R method. Gibson and Levin (1975, Chapter 11) provide a review of memory research relevant to reading. Also, the book by Thomas and Robinson (1972) sets forth the PQ4R method, and an earlier book by another Robinson (1961) describes the SQ3R method, which seems to have been the source for the PQ4R method.

Chapter 8

Problem Solving

Summary

1. Declarative knowledge refers to knowledge about facts and things; procedural knowledge refers to knowledge about how to perform various cognitive activities. Procedural knowledge fundamentally has a problem-solving organization.

2. Problem solving is defined as a behavior directed toward achieving a goal. Problem solving involves decomposing the original goal into subgoals and these into subgoals until subgoals are reached that can be achieved by direct action. The term *operator* refers to an action that will directly achieve a goal.

3. Problem solving can be conceived of as a search of a problem space. The problem space consists of physical states or knowledge states that are achievable by the problem solver. The problem-solving task involves finding a sequence of operators to transform the initial state into a goal state, in which the goal is achieved.

4. People often use general problem solving methods for deciding what sequence of operators to use in solving a problem. These methods are called *heuristics* when they often lead to problem solution but are not guaranteed to succeed.

5. The difference-reduction method for problem solving involves setting subgoals of reducing differences between the current state and the goal state.

6. The means–ends method for problem solving involves selecting operators to reduce the differences between the current state and the goal state as well as transforming the current state so that needed operators can apply.

7. The working-backward method for problem solving involves breaking a

goal into a set of subgoals whose solutions logically imply solutions of the original goal.

8. Problem solving by analogy involves using the structure of the solution to one problem to guide the solution to another problem.

9. The knowledge underlying problem solving can be formalized as a set of productions that specify actions that will achieve goals under particular conditions.

10. The key to solving problems in many cases is to represent them in a way that the needed operators can apply. Functional fixedness is the failure to solve a problem because the person fails to represent an object as having a novel function so that it can be used in solving the problem.

11. The amount and type of knowledge available for solving a problem will vary with a person's problem solving experience. Increasing the availability of relevant knowledge can facilitate problem solving; conversely, increasing the availability of irrelevant knowledge can inhibit problem solving. Effects of knowledge availability on problem solving are referred to as *set effects.*

This chapter represents a watershed in the book. To this point, we have concerned ourselves with how knowledge about the world gets into the system, how this knowledge is represented, and how it is stored in and retrieved from long-term memory. In cognitive psychology this kind of knowledge is frequently referred to as *declarative knowledge*—knowledge about facts and things. In this chapter we begin to consider *procedural knowledge*—knowledge about how to perform various cognitive activities. This chapter is about the knowledge underlying problem-solving activities. Later chapters will be concerned with knowledge underlying reasoning, decision making, language comprehension, and language generation.

Procedural Knowledge and Problem Solving

In understanding procedural knowledge we start with problem solving because it seems that all cognitive activities are fundamentally problem solving in nature. The basic argument (Anderson, 1983; Newell, 1980; Tolman, 1932) is that human cognition is always purposeful, directed to achieving goals and to removing obstacles to those goals. In order to understand what this claim means, it is useful to understand what we mean when we say that a behavior is an instance of problem solving.

To get a perspective on what is meant by problem solving, we will look at one of the classic studies of problem solving in another species—apes (Köhler, 1927). Köhler, a famous German Gestalt psychologist who came to America in the 1930s, found himself trapped on Tenerife in the Canary Islands during World War I. On this island he found a colony of captive chimpanzees, which he studied, taking particular interest in the problem-solving behavior of the animals. His prize subject was a chimpanzee named Sultan. One problem posed to Sultan was to get some bananas that were outside his cage. Sultan had no difficulty if he was given a stick that could reach the bananas. He simply used the stick to pull the bananas into his cage. However, the critical problem occurred when Sultan was provided with two poles, neither of which would reach the food. After vainly reaching with the poles, the frustrated ape sulked in his cage. Suddenly, he went over to the poles and put one inside the other, creating a pole long enough to reach the food; with this extended pole, he was able to reach his prize (see Figure 8-1). This was clearly a creative problem-solving activity on the part of Sultan. Köhler used the term *insight* to refer to the ape's discovery.

What are the essential features that qualify this episode as an instance of problem solving? There seem to be three essential features:

1. *Goal Directedness.* The behavior is clearly organized toward a goal—in this case, of getting the food.

2. *Subgoal Decomposition.* If the ape could have gotten the food by simply reaching for it, the behavior would have been problem solving in only the most primitive sense. The essence of the problem solution is that the ape had to decompose the original goal into subtasks, or subgoals, such as getting the poles and putting them together.

3. *Operator Selection.* Decomposing the overall goal into subgoals like putting the sticks together is useful because the ape knows actions to achieve these subgoals. The term *operator* refers to an action that will achieve a goal. The solution of the overall problem is a sequence of these known operators.

An interesting question is, what would have happened had Sultan been required to solve the same problem over and over again? Eventually, the whole situation would have become packaged as a single operation, and Sultan would have been able to achieve his goal without decomposing it into subgoals; he would simply breeze through the sequence of steps required to achieve the goal. One of the issues in the next chapter will be how the character of problem solving changes with repeated practice.

Figure 8-1   Köhler's ape solving the two-stick problem: He combines two short sticks to form a pole long enough to reach the food. (From Köhler, 1956.)

The Problem Space

States in the Problem Space

Frequently, problem solving is described in terms of searching a *problem space*, which consists of various states of the problem. The initial situation of the problem solver is referred to as the *initial state*, the situations on the way to the goal as *intermediate states*, and the goal as the *goal state*. Starting from the initial state, there are many ways the problem solver can choose to change his or her state. Sultan could reach for a stick, stand on his head, sulk, and so on. Suppose the ape reaches for the stick. Now he is in a new state. He can transform this to another state, for example, by letting go of the stick (thereby returning to the earlier state), reaching with the stick for the food, throwing the stick at the food, or reaching for the other stick. Suppose he reaches for another stick. Again he is in a new state. From this state Sultan can choose to try, say, walking on the sticks, putting them together, or eating the sticks. Suppose he chooses to put the sticks together. He can then choose to reach for the food, throw the sticks away, or undo them. If he reaches for the food, he will achieve his goal state.

The states in this example are actual physical states of the world. However, often in problem solving, the term *states* refers to states of knowledge. For instance, consider the following problem:

> The country of Marr is inhabited by two types of people, liars and truars (truth tellers). Liars always lie and truars always tell the truth. As the newly appointed United States ambassador to Marr, you have been invited to a local cocktail party. While consuming some of the native spirits, you are engaged in conversation with three of Marr's most prominent citizens: Joan Landill, Shawn Farrar, and Peter Fant. At one point in the conversation, Joan remarks that Shawn and Peter are both liars. Shawn vehemently denies that he is a liar, but Peter replies that Shawn is indeed a liar. From this information can you determine how many of the three are liars and how many are truars? (Wickelgren, 1974b, p. 36).

Stop reading for a few minutes and try to solve this problem.

To solve this problem, we must consider different possible states of knowledge about Joan, Shawn, and Peter. For instance, we might start out with the following knowledge state:

1. Assume that Joan is a truar.

From this, since Joan asserts that Shawn and Peter are both liars, we can infer the following knowledge state:

2. If Joan is a truar, Shawn and Peter are liars.

However, Peter claims Shawn is a liar. Since Peter is a liar, Shawn must actually be a truar, but this conclusion contradicts the above assumption that Shawn is a liar. Because of the contradiction, we can now infer that assumption 1 is false. Hence:

3. Joan must be a liar.

If so, her assertion that Shawn and Peter are both liars must be false. Hence, we have the following knowledge state:

4. Joan is a liar and Shawn or Peter or both are truars.

To further explore the issue, we assume the following knowledge state:

5. Suppose that both Shawn and Peter are truars.

Again, with this assumption we run into the problem that Peter claims that Shawn is a liar. If Peter is a truar, Shawn must be a liar. Therefore state 5 leads to a contradiction. Combining state 4 with 5, we get

6. Joan is a liar and only one of Shawn and Peter is a truar.

From state 6 we can reach the knowledge state that is the answer to the problem.

7. Two of the three are liars and one is a truar.

Just as Sultan found his way through states of the physical world to solve his problem, in this example the problem solvers must find their ways through states of knowledge 1 through 7.

Searching the Problem Space

The various states that the problem solver can achieve are referred to as defining a problem space, or state space. Problem-solving operators can be conceived of as changing one state in the space into another. The problem is to find some possible sequence of state changes that goes from the initial state to the goal state in the problem space. We can conceive of the problem space as a maze of states and of the operators as paths for moving among the states. In this conception, the solution to a problem is achieved through a *search* process; that is, the problem solver must find an appropriate path through a maze of states. This conception of problem solving as a search through a state space was developed by Allen Newell and Herbert Simon of Carnegie-Mellon University and has become the dominant analysis of problem solving, in both cognitive psychology and artificial intelligence.

A problem-space characterization consists of a set of states and operators for moving among states. A good problem for illustrating the problem-space characterization is the eight-tile puzzle, consisting of eight numbered, movable tiles set in a 3 × 3 frame. One cell of the frame is always empty, making it possible to move an adjacent numbered tile into the empty cell and thereby to "move" the empty cell as well. The goal is to achieve a particular configuration of tiles, starting from a different configuration. For instance, a problem might be to transform

The possible states of this problem are represented as configurations of tiles in the eight-tile puzzle. So, the first configuration shown is the initial state, and the second is the goal state. The operators that change the states are movements of tiles into empty spaces. Figure 8-2 reproduces an attempt of mine to solve this problem. This solution involved 26 moves, each move being an operator that changes the state of the problem. This sequence of operators is considerably longer than necessary. Try to find a shorter sequence of moves. (The shortest sequence possible is given at the end of the chapter, in Figure 8-17.)

Often, discussions of problem solving involve the use of *search graphs* or *search trees*. Figure 8-3 gives a partial search tree for the following eight-tile problem:

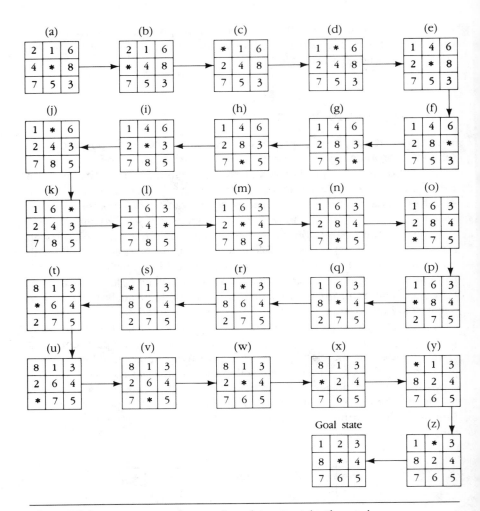

Figure 8-2 A sequence of moves for solving an eight-tile puzzle.

 into

Figure 8-3 is like an upside-down tree with a single trunk and branches leading out from that. This tree begins with the *start state*, represents all states reachable from this state, then all states reachable from those states, and so on. Any path through such a tree represents a possible sequence of moves that a problem solver might make. By generating a complete tree, we can also find the shortest sequence of operators between the start state and the goal state. Figure 8-3 illustrates some of the problem space. Frequently, in discussions of such examples, only the path through the problem space that leads to the solution is presented (for instance, in Figure 8-2). Figure 8-3 gives a better idea of the size of the space of possible moves that exist for a problem.

General Problem-Solving Methods

This search-space terminology is a descriptive way of characterizing possible steps that the problem solver might take. It does not explain the steps that the problem solver does take. Much of the theory of problem solving is concerned with identifying the principles that govern people's search through a problem space. These principles are concerned with how subjects select subgoals when they cannot directly achieve the whole goal. A major contribution of the research on cognitive science has been a cataloging of some of the methods human subjects use.

In discussing methods for selecting subgoals, it is useful to make the distinction between *algorithms* and *heuristics*. Algorithms are procedures guaranteed to result in the solution of a problem. The procedure for multiplication is an algorithm, because it identifies a series of subgoals that, if correctly achieved, will always result in the correct answer. In contrast, a heuristic is a rule of thumb that often (but not always) leads to a solution. For instance, most people in trying to solve the eight-tile puzzle wind up using heuristics of one sort or another. Often heuristics lead to more rapid solutions than algorithms. The problem-solving methods we will describe are all heuristics.

Consider the following as an example of the difference between an algorithm and a heuristic. Suppose you arrive in a strange town and want to find out if your family has any relations there. Your family has been so prolific that you have lost track of all your second cousins, great-aunts, and such. One solution would be to call up everyone in the phone book and interrogate them as to their family tree. Assuming that all the townsfolk were cooperative and listed in the phone book, you would have an algorithtm for finding your lost relatives. However, this could cost you a lot of time. A heuristic would be to call up only those townsfolk in the phone book who have your family name. You might miss relatives who have changed their name through marriage or for other reasons, but the procedure would certainly be much less costly and would have a good chance of turning up a lost relative if one

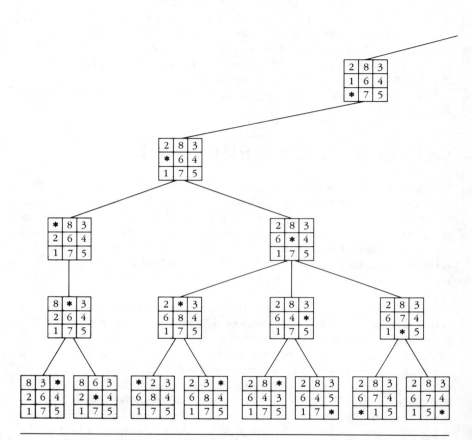

Figure 8-3 Part of the search tree, five moves deep, for an eight-tile problem. (From Nilsson, 1971.)

existed in the town. (Just how good a heuristic it is depends on how common your family name is; compare Anderson with Reder.)

The Difference-Reduction Method

A frequent method of problem solving, particularly in unfamiliar domains, is to try to reduce the difference between the current state and the goal state. That is, problem solvers set as their subgoal the reduction of the difference between the current state and the goal state. For instance, consider my so-

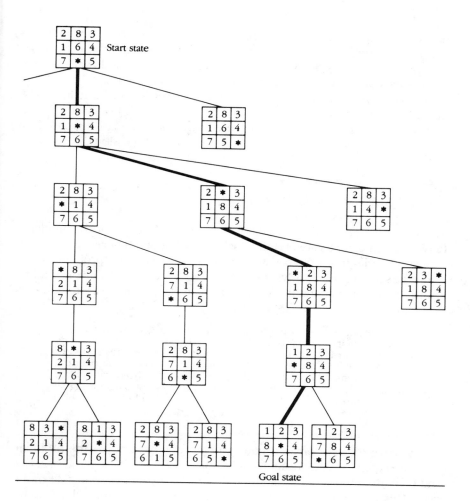

Goal state

lution to the eight-tile puzzle in Figure 8-2. There were four options possible for the first move. One possible operator was to move the 1 into the empty square, another was to move the 8, a third was to move the 5, and the fourth was to move the 4. I chose the last operator. Why? The answer is that it seemed to get me closer to my end goal. I was moving the 4 tile closer to its final destination. Human problem solvers are often strongly governed by *similarity*. They choose operators that transform the problem state into a state that resembles the goal state more closely than the initial state.

One of the ways problem solvers improve is by using more sophisticated measures of similarity. My move above was intended simply to get a tile closer to its final destination. After working with many tile problems, we begin to notice the importance of *sequence*—that is, whether noncentral tiles are followed by their appropriate successors. For instance, in state 0 of Figure 8-2, the 3 and 4 tiles are in sequence because they are followed by their successors 4 and 5, but the 5 is not in sequence because it is followed by 7 rather than 6. Trying to move tiles into sequence proves to be more important than trying to move them to their final destination. Thus, using sequence as a measure of similarity leads to more effective problem solving based on difference reduction (see Nilsson, 1971, for further discussion).

Where Similarity Is Wrong

The difference-reduction technique relies on evaluations of the similarity between the current state and the goal state. Although difference reduction probably works more often than not, it can also lead the problem solver astray. In some problem solving situations, a correct solution involves going against the grain of similarity. A good example is called the hobbits and orcs problem:

> On one side of a river are three hobbits and three orcs. They have a boat on their side that is capable of carrying two creatures at a time across the river. The goal is to transport all six creatures across to the other side of the river. At no point on either side of the river can orcs outnumber hobbits (or the orcs would eat the outnumbered hobbits). The problem, then, is to find a method of transporting all six creatures across the river without the hobbits ever being outnumbered.

Stop reading and try to solve this problem.

Figure 8-4 shows a correct sequence of moves for solution of this problem. Illustrated there are the locations of hobbits (H), orcs (O), and the boat (b). The boat, the three hobbits, and the three orcs all start on one side of the river. This condition is represented in state 1 by the fact that all are above the line. Then, a hobbit, an orc, and the boat proceed to the other side of the river. The outcome of this action is represented in state 2 by placement of the boat (b), the hobbit (H), and the orc (O) on the other side of the line. In state 3, one hobbit has taken the boat back, and the diagram continues in the same way. Each state in Figure 8-4 represents another configuration of hobbits, orcs, and boat. Subjects (e.g., those studied by Greeno, 1974) have a particular problem with the transition from state 6 to state 7 (see also Jeffries, Polson, Razran, & Atwood, 1977). One reason for this difficulty is that the action involves moving two creatures back to the wrong side of the river. The move seems to be away from a solution. At this point, subjects will often back up and look for some other solution.

Atwood and Polson (1976) provide another experimental demonstration

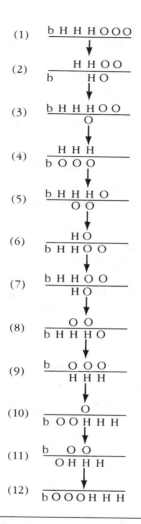

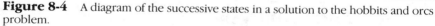

Figure 8-4 A diagram of the successive states in a solution to the hobbits and orcs problem.

of subjects' reliance on similarity and how that reliance can be beneficial or harmful. Subjects were given the following water-jug problem:

> You have three jugs, which we will call *A*, *B*, and *C*. Jug *A* can hold exactly 8 cups of water, *B* can hold exactly 5 cups, and *C* can hold exactly 3 cups. *A* is filled to capacity with 8 cups of water. *B* and *C* are empty. We want you to find a way of dividing the contents of *A* equally between *A* and *B* so that both have 4 cups. You are allowed to pour water from jug to jug.

Figure 8-5 illustrates two paths of solution to this problem. At the top of the figure all the water is in jug *A*—represented by *A* (8); no water is in jug *B* or *C*—represented by *B* (0) *C* (0). The two possible actions are to pour *A* into *C*, in which case we get *A*(5) *B*(0) *C*(3), or to pour *A* into *B*, in which case we get *A*(3) *B*(5) *C*(0). From these two states more moves can be made. Numerous other sequences of moves are possible besides the two paths illustrated in Figure 8-5. However, Figure 8-5 does illustrate the two shortest sequences to the goal.

Atwood and Polson used the representation in Figure 8-5 to analyze subjects' behavior. For instance, Atwood and Polson asked which move subjects would prefer in starting from the initial state 1. That is, would they prefer to pour *A* into *C* and get state 2, or *A* into *B* and get state 9? The answer is that subjects preferred the latter move. Twice as many subjects moved to state 9 as moved to state 2. Note that state 9 is quite similar to the goal. The goal is to have 4 cups in both *A* and *B*, and state 9 has 3 cups in *A* and 5 cups in *B*. In contrast, state 2 has no cups of water in *B*. Throughout their problem, Atwood and Polson found a strong tendency for subjects to move to states that were similar to the goal state. Usually, similarity was a good heuristic, but there are critical cases where similarity is misleading. For instance, the transitions from state 5 to state 6 and from state 11 to state 12 both lead to significant decreases in similarity to the goal. However, both transitions are critical to their solution paths. Atwood and Polson found that more than 50 percent of the time subjects deviated from the correct sequence of moves at these critical points. Rather, subjects chose some move that seemed closer to the goal but actually took them away from the solution.

These examples illustrate the heuristic character of similarity. While it frequently does a good job in leading the problem solver to a solution, in some situations it does not work and can even be misleading. To repeat, heuristics are only rules of thumb and can be wrong on occasion.

Means–Ends Analysis

A more sophisticated method of subgoal selection is referred to as means–ends analysis. This method has been extensively studied by Newell and Simon, who have used it in a computer simulation program (called the General Problem Solver or GPS) that models human problem solving. The following is Newell and Simon's description of means–ends analyis.

> The main methods of GPS jointly embody the heuristic of means–end analysis. Means–end analysis is typified by the following kind of common-sense argument:

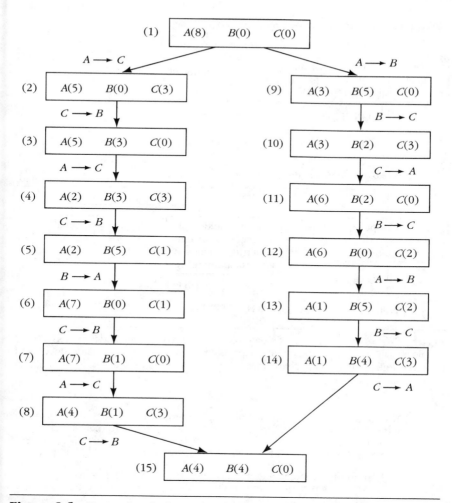

Figure 8-5 Two paths of solution for the water-jug problem posed in Atwood and Polson (1976). Each state is represented in terms of the contents of the three jugs. The transitions between states are labeled in terms of which jug is poured into which.

I want to take my son to nursery school. What's the difference between what I have and what I want? One of distance. What changes distance? My automobile. My automobile won't work. What is needed to make it work? A new battery. What has new batteries? An auto repair shop. I want the repair shop to put in a new battery; but the shop doesn't know I need one. What is the difficulty? One of communication. What allows communication? A telephone . . . and so on.

Flowchart I Goal: Transform current state into goal state

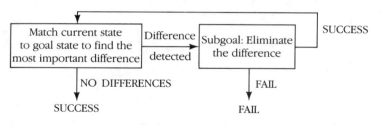

Flowchart II Goal: Eliminate the difference

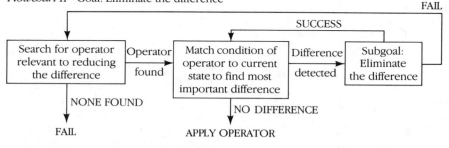

Figure 8-6   The application of means–ends analysis by Newell and Simon's General Problem Solver. Flowchart I breaks a problem down into a set of differences and tries to eliminate each. Flowchart II searches for an operator relevant to eliminating a difference.

This kind of analysis—classifying things in terms of the functions they serve and oscillating among ends, functions required, and means that perform them—forms the basic system of heuristic of GPS. More precisely, this means–ends system of heuristic assumes the following:

1. If an object is given that is not the desired one, differences will be detectable between the available object and the desired object.

2. Operators affect some features of their operands and leave others unchanged. Hence operators can be characterized by the changes they produce and can be used to try to eliminate differences between the objects to which they are applied and desired objects.

3. If a desired operator is not applicable, it may be profitable to modify the inputs so that it becomes applicable.

4. Some differences will prove more difficult to affect than others.

It is profitable, therefore, to try to eliminate "difficult" differences, even at the cost of introducing new differences of lesser difficulty. This process can be repeated as long as progress is being made toward eliminating the more difficult differences (Newell & Simon, 1972, p. 416)

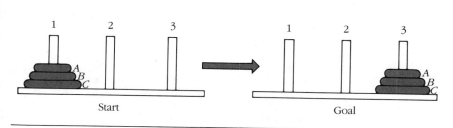

Figure 8-7   The three-disk version of the tower of Hanoi problem.

Figure 8-6 displays in flowchart form the procedures used in the means–ends analysis employed by GPS. A general feature of this means–ends analysis is that it breaks a larger goal into subgoals. GPS creates subgoals in two ways. First, in flowchart I, GPS breaks the current state into a set of differences and sets the reduction of each difference as a separate subgoal. It chooses to try to eliminate first what it perceives as the most important difference. Second, in flowchart II, GPS tries to find an operator that will eliminate the difference. However, this operator may be unable to apply immediately because a difference exists between the operator's condition and the state of the environment. Thus, before the operator can be applied, eliminating another difference may be necessary. To eliminate the difference that is blocking the operator's application, flowchart II will have to be called again to find another operator relevant to eliminating that difference.

The Tower of Hanoi Problem

Means–ends analysis has proved to be an extremely general and powerful method of problem solving. Ernst and Newell (1969) discuss its applications to the modeling of monkey and bananas problems (such as Sultan's predicament described at the beginning of the chapter), algebra problems, calculus problems, and logic problems. However, we will illustrate means–ends analysis here by applying it to the *tower of Hanoi problem*. A simple version of this problem is illustrated in Figure 8-7. There are three pegs and three disks of differing sizes, *A*, *B*, and *C*. The disks have holes in them, so they can be stacked on the pegs. The disks can be moved from any peg to any other peg. Only the top disk on a peg can be moved, and it can never be placed on a smaller disk. The disks all start out on peg 1, but the goal is to move them all to peg 3, one disk at a time, by means of transferring disks among pegs.

Figure 8-8 traces out the application of the GPS techniques to this problem. The first line gives the general goal of moving *A*, *B*, and *C* to peg 3. This goal leads us to the first flowchart of Figure 8-6. One difference between the goal and the current state is that *C* is not on 3. This difference is chosen first

1. Goal: Move *A*, *B*, and *C* to Peg 3
2. :Difference is that *C* is not on 3
3. :Subgoal: Make *C* on 3
4. :Operator is to move *C* to 3
5. :Difference is that *A* and *B* are on *C*
6. :Subgoal: Remove *B* from *C*
7. :Operator is to move *B* to 2
8. :Difference is that *A* is on *B*
9. :Subgoal: Remove *A* from *B*
10. :Operator is to move *A* to 3
11. :No difference with operator's condition
12. :Apply operator (move *A* to 3)
13. :Subgoal achieved
14. :No differences with operator's condition
15. :Apply operator (move *B* to 2)
16. :Subgoal achieved
17. :Difference is that *A* is on 3
18. :Subgoal: Remove *A* from peg 3
19. :Operator is to move *A* to 2
20. :No difference with operator's condition
21. :Apply operator (move *A* to 2)
22. :Subgoal achieved
23. :No difference with operator's condition
24. :Apply operator (move *C* to 3)
25. :Subgoal achieved
26. :Difference is that *B* is not on 3
27. :Subgoal: Make *B* on 3
28. :Operator is to move *B* to 3
29. :Difference is that *A* is on *B*
30. :Subgoal: Remove *A* from *B*
31. :Operator is to move *A* to 1
32. :No difference with operator's condition
33. :Apply operator (move *A* to 1)
34. :Subgoal achieved
35. :No difference with operator's condition
36. :Apply operator (move *B* to 3)
37. :Subgoal achieved
38. :Difference is that *A* is not on 3
39. :Subgoal: Make *A* on 3
40. :Operator is to move *A* to 3
41. :No difference with operator's condition
42. :Apply operator (Move *A* to 3)
43. :Subgoal achieved
44. :No difference
45. Goal Achieved

Figure 8-8 A trace of the application of GPS to the tower of Hanoi problem in Figure 8-7.

because GPS tries to remove the most important differences first, and we are assuming that the largest misplaced disk will be viewed as the most important difference. Therefore, a subgoal is set up to eliminate this difference. This takes us to the second flowchart, which tries to find an operator to reduce the difference. The operator chosen is to *move C to 3*. The condition for applying a move operator is that nothing be on the disk. Since *A* and *B* are on *C*, there is a difference between the condition of the operator and the current state. Therefore, a new subgoal is created to reduce one of the differences—*B* on *C*. This subgoal gets us back to the start of flowchart II, but now with the goal of removing *B* from *C* (line 6 in Figure 8-8). Note that we have gone from use of flowchart I to use of II to a new use of II. This action is called *recursion* because to apply flowchart II to find a way to move *C* to 3 we need to apply flowchart II to find a way to remove *B* from *C*. Thus, one procedure is using itself as a subprocedure.

The operator chosen the second time in flowchart II is to *move B to 2*. However, we cannot immediately apply the operator of moving *B* to 2, since *B* is covered by *A*. Therefore, another subgoal is set up—that of removing *A*—and flowchart II is used to remove this difference. The operator relevant to achieving this is to *move A to 3*. There are no differences between the conditions for this operator and the current state. Finally, we have an operator we can apply (line 12 in Figure 8-8). Thus, we achieve the subgoal of moving *A* to 3. Now we return to the earlier intention of moving *B* to 2. There are no more differences between the operator for this move and the current state, so the action takes place. The subgoal of removing *B* from *C* is then satisfied (line 16 in Figure 8-8).

We have now returned to the original intention of moving *C* to 3. However, disk *A* is now on peg 3, which prevents the action. Thus, we have another difference to be eliminated between the now current state and the operator's condition. We move *A* onto peg 2 to remove this difference. now the original operator of moving *C* to 3 can be applied (line 24 in Figure 8-8).

The state of this point is that disk *C* is on peg 3 and *A* and *B* are on peg 2. At this point, GPS returns to its original goal of moving the three disks to 3. It notes that another difference is that *B* is not on 3 and sets up another subgoal of eliminating this difference. It achieves this subgoal by first moving *A* to 1 and then *B* to 3. This gets us to line 37 in the trace. The remaining difference is that *A* is not on 3. This difference is eliminated in the lines 38 through 42. With this step, no more differences exist and the original goal is achieved.

Note that subgoals are created in service of other subgoals. For instance, to achieve the subgoal of moving the largest disk, a subgoal is created of moving the second largest disk, which is on top of it. We indicated this logical dependency of one subgoal on another in Figure 8-8 by indenting the processing of the dependent subgoal. At line 9 of Figure 8-8, four goals and

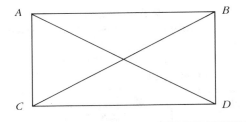

Figure 8-9 A geometry problem: Given that □*ABDC* is a rectangle, prove that $\overline{AD}$ and $\overline{CB}$ are congruent.

subgoals had to be remembered. As Simon (1975) has pointed out, the number of subgoals that must be remembered simultaneously will increase as we increase the number of disks. With every disk added to the problem, another subgoal will have to be maintained. From what we studied earlier about the limitations of short-term memory (Chapter 6), we can predict that subjects should have difficulty keeping many goals and subgoals active in short-term memory. In fact, the evidence is that when subjects try to use such problem-solving methods, they often fail because they lose track of the subgoals and how they interrelate.

Working Backward

A useful method of solving some problems is to work backward from the goal. This can be a particularly useful search heuristic in areas such as finding proofs in mathematics. Consider the geometry problem illustrated in Figure 8-9. The student is given that *ABDC* is a rectangle and is asked to prove that *AD* and *CB* are of the same length (are congruent). In working backward, the student would ask, "What would prove that *AD* and *CB* are congruent? I could prove this if I could prove that the triangles *ACD* and *BDC* are congruent." Thus, the student would work backward from the goal of proving line congruence to that of proving triangle congruence. The next step is reasoning, "I could prove that triangles *ACD* and *BDC* are congruent if I could prove that two sides and an included angle (the side-angle-side postulate) are congruent." Thus, the student would reason back from this subgoal to another subgoal.

The key to working backward is to decompose the initial goal into a set of subgoals that imply solution of the original goal. The problem solver can then focus on solving each of the subgoals independently. The method runs into difficulty when solving one of the subgoals prevents solution of another goal—that is, when the subgoals prove not to be independent.

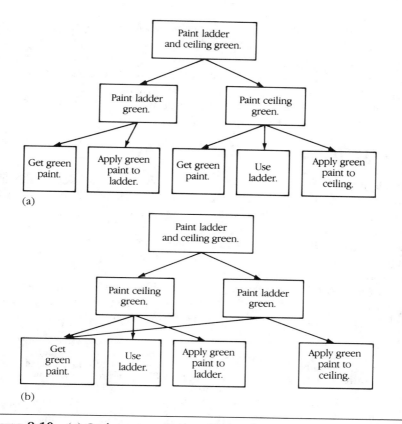

Figure 8-10 (a) Goal structure generated by working backward from the goal of painting the ladder and ceiling. (b) Reorganization of the goal structure to deal with the conflicts between nonindependent goals in part (a). (Adapted from Sacerdoti, 1977.)

A good example of dealing with nonindependent subgoals is Sacerdoti's (1977) work on NOAH, an artificial-intelligence problem solver. Part (a) of Figure 8-10 illustrates the plan first generated by NOAH to solve the problem of painting a ladder and a ceiling green. It decomposed these goals into separate subgoals: (1) painting the ladder green and (2) painting the ceiling green. Painting the ladder was decomposed into getting the green paint and applying the green paint. Painting the ceiling was decomposed into getting the paint, using the ladder, and applying the paint to the ceiling. Unfortunately, applying the paint to the ladder made it unavailable for painting the ceiling. NOAH responds to such goal conflicts by reorganizing the goals in this case to the plan shown in (b). Now the ceiling is painted first. Note, too, that the reorganized plan will get the green paint only once.

Many of the difficulties in our daily problem solving arise because of such nonindependence of goals. For instance, as a student, I often encountered problems because the Stanley Cup finals were always scheduled around the time of final exams. I had to make difficult, but inventive, choices about how to satisfy both my need to watch hockey and my need to get good grades. Fortunately, it is not so much of a problem now that I give exams.

Problem Solving by Analogy

Another important method of solving a problem is by analogy. With this method, the problem solver attempts to use the structure of the solution to one problem to guide solutions to another problem. This method is frequently employed, for instance, in solving exercises in mathematics text, where students will use the structure of one example worked out in the text to guide solutions of other problems. Here, the subgoals set are to transform the steps of the example into steps for the current problem.

An example of the power of analogy in problem solving is provided in an experiment of Gick and Holyoak (1980). They presented their subjects with the following problem, which is adapted from Duncker (1945):

> Suppose you are a doctor faced with a patient who has a malignant tumor in his stomach. It is impossible to operate on the patient, but unless the tumor is destroyed the patient will die. There is a kind of ray that can be used to destroy the tumor. If the rays reach the tumor all at once at a sufficiently high intensity, the tumor will be destroyed. Unfortunately, at this intensity the healthy tissue that the rays pass through on the way to the tumor will also be destroyed. At lower intensities the rays are harmless to healthy tissue, but they will not affect the tumor either. What type of procedure might be used to destroy the tumor with the rays, and at the same time avoid destroying the healthy tissue? (pp. 307–308)

This is a very difficult problem, and few subjects are able to solve it. However, Gick and Holyoak presented their subjects with the following story as an analogy for solution:

> A small country was ruled from a strong fortress by a dictator. The fortress was situated in the middle of the country, surrounded by farms and villages. Many roads led to the fortress through the countryside. A rebel general vowed to capture the fortress. The general knew that an attack by his entire army would capture the fortress. He gathered his army at the head of one of the roads, ready to launch a full-scale direct attack. However, the general then learned that the dictator had planted mines on each of the roads. The mines were set so that small bodies of men could pass over them safely, since the dictator needed to move his troops and workers to and from the fortress. However, any large force would detonate the mines. Not only would this blow up the road, but it would also destroy many neighboring villages. It therefore seemed impossible to capture the fortress.

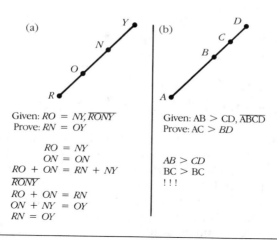

Given: $RO = NY$, $\overline{RONY}$
Prove: $RN = OY$

$RO = NY$
$ON = ON$
$RO + ON = RN + NY$
$\overline{RONY}$
$RO + ON = RN$
$ON + NY = OY$
$RN = OY$

Given: $AB > CD$, $\overline{ABCD}$
Prove: $AC > BD$

$AB > CD$
$BC > BC$
$!!!$

Figure 8-11   (a) A worked-out proof problem given in a geometry text. (b) One student's attempt to use the structure of this problem's solution to guide his solution of a similar problem.

However, the general divised a simple plan. He divided his army into small groups and dispatched each group to the head of a different road. When all was ready he gave the signal and each group marched down a different road. Each group continued down its road to the fortress so that the entire army arrived together at the fortress at the same time. In this way, the general captured the fortress and overthrew the dictator. (Gick & Holyoak, 1980, p. 351)

With this story as a hint nearly 100 percent of the subjects were able to develop an analogous solution to the tumor problem.

An interesting example of problem solving by analogy that did not quite work is a problem encountered by one geometry student whom we have studied. Part (a) of Figure 8.11 illustrates the steps of a geometry solution that the text gave as an example, and part (b) illustrates the student's attempts to use that worked-out proof to guide his solutions to a homework problem. In part (a), two segments of a line are given as equal length and the goal is to prove that two larger segments have equal length. In part (b) the student was given two segments with AB longer than CD and his task was to prove the same inequality for two larger segments, AC and BD.

Our subject noted the obvious similarity between the two problems and proceeded to develop the apparent analogy. He thought he could simply substitute points in one line for points on another, and inequality for equality. That is, he tried the following, simply substituting A for R, B for O, C for N, D for Y, and $>$ for $=$. With these solutions he got the first line correct: Analogous to $RO = NY$, he wrote $AB > CD$. Then he had to write something analogous to $ON = ON$. He wrote $BC > BC$! This example illustrates both how analogy can be used to guide problem solving, and that it requires a little sophistication to use analogy correctly.

Production Systems: A General Problem-Solving Formalism

How to formalize the knowledge that underlies problem solving is an important issue. There is a general theoretical construct, called *production systems*, that has proven to be particularly useful in representing problem-solving knowledge. Production systems consist of a set of *productions*, which are rules for solving a problem. A typical problem-solving production (Anderson, 1983; Brown & Van Lehn, 1980; Card et al., 1983) consists of a goal, some application tests, and an action. The following is a fairly simple production rule:

> IF the goal is to drive a standard transmission car
> and the car is in first gear
> and the car is going more than 10 miles an hour
> THEN shift the car into second gear

Such a production is organized into a condition and an action. The *condition* consists of a statement of the goal (i.e., to drive a standard transmission car) and of certain tests to determine if the rule is applicable to the goal. If these tests are met, the rule will apply and the action (i.e., shifting the car into second gear) will be performed.

Later chapters will illustrate the utility of such rules in modeling a wide range of cognitive behavior. For current purposes, however, it is important to note an important distinction between two types of production rules—between domain-general and domain-specific rules. The foregoing rule is domain specific. It applies only in the context of driving a car. If we had only domain-specific production rules, we would be incapable of solving problems in novel domains. The various general problem-solving strategies or methods that we have just reviewed demand domain-general productions. For instance, consider the means–ends problem-solving strategy represented in Figure 8-6. It can be encoded by the following domain-general production rules:

> P1   IF the goal is to transform the current state into the goal
>   state
>   and D is the largest difference between the states
>   THEN set as subgoals
>   1. To eliminate the difference D
>   2. To convert the resulting state into the goal state

P2   IF the goal is to eliminate a difference *D*
          and *O* is an operator relevant to reducing the difference
      THEN set as a subgoal
            1. To apply *O*

P3   IF the goal is to apply an operator *O*
          and *D* is the most important difference between the
          application condition of *O* and the current state
      THEN set as subgoals
            1. To eliminate the difference *D*
            2. To apply the operator *O*

The first production rule selects differences to be reduced. The second production rule selects operators to apply. The third eliminates any features that prevent the operators from applying. Note that P2 sets a subgoal that can lead to P3, which sets a subgoal that can lead to P2. In this way, we get the embedding of goals as observed in figure 8-6. Eventually, we get to a point where there are no more differences and operators can apply. In that case, the following rule would apply:

P4   IF the goal is to apply operator *O*
          and there are no differences between the application
          condition of *O* and the current state
          and operator *O* calls for action *A*
      THEN set as a goal to perform *A*

In the context of solving tower of Hanoi problems, this production would lead to goals such as moving disk *A* to peg 3. Now domain-specific rules for moving objects can apply, such as:

P5   IF the goal is to move an object to a peg
      THEN set as subgoals
            1. To pick up the object
            2. Place it on a peg

Thus, the general character of problem solving in novel domains is that these general-strategy productions will break the task down into subgoals, and these into subgoals, and so on until subgoals are set that correspond to domain-specific rules at which point the domain-specific rules can take over. As we will see in the next chapter, one way to develop expertise in a problem-solving domain involves creating rules specific to that domain to replace domain-general rules.

Figure 8-12   The mutilated checkerboard. (Adapted from W. A. Wickelgren. *How to Solve Problems.* W. H. Freeman and Company. Copyright 1974.)

Representation

The Importance of the Correct Representation

We have analyzed problem solution into problem states and operators for changing states. So far, we have discussed problem solving as if the only problem were operator selection. Difference reduction, means–ends analysis, working backward, and use of analogy all serve to help the problem solver select the right operator. However, the way in which states of the problem are represented also has significant effects.

A famous example illustrating the importance of representation is the *mutilated-checkerboard problem.* Suppose we have a checkerboard in which the two diagonally opposite corner squares have been cut out. Figure 8-12 illustrates this mutilated checkerboard, on which 62 squares remain. Now suppose that we have 31 dominos, each of which covers exactly two squares of the board. Can we find some way of arranging these 31 dominos on the board so that they cover all 62 squares? If it can be done, explain how. If it cannot be done, prove that it cannot. Perhaps you would like to ponder this problem before reading on. Few people are able to solve this problem and very few see the answer quickly.

The answer is that the checkerboard cannot be covered by the dominos. The trick to seeing this is to include in your representation of the problem

Figure 8-13   The two-string problem used by Maier.

the fact that each domino must cover one black and one red square, not just any two squares. There is just no way to place a domino on two squares of the checkerboard without having it cover one black and one red square. This means that with 31 dominos we can cover 31 black squares and 31 red squares. But the mutilation has removed two black squares. Thus, there are 32 red squares and 30 black. It follows that the mutilated checkerboard cannot be covered by 31 dominos.

Why is the mutilated-checkerboard problem easier to solve when we represent each domino as covering a red and a black space? The answer is that in so representing the problem we are encouraged to count and compare the number of red and black squares on the board. Thus, the effect of the problem representation is that it allows the critical operator to apply (i.e., counting red and black squares to check for parity.)

Another problem that depends on correct representation is the *27 cubic apples problem*. Imagine 27 apples, each of which is shaped as a perfect cube. They are packed together in a crate 3 apples high, 3 apples wide, and 3 apples deep. A worm is in the center apple. Its life's ambition is to eat its way to all

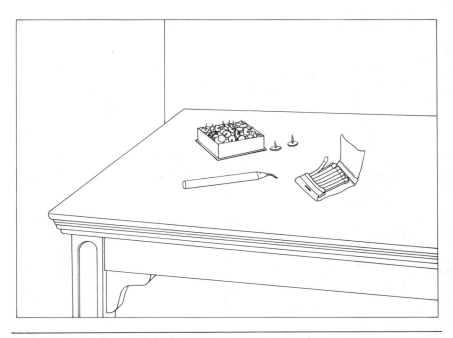

Figure 8-14   The candle problem used by Dunker. (Adapted from Glucksberg and Weisberg, 1966. Copyright 1966 by the American Psychological Association. Reprinted by permission.)

the apples in the crate, but it does not want to waste time by visiting any apple twice. The worm can move from apple to apple only by going from the side of one into the side of another. It cannot go from the corner of one apple to the corner of another or from the edge of one into the edge of another. Can you find some path by which the worm, starting from the center apple, can reach all the apples without going through any apple twice? If not, can you prove it is impossible? The solution is left to you. (*Hint*: The solution is based on a partial three-dimensional analogy to the solution for the mutilated-checkerboard problem; it is given at the end of the chapter.)

Functional Fixedness

Often, solutions to problems depend on the solver's ability to represent the objects in his or her environment in novel ways. This fact has been demonstrated in a series of studies by different experimenters. A typical experiment in the series is the two-string problem of Maier (1931), illustrated in Figure 8-13. Two strings hanging from the ceiling are to be tied together, but they are so far apart that the subject cannot grasp both at once. Among the objects in the room are a chair and a pair of pliers. Subjects try various solutions involving the chair but these do not work. The only solution is to tie the pliers to one string and set that string swinging like a pendulum, and then to get the second string, bring it to the center of the room, and wait for the first string to swing close enough to grasp. Only 39 percent of Maier's subjects were able to see this solution within 10 minutes. The difficulty is that subjects do not perceive the pliers as a weight that can be used as a pendulum. This phenomenon is called *functional fixedness.* It is so named because subjects are fixed on representing the object according to its conventional function and fail to represent its novel function.

Another demonstration of functional fixedness is an experiment by Duncker (1945). The task he posed to subjects is to support a candle on a door, ostensibly for an experiment on vision. The problem is illustrated in Figure 8-14. On the table are a box of tacks, some matches, and the candle. The correct solution is to tack the box to the door and use the box as a platform for the candle. This task is difficult for subjects because they see the box as a container, not as a platform. Subjects have greater difficulty with the task if the box is filled with tacks, reinforcing perception of the box as a container.

Another demonstration of functional fixedness, introduced by Glucksberg and Danks (1968), involved a problem that required a screwdriver blade to function as wire in an electric circuit. Again, the solution is difficult to conceive because subjects do not normally perceive a blade as having this function. In an interesting follow-up to this study, Teborg (1968) gave subjects practice classifying objects such as paper clips and crayons according to their conducting properties. This practice turned out to be very useful in dissipating the functional fixedness and enabling subjects to perceive the needed function of the screwdriver blade.

These demonstrations of functional fixedness are consistent with the interpretation that representation has its effect on operator selection. For instance, in Duncker's candle problem (Figure 8-14), subjects had to represent the match box so that it could be used by the problem-solving operators that were looking for a support for the candle. When the box was conceived of as a container and not as a support, it was not available to the support-seeking operators.

Set Effects

We have just discussed how problem representations can enable or block application of the operators that will lead to problem solution. It is also the case that problem solvers can become biased by their experiences to prefer certain problem-solving operators in solving a problem. Such biasing of the problem solution is referred to as a *set effect*. A good illustration involves the water-jug problem studied by Luchins (1942; Luchins & Luchins, 1959). In Luchins's water-jug experiments, a subject was given a set of jugs of various capacities and unlimited water supply. The subject's task was to measure out a specified quantity of water. Two examples are given below:

Problems	Capacity of Jug A	Capacity of Jug B	Capacity of Jug C	Desired quantity
1	5 cups	40 cups	18 cups	28 cups
2	21 cups	127 cups	3 cups	100 cups

Assume that subjects have a tap and a sink so that they can fill jugs and empty them. The jugs start out empty. Subjects are allowed only to fill the jugs, empty them, and pour water from one jug to another. In problem 1, subjects are told that they have three jugs—jug A, with a capacity of 5 cups; jug B, with a capacity of 40 cups; and jug C, with a capacity of 18 cups. To solve this problem, subjects would fill A and pour it into B, fill A again and pour it into B, and fill C and pour it into B. The solution to this problem is denoted by $2A + C$. The solution for the second problem is to first fill jug B with 127 cups; fill A from B so that 106 cups are left in B; fill C from B so that 103 cups are left in B; empty C, fill C again from B so that the goal of 100 cups in B is achieved. The solution to this problem can be denoted by $B - A - 2C$. The first solution is called an *addition* solution because it involves adding the contents of the jugs together; the second solution is referred to as a *subtraction* solution becauase it involves subtracting the contents of one jug from another. Luchins studied the effect of giving subjects a series of problems, all of which could be solved by addition. This created an "addition set" such that subjects solved new addition problems faster than control subjects, who had no practice, and solved subtraction problems more slowly.

The set effect that Luchins is most famous for demonstrating is the *Einstellung effect*, or *mechanization of thought*, which is illustrated by the series of problems in Table 8-1. Subjects were given these problems in this order and required to find solutions for each. Take time out from reading this text and try to solve each problem.

All problems except 8 can be solved by using the $B - 2C - A$ method (i.e., filling B, twice pouring B into C to fill C, and once pouring B into A). For problems 1 through 5, this solution is the simplest, but for problems 7 and 9 the simpler solution of $A + C$ applies. Problem 8 cannot be solved by the $B - 2C - A$ method, but can be solved by the simpler solution of $A - C$. Problems 6 and 10 are also solved more simply as $A - C$ than $B - 2C - A$. Of Luchins's subjects who received the whole setup of 10 problems,

Table 8-1 *Luchins's 1939 water-jug problems*

Problems	Capacity of Jug A	Capacity of Jug B	Capacity of Jug C	Desired quantity
1	21	127	3	100
2	14	163	25	99
3	18	43	10	5
4	9	42	6	21
5	20	59	4	31
6	23	49	3	20
7	15	39	3	18
8	28	76	3	25
9	18	48	4	22
10	14	36	8	6

Note. All volumes are in cups.

83 percent used the $B - 2C - A$ method on problems 6 and 7, 64 percent failed to solve problem 8, and 79 percent used the $B - 2C - A$ method for problems 9 and 10. The performance of subjects who worked on all 10 problems was compared with the performance of control subjects who saw only the last five problems. These control subjects did not see the biasing $B - 2C - A$ problems. Fewer than 1 percent of the control subjects used $B - 2C - A$ solutions, and only 5 percent failed to solve problem 8. Thus, the first five problems can create a powerful bias for a particular solution. This bias hurt solution of problems 6 through 10.

Note that the Einstellung effect does not involve creating a general bias for subtraction over addition. The critical problem, 8, involved subtraction too. Rather, subjects are remembering a particular sequence of operations, and it is memory for this sequence that is blinding them to other possibilities. While these effects are quite dramatic, they are relatively easy to reverse with the exercise of cognitive control. Luchins found that simply by warning subjects by saying, "Don't be blind," after problem 5, more than 50 percent of the subjects overcame set for the $B - 2C - A$ solution.

Another kind of set effect in problem solving has to do with the influence of general semantic factors. This effect is nicely illustrated in the experiment of Safren (1962) on anagram solution. Safren presented subjects with lists such as the following in which each set of letters was to be unscrambled and made into a word:

kmli   graus   teews

recma   foefce   ikrdn

This is an example of an organized list, in that the individual words are all

Given state

Goal state

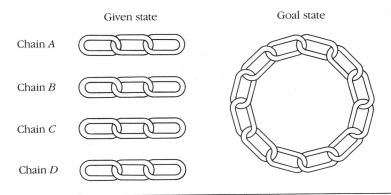

Chain A

Chain B

Chain C

Chain D

Figure 8-15 The cheap-necklace problem. (Figure 4-5 from W. A. Wickelgren. *How to Solve Problems*. W. H. Freeman and Company. Copyright 1974.)

associated with drinking coffee. Safren compared solution times for organized lists such as these with those for unorganized lists. Median solution time was 12.2 sec for anagrams from unorganized lists but 7.4 sec for anagrams from organized lists. Presumably, the facilitation evident with the organized lists occurred because the earlier items in the list associatively primed, and so made more available, the later words. Note that this anagram experiment contrasts with the water-jug experiment in that no particular procedure is being strengthened. Rather, what is being strengthened is part of the subject's factual (declarative) knowledge about spellings of associatively related words.

In general, set effects occur when some knowledge structures become more available at the expense of others. These knowledge structures can be either procedures, as in the water-jug problem, or declarative information, as in the anagram problem. If the available knowledge is what subjects need for solving the problem, their problem solving will be facilitated. If the available knowledge is not what is needed, problem solving will be inhibited. It is good to realize that set effects can sometimes be easily dissipated (as with Luchin's "Don't be blind" instruction). If you find yourself stuck on a problem and you keep generating similar unsuccessful approaches, it is often useful to force yourself to back off, change set, and try a different kind of solution.

Incubation Effects

Problem solvers frequently report that after trying and getting nowhere on a problem, they can put the problem aside for hours, days, or weeks and then, upon returning to it, can see the solution quickly. Numerous examples of this pattern were reported by the famous French mathematician Poincaré (1929), for instance the following:

> Then I turned my attention to the study of some arithmetical questions apparently without much success and without a suspicion of any connection with my preceding researches. Disgusted with my failure, I went to spend a few days at the seaside, and thought of something else. One morning, walking on the bluff, the idea came to me, with just the same characteristics of brevity, suddenness and immediate certainty, that the arithmetic transformations of indeterminate ternary quadratic forms were identical with those of non-Euclidean geometry. (p. 388)

Such phenomena are referred to as *incubation effects*. An incubation effect was nicely demonstrated in an experiment by Silveira (1971). The problem she posed to subjects, called the *cheap-necklace problem*, is illustrated in Figure 8-15. Subjects were given the following instructions:

> You are given four separate pieces of chain that are each three links in length. It costs 2¢ to open a link and 3¢ to close a link. All links are closed at the beginning of the problem. Your goal is to join all 12 links of chain into a single circle at a cost of no more than 15¢.

Try to solve this problem yourself. A solution is provided in the section headed "Appendix" at the end of this chapter. Silveira tested three groups. A control group worked on the problem for half an hour; 55 percent of these subjects solved the problem. For one experimental group, their half hour spent on the problem was interrupted by a half-hour break in which they performed other activities; 64 percent of these subjects solved the problem. A third group had a 4-hour break; and 85 percent of these subjects solved the problem. Silveira required her subjects to talk aloud as they solved the cheap-necklace problem. She found that subjects did not come back to the problems with solutions completely worked out. Rather, they started out trying to work out the problem much as before.

The best explanation for incubation effects relates them to set effects. During initial attempts on a problem, subjects set themselves to think about the problem in certain ways and bring to bear certain knowledge structures. If this initial set is appropriate, subjects will solve the problem. If the initial set is not appropriate, however, subjects will be stuck throughout the session with inappropriate procedures. By going away from the problem, the activation of the inappropriate knowledge structures will dissipate and subjects will be able to take a fresh approach to the problem.

Numerous other attempts have been made to display incubation effects by interrupting problem solving, only some of which have proven successful (for discussions see Dominowski & Jenrick, 1972; Murray & Denny, 1969). Sometimes worse performance is found with an interruption. A good example of a situation in which interruption is harmful is in the solving of a set of simultaneous equations. The only effect of interruption here would be sub-

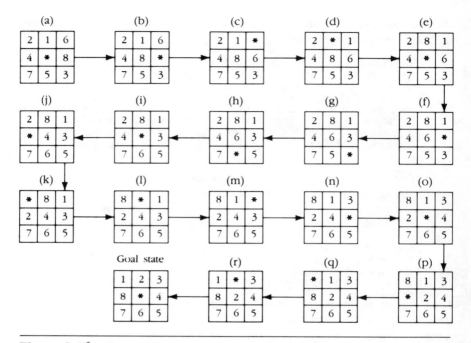

Figure 8-16 The minimum-path solution for the eight-tile problem that was solved less efficiently in Figure 8-2.

ject's losing their places in the solution. Incubation effects are most likely to be found in problems such as the cheap-necklace problem, which depend on a single key insight.

Remarks and Suggested Readings

A number of textbooks provide extensive reviews on problem solving. Many exhibit a certain tendency to equate the topic of thinking with problem solving. So, texts with the topic *thinking* in their title, such as Johnson (1972) or Vinacke (1974), include extensive discussions of the traditional problem-solving literature. A more modern review of problem-solving research is to be found in Hayes (1978). Newell and Simon have been the most influential workers on problem solving in the modern era. Their work is extensively presented in their 1972 book. A more thorough discussion of GPS is to be found in Ernst and Newell (1969). Recent work on the use of analogies in problem solving has been done by Carbonell (1983) and Gick and Holyoak

(1983). Overviews of the problem-solving literature are to be found in Greeno (1978) and Simon (1978a). Gregg (1974) edited a collection of papers on problem solving.

A great deal of research in artificial intelligence could be classified under the topic of problem solving. This work has had particularly strong influence on the thinking of cognitive psychologists, partly because of the efforts of Newell and Simon. The texts by Hunt (1975), Nilsson (1980), and Winston (1977) all provide discussions of the problem-solving techniques in artificial intelligence.

Appendix

A number of problems were presented in this chapter without solution. Figure 8-16 gives the minimum-path solution to the problem solved less efficiently in Figure 8-2.

With regard to the problem of the 27 cubic apples, the worm cannot succeed. To see that this is the case, imagine that the apples alternate in color, green and red, in a three-dimensional checkerboard pattern. If the center apple, from which the worm starts, is red, there are 13 red apples and 14 green apples in all. Every time the worm moves from one apple to another, he must change colors. Since the worm starts from the red, this means that it cannot reach more green apples than red apples. Thus, it cannot visit all 14 green apples if it also visits each of the 13 red apples just once.

Solve the cheap-necklace problem in figure 8-15 by opening all three links in one chain (at a cost of 6¢) and then using the three open links to connect together the remaining three chains (at a cost of 9¢).

Chapter 9

Development of Expertise

Summary

1. Skill learning occurs in three steps: (1) a cognitive stage, in which a description of the procedure is learned; (2) an associative stage, in which a method for performing the skill is worked out; and (3) an autonomous stage, in which the skill becomes more and more rapid and automatic.

2. Time to perform a task is a power function of the amount of practice on the task. Such a function implies that continued practice is of continued but ever diminishing benefit to the task performance.

3. There are a number of factors modulating the effects of practice: Spacing of practice increases learning; there is frequently positive transfer among related skills; skills can be learned better if independent parts are taught separately; subjects learn more rapidly if they are given immediate feedback.

4. Master chess players are not more intelligent generally than average players; they have achieved their expertise through practice. Expert players have better memory for chess positions and have memorized the analysis of thousands of chess positions.

5. Students become expert in geometry by converting the inference rules of geometry into mental procedures (productions), by tuning these procedures so that they apply appropriately, and by developing forward-inference procedures that will apply in the absence of a specific goal.

6. As people become expert in physics they learn to reason forward from the givens of a physics problem rather than backward from the problem statement, and they learn to represent a physics problem in terms of abstract concepts that are predictive of the method of solution.

7. As programmers become more expert they learn to represent problems in terms of abstract programming constructs, they do more breadth-first program development, and they develop better memories for programs and program patterns.

8. Underlying the development of expertise is the transformation of problem solving from a basis in serial processing and deduction to a basis in memory retrieval and pattern matching.

It may sometimes seem that at every turn we are being faced with a novel problem, but generally we are achieving goals in domains that are highly familiar—speaking a language, driving a car, solving column addition, and the like. Here our behavior is often so automatic that it is difficult to even recognize that we are solving a problem. However, if we look at novices—someone trying to communicate in an unfamiliar language, a person behind the wheel of a car for the first time, a child learning addition—we can see that these are difficult and quite novel problem domains for novices. Through practice, however, we have become relatively expert. The skills just mentioned are ones at which a large fraction of the population becomes expert. There are other skills at which only a small fraction become expert—playing chess, doing science, hitting major league pitching, and so on. Nevertheless, it appears that development of expertise in these specialized areas is really no different than in the more general areas.

William G. Chase, late of Carnegie-Mellon University, was one of our local experts on expertise. He had two mottos that summarize much of the nature of expertise and its development:

No pain, no gain.

When the going gets tough, the tough get going.

The first motto reflects the fact that no one develops expertise without a great deal of hard work. Richard Hayes (in press), another CMU faculty member, has studied geniuses in fields varying from music to science to chess. He found that no one reached genius levels of performance without at least 10 years of practice[1]. Chase's second motto reflects the fact that the difference between relative novices and relative experts increases as we look at more difficult problems. For instance, there are many chess duffers who could play a credible, if losing, game against a master when they are given unlimited time to choose moves. However, they would lose embarrassingly if forced to play lightning chess, where they have only 5 sec per move.

---

[1]Frequently cited as an exception to this generalization is Mozart, who wrote his first symphony when he was 8. However, his early works are not of genius caliber and are largely of historical value only. Schonberg (1970) claims Mozart's great works were produced after the twentieth year of his career.

Chapter 8 reviewed some of the general principles governing problem solving, particularly in novel domains. This research has provided a framework for analyzing the development of expertise in problem solving. Research on expertise has been one of the major new research developments in cognitive science. This is a particularly exciting development because it promises to have implications for education of technical or formal skill in areas such as mathematics, science, and engineering.

This chapter begins with a look at the general characteristics of the development of expertise in a skill. Then we will consider what is known about the development of skill in four domains—chess, physics, geometry, and computer programming. From these case studies we will identify the major principles that underlie skill acquisition.

Stages of Skill Acquisition

It is typical to distinguish among three stages in the development of a skill (Anderson, 1983; Fitts & Posner,1967). Fitts and Posner call the first stage the *cognitive stage*. In this stage subjects develop a declarative encoding (see the distinction between declarative and procedural representations at the beginning of Chapter 8) of the skill; that is, they commit to memory a set of facts relevant to the skill. Learners typically rehearse these facts as they first perform the skill. For instance, when I was first learning to shift gears in a standard transmission car, I memorized the location of the gears (e.g., "up, left") and the correct sequence of engaging the clutch and moving the stick shift. I rehearsed this information as I performed the skill.

In this stage the learners are using domain-general problem-solving procedures (see the distinction between domain-general and domain-specific procedures in Chapter 8) to perform and are using the facts they have learned about the domain to guide their problem solving. Thus, they might have a general mean–ends production, such as

IF   the goal is to achieve a state X
     and M is a method for achieving state X
THEN   set as a subgoal to apply M

Applied to driving, if the goal is to go in reverse and if the learner knows that moving the stick shift to the upper left will put the car into reverse, then this production would set the subgoal of moving the gear to the upper left. The knowledge acquired in the cognitive stage is quite inadequate for skilled performance. There follows what is called the *associative stage*. Two main things happen in this second stage. First, errors in the initial understanding are gradually detected and eliminated. So, I slowly learned to coordinate the release of the clutch in first gear with the application of gas in order not to kill the engine. Second, the connections among the various elements required for successful performance are strengthened. Thus, I no longer had to sit for a few seconds trying to remember how to get to second gear from first. Basically, the outcome of the associative stage is successful procedure for performing the skill. In this stage, the declarative information is transformed into a procedural form. However, it is not always the case that the procedural representation of the knowledge replaces the declarative. Sometimes the two forms of knowledge can coexist side by side, as when we can speak a foreign language fluently and still remember many rules of grammar. However, it is the procedural, not the declarative, knowledge that governs the skilled performance.

The output of the associative stage are procedures specific to the domain. So, for instance, rather than using the general means–ends production above in driving, the learner may develop a special production for moving into reverse:

IF the goal is to go in reverse
THEN set as subgoals
    1. To disengage the clutch
    2. Then to move the gear to the upper left
    3. Then to engage the clutch
    4. Then to push down on the gas

The third stage in the standard analysis of skill acquisition is the *autonomous stage*. In this stage, the procedure becomes more and more automated and rapid. No sharp distinction exists between the autonomous and associative stage. The autonomous might be considered an extension of the associative stage. Because facility in the skill increases, verbal mediation in the performance of the task often disappears at this point. In fact, the ability to verbalize knowledge of the skill can be lost altogether. This autonomous stage appears to extend indefinitely. Throughout it, the skill gradually improves.

Two of the dimensions of improvement with practice are speed and accuracy. The procedures come to apply more rapidly and more appropriately. Anderson (1982) and Rumelhart and Norman (1978) refer to the increasing appropriateness of the procedures as *tuning*. For instance, consider our production for moving into reverse. It is only applicable to an ordinary three-speed gear. The process of tuning would result in a production that had additional tests for the appropriateness of this operation. Such a production might be

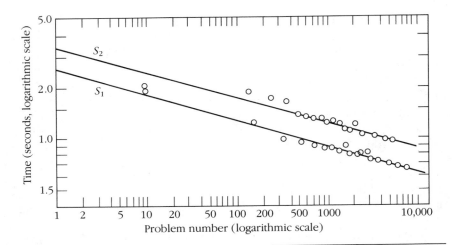

Figure 9-1 Improvement with practice in time taken to add two numbers. Data are given separately for two subjects. Plot by Crossman (1959) of data from Blackburn (1936). Both time and problem number are plotted on a logarithmic scale.

IF   the goal is to go in reverse
and there is a three-speed standard transmission
THEN set as subgoals
1. To disengage the clutch
2. Then to move the gear to the upper left
3. Then to engage the clutch
4. Then to push down on the gas

The Power Law of Practice

Figure 9-1 is a graph of some data from Blackburn (1936) showing the improvement in performance of mental addition as a function of practice. Blackburn had two subjects, S_1 and S_2, perform 10,000 addition problems! The data are plotted on a log–log scale. That is, the abscissa is the logarithm of practice (number of additions) and the ordinate is the logarithm of time per addition. On this log–log plot, the data for two subjects approximate a straight line. Similar straight-line functions relating practice to performance time have been found over a wide range of tasks. In fact, virtually every study of skill acquisition has found a straight-line function on a log–log plot. There is usually some limit to how much improvement can be achieved, determined by the capability of musculature involved, age, level of motivation, and so on. There do not appear to be any cognitive limits on the speed with which a skill can be performed. In fact, one famous study followed the improvement of a woman whose job was to roll cigars in a factory. Her speed of cigar making followed this log–log relationship over a period of 10 years. When she finally stopped improving, it was discovered that she had reached the physical limit of the machinery with which she was working!

The linear relationship between time (T) and log practice (P) can be expressed as

$$\log(T) = A - b \log(P)$$

which can be transformed into

$$T = aP^{-b}$$

where $a = 10^A$. In Chapter 6 we discussed such power functions in memory (see Figure 6-4). Basically, these are functions where the decrease in processing time with further practice becomes small very rapidly.

Effects of practice have also been studied in domains involving complex problem solving, such as giving justifications for geometrylike proofs (Neves & Anderson, 1981). Figure 9-2 shows a power function for that domain, in terms of both a normal scale and a log–log scale. Such functions illustrate that the benefit of further practice rapidly diminishes, but that no matter how much practice we have had, further practice will help a little.

Kolers (1979) investigated the acquisition of reading skill using materials such as those illustrated in Figure 9-3. The first type of text (N) is normal, but the others have been transformed in various ways. In the R transformation, the whole line has been turned upside down; in the I transformation, each letter has been inverted; in the M transformation, the sentence has been set as a mirror image of standard type. The rest are combinations of the several transformations. In one study, Kolers looked at the effect of massive practice on reading inverted (I) text. Subjects took more than 16 min to read their first page of inverted text as compared with 1.5 min for normal text. Following the initial test of reading speed, subjects practiced on 200 pages of inverted text. Figure 9-4 provides a log–log plot of reading time against amount of practice. In this figure, practice is measured in terms of number of pages read. The change in speed with practice is given by the curve labeled *original training on the inverted text*. Kolers interspersed a few tests on normal text; data for these are given by the curve labeled *original tests on normal text*. We see the same kind of improvement for inverted text as in the Blackburn study (i.e., a straight-line function on a log–log plot). After reading 200 pages, Koler's subjects were reading at the rate of 1.6 min per page, almost the same rate as subjects reading normal text.

Kolers brought his subjects back a year later and had them read inverted text again. These data are given by the curve in Figure 9-4 labeled *retraining on inverted text*. This time for the first page of the inverted text, subjects took about 3 min. Compared with their performance of 16 min on their first page

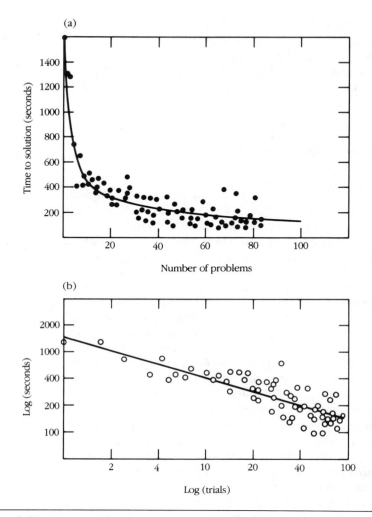

Figure 9-2 Time to generate proofs in a geometrylike proof system as a function of the number of proofs already done. (a) Function on a normal scale, $RT = 1410P^{-.55}$; (b) function on a log–log scale.

a year earlier, subjects were displaying an enormous savings, but it was now taking them almost twice as long to read the text as it did after their 200 pages of training a year earlier. They had clearly forgotten something. As Figure 9-4 illustrates, subjects' improvement on the retraining trials showed a log–log relationship between practice and performance, as had their original training. Subjects took 100 pages to reach the same level of performance that they had initially reached after 200 pages of training.

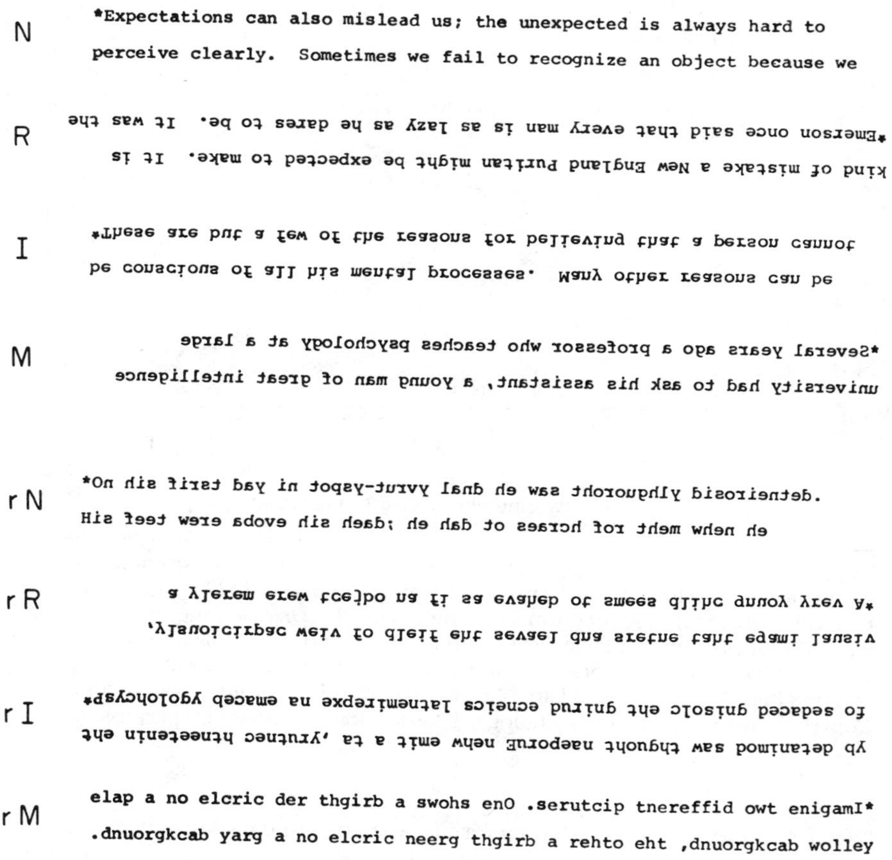

N *Expectations can also mislead us; the unexpected is always hard to
   perceive clearly. Sometimes we fail to recognize an object because we

R *Emerson once said that every man is as lazy as he dares to be. It was the
   kind of mistake a New England Puritan might be expected to make. It is

I *There are but a few of the reasons for believing that a person cannot
   be conscious of all his mental processes. Many other reasons can be

M *Several years ago a professor who teaches psychology at a large
   university had to ask his assistant, a young man of great intelligence

r N *On his first day in court-yesterday dual he was thoroughly disoriented.
     His feet were above his head; he had no sense for weight when he

r R *A very young child sees it as if as exactly as dashes or seems alike quite rarely. A
     visual image that leaves the field of view repeatedly,

r I *Psychology became an experimental science during the latter
     the nineteenth century, at a time when purging the solsto

r M *Imagine two different pictures. One shows a bright red circle on a pale
     yellow background, the other a bright green circle on a gray background.

Figure 9-3 Some examples of the spatially transformed texts used in Kolers's studies of the acquisition of reading skills. The asterisks indicate the starting point for reading. (From Kolers & Perkins, 1975.)

Factors Affecting Practice

Although practice is very important for the development of a skill, you should not think that this is all that is involved. The nature of the practice and the circumstances surrounding it can be very important. This is just the same as the effect of practice on the development of factual or declarative memories (Chapters 6 and 7). Practice was important there, too, but there were numerous modulating factors. In fact, it seems that some of the principles that apply to declarative memory also apply to memory for procedures. For instance, we discussed in Chapter 7 the powerful effects that spaced study can

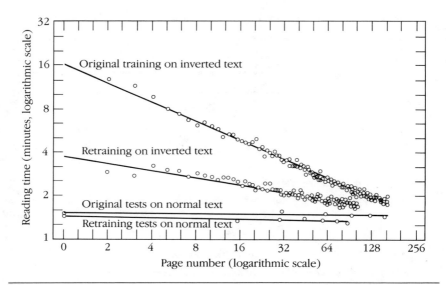

Figure 9-4   The results for readers in Kolers's reading-skills experiment (1979) on two tests more than a year apart. Subjects were trained with 200 pages of inverted text with occasional pages of normal text interspersed. A year later they were retrained with 100 pages of inverted text, again with normal text occasionally interspersed. The results show the effect of practice on the acquisition of the skill. Both reading time and number of pages practiced are plotted on a logarithmic scale. (From Kolers, 1976. Copyright by the American Psychological Association. Reprinted by permission.)

have on the learning of verbal materials. Spacing appears to have even more profound effects on skill learning. The inefficiency of massed practice was shown in one study involving intensive training in Morse code during World War II (reported in Bray, 1948). Students were found to learn as rapidly with 4 hours a day of practice as with 7 hours of practice. The 7-hour subjects were effectively wasting the 3 extra hours of practice crammed into the day. Similar advantages of spaced practice are found for the learning of more cognitive skills. For instance, Gay (1973) has shown that spaced practice of algebra rules results in better retention than massed practice.

The Transfer of Practice

We saw in the declarative domain (Chapter 6) that one fact could interfere with another. Can one procedure also interfere with another? Lewis, McAllister, and Adams (1951) have shown for motor skills that procedures do interfere with each other. Their subjects used what is called a Modified

Mashburn Apparatus, which was used for pilot selection in World War II. This apparatus simulates an aircraft, containing a stick about the size of an airplane's for two-dimensional manipulation and a rudder bar for one-dimensional foot operation.

A set of display lights defined the amount that the stick and rudder were to be moved. After they spent 30 trials learning to make the prescribed movement, subjects were switched to a second task, during which movements were required that were antagonistic to original movement. This second task, or *interpolated learning*, involved 10, 20, 30, or 50 trials. Then subjects were transferred back to the original task. It was found that their performance of the original skill had deteriorated and that this deterioration increased with an increase in interpolated learning. Thus, interfering effects occur with the learning of procedures like those found for declarative facts.

Such interference, or *negative transfer* as it is often called, among skills can be quite significant when a skill is placed in direct conflict with a well-engrained old skill. For instance, Conrad and Hull (1968) considered two spatial layouts for labeling numbers on machine keys. One is used with adding machines and other with touch telephones:

Adding Machines	Telephone
789	123
456	456
123	789
0	0

The second layout corresponds to the standard left-to-right, top-down manner of reading. That is, if the telephone array is read from left to right from the top down, it is in the order 1-2-3-4-5-6-7-8-9, whereas the adding machine would come out in the order 7-8-9-4-5-6-1-2-3. The telephone array also incorporates the common practices of ordering 0 after 9 (e.g., on typewriters) and starting the series with 1. Conrad and Hull found that the telephone layout resulted in fewer errors in the keying of eight-digit sequences. Thus, learning to key numbers is easier on a telephone than on an adding machine because the numbers are ordered on the telephone in the generally practiced order, while this is not the case for the adding machine. Thus, in the adding machine case, there is negative transfer from prior habits.

While negative interference can be obtained, the more frequent outcome is beneficial transfer from one skill to another. For instance, Singley and Anderson (in press) looked at transfer among computer text editors.[2] Depending on how similar the two text editors were, they found that learning one text editor eliminated between 60 and 90 percent of the work in learning

---

[2]A text editor is a computer system for creating and correcting manuscripts and computer programs.

a second text editor. Looking at the performance of their subjects, they were able to identify a few cases where something learned with the first editor interfered with the second, but the overwhelming effect was positive.

Part versus Whole Learning

Students working to acquire a skill frequently ask whether it is better to try to learn and practice the whole skill or to learn and practice parts of the skill, putting them together later. In the area of motor skills, the answer to this question depends on whether the parts to be practiced are independent. If they are, it is better to practice the parts separately. For instance, Koch (1923) taught subjects a rather bizarre skill—to type finger exercises using two typewriters simultaneously, one hand per typewriter. There were two groups of subjects—those who practiced each hand first and those who tried immediately to use both hands. The group that started by practicing with separate hands was better when they switched to both hands than the group that started with both hands, and they maintained this superiority with further practice. In contrast, experiments on tasks that require careful integration show superiority for whole learning over part learning. For example, in playing the piano it is better to try to learn the whole sequence rather than to try to integrate subsections of a sequence.

Much of education seems designed to decompose a complex skill into independent subcomponents, and to teach each separately. Gagne (1973) has argued that many skills in education can be decomposed into subskills and these into subsubskills, and so on. The lower level skills are prerequisites to the higher skills. For instance, calculus assumes algebra as a subcomponent, which assumes arithmetic as a subcomponent, which assumes basic counting skills as a subcomponent. Gagne argued that the key to successful educational plans was to identify the correct hierarchy of subskills. The educational curriculum should be designed to teach separately each of the subskills in the hierarchy.

Knowledge of Results

Subjects learn a skill more rapidly if they receive feedback as to whether their skill attempts are correct and how they are in error (for a review of research on feedback see Bilodeau, 1969). The amount of time between the action and the feedbacks is important—an expected relationship, since for feedback to be useful, the action must be active in memory. After a delay, it may be hard to recall just what led to incorrect action.

Recently, Lewis and Anderson (submitted) looked at this relationship in learning to play a maze game on the order of Dungeons and Dragons. In one condition, players received immediate feedback after making a wrong move. In a second condition, the consequences of a wrong move became apparent only after the next move, when players found themselves in a bad situation. As predicted, subjects learned to play the game better in the condition of immediate feedback.

One of the problems in education is that of providing students with immediate and direct feedback on their problem-solving effects. Whether on a computer program, a mathematics exercise, or an English composition, students usually receive feedback about an error only long after they have made it. They also receive only general feedback, such as information that the final answer to the mathematics problem was wrong. Private tutors, who can monitor the student during an exercise, can provide detailed feedback immediately, but of course private tutors are very expensive.

One of the promises of computer-assisted instruction is that it would be an economical means of providing students with immediate feedback on their problem-solving efforts. Of course, it also requires a great deal of intelligence to provide such feedback. Endowing computers with sufficient intelligence has been a major stumbling block. However, there have been some recent successes (Anderson, Boyle, Farrell, & Reiser, 1984; Sleeman & Brown, 1982). These successes have relied heavily on cognitive psychology and artificial-intelligence research.

Expertise in Chess

Chess certainly illustrates the maxim that practice makes perfect. All chess masters have spent many years studying and playing countless games. No matter what your intelligence, you cannot become a good chess player simply by thinking carefully. Indeed, many chess masters are not particularly intelligent in other dimensions. De Groot (1965, 1966) attempted to determine what separated expert chess players from novices. He found hardly any difference between expert players and weaker players—except, of course, that the expert players chose much better moves. For instance, chess masters consider about the same number of possible moves before selecting their move. In fact, if anything, masters consider fewer moves than chess duffers.

However, de Groot did find one intriguing difference between masters and weaker players. He presented chess masters with chess positions (i.e., chessboards with pieces in a configuration that occurred in a game) for just 5 sec and then removed the chess position. The chess masters were able to reconstruct the positions of more than 20 pieces after just 5 sec of study. In contrast, the chess duffer could reconstruct only four or five pieces—an

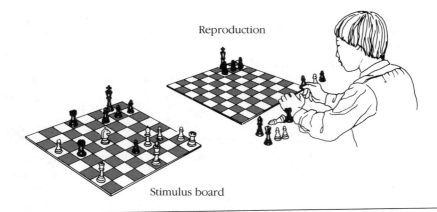

Reproduction

Stimulus board

Figure 9-5   The reproduction task in Chase and Simon (1973). Subjects were to reproduce the configuration of pieces on the reproduction board. (Adapted from Klatzky, 1979.)

amount much more in line with the traditional capacity of short-term memory (see Chapter 6). It appears that chess masters build up chunks of four or five pieces that reflect common board configurations as a function of their massive amount of experience with the task. Thus, they remember not individual pieces but rather chunks. In line with this analysis, if the players are presented with random chessboard positions rather than ones that are actually encountered in games, no difference is demonstrated between masters and duffers. Both types of subjects can reconstruct only a few chess pieces. The masters complain about being very uncomfortable and disturbed by such chaotic board positions.

We might think that the memory advantage shown by chess experts is just a short-term memory advantage, but recent research has shown that it is not this simple. Charness (1976) compared experts' memory for chess positions immediately after they had viewed the position, or after a 30-sec delay filled win an interfering task (like the Peterson and Peterson task discussed in Chapter 6). Class A chess players show no loss in recall over the 30-sec interval, unlike other subjects, who show a great deal of forgetting. Thus, expert chess players, unlike duffers, have an increased capacity to store information about the domain. Interestingly, these subjects show the same poor memory for three-letter trigrams as ordinary subjects. Thus, their increased long memory is *only* for the domain of expertise.

Chase and Simon (1973) examined the nature of the chunks used by masters. They used a chessboard-reproduction task, as illustrated in Figure 9-5. The subject's task was simply to reproduce the positions of pieces of a target chessboard on a test chessboard. In this task, subjects glanced at the target board, placed some pieces on the test board, glanced back to the target board, placed some more pieces on the test board, and so on. Chase and Simon defined as a chunk those pieces that subjects moved following one glance. They found that these chunks tended to define meaningful game relations among the pieces. For instance, more than half of the masters' chunks were pawn chains (configurations of pawns that occur frequently in chess).

Simon and Gilmartin (1973) estimate that masters have acquired on the order of 50,000 different chess patterns, that they can quickly recognize such patterns on a chessboard, and that this ability is what underlies their superior memory performance in chess. This 50,000 figure is not unreasonable when we consider the years of devoted study that becoming a chess master takes.

What might be the relationship between memory for so many chess patterns and superior performance in chess? Newell and Simon (1972) speculated that, in addition to learning many patterns, masters have also learned what to do in the presence of such patterns. Basically, they must have something on the order of 50,000 productions in which the condition (the IF part) of a production is a chess pattern and its action (the THEN part) is the appropriate response to that pattern. For instance, if the chunk pattern is symptomatic of a weak side, the response of the production might be to suggest an attack on the weak side. Thus, masters effectively "see" possibilities for moves; they do not have to think them out. This explains why chess masters do so well at lightning chess, in which they have only a few seconds to move.

So, to summarize, chess experts have stored the solutions to many problems that duffers must solve as novel problems. Duffers have to analyze different configurations, try to figure out their consequences, and act accordingly. Masters have all this information stored in memory, thereby claiming two advantages. First, they do not risk making errors in solving these problems, since they have stored the correct solution. Second, because they have stored the correct analysis of so many positions, they can focus their problem-solving efforts on more sophisticated aspects and strategies of chess. It bears repeating that chess players only become masters after years of playing. They have to be able to store a great deal of information about chess to be experts. Native intelligence is no substitute for knowledge.

Geometry

Unlike chess, high school geometry is a domain where a significant fraction of the population acquire a fair amount of expertise. A typical course in high school geometry involves many aspects, but most of the research has studied the acquisition of skills involved in generating formal proofs (Greeno, in press; Greeno, Magone, & Chaiklin, 1979). The rate of improvement in this

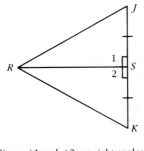

Given: ∠1 and ∠2 are right angles
$\overline{JS} \cong \overline{KS}$
Prove: △RSJ ≅ △RSK

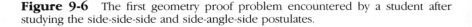

Figure 9-6 The first geometry proof problem encountered by a student after studying the side-side-side and side-angle-side postulates.

skill can be quite dramatic. Within about 50 hours some students progress from not knowing what a proof is to being able to generate some nonobvious proofs.

Proceduralizing Knowledge

One student we studied (Anderson, 1982) had just learned two postulates for proving triangles congruent—the side-side-side (SSS) postulate and the side-angle-side (SAS) postulate. The side-side-side postulate states that if three sides of one triangle are congruent to the corresponding sides of another triangle, the triangles are congruent. The side-angle-side postulate states if two sides and the included angle of one triangle are congruent to the corresponding parts of another triangle, the triangles are congruent. Figure 9-6 illustrates the first problem the student had to solve. The first thing he did in trying to solve this problem was to decide which postulate to use. The following is the portion of his thinking-aloud protocol, during which he decided on the appropriate postulate:

> "If you looked at the side-angle-side postulate [long pause] well *RK* and *RJ* could almost be [long pause] what the missing [long pause] the missing side. I think somehow the side-angle-side postulate works its way into here [long pause]. Let's see what it says: 'Two sides and the included angle.' What would I have to have to have two sides. *JS* and *KS* are one of them. Then you could go back to *RS*=*RS*. So that would bring up the side-angle-side postulate [long pause]. But where would Angle 1 and Angle 2 are right angles fit in [long pause] wait I see how they work [long pause] *JS* is congruent to *KS* [long pause] and with Angle 1 and Angle 2 are right angles that's a little problem [long pause]. OK, what does it say—check it one more time: 'If two

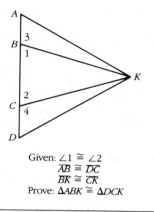

Given: $\angle 1 \cong \angle 2$
$\overline{AB} \cong \overline{DC}$
$\overline{BK} \cong \overline{CK}$
Prove: $\triangle ABK \cong \triangle DCK$

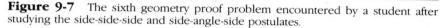

Figure 9-7   The sixth geometry proof problem encountered by a student after studying the side-side-side and side-angle-side postulates.

> sides and the included angle of one triangle are congruent to the corresponding parts.' So I have got to find the two sides and the included angle. With the included angle you get Angle 1 and Angle 2. I suppose [long pause] they are both right angles, which means they are congruent to each other. My first side is *JS* is to *KS*. And the next time one is *RS* to *RS*. So these are the two sides. Yes, I think it is the side-angle-side postulate." (Anderson, 1982, pp. 381–382)

After reaching this point the student still went through a long process of actually writing out the proof, but this is the relevant portion in terms of assessing what goes into recognizing the relevance of the SAS postulate.

After a series of four more problems (two were solved by SAS and two by SSS), we came to the student's application of the SAS postulate for the problem illustrated in Figure 9-7. The method-recognition portion of the protocol follows:

> "Right off the top of my head I am going to take a guess at what I am supposed to do: Angle *DCK* is congruent to Angle *ABK*. There is only one of two and the side-angle-side postulate is what they are getting to." (Anderson, 1982, p. 382)

A number of things seem striking about the contrast between these two protocols. One is that there has been a clear speedup in the application of the postulate. A second is that there is no verbal rehearsal of the statement of the postulate in the second case. The student is no longer calling a declarative representation of the postulate into working memory. Note also in the first protocol that there are a number of failures of working memory—points where the student had to recover information that he had forgotten. The third feature of difference is that in the first protocol there is a clear piecemeal application of the postulate by which the student is separately identifying every element of the postulate. This is absent in the second protocol. It appears that the postulate is being matched in a single step.

These transitions are like the ones that Fitts characterized as belonging to the associative stage of skill acquisition. The student is no longer relying on a verbal recall of the postulate, but has advanced to the point where he can simply recognize the application of the postulate as a pattern. So, we have another instance of the association of skill acquisition with the development of pattern-recognition ability. Students develop the ability to directly recognize the applicability of a particular postulate. We can represent this ability by the following production rule:

> IF the goal is to prove triangle 1 is congruent to triangle 2
> and triangle 1 has two sides and an included angle that appear congruent to two sides and an included angle of triangle 2
> THEN set as subgoals to prove the corresponding sides and angles congruent
> and then to use the side-angle-side postulate to prove triangle 1 congruent to triangle 2

Thus, the student has converted the verbal or declarative knowledge of the postulate into a procedural knowledge as embodied in the production rule above.

Forward Search versus Backward Search

There is another type of skill development in geometry that cannot be simply described as tuning the conditions of existing productions. This is nicely illustrated by the problem in Figure 9-8. Try to solve it for yourself. Good geometry problem solvers will note that there are two pairs of congruent segments: $\overline{AM} \cong \overline{MB}$ and $\overline{CM} \cong \overline{MD}$. They will also note that there is a pair of congruent angles: $\angle AMC \cong \angle BMD$ because the two are vertical, or opposite, angles. They will then use the SAS postulate to infer that $\triangle AMC \cong \triangle BMD$. The important feature of this method of solution is that the students make this inference without any idea of how it will figure in the final proof that M is the midpoint of $\overline{EF}$. However, this is a critical step in the final proof.

Reasoning from the givens is referred to as *forward search* and is to be *contrasted* with *backward search*, which is reasoning back from the to-be-proven conclusion. An example of backward search is the production rule above, which went from the goal of proving triangles congruent to the goals of proving that the side and angle components are congruent. Experts appear to differ from novices in geometry in that their proof behavior involves much

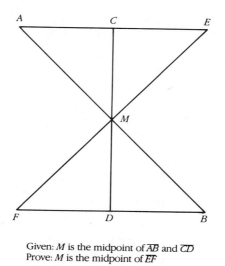

Given: *M* is the midpoint of $\overline{AB}$ and $\overline{CD}$
Prove: *M* is the midpoint of $\overline{EF}$

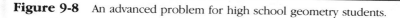

Figure 9-8 An advanced problem for high school geometry students.

more *forward search* and their choice about which inferences to make in forward search usually is appropriate. For instance, experts correctly decide to use the vertical-angle postulate to infer that $\angle AMC \cong \angle BMD$ in Figure 9-8, but do not use the postulate to make the useless inference $\angle AMF \cong \angle EMB$. We can characterize these forward-inference rules as productions also. Thus, the good geometry student might have the rule

> IF there are two triangles
> and they have two pairs of congruent sides
> and these sides combine to form a vertical-angle configuration
> THEN conclude the angles are congruent because of vertical angles
> and conclude the triangles are congruent because of the postulate side-angle-side

Figure 9-9 illustrates the pattern described by the postulate. This is a sub-pattern in the larger problem in Figure 9-8, and it is the recognition of this subpattern that enables this forward inference. Note that this production is like the others we have except that there is no mention of an explicit goal. Thus, another feature of expertise in geometry is development of these forward-search rules that omit mention of specific goals.

What underlies this development from backward to forward search? Anderson (1981b) and Larkin (1981) speculate that it is basically a result of

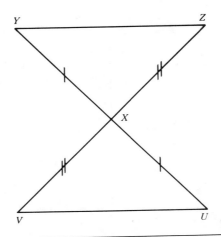

Figure 9-9   A pattern that advanced students will use to generate forward inferences.

subjects' recording past experience. In the past, certain configurations of information led to certain patterns of successful inference. Initially, these patterns are discovered in backward search, but once discovered, subjects form rules like the foregoing production that will generate the rule as a step of forward search.

Physics

Physics is another academic domain that has been studied. It is a more advanced topic than geometry and one that requires many years for the development of expertise. Typical studies comparing novices and experts have contrasted college students after their first one-semester course with the professors that teach the course. This is contrasting students with under 200 hours of exposure with teachers who have around 10,000 hours of exposure to physics. Not surprisingly, there are some sharp contrasts.

Forward Search versus Backward Search

Larkin (1981) compared novice and expert solutions on problems like the one in Figure 9-10. In the figure a block is sliding down an inclined plane of length *l* where θ is the angle between the plane and the horizontal. The coefficient of friction is μ. The subject's task is to find the velocity of the

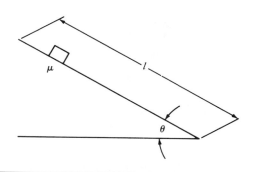

Figure 9-10   A sketch of a sample physics problem from Larkin (1981).

block when it reaches the bottom of the plane. Table 9-1 gives a typical novice solution to the problem and Table 9-2 gives a typical expert solution.

The novice solution typifies the method of *working backward*. It starts with the unknown, which is the velocity, v. Then the novice finds an equation to calculate v. However, to calculate v by this equation it is necessary to calculate a, the acceleration. So an equation is found involving a; and so the novice chains backward until a set of equations is found that enable solution of the problem. This is very much like the backward search involved in novice solutions of geometry problems.

The expert, on the other hand, uses similar equations but in the completely opposite order. The expert starts with quantities that can be directly computed, such as gravitational force, and works toward the desired velocity. This is much like the forward search we saw for good solvers of geometry problems.

Larkin (1981) has shown that on such problems, experts and novices typically apply physics principles in just the opposite orders. She developed a computer model that is able to simulate the development from a novice to expert with practice. This was done within a production-system framework. Novices start out with productions for working backward and slowly develop productions that make forward inferences.

Novice students are simulated by means–ends productions like

> IF   the goal is to calculate quantity x
> and there is a physics principle that involves x
> THEN   try to use that principle to calculate x

So, given the goal of calculating the acceleration, a, this production might invoke the use of the equation $v = v_0 + at$ (velocity equals initial velocity plus acceleration times time). With experience however, her system devel-

Table 9-1 *Typical novice solution to a physics problem*

To find the desired final speed v requires a principal with v in it, say

$$v = v_0 + 2at.$$

But both a and t are unknown, so that seems hopeless. Try instead

$$v^2 - v_0^2 = 2ax.$$

In that equation v_0 is zero and x is known, so it remains to find a. Therefore try

$$F = ma.$$

In that equation m is given, and only F is unknown, therefore use

$$F = \Sigma F\text{'s}.$$

which in this case means

$$F = F_g'' - f$$

where F_g'' and f can be found from

$$F_g'' = mg \sin \theta,$$
$$f = \mu N.$$
$$N = mg \cos \theta.$$

With a variety of substitutions, a correct expression for speed,

$$v = \sqrt{2(g \sin \theta - \mu g \cos \theta)},$$

can be found.

Adapted from Larkin, 1981.

oped productions that modeled expert students:

> IF   the quantities v, v_0, and t are known
> THEN   assert that the acceleration a is also known

There are real advantages to be had by forward reasoning in domains like geometry and physics. Reasoning backward involves setting goals and subgoals and keeping track of them. For instance, the student must remember that he or she is calculating F so a can be calculated so v can be calculated. This puts a severe strain on working memory and can lead to errors. Reasoning forward eliminates the need to keep track of subgoals. However, the trick in forward reasoning is to know which of the many possible forward inferences are relevant to the final solution. This is what the expert learns with experience. The expert learns to associate various inferences with various patterns of features in the problem. In this respect physics is another case where

Table 9-2 *Skilled solution to a physics problem*

The motion of the block is accounted for by the gravitational force,

$$F_g'' = mg \sin \theta$$

directed downward along the plane, and the frictional force,

$$f = \mu mg \cos \theta$$

directed upward along the plane. The block's acceleration a is then related to the (signed) sum of these forces by

$$F = ma$$

or

$$mg \sin \theta - \mu mg \cos \theta = ma.$$

Knowing the acceleration a, it is then possible to find the block's final speed v from the relations

$$l = \tfrac{1}{2}at^2$$

and

$$v = at$$

Adapted from Larkin, 1981.

development of expertise depends on the development of more sophisticated pattern-recognition abilities.

Problem Representation

There are also important developments in terms of the way experts represent problems in physics. Physics, being an intellectually deep subject, has principles that are only implicit in the surface features of the problem. Experts learn to see these implicit principles and represent problems in terms of them.

Chi, Feltovich, and Glaser (1981) asked subjects to classify a large set of problems into similar categories. Figure 9-11 shows sets of problems that their novices thought were similar and the novices' explanations for the similarity groupings. As can be seen, the novices chose surface features, such as rotations or inclined planes, as their bases for classification. Being a physics novice myself, I have to admit these seem very intuitive bases for similarity. Contrast these classifications with pairs of problems that the expert subjects saw as similar in Figure 9-12. Problems that are completely different on the surface were seen as similar because they both involved conservation of energy or they both used Newton's second law. Thus experts have the ability

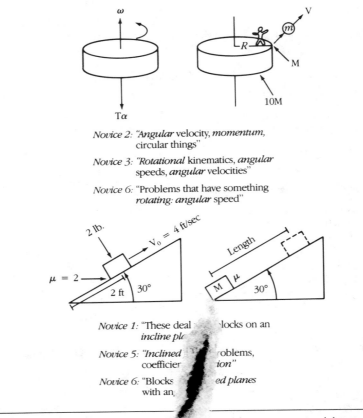

Novice 2: "*Angular* velocity, *momentum*, circular things"

Novice 3: "*Rotational* kinematics, *angular* speeds, *angular* velocities"

Novice 6: "Problems that have something *rotating: angular* speed"

Novice 1: "These deal   locks on an incline pl

Novice 5: "Inclined   roblems, coefficier   ion"

Novice 6: "Blocks   ed planes with an,

Figure 9-11 Diagrams depicting   problems categorized by novices as similar and samples of their explana   he similarity. Adapted from Chi et al. (1981).

to map surface features of a problem onto these deeper principles. This is very useful because the deeper principles are more predictive of the method of solution.

Computer Programming

As we all know, computer literacy is becoming a more and more important issue in society. Computers are affecting all aspects of our lives, and success depends on being able to deal with them at many levels. Computer systems have often not been designed to facilitate interaction with human users; but each year, systems are becoming more and more user friendly, with the result

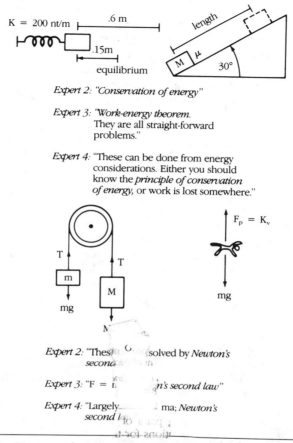

Figure 9-12 Diagrams depicting pairs of problems categorized by experts as similar and samples of their explanations for the similarity. Adapted from Chi et al. (1981).

that dealing with them is much easier. However, certain aspects of computer–user interaction remain very demanding and probably will continue to be demanding for some time. The prime example of this is computer programming—the task of specifying instructions to a program in a language flexible enough to permit the computer to display its full range of capability.

Programming languages are often difficult to learn to deal with. It takes about a 100 hours for a novice to develop even modest proficiency in a first programming language. Programming problems are also often inherently hard. They can make very high demands on problem-solving skill. There is a wide range of programming expertise in society, from people who have none, to people who have had a little experience with a personal computer or college course, to people who have had one rigorous college course, to people who have had a few courses, to people who have had many courses and thousands of hours of programming experience.

When people become expert at programming, they develop a number of new capabilities. A recent flurry of research has tried to understand the nature of these developments. Among the features that have been noted are changes in problem representation, program development, and memory.

Problem Representation

One aspect of acquiring programming expertise is the development of *language independence*. There are many programming languages that have different means of achieving the same final effect. For instance, most languages have multiple mechanisms for achieving *iteration*, which refers to the repetition of a sequence of instructions. Novices think of iteration in terms of the mechanisms of a particular language. Experts think of iteration in the abstract, independent of any particular language. This is much like the development observed in physics, where experts perceive problems in terms of abstract principles.

A further illustration of language independence is the appearance of a great deal of high-level vocabulary to describe a problem solution. Below I have reproduced an "expert" description of a problem solution. Unless you are a good programmer, you should not feel that you should be able to understand it. However, note the high frequency of what might appear to be jargon. (I have italicized some of the more striking instances.) Actually, each of these instances of jargon is attached to an important programming construct and enables the programmer to more economically represent and think about the plan for the program:

> BKT-DELETE is implemented as the *standard list deletion plan*. Inputs are a *key* and a *list of entries*. The plan is a *search loop* using two *pointers*: a pointer to the *current entry* which is *initialized* to the *input list*, and a *trailing pointer* which is initialized to *NIL*. On each *iteration*, it *tests the key* of the *first element* of the current list. If it is equal to the input key, it *splices* the *current element* out of the list by *RPLACD'ing* the *previous pointer*.

Thus, one important dimension of growing expertise is the development of a set of new constructs for representing the key aspects of a problem. The representation an expert develops for a problem is largely independent of the programming language in which the problem is going to be solved.

Program Development

Novice and expert programmers show both interesting differences and interesting similarities in the way they create or develop computer programs (Anderson, Farrell, & Sauers, 1984; Jeffries, Turner, Polson, & Atwood, 1981). Both types of programmers develop programs in what is called a *top-down* manner. That is, they work from the statement of the problem to subproblems to sub-subproblems, and so on, until they solve the problem. For instance, Figure 9-13 illustrates part of the development of a plan for a program to calculate the difference in mean height between boys and girls in a classroom. First, the problem is developed into the subproblems of (1) calculating the mean height of the boys; (2) calculating the mean height of the girls; (3) subtracting the two. The problem of calculating the mean height of the boys is divided into the goals of adding up the heights and dividing by the number of boys. And so the program development continues until we get down to statements in the language like:

AVERAGE = TOTAL/NUMBER.

This top-down development is basically the same thing as what is called *working backward* in the context of geometry or physics. It is noteworthy that there is not much change to working forward as programmers become more expert. This is in sharp contrast to geometry and physics, where experts do change to working forward. This contrast can be understood by considering the differences in the problem domains. Physics and geometry problems have a rich set of givens that are more predictive of solutions than is the goal. In contrast, the "givens" of a programming problem are the properties of the language, which are not predictive, whereas the goal is a rich problem statement that is highly predictive. Thus, we see that development of expertise does not follow the same course in all domains. Rather, experts adapt themselves to the characteristics of a particular domain.

One difference has been noted between expert and novice problem development (Anderson, 1983; Jeffries, Turner, Polson, & Atwood, 1981). Experts tend to develop problem solutions breadth first, whereas novices develop their solutions depth first. The differences are not striking with a simple problem like Figure 9-13, but can become quite dramatic with more complex programs that have more complex plans. The expert tends to expand a full level of the plan tree before going down to expand the next level, whereas the novice will expand the first problem down to its lowest levels. Thus, an expert will have decided on a basic plan for calculating both the boys' and the girls' heights in Figure 9-13 before working out all the details of calculating the boys' heights, whereas the novice will completely work out the plan for the boys' heights before considering the plan for the girls' heights. The

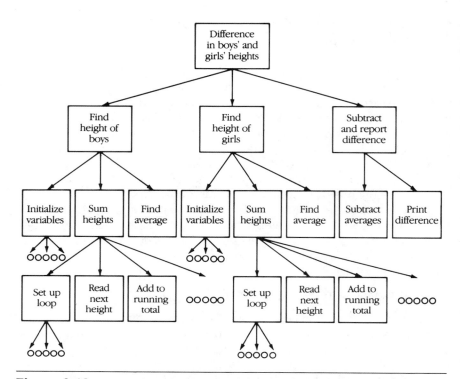

Figure 9-13 A partial representation of the plan for a program to calculate the difference in mean height between boys and girls in a classroom.

expert's approach is called breadth first because a whole layer of tree is created at a time. The novice's approach is called depth first because of the tendency to first create the leftmost branch of the tree right to the bottom. There are good reasons for the experts' approach. Programming problems are typically nonindependent (see the discussion on p. 216). Therefore, solution of a later problem can often impact on the solution of an earlier problem. For instance, you might want to write a program to calculate the boys' heights in such a way that the same program could be used to calculate the girls' heights. Experts, because of breadth-first expansion, are likely to see these dependencies among subproblems.

Memory for Programs

Another strength of experts is that they have much better memory for features of computer programs. McKeithen, Reitman, Rueter, & Hirtle (1981) and Shneiderman (1976) have done the analog of the Chase and Simon chess experiment with computer programs. They had experts and novices try to reconstruct computer programs after brief presentations. The experts show much better memory. However, when presented with scrambled programs, the experts show a great reduction in their memory. Jeffries et al. have noted how experts appear to have infallible memory for parts of their plan for a program, even a half hour after developing it. Anderson (1983), looking at novices, has noted how they can forget key aspects of their plan from one moment to the next.

Like chess players, programmers have developed patterns, or templates, for aspects of a program that reoccur over and over again. Soloway (1980) has argued that development of programming expertise depends on development of a great many of these templates, just as development of chess expertise depends on the acquisition of a great many chess patterns. Programmers learn to associate these templates to programming goals. When they have these goals, they can generate the template. When they see this template in a program, they can infer what the programmer's goals were. Soloway, Ehrlich, and Gold (1983) have shown that experts' ability to understand and debug novel programs depends on whether these programs contain common templates.

Conclusions

By looking at these four domains—chess, geometry, physics, and computer programming—we can identify some of the general principles underlying the development of problem-solving expertise:

1. Experts learn to perceive recurring patterns in the problem and to associate their problem solutions to these patterns.

2. Experts learn to represent the problem in terms of more abstract features, which are more predictive of problem solution.

3. Experts reorganize their approach to the problem in order to capitalize on features of the domain. In geometry and physics this reorganization takes the form of transforming working backward into working forward. In programming it takes the form of transforming depth-first development into breadth-first development.

4. Experts develop better memories for information that is involved in the solution of problems.

The general theme that seems to underlie many of the trends in the development of expertise is the movement from deductive processing toward memory retrieval and pattern recognition. People become expert in a domain to the extent that they can find ways to approach and represent its problems that allow them to solve these problems by simple retrieval and pattern recognition. We discussed in Chapter 2 the evidence that human brains are parallel computational devices that do things like spreading activation and recognizing patterns well, but are poor at long chains of deductions that involve serial processing. The more general problem-solving strategies that we display in novel domains depend heavily on serial processing. It appears that development of expertise depends on movement to a mode of information processing for which our neural hardware is better adapted. Specifically, knowledge is converted into patterns for pattern matching. These patterns are specific to the particular domain. This is why an expert problem solver in a domain like chess is ordinary in other domains.

Remarks and Suggested Readings

The work on the development of expertise in cognitive skills is a relatively recent phenomenon. The papers by Chase and Simon (1973) and Larkin, McDermott, Simon, and Simon (1980) are already considered classics. Lesgold (1984) reviews many of the concepts. The books edited by Anderson (1981a) and Chi, Glazer, and Farr (in press) contain numerous recent papers on the topic. Card et al. (1983) have written a book describing interaction with computer systems, especially text editors. Shneiderman (1980) reviews many aspects of computer programming. Soloway, Bonar, and Ehrlich (1983) have done some excellent research on programming in Pascal.

This chapter has focused mainly on the development of cognitive skills. However, considerable research has been done on the development of motor skills. Reviews of this research can be found in Fitts and Posner (1967), Keele (1973), Kelso (1982), Schmidt (1982), Stelmach and Reguin (1980), and Welford (1968). Rosenbloom and Newell (1983) have done a production-system analysis of practice and transfer in the domain of perceptual-motor skills.

Chapter 10

Reasoning

Summary

1. Research on deductive reasoning has frequently compared human reasoning with the prescriptions of a logical system. A logical system consists of rules of inference, which permit true conclusions to be derived from true premises.

2. Conditional reasoning is deduction involving statements of the form *If A then B*, where *A* and *B* are propositions. People make errors in conditional-reasoning tasks because they misinterpret the meaning of the connective *if*, and because they do not use the rule of inference known as modus tollens. Modus tollens allow a person to reason from the premises *If A then B* and *B is false* to the conclusion *A is false*.

3. Categorical syllogisms are reasoning problems involving the quantifiers *all, some, no,* and *some not*. Venn diagrams in which the categories are represented by circles, can be helpful in reasoning about categorical syllogisms.

4. People make many errors when dealing with categorical syllogisms, particularly errors that involve the acceptance of invalid conclusions. This pattern of errors is partially described by the atmosphere hypothesis, which asserts that people are inclined to accept conclusions similar to the premise.

5. In dealing with categorical syllogisms, people appear to be relying on a number of problem-solving heuristics that result in fairly good performance but that produce errors on certain critical problems

6. For an argument to be inductively valid, the conclusion must be probable if the premises are true. This criterion contrasts with that for a deductively valid argument, in which the conclusion must be certain if the premises are true.

7. The components of the inductive-reasoning process are hypothesis formation and hypothesis evaluation.

8. Concept formation studies how people form hypotheses about the definition of a concept when given instances of the concept. A major limitation on human concept formation involves keeping track of all the relevant information and using that information correctly.

9. People have particular difficulty in acquiring and utilizing negative information in forming hypotheses. Negative information refers to data that are inconsistent with a hypothesis.

10. Bayes's theorem prescribes a way for evaluating a hypothesis. It updates the probability of a hypothesis in light of new evidence. In the terminology of Bayes's theorem, the original probability of a hypothesis is referred to as the *prior probability*, the updated probability as the *posterior probability*, and the probability of the evidence given the hypotheses as the *conditional probability*.

11. In evaluating hypotheses, human beings deviate from the norm prescribed by Bayes's theorem in that they do not adjust the posterior probabilities as radically as they should and they tend to ignore information about prior probabilities.

12. When people cannot directly observe the probability of a particular type of event, they try to estimate its probability by means of various heuristics. These heuristics are biased and can lead to serious distortions in probability estimates. It is the use of such heuristics that accounts for the deviations from the prescription of Bayes's theorem.

Logic and Reasoning

Reasoning refers to the processes by which people evaluate and generate logical arguments. *Logic* is a subdiscipline of philosophy and mathematics that tries to formally specify what it means for an argument to be logically correct. To understand the psychological research on reasoning, we have to understand the relationship of this research to logic. Until the twentieth century, logic and the psychology of thought were often considered one and the same. The famous Irish mathematician George Boole (1854) called his book on logical calculus *An Investigation into the Laws of Thought*, and designed it "in the first place, to investigate the fundamental laws of those operations of the mind by which reasoning is performed." Of course, humans did not always operate according to the prescriptions of logic, but such lapses were seen as the malfunctioning of mental machinery that was logical when it worked properly. In trying to improve the mind, people tried to train themselves to be logical. A hundred years ago, a section on "cognitive processes" in a psychology text would have been about "logical thinking." The fact that only one chapter in this book is on reasoning reflects the current understanding that a large portion of human thought is not logical reasoning in any useful sense. However, the belief persists that in studying reasoning we are dealing with mental operations that are fundamentally logical in nature.

Deductive Reasoning

Much of the research on deductive reasoning has been explicitly designed to compare human performance with the prescriptions of logic. In such experiments, the reasoning problems presented to subjects are analyzed in the terms used in logic. Therefore, it is essential to have some familiarity with the nature of systems of logic and the terminology of logic.

We will first consider research on deductive logic and deductive reasoning. In a deductive system, it is possible to reason with certainty from the premises of an argument to the conclusion. This is to be contrasted with inductive reasoning, where we go from the premises to the conclusions with a certain probability. We will discuss inductive reasoning later in the chapter.

In a logical system, *rules of inference* prescribe when it is possible to infer a conclusion from a set of premises. A particularly useful rule of inference is *modus ponens*. It states that given the proposition A implies B and given A, we can infer B. The statement A *implies* B is often rendered *If A then B*. So, suppose we are told the following:

1. If it rains tomorrow, then the game will be canceled.

2. If the game is canceled, then our team will surely lose the pennant.

3. It will rain tomorrow.

From 1 and 3 we can infer 4 by modus ponens:

4. The game will be canceled.

From 2 and 4 we can infer 5:

5. Our team will surely lose the penant.

This example is an instance of valid deduction. By *valid* we mean that if premises 1 through 3 are true, the conclusion 5 must be true. Of course, the premises might not be true, in which case the conclusion need not be true. Logic and deductive reasoning are not concerned with examining the truth of the premises in a logical argument. Rather, the concern is with whether the premises logically imply the conclusions.

Another rule of inference is *modus tollens*. This rule states that if we are given the proposition *A implies B* and the fact that *B* is false, then we can infer that *A* is false. The following is an inference exercise that requires the use of modus tollens. Suppose we are given the premises

6. If it snows tomorrow, then we will go skiing.

7. If we go skiing, then we will be happy.

8. We are not going to be happy.

Then it follows from 7 and 8 by modus tollens that

9. We will not be going skiing.

and it follows from 6 and 9 by modus tollens that

10. It is not going to snow tomorrow.

Is Human Reasoning Logical?

One of the recurring themes in the research on human deduction is that human reasoning does not always correspond to the prescriptions of logic. People commit both errors of omission and errors of commission. That is, they fail to see as valid certain conclusions that are valid, and they see as valid conclusions that are not. Thus, the rules of inference that people follow are not always correct. Much of the research on human reasoning has been concerned with determining the rules of inference that people have available, when these rules apply, and how these rules originated. There is some evidence that people can be trained to correct their errors of reasoning, but such remedial training is hard.

People approach reasoning as a problem-solving task where the problem is to evaluate a logical argument or to generate a deduction. People have various general-purpose operators for solving these problems. These operators have the status of *heuristics*, which sometimes work and sometimes do not, in the latter case leading to logical error. The effect of logical training is to create domain-specific operators for correct logical reasoning. It is important to emphasize that these operators are domain specific. Logicians who reason flawlessly in their formal domain are still subject to logical error in their everyday reasoning.

Conditional Reasoning

Conditional reasoning refers to how people reason with implications or conditional statements, for example,

> If the maid hid the gun, then the butler was not at the scene of the crime.

Such conditional statements are important in mathematics and science, and as this example suggests, they can be significant in the evaluation of evidence. Therefore, it is important to understand how people tend to reason about such statements and what efforts they are prone in their reasoning. A considerable amount of research has focused on reasoning with conditional syllogisms (e.g., Marcus & Rips, 1979; Rips & Marcus, 1977; Staudenmayer, 1975; Taplin, 1971; Taplin & Staudenmayer, 1973). Examples of conditional syllogisms include the following:

1. If the ball rolls left, the green lamp comes on.
   The ball rolls left.
   Therefore, the green lamp comes on.

2. If God exists, life will be beautiful.
   God does not exist.
   Therefore, life is not beautiful.

Or, more abstractly, we may represent these syllogisms in the following way:

1. $P \supset Q$
   $\underline{P}$
   $\therefore Q$

2. $P \supset Q$
   $\underline{\sim P}$
   $\therefore \sim Q$

where the symbol $\supset$ stands for implication, and $\sim$ stands for negation. Conditional syllogisms involve such arguments as these, where one premise is an implication between two propositions, the second premise is one of these propositions or its negation, and the conclusion is the other proposition or its negation. Subjects are asked to determine whether these syllogisms are logically valid. In the above case, syllogism 1 is valid and 2 is not.

Table 10-1 *Percentage of total responses for eight types of conditional syllogisms*

Syllogism	Always	Sometimes	Never
1. $P \supset Q$ $\underline{P}$ $\therefore Q$	100[a]	0	0
2. $P \supset Q$ $\underline{P}$ $\therefore \sim Q$	0	0	100[a]
3. $P \supset Q$ $\underline{\sim P}$ $\therefore Q$	5	79[a]	16
4. $P \supset Q$ $\underline{\sim P}$ $\therefore \sim Q$	21	77[a]	2
5. $P \supset Q$ $\underline{Q}$ $\therefore P$	23	77[a]	0
6. $P \supset Q$ $\underline{Q}$ $\therefore \sim P$	4	82[a]	14
7. $P \supset Q$ $\underline{\sim Q}$ $\therefore P$	0	23	77[a]
8. $P \supset Q$ $\underline{\sim Q}$ $\therefore \sim P$	57[a]	39	4

Adapted from Rips and Marcus, 1977.
[a]The correct response.

Consider a representitive experiment by Rips and Marcus (1977) in which subjects from the University of Chicago were asked to evaluate eight types of syllogisms. Though the syllogisms are presented abstractly in Table 10-1 the subjects were actually tested with concrete propositions. An example would be

> If the ball rolls left, the green lamp comes on.
> The green lamp comes on.
> Therefore, the ball rolled left.

Subjects were asked to judge whether the conclusion was always true, sometimes true, or never true given the premises. Table 10-1 gives the percentage of responses in each category for each type of syllogism.

Problems 1 and 2 in Table 10-1 indicate that subjects could apply modus ponens quite successfully. However, they had much greater difficulty with the other form of the conditional syllogism permitting a valid conclusion. This is the form in problems 7 and 8, which required application of the rule of modus tollens. Here more than 30 percent of the subject population failed to realize that we can reason from the negation of the second term in a conditional to the negation of the first term. Syllogisms 3 and 4 display evidence for a fallacy in conditional reasoning known as *denial of the antecedent* (the first term in the conditional). Almost 20 percent of the subject population believed that we can conclude that Q is not true if we know that P implies Q and that P is not true. Problems 5 and 6 display a tendency for a fallacy known as *affirmation of the consequent* (the second term in the conditional). On these problems almost 20 percent of the subject population believed that we can conclude that P is true from knowing P *implies* Q and Q.

It seems that one source of the fallacies displayed in problems 3 through 6 is that subjects do not interpret conditionals in the same way that logicians do. This discrepancy has been demonstrated in a series of experiments by Taplin (1971), Taplin and Staudenmayer (1973), and Staudenmayer (1975). They showed that many subjects interpreted the conditional as being what logicians would call the *biconditional*. The biconditional if rendered in English unambiguously by the rather awkward construction *if and only if*. For instance,

> Israel will use atomic weapons if and only if it is faced with annihilation.

With the biconditional, if either the first or second premise is true, the other will be true. Similarly, if either the first or second premise is false, the other will be false.

The Failure to Apply Modus Tollens

The hypothesis that subjects interpret the conditional as a biconditional explains why some subjects display the fallacies of affirming the consequent or denying the antecedent, but leaves unexplained the difficulty they have in applying modus tollens in problems 7 and 8 of Table 10-1. Modus tollens is a valid inference even if the conditional is interpreted as a biconditional. Table 10-1 actually is a rather mild case of failure to apply modus tollens. In other situations the failure can be much more grievous.

A very stiking demonstration of failure to apply modus tollens comes from a series of experiments performed by Wason (for a review see Wason & Johnson-Laird, 1972, Chapters 13 and 14). In one of the principal experiments from this research, four cards showing the following symbols were placed in front of subjects:

Subjects were told that a letter appeared on one side of each card and a number on the other. The task was to judge the validity of the following rule, which referred only to these four cards:

> If a card has a vowel on one side, then it has an even number on the other side.

The subjects' task was to turn over only those cards that had to be turned over for the correctness of the rule to be judged. Forty-six percent of the subjects elected to turn over both E and 4, which is a wrong combination of choices. The E had to be turned over, but the 4 did not have to be turned over, since neither a vowel nor a consonant on the other side would have falsified the rule. Only 4 percent elected to turn over E and 7, which are the correct choices. An odd number behind the E or a vowel behind the 7 would have falsified the rule. Another 33 percent of the subjects elected to turn over the E only. The remaining 17 percent of the subjects made other incorrect choices.

So, subjects displayed two types of errors in the task. First, they often turned over the 4, another example of the fallacy of affirming the consequent. Again, this response might just have reflected an interpretation by subjects of the conditional as biconditional. However, even more striking was the almost total failure to take the modus tollens step of disconfirming the consequent and determining whether the antecedent was also disconfirmed (in other words, turning over the 7).

These failures of reasoning have been observed over a wide range of situations, but interesting exceptions have been demonstrated. Johnson-Laird. Legrenzi, and Legrenzi (1972) presented subjects with the material in Figure 10-1. They asked subjects to imagine that they were Post Office workers engaged in sorting letters. The task was to discover whether the postal regulation requiring an extra 10 lire of postage on sealed letters had been violated. Thus, subjects were to test this rule:

> If a letter is sealed, then it has a 50-lire stamp on it.

They were asked which letters should be turned over. Here, 21 of the 24 subjects made the right choice, turning over the sealed letter and the letter with the 40-lire stamp. The fact that they had little difficulty in seeing that the 40-lire envelope should be turned over indicated that use of a rule such as modus tollens can depend on context. While the rule of modus tollens may not be generally available, it does seem available in the context where a person is trying to "catch cheaters."

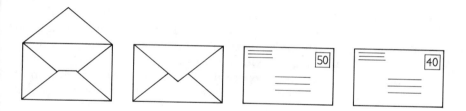

Figure 10-1 Material used in the envelope experiment by Johnson-Laird et al. (1972). Subjects were asked which envelopes should be turned over to test the rule *If a letter is sealed, then it has a 50-lire stamp on it.*

Inability to reason with modus tollens is a major weakness of human deduction. For instance, students coming into college math courses, where they need to be able to use the rule, often need special coaching on the rule. This widespread failure to use modus tollens probably reflects the fact that we are not practiced in thinking about what is not the case. The rule requires us to realize that $P \supset Q$ is equivalent to $\sim Q \supset \sim P$. Although we are not generally practiced in reasoning about negation of a proposition, the experimental results cited above illustrate that we are practiced in certain contexts. The fact that availability of an inference rule depends on context illustrates another way in which human reasoning is different from logical deduction. Such a rule as modus tollens would apply in all appropriate situations in logic.

Reasoning about Quantifiers

Much of human knowledge is cast with logical quantifiers such as *all* or *some*. Witness Lincoln's famous statement: "You may fool all the people some of the time; you can even fool some of the people all of the time; but you can't fool all of the people all of the time." Our scientific laws are cast with such quantifiers also. It is extremely important to understand how people reason with such quantifiers.

The Categorical Syllogism

Modern logic is greatly concerned with analyzing the meaning of quantifiers such as *all* and *some*, as in, for example, the statement *All philosophers read some books*. At the turn of this century, the sophistication with which such quantified statements were analyzed increased considerably (see Church,

1956, for a historical discussion). This more advanced treatment of quantifiers is covered in most modern logic courses. However, most of the research on quantifiers in psychology has focused on a simpler and older kind of quantified deduction, called the *categorical syllogism*. Much of Aristotle's writing on reasoning concerned the categorical syllogism. Extensive discussion of categorical syllogisms can be found in textbooks on logic as recent as that of Cohen and Nagel (1934).

Categorical syllogisms involve statements containing the quantifiers *some, all, no,* and *some not*. Examples of such categorical statements are

1. All doctors are rich.

2. Some lawyers are dishonest.

3. No politician is trustworthy.

4. Some actors are not handsome.

In experiments, the categories (e.g., doctors, rich people, lawyers, dishonest people) in such statements are frequently represented by letters, say *A, B, C*. This system serves as a handy shorthand for describing the material. In the traditional analysis of categorical statements, the foregoing sentences would be analyzed into *subject* and *predicate*, the first category (e.g., doctor) being subject and the second category (rich people) the predicate. Thus, the statements might be rendered in this way:

1.' All *A*'s are *B*'s.

2.' Some *C*'s are *D*'s.

3.' No *E*'s are *F*'s.

4.' Some *G*'s are not *H*'s.

A *Venn diagram* is a graphic interpretation of such a categorical statement. Figure 10-2 presents Venn diagrams for these four types of statements; parts (a) through (d) correspond to sentences 1' through 4'. In the Venn diagrams, each category is represented by a circle, and the area within a circle represents all the individuals in the category. Where two circles overlap, this overlap represents individuals in both categories.

There are four possible Venn diagrams. First the circles for the two categories can be identical. This means that the two categories contain the same individuals. Second, one circle can be within the other. This means that all the individuals in the first category are in the second but some individuals in the second are not in the first. Third, the two circles can partially overlap. This means that some individuals are in both categories but some individuals in each category are not in the other category. Finally, the two circles can be completely disjoint. This means that there are no individuals who are in both categories.

Figure 10-2a illustrates that the quantifier *all* can have two possible inter-

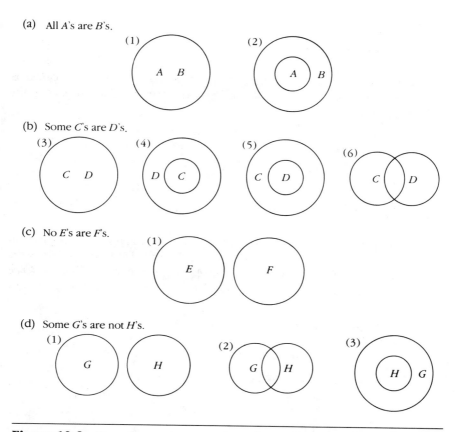

(a) All *A*'s are *B*'s.

(b) Some *C*'s are *D*'s.

(c) No *E*'s are *F*'s.

(d) Some *G*'s are not *H*'s.

Figure 10-2 Venn-diagram interpretations of categorical statements 1' through 4'.

pretations: either (1) *A* and *B* are identical or (2) *B* includes *A* and things other than *A* (i.e., the *B* circle contains the *A* circle). Part (b) shows that *some* has four possible interpretations. People often interpret *some* as only implying the meaning conveyed by Venn diagram 6, in which *C* and *D* overlap, but some *C* are not *D* and some *D* are not *C*. However, the standard logical meaning of *some* allows the ambiguity in Figure 10-2b. In reasoning experiments, subjects often have to be told explicitly that *some* has this broader meaning. Part (c) of the figure gives the one interpretation for *no*. Finally, part (d) illustrates the three meanings of *some not*. We will return to these Venn diagrams after discussing results from some experiments studying how subjects reason with categorical syllogisms.

A categorical syllogism typically contains two premises and a conclusion. All three statements are of a categorical nature. The following is a simple example:

1. All A's are B's.
   <u>All B's are C's.</u>
   ∴ All A's are C's.

This syllogism, incidentally, is one that most people correctly recognize as valid. On the other hand, people accept with almost equal frequency the following invalid syllogism:

2. Some A's are B's.
   <u>Some B's are C's.</u>
   ∴ Some A's are C's.

The Atmosphere Hypothesis

The general problem subjects seem to have with categorical syllogisms is that they are too willing to accept false conclusions. However, subjects are not completely indiscriminate in their acceptance of syllogisms. That is, while they will accept 2, they will not accept 3; and while they will accept 4, they will not accept 5.

3. Some A's are B's.
   <u>Some B's are C's.</u>
   ∴ No A's are C's.

4. No A's are B's.
   <u>No B's are C's.</u>
   ∴ No A's are C's.

5. No A's are B's.
   <u>No B's are C's.</u>
   ∴ All A's are C's.

To account for this pattern of errors, Woodworth and Sells (1935) proposed the *atmosphere hypothesis*. This hypothesis stated that the logical terms (*some, all, no, not*) used in the syllogism created an "atmosphere" that predisposed subjects to accept conclusions with the same terms. There are two parts to the atmosphere hypothesis. One part asserts that subjects would accept a positive conclusion to positive premises and a negative conclusion to negative premises. When the premises were mixed, the subjects would prefer a negative conclusion. Thus, they would tend to accept the following conclusion:

6. No A's are B's.
   <u>All B's are C's.</u>
   ∴ No A's are C's.

The other part of the atmosphere hypothesis concerns a subject's response to particular statements (*some, some not*) versus universal statements (*all* or *no*). As the above examples illustrate, subjects will accept a universal conclusion if the premises are universal. They will accept a particular conclusion if the premises are particular. So they tend to accept syllogisms 7 and 8 but not 9 and 10.

> 7. Some *A*'s are *B*'s.
>   Some *B*'s are *C*'s.
>   ∴ Some *A*'s are *C*'s.

> 8. Some *A*'s are not *B*'s.
>   Some *B*'s are not *C*'s.
>   ∴ Some *A*'s are not *C*'s.

> 9. Some *A*'s are *B*'s.
>   Some *B*'s are *C*'s.
>   ∴ All *A*'s are *C*'s.

> 10. Some *A*'s are not *B*'s.
>   Some *B*'s are not *C*'s.
>   ∴ No *A*'s are *C*'s.

When one premise is particular and the other universal, subjects prefer a particular conclusion. So they will accept the following:

> 11. All *A*'s are *B*'s.
>   Some *B*'s are *C*'s.
>   ∴ Some *A*'s are *C*'s.

Limitations of the Atmosphere Hypothesis

The atmosphere hypothesis has been quite successful in capturing many of the main trends in the data on syllogistic reasoning. However, it is becoming increasingly clear that this hypothesis does not represent the whole story. For one thing, according to the atmosphere hypothesis, subjects would be just as likely to accept the atmosphere-favored conclusion when it was not valid as when it was valid. That is, it predicts that subjects would be just as likely to accept

> All *A*'s are *B*'s.
> Some *B*'s are *C*'s.
> ∴ Some *A*'s are *C*'s.

which is not valid, as they would be to accept

> Some *A*'s are *B*'s
> All *B*'s are *C*'s.
> ∴ Some *A*'s are *C*'s.

which is valid. In fact, subjects are more likely to accept the conclusion in the valid case. Thus, subjects do display some ability to evaluate a syllogism accurately.

An even more serious limitation of the atmosphere hypothesis is that it fails to predict the effects that the form of a syllogism has on subjects' validity judgments. For instance, the hypothesis predicts that subjects would be no more likely to erroneously accept

> Some *A*'s are *B*'s.
> Some *B*'s are *C*'s.
> ∴ Some *A*'s are *C*'s.

than they would be to erroneously accept

> Some *B*'s are *A*'s.
> Some *C*'s are *B*'s.
> ∴ Some *A*'s are *C*'s.

In fact, it has now been established (Johnson-Laird and Steedman, 1978) that subjects are more willing to erroneously accept the conclusion in the former case. In general, subjects are more willing to accept a conclusion from *A* to *C* (i.e., one that involves *A* as subject and *C* as predicate) if they can find a chain leading from *A* to *B* in one premise and from *B* to *C* in the second premise. Other effects of the form of the argument rather than the quantifiers have been shown by Dickstein (1978).

In conclusion, although the atmosphere hypothesis clearly describes many qualitative features of the data on syllogism evaluation, the hypothesis obviously does not constitute the whole story. As the next section will argue, subjects appear to be using a variety of problem-solving heuristics in evaluating syllogisms, and the atmosphere hypothesis simply captures descriptively the central tendency of many of these heuristics.

Problem Solving and Categorical Syllogisms

To return to our problem-solving framework, it appears again that subjects are frequently unable to find the steps of inference that let them reason through to the truth or falsity of a conclusion. Consider one of the valid syllogisms that subjects often have great difficulty with:

> Some *B*'s are *A*'s.
> No *C*'s are *B*'s.
> ∴ Some *A*s are not *C*'s.

In a study I did on problems like this with University of Michigan undergraduates as subjects, only 60 percent agreed that the foregoing conclusion was valid. To help subjects reason through to the conclusion, I gave them a couple of intermediate steps on the way to the conclusion:

	1. Some B's are A's.
	2. No C's are B's.
From 1 it follows that	3. Some A's are B's.
From 2 it follows that	4. No B's are C's.
From 3 and 4 it follows that	5. Some A's are not C's.

In this form, 80 percent of the subjects got this problem right.

Similarly, subjects have problems with invalid syllogisms because they tend to have no systematic way of showing that the conclusion need not be true. The way to prove that a syllogism is not valid is to look for counterexamples where the premises are true but the conclusion is not. One way to do this is by means of Venn diagrams. By considering various possible combinations of Venn diagrams, we are able to find counterexamples to categorical syllogisms.[1] To illustrate how this works, consider the following invalid syllogism:

No A's are B's.
All B's are C's
∴. No A's are C's.

Figure 10-3 gives the only Venn diagram of the first premise (1) and the two Venn diagrams of the second premise, 2 and 3. In the Venn diagram (1) for the first premise, the two categories, A and B are disjoint. In the first Venn diagram for the second premise (2), the category B is contained within C. In the other Venn diagram for the second premise (3), C and B are identical. Venn diagrams 4 through 7 represent various possible combinations of diagram 1 for the first premise with one of diagrams 2 and 3 for the second premise. In diagram 4, 1 and 2 are combined such that the circle for C in 2 does not touch A. In this diagram, A and C are disjoint. However, as 5 illustrates, it is also possible for the circle for C to overlap with A, and as 6 illustrates, it is even possible for C to include A completely. Diagram 7 represents the combination of 1 and 3. There is only one possibility for this combination. Since C and B are identical in 3, and A is disjoint from B in 1, A must be disjoint from C in 7. The conclusion *No A's are C's* in the syllogism above, although it describes combinations 4 and 7, does not describe diagrams 5 and 6. Thus, diagrams 5 and 6 are counterexamples to the conclusion; they show that possible interpretations of the premises are incompatible with the conclusion.

Simply stated, then, categorical syllogisms make difficult problem-solving demands on a subject. A *representation problem* exists (see Chapter 8) in that subjects often do not know how to represent a state space for the problem (i.e., steps in a deduction, combinations of Venn diagrams) so that they can

---

[1]Quine (1950) suggests a different way of using Venn diagrams in evaluating categorical syllogisms.

No *A*'s are *B*'s.

All *B*'s are *C*'s.

Possible combinations

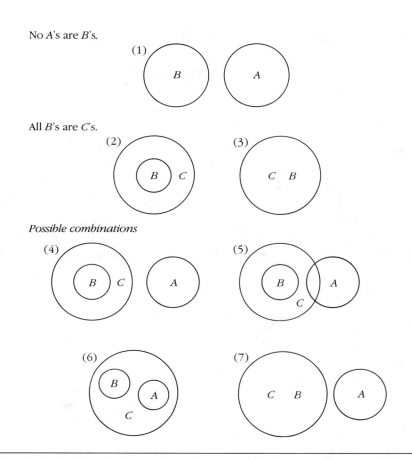

Figure 10-3 Combinations of Venn-diagram representations of premises. If a valid conclusion follows from the premises, it must be consistent with all Venn-diagram combinations.

solve the problem. Even if they do know of a state space for representing the problem, they will have difficulty in searching the space. Subjects often face a large space of possibilities to search and do not know how to conduct the search.

Errors Resulting from Heuristics

While it is understandable that subjects make as many errors as they do, it remains to be explained why they accept only some, and not all, invalid

syllogisms. This phenomenon also seems to have a problem-solving explanation. Subjects use various heuristics (discussed in Chapter 8) to help them
in their representation and search. These heuristics lead to errors on a few
problems only, as with any good heuristic. Many of the heuristics that researchers have attributed to subjects lead to atmosphere errors.

It may be that when the problem gets hard, some subjects don't think
about the meaning of the statement but rather simply use the words *all, some,
some not,* and *no* to evaluate the conclusion—just as the atmosphere hypothesis suggests. In itself, the atmosphere hypothesis proves not to be a bad
heuristic. Using this method, subjects reject about 75 percent of the contingent
syllogisms and identify most of the valid syllogisms. Thus, used by itself, the
atmosphere heuristic leads to a performance of more than 80 percent correct.
This is not bad for such a crude heuristic.

Another explanation of errors is known as the *conversion hypothesis* (Chapman & Chapman, 1959, Henle, 1962). According to this explanation, subjects
interpret *All A's are B's* to mean *A is the same as B. Some A's are B's* will be
interpreted as meaning *Some A's are B's but not all A's are B's and not all
B's are A's. Some A's are not B's* will get the same interpretation as *Some A's
are B's.* Figure 10-4 shows the Venn-diagram representations of these favored
interpretations. Each statement now is interpreted by a single Venn diagram.
In contrast, as illustrated in Figure 10-2, the correct interpretation of these
statements often involves multiple Venn diagrams. Thus, subjects have simplified the Venn-diagram interpretations of the statements by conversion.
These simplified interpretations make reasoning about syllogisms easier, if
less correct. Figure 10-4 also shows how, given these representations, subjects
would make an atmosphere error of accepting the following syllogism:

>All *A*'s are *B*'s.
>All *C*'s are *B*'s.
>∴ All *A*'s are *C*'s.

Ceraso and Provitera (1971) have shown that when the premises were
stated less ambiguously, subjects made many fewer errors. For instance, in
their experiment, *All A's are B's* was stated as *All A's are B's but some B's are
not A's.* This more explicit expression should discourage subjects from making erroneous conversions.

Like the atmosphere heuristic itself, this conversion heuristic will lead to
fairly good performance but will yield errors on certain critical problems.
These errors will tend to be in accord with the atmosphere hypothesis.

Another explanation of subjects' reasoning behavior, developed by Johnson-Laird and Steedman (1978), is that the subject actually creates a little
world that satisfies the premises. (A similar idea has been proposed by Guyote
and Sternberg, 1981). Consider these premises:

(a)

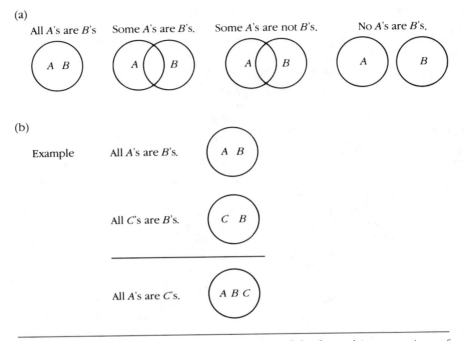

(b)

Figure 10-4 (a) Venn-diagram representations of the favored interpretations of each of the categorical statements. (b) An example of the combination of these interpretations.

> All the artists are beekeepers.
>
> Some of the beekeepers are chemists.

A subject might imagine a group of artists who are beekeepers, perhaps add some additional beekeepers who are not artists, and then imagine that some of the beekeepers are chemists. To illustrate this possibility more specifically, let us suppose that for the premises above the subject imagines four individuals. Individuals 1, 2, and 3 are artists but 4 is not. All four are beekeepers. Individuals 2 and 4 are chemists. The subject inspects this group, notes that individual 2 is both an artist and a chemist and concludes,

> Some artists are chemists.

Thus, the subject is building a specific model for the premises and inspecting this to see what is true in that model. Again, this kind of reasoning pattern is a fairly good heuristic but will lead to errors, as in the example above. Johnson-Laird has developed this idea to explain why subjects are more likely to come up with conclusions when the premises have one form rather than another (refer to the discussion on p. 274).

Yet another hypothesis, suggested by Chapman and Chapman (1959) and Henle (1962), is that subjects decide not to work within the difficult framework of logical reasoning, but that they revert to the probabilistic kind of reasoning that serves them well in many natural-world situations. For instance, they might reason

Some plants with leaves of three are poisonous.

Some of the plants in my yard have leaves of three.

Therefore, some of the plants in my yard are probably poisonous.

This kind of reasoning pattern is very useful in a world where little is certain. Such a reasoning pattern might be imported into the laboratory situation when the subject cannot find any other way to reason. Again, this probabilistic heuristic will lead to atmosphere errors.

Categorical Syllogisms: A Summary

Current theory on categorical syllogisms is quite fragmented. One researcher will propose that subjects use an atmosphere heuristic, another that they search Venn-diagram-like models, and another that they use probabilistic reasoning. Many baroque combinations and variations of these hypotheses appear as well. It seems clear to me that subjects use many different heuristics. Dominowski (1977), looking at patterns of response for individual subjects, found evidence that different subjects were using different heuristics.

Inductive Reasoning

We now turn from considering deductive reasoning to considering inductive reasoning. To illustrate the difference between inductively valid and deductively valid conclusions, consider the following argument:

The Abkhasian Republic of the USSR has 10 men over 160.

No other place in the world has a man over 160.

1. The oldest man in the world today is in the USSR.

2. The oldest man in the world tomorrow will be in the USSR.

Conclusion 1 is deductively valid. If the premises are true (and I don't know if they are, but this is irrelevant), then the conclusion must be true. However, conclusion 2 is only inductively valid; that is, it is a highly likely conclusion if the premises are true, but is conceivable that all 10 men could die before tomorrow.

Two major difficulties can be identified with respect to inductive reasoning. First, evaluating a particular inductive conclusion is often hard. Consider the predicament of Jane as she tries to evaluate the following argument:

Often when Jane turns around in class, Dick is looking at her.

Dick keeps asking Jane for suggestions on his homework.

Dick has stopped seeing Janice.

Therefore, Dick has a crush on Jane.

Many other possible explanations for Dick's behavior certainly exist, and evaluating the probability of the conclusion given the premises is extremely difficult for Jane. Indeed, in trying to evaluate this hypothesis, basically Jane would be engaging in a problem-solving activity.

The second difficulty in inductive reasoning occurs when only the premises are provided and we must come up with a conclusion. This is the process of hypothesis formation. As with deductive reasoning, deciding what conclusion, if any, should be drawn can be quite difficult. Consider the following premises:

The first number in the series is 1.

The second number in the series is 3.

The third number in the series is 7.

What conclusions follows: One possible conclusion is that

1. The fourth number in the series is 15.

However, a better conclusion would probably be

2. The nth number in the series is $2^n - 1$.

This conclusion seems better because it is general and so describes the whole series. However, it might not be the correct conclusion. For instance, the series might actually obey the following rule:

3. The nth number is $n^2 - n + 1$.

Of course, this conclusion predicts that the fourth number in the series will be 13, whereas conclusion 2 predicts that the fourth number will be 15. However, the original three premises provide no means of selecting between the two extrapolations. This fact reflects the important feature of induction: We can never know for sure whether a conclusion is true or whether some other conclusion would be better. Thus, it is often hard to find an inductive conclusion; and once a set of possible conclusions has been found, it is often hard to decide which is the best of the set.

Research in cognitive psychology has tended to study separately each of these two aspects of inductive reasoning, *hypothesis formation* and *hypothesis evaluation*. The remaining two sections of this chapter will cover these two major research domains.

Hypothesis Formation
Concept Identification

We begin our discussion of hypothesis formation with a review of some of the significant results from the *concept-identification* or *concept-formation* literature. This material derives from one of the older research traditions in cognitive psychology. Historically, this domain is important not only because it studies hypothesis formation, but also because it was one area in which cognitive psychology first successfully broke from the predominant behaviorist traditions of the 1950s and early 1960s. It is generally regarded now as shedding light on how people do conscious hypothesis formation and not as relevant to how natural categories like *dog* are formed. The ideas about schemas in Chapter 5 are more relevant to the formation of natural categories.

As an example of a concept-formation task, consider the following:

A dax can be large, bright, red, and square.

A dax can be large, dull, red, and square.

A dax cannot be small, dull, red, and square.

A dax cannot be large, bright, red, and triangular.

A dax can be large, dull, blue, and square.

What is a dax?

The best answer is probably that a dax is a large square. With carefully controlled material such as that in the concept-formation example above, researchers have discovered a good deal about how people form inductive hypotheses.

A classic series of studies of concept identification was reported by Bruner, Goodnow, and Austin (1956). Figure 10-5 illustrates the kind of material that they used. The stimuli were all rectangular boxes containing various objects. The stimuli varied on four dimensions: number of objects (one, two, or three); number of borders around the boxes (one, two, or three); shape (cross, circle, or square); and color (green, black, and red, represented in the figure

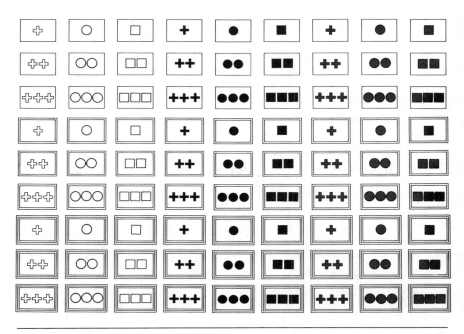

Figure 10-5 Material used by Bruner et al. in one of their studies of concept identification (1956). The array consists of instances formed by combinations of four attributes, each exhibiting three values. Open (white) shapes represent green figures, solid shapes represent black figures, and gray shapes represent red figures. (*A Study of Thinking*. Copyright 1956. Reprinted by permission of John Wiley & Sons, Inc.)

by white, black, and gray, respectively). Subjects were told that they were to discover some concept that described a particular subset of these instances. For instance, the concept might have been black crosses. Subjects were to discover the correct concept on the basis of information they were given about what were and what were not instances of the concept.

Figure 10-6 contains three illustrations (the three columns) of the information subjects might have been presented. Each column consists of a sequence of instances identified either as members of the concept (positive, +) or not (negative, −). Each column represents a different concept. Subjects would be presented with the instances in a column one at a time. From these instances subjects would determine what the concept was. Stop reading and try to determine the concept for each column.

The concept in the first example is *two crosses*. This concept is referred to as a *conjunctive* concept, since the conjunction of a number of features (in this case the features are *two* and *cross*) must be present for the instance to be positive. Subjects typically find conjunctive concepts easiest to discover. In some sense conjunctive hypotheses seem to be the most "natural" kind

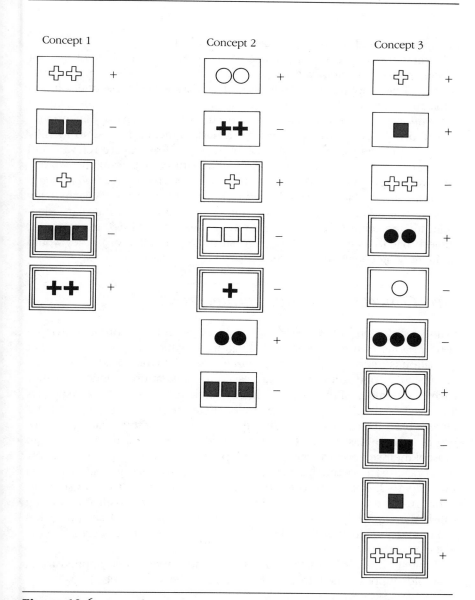

Figure 10-6 Examples of sequences of instances from which a subject is to identify concepts. Each column gives a sequence of instances and noninstances for a different concept. A plus (+) signals a positive instance and a minus (−) a negative instance.

of hypotheses and the type that has been researched most extensively. The solution to the second example is *two borders or circles*. This kind of concept is referred to as a *disjunctive concept*, since an instance is a member of the concept if either of the features is present. In the final example, the solution is that the number of objects must equal the number of borders. This example is a *relational concept*, since it specifies a relationship between two dimensions.

The problems in this series are particularly difficult, because to identify the concept a subject must both determine which features are relevant and discover the kind of rule that connects the features (e.g., conjunctive, disjunctive, or relational). The former problem is referred to as *attribute identification* and the latter as *rule learning* (Haygood & Bourne, 1965). In many experiments, either the form of the rule or the relevant attributes are identified for the subject. For instance, in the Bruner et al. (1956) experiments, subjects had to identify only the correct attributes. They knew that they would be identifying conjunctive concepts.

Two Concept-Formation Strategies

Bruner et al. were interested in how subjects would go about identifying a concept. One of the experimental situations in which they studied concept formation is referred to as the *reception paradigm*. In this paradigm, subjects see instances one at a time and are asked to judge at presentation whether each is a member of the category. After making their classifications, subjects are given feedback as to whether their classifications were correct. It is inferred that subjects have identified the concept when they make no more errors in their classification. Bruner et al. discovered that in this paradigm most of their subjects spontaneously adopted one of two strategies to identify the concept. The optimal strategy, called the *wholist strategy* and described in Table 10-2, was adopted to some degree by 65 percent of the subjects. Table 10-2 is a 2 × 2 matrix in which the situations are classified according to whether a positive or negative instance of the concept has been presented (columns) and whether the subject has correctly or incorrectly classified the instance (rows).

Table 10-2 is a bit abstract and is best understood when applied to an example. Suppose, then, that the first stimulus the subject sees is

> one border, one green square,

and that this is a positive instance. The table specifies that all the features in this first positive instance be taken as the hypothesis. That is, subjects will hypothesize that the concept is defined by the conjunction of the features *one border, one object, green color,* and *square shape*. If subjects are then presented with

Table 10-2   *The wholist strategy for concept identification*

Summary of strategy:
Take the set of all the features of the first positive instance as the initial hypothesis.
Then, as more instances are presented eliminate any feature in this set that does
not occur with a positive instance.

Classifications	Positive instance	Negative instance
Correct	Maintain the hypothesis now in force.	Maintain the hypothesis now in force.
Incorrect	Take as the next hypothesis what the old hypothesis and the present instance have in common.	Impossible unless we have misreckoned.

one border, two red circles,

they would judge this instance not to be a member of the category because it does not match the hypothesis. Suppose this judgment is correct; this condition is described in the upper right cell of Table 10-2, and the hypothesis is kept. Then suppose subjects are presented with

two borders, one green square.

They would also judge this instance not to be a member of the category. But suppose they are wrong and that this is a positive instance. This case is described in the lower left cell, and subjects take as their new hypothesis what the old hypothesis and the current instance have in common:

one green square.

Suppose they are now presented with

three borders, one green square.

They would classify this as an instance of the category and would be told that they are correct. They would then be in the condition described by the upper left cell, and would keep the hypothesis. Finally, assume that subjects are presented with

one border, two green crosses.

They would say that this is not an instance of the category, but suppose it is. Again, the situation is that of the lower left cell of Table 10-2, and subjects would make a new hypothesis,

green,

the feature that the old hypothesis and new instance have in common.

Table 10-3 *Partist strategy for concept identification*

Summary of strategy:
Begin with part of the first positive instance as a hypothesis (i.e., choose just a subset of the features in the instance). Then, as more instances are presented, retain the hypothesis or change it to be consistent with the instances.

Classifications	Positive instance	Negative instance
Correct	Maintain hypothesis now in force.	Maintain hypothesis now in force.
Incorrect	Change hypothesis to make it consistent with past instances; in other words, choose a hypothesis not previously disconfirmed.	Change hypothesis to make it consistent with past instances; in other words, choose a hypothesis not previously disconfirmed.

It is impossible, if subjects follow this wholist strategy faithfully, for them ever to make an error on a negative instance (lower right cell of Table 10-2). Note that subjects have to revise the hypothesis only when they fail to identify an instance (lower left cell). They never have to change the hypothesis when they are correct (upper cells). The wholist strategy is relatively easy to follow, for it requires that subjects remember only the current hypothesis, not past instances. Of the subjects who attempted to follow the wholist strategy in the Bruner et al. study, 47 percent were able to do so without ever deviating from the prescriptions of Table 10-2.

The other common subject strategy Bruner et al. detected they called the *partist strategy*. In this strategy, subjects started with a conjunctive hypothesis that was consistent with the first positive instance. It would involve some subset of the features contained in that instance. Thus, this strategy differs at the start from the wholist strategy, where subjects take as their first hypothesis *all* the features in the first positive instance. Table 10-3 describes the behavior of an "ideal" partist subject after the first trial (I use the word *ideal* because subjects often did not conform perfectly to this strategy). Subjects' behavior is presented in the same format as in Table 10-2 in order to facilitate comparison. When subjects are correct, they maintain the hypothesis. Here the partist strategy does not differ from the wholist strategy. When subjects are wrong, however, they try to select a new hypothesis consistent with the past items. This process requires memory for all the past items, and subjects often fail at this point because they are unable to remember past items. Bruner et al. classified 35 percent of their subjects as following a partist strategy. Of these, only 38 percent were able to behave in accord with Table 10-3 consistently over five trials.

The reason that the partist strategy is less useful than the wholist strategy for identifying conjunctive concepts lies in the initially formed hypothesis.

In the wholist strategy, all the potentially relevant information from the first instance is kept in the initial hypothesis, whereas in the partist strategy some potentially relevant features are dropped out. In the wholist strategy, a feature is dropped from the hypothesis only when it is proven irrelevant. The partist strategy can be seen as the outcome of an inappropriate application of a similarity heuristic (discussed in Chapter 8) to the task of hypothesis search. Subjects believe that the correct concept will involve a conjunction of one, two, or at most three of the features in the first instance. Therefore, they try to maximize the similarity between the first hypothesis and the eventual correct hypothesis by including only one, two, or three features in the initial hypothesis.

Using Negative Information

Subjects have particular difficulty in the proper use of negative information, that is, information about what is *not* an instance of a category. Consider a concept-learning experiment in which the stimuli vary on three binary (two-valued) dimensions—size (large and small), shape (circle and triangle), and color (red and yellow). Suppose subjects are trying to learn a concept defined on a single feature (e.g., small) and are presented with the following negative instance:

large red triangle.

It is the case that subjects could calculate from this negative instance that the following is a positive instance:

small yellow circle,

which is just the opposite of the first instance on each dimension. The relationship of these instances illustrate a general rule applying to single-feature concepts with binary dimensions:

Each negative instance is equivalent to a positive instance with all values switched.

This rule also means that if subjects are presented with

small yellow triangle

as a positive instance, they can know that one negative instance is the stimulus with the above values switched:

large red circle

Thus, in this experimental situation, positive and negative examples are perfectly equivalent in the information they offer subjects. However, subjects do better given positive evidence, examples of the category, than given negative evidence, nonexamples of the category (Hovland & Weiss, 1953; Johnson, 1972). Subjects obviously are not aware of the informational equivalence of positive and negative instances, and they find it difficult to use examples that violate the concept to infer what the concept is.

Seeking Disconforming Information

An experiment by Wason (1960) shows that, in addition to being poor at using negative information, subjects fail to seek negative information. In his experiment, subjects were told that three numbers—2, 4, and 6—conformed to a simple relational rule. Subjects were to discover that rule by generating various triads of numbers and giving their reason for each of their choices. They were told whether each triad generated conformed to the rule. They were to announce the rule when they thought they had identified it. The protocol below comes from one of Wason's subjects. Each triad the subject produced and the reason for the choice are included, along with the experimenter's feedback as to whether the triad conformed to the rule. The sequence of triads was occasionally broken when the subject decided to announce a hypothesis. The experimenter's feedback for each hypothesis is given in parentheses.

Triad	Reason Given for Triad	Feedback
8 10 12	Two added each time.	yes
14 16 18	Even numbers in order of magnitude.	yes
20 22 24	Same reason.	yes
1 3 5	Two added to preceding number.	yes

Announcement: *The rule is that by starting with any number, 2 is added each time to form the next number.* (Incorrect)

2 6 10	The middle number is the arithmetic mean of the other two.	yes
1 50 99	Same reason.	yes

Announcement: *The rule is that the middle number is the arithmetric mean of the other two.* (Incorrect)

3 10 17	Same number, 7, added each time.	yes
0 3 6	Three added each time.	yes

Announcement: *The rule is that the difference between two numbers next to each other is the same.* (Incorrect)

12 8 4	The same number is subtracted each time to form the next number.	no

Announcement: *The rule is adding a number, always the same one, to form the next number.* (Incorrect)

1 4 9 Any three numbers in order of magnitude   yes
Announcement: *The rule is any three numbers in order of magnitude.* (Correct)

The important feature to note about this protocol is that the subject tested the hypothesis by generating sequences mainly consistent with it. The correct procedure would have been to try sequences that were inconsistent also. That is, the subject should have looked for negative evidence. It is easy to start out with a hypothesis that is too narrow and to miss the more general correct hypothesis. The only way to discover this error is to try examples that disconfirm your hypothesis, but this is just what people have great difficulty doing.

In another experiment, Wason (1968) asked 16 subjects, after they had announced their hypotheses, what they would do to determine whether their hypotheses were incorrect. Nine subjects said they would generate only instances consistent with their hypotheses and wait for one to be identified as not an instance of the concept. Only four subjects said that they would generate instances inconsistent with the hypothesis to see if they were identified as members of the concept. The remaining three insisted that their hypotheses could not be incorrect.

Summary of Hypothesis Formation

Subjects seem to have at least two difficulties in hypothesis formation. One is keeping track of the requisite information. A subject may have to keep track of many instances, each of which has many features. The power of strategies such as the wholist strategy is that they summarize the information for the subject in a condensed form that is easier to remember. The second difficulty subjects have is realizing the information value in negative information and utilizing that negative information. This deficit may be the same as their inability to use modus tollens in deductive reasoning.

Hypothesis Evaluation

In the discussions of concept-identification and rule-induction tasks, the means of deciding if a hypothesis fit the facts and the degree to which it fit were fairly obvious. Consider, however, the following case. Suppose I come home and find the door to my house ajar. I am interested in the hypothesis that this might be the work of a burglar. How do I evaluate this hypothesis? The problem of hypothesis evaluation in this situation is more complicated than in a concept-formation experiment for two reasons. First, in concept-identification situations such as those discussed in the preceding section, each hypothesis (that is a square, black, a triangle, and so on) is equally likely to be true from the beginning. This is not the case in the open-door mystery (where the two competing hypotheses are that the home has been burglarized and that it has not been burglarized). Before I noted that the door was open, I would have estimated the probability that my home had not been burglarized as high and the probability that it had been burglarized as correspondingly low. These unequal prior probabilities should have some influence on my hypothesis evaluation.

Second, the connection between hypotheses and observations is not absolute, as it is in a concept-identification experiment. In the latter, if the correct hypothesis is that the concept is black, then a large black triangle with two borders must be an instance of the concept. However, even if the hypothesis that my house has been burglarized is correct, it need not be the case that the door will be open. Perhaps the probability of this connection is only 80 percent.

Bayes's Theorem

Bayes's theorem provides a method for evaluating hypotheses in situations, such as that cited above, in which hypotheses vary in their prior probability and the connection between evidence and hypothesis is only probabilistic. The theorem is a mathematical prescription for estimating the posterior probability that a hypothesis is true from the prior probability that the hypothesis is true and the conditional probability of a piece of evidence given the hypothesis.

Prior probabilities are the probabilities that a hypothesis is true before evidence. Let us refer to the hypothesis that my house has been burglarized as H. Suppose that I know from police statistics that the probability (P) of a house in my neighborhood being burglarized on any particular day is 1 in 1000. This probability is expressed as

$$P(H) = .001.$$

This equation expresses the prior probability of the hypothesis, or the probability of the hypothesis's being true before the evidence. We will refer to this hypothesis as H. The other prior probability needed is the probability that the house has not been burglarized. This alternate hypothesis is denoted $\overline{H}$. This value is 1 minus $P(H)$ and is

$P(\overline{H}) = .999.$

A *conditional probability* is the probability that a particular type of evidence is true if a particular hypothesis is true. Let us consider what the conditional probabilities of the evidence (door ajar) would be under the two hypotheses. Suppose I believe that the probability of the door's being ajar is quite high if I have been burglarized, say 4 out of 5. Let E denote the evidence, or the event of the door being ajar. Then we will denote this conditional probability by

$P(E|H) = .8,$

which should be read *the probability of* E *given that* H is true. Second, we determine the probability of E if H is not true. Suppose I know that chances are only 1 out of 100 that the door would be ajar if no burglary had occurred (e.g., by accident, neighbors with a key). This we denote by

$P(E|\overline{H}) = .01,$

the probability of E *given that* H *is not true.*

The *posterior probability* is the probability of a hypothesis's being true after some evidence. The notation $P(H|E)$ is the posterior probability of hypothesis H given evidence E. According to Bayes's theorem, we can calculate the posterior probability of H, that the house has been burglarized, in light of the evidence thus:

$$P(H|E) = \frac{P(E|H) \cdot P(H)}{P(E|H) \cdot P(H) + P(E|\overline{H}) \cdot P(\overline{H})}. \tag{1}$$

Given our assumed values, we can solve for $P(H|E)$ by substituting into equation 1:

$$P(H|E) = \frac{(.8)(.001)}{(.8)(.001) + (.01)(.999)} = .074.$$

Thus, the probability that my house has been burglarized is still less than 8 in 100. Note that this probability is true even though an open door is good evidence for a burglary and not for a normal state of affairs, $P(E|H) = .8$, and $P(E|\overline{H}) = .01$. The posterior probability is still quite low because the prior probability of H—$P(H) = .001$—was low to begin with. Relative to that low start, the posterior probability has been drastically revised upward.

A formal derivation of Bayes's theorem is given in the appendix to this chapter. Table 10-4 offers an informal explanation of Bayes's theorem as applied to the burglary example (adapted from Hayes, 1981). There are four possible states of affairs, determined by whether the burglary hypothesis is true or not and by whether there is the evidence of an open door or not. The probability of each state of affairs is set forth in the four cells of Table

Table 10-4 *An analysis of Bayes's theorem*

Evidence	Burglarized (H)	Not burglarized ($\overline{H}$)	Sum of probabilites
Door open (E)	$P(E\|H)P(H)$ = .00080	$P(E\|\overline{H})P(\overline{H})$ = .00999	.01079
Door not open ($\overline{E}$)	$P(\overline{E}\|H)P(H)$ = .00020	$P(\overline{E}\|\overline{H})P(\overline{H})$ = .98901	.98921
Sum of probabilities	.00100	.99900	1.00000

10-4. The probability of each state is the prior probability of that hypothesis times the conditional probability of the event given the hypothesis. For instance, consider the upper left cell. Since $P(H)$ is .001 and $P(E|H)$ is .8, the probability in that cell is .0008. The four probabilities in these cells must sum to 1. Given the evidence that the door is open, we can eliminate the two cells in the lower row of the table. Since one of the two remaining states of affairs must be the case, the posterior probabilities of the two remaining states must sum to 1. Bayes's theorem provides us with a means for recalculating the probabilities of the states in light of evidence that makes impossible one row of the matrix. What we have done in equation 1 in calculating the posterior probability is taken the probability of the upper left cell, where hypotheses H is true, and divided it by the sum of the probabilities in the two upper cells, which represent the only two possible states of affairs.

Bayes's theorem rests on a mathematical analysis of the nature of probability. The formula has been proven to evaluate hypotheses correctly; thus it enables us to determine precisely the posterior probability of a hypothesis given the prior and conditional probabilities. The theorem serves as a *prescriptive*, or *normative*, *model* specifying the means of evaluating the probability of a hypothesis. Such a model contrasts with a *descriptive model*, which specifies what people actually do.

Deviations from Bayes's Theorem

It should come as no surprise to learn that humans typically do not behave perfectly in accord with the Bayesian model. Ward Edwards (1968) has extensively investigated how people use new information to adjust their estimates of the probabilities of various hypotheses. In one experiment, he presented subjects with two bags, each containing 100 poker chips. One of the bags contained 70 red chips and 30 blue and the other contained 70 blue chips and 30 red. The experimenter chose one of the bags at random and the subjects' task was to decide which bag had been chosen.

In the absence of any prior information, the probability that the chosen bag contained predominantly red chips was 50 percent. Thus,

$$P(H_R) = .50 \text{ and } P(H_B) = .50$$

where H_R is the hypothesis of a predominantly red bag and H_B is the hypothesis of a predominantly blue bag. To obtain further information, subjects sampled chips at random from the bag. Suppose the first chip drawn was red. The conditional probability of drawing a red chip if most of the chips in the bag are red is

$$P(R|H_R) = .70.$$

Similarly, the conditional probability of drawing a red chip from a blue-majority bag is

$$P(R|H_B) = .30.$$

Now, we can calculate the posterior probability of the bag's being predominantly red given the red chip by applying equation 1 to this situation:

$$P(H_R|R) = \frac{P(R|H_R) \cdot P(H_R)}{P(R|H_R) \cdot P(H_R) + P(R|H_B) \cdot P(H_B)}$$
$$= \frac{(.70) \cdot (.50)}{(.70) \cdot (.50) + (.30) \cdot (.50)} = .70.$$

This result seems, to both naive and sophisticated observers, to be a rather sharp increase in probabilities. Typically, human subjects do not increase their probability of a red-majority bag to .70; rather, they make a more conservative revision to a value such as .60.

After this first drawing, the experiment continues: The poker is put back in the bag and a second chip is drawn at random. Suppose this chip too is red. Again, by applying Bayes's theorem, we can show that the posterior probability of a red bag is .84. Suppose our observations continued for 10 more trials and after all 12 we have observed 8 reds and 4 blues. By continuing the Bayesian analysis, we could show that the new posterior probability of the hypothesis of a red bag is .97. Subjects who see this sequence of 12 trials only estimate subjectively a posterior probability of .75 or less for the red bag. Edwards has used the term *conservative* to refer to subjects' tendency to underestimate the force of evidence. He estimates that they use between a half and a fifth of the available evidence from each chip.

Another problem is that subjects sometimes ignore prior probabilities. Kahneman and Tversky (1973) told one group of subjects that an individual had been chosen at random from a set of 100 individuals consisting of 70 engineers and 30 lawyers. This group of subjects was termed the engineer-high group. A second group, the engineer-low group, was told that the individual came from a set of 30 engineers and 70 lawyers. Both groups were asked to determine the probability that the individual chosen at random from the group would be an engineer given no information about the individual. Subjects were able to respond with the right prior probabilities: The engineer-high group estimated .70 and the engineer-low group estimated .30. Then subjects were told that another person was chosen from the population and they were given the following description:

> Jack is a 45-year-old man. He is married and has four children. He is generally conservative, careful, and ambitious. He shows no interest in political and social issues and spends most of his free time on his many hobbies, which include home carpentry, sailing, and mathematical puzzles.

Subjects in both groups gave a .90 probability estimate to the hypothesis that this person was an engineer. No difference was displayed between the two groups, which had been given different prior probabilities for an engineer hypothesis. But Bayes's theorem prescribes that prior probability should have a strong effect, resulting in a higher posterior probability from the engineer-high group than the engineer-low group.

The following sample description was also used by Kahneman and Tversky:

> Dick is a 30-year-old man. He is married with no children. A man of high ability and high motivation, he promises to be quite successful in his field. He is well liked by his colleagues.

This example was designed to provide no diagnostic information either way with respect to Dick's profession. According to Bayes's theorem, the posterior probability of the engineer hypothesis should be the same as the prior probability, since this description is not informative. However, both the engineer-high and the engineer-low groups estimated that the probabiltiy was .50 that the individual described was an engineer. Thus, they allowed a completely uninformative event to change their probabilities. Again, subjects were shown to be completely unable to use prior probabilities in assessing the posterior probability of a hypothesis.

The failure to take prior probabilities into account can lead an individual to make some totally unwarranted conclusions. For instance, suppose you take a test for cancer. It is known that a particular type of cancer will result in a positive test 95 percent of the time. On the other hand, if a person does not have the cancer, there is only a 5 percent probability of a positive result. Suppose you are informed that your result is positive. If you are like most people, you will assume that your chances of having the cancer are 95 out of 100, and begin saying good-bye to your friends (Hammerton, 1973). You would be overreacting in assuming that the cancer would be fatal, but you would also be making a fundamental error in probability estimation. What is the error?

You would have failed to consider the base rate for the particular type of cancer in question. Suppose, only 1 in 10,000 people have this cancer. This would be your prior probability. Now, with this information you would be able to determine the posterior probability of your having the cancer. Bringing out the Bayesian formula, you would express the problem this way:

$$P(H|E) = \frac{P(H)P(E|H)}{P(H)P(E|H) + P(\overline{H})P(E|\overline{H})}$$

where the prior probability of the cancer hypothesis is $P(H) = .0001$, and $P(\overline{H}) = .9999$, $P(E|H) = .95$, and $P(E|\overline{H}) = .05$. Thus,

$$P(H|E) = \frac{(.0001)(.95)}{(.0001)(.95) + (.9999)(.05)} = .0019.$$

That is, the posterior probability of your having the cancer would still be less than 1 in 500.

Judgments of Probability

To understand why subjects do not operate according to Bayes's theorem in evaluating evidence, it is necessary to understand how they reason about probabilities. They certainly do not think about probabilities by performing mentally the kinds of arithmetic operations (additions, multiplications, and divisions) called for by Bayes's theorem. A number of experiments have asked subjects to make judgments of probabilities. In some circumstances they can do this quite accurately. Consider an experiment by Shuford (1961). He presented arrays such as that in Figure 10-7 to subjects for 1 sec. He then asked subjects to judge the proportion of vertical bars relative to horizontal bars. The numbers of vertical bars varied from 10 to 90 percent in different matrices. Shuford's results are shown in Figure 10-8. As can be seen, subjects' estimates are quite close to the true proportions.

Another experiment to assess judgments as to proportion was performed by Robinson (1964). He presented his subjects with a sequence of flashes from a left light and a right light. The task was to estimate the proportion of left or right flashes in the sequence. Again, subjects were very accurate in making these estimates. Their estimates fell within .02 of the true proportions.

In both of these experiments, subjects were not actually estimating *prob-*

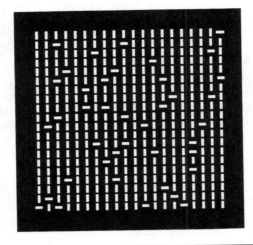

Figure 10-7   A random matrix composed of 90 percent vertical bars and 10 percent horizontal bars, presented to subjects to determine their accuracy in judging proportions. (From Shuford, 1961. Copyright 1961 by the American Psychological Association. Reprinted by permission.)

abilities: rather, they were estimating the *proportions* of a type of event in a population. However, it seems that people think of probabilities in terms of proportion in a population—and, indeed, the mathematics of probability is based on a concept very close to this. In the two experiments cited, subjects were able to make an unbiased inspection of the population; thus, their estimates were unbiased. They could see all the instances. However, as we will see, in many probability-estimation situations, we do not have total and unbiased access to the underlying population. It is in such situations that distortions in probability estimates occur.

Availability

Consider the following experiment reported by Tversky and Kahneman (1974), which demonstrates that probability judgments can be biased by differential availability of examples. They asked subjects to judge the proportion of words in the language that fit certain characteristics. For instance, they asked subjects to estimate the proportion of English words that begin with a *k* versus words with a *k* in third position. How might subjects perform this task? One obvious heuristic is to briefly try to think of words that satisfy the specification and words that do not and to estimate the relative proportion of target words. How many words can you think of that begin with *k*? How many words can

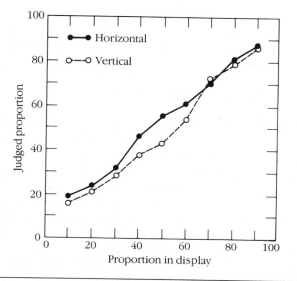

Figure 10-8 Mean estimated proportion as a function of the true proportion. Subjects exhibited a fairly accurate ability to estimate the proportions of vertical and horizontal bars in Figure 10-7. (From Shuford, 1961. Copyright 1961 by the American Psychological Association. Reprinted by permission.)

you think of that don't? What is your estimate of their relative proportion? Now how many words can you think of that have *k* in the third position? How many words can you think of that don't? What is their relative proportion? Subjects estimated that more words begin with *k* than have *k* in their third position. In actual fact, three times as many words have *k* in third positions as begin with *k*.

As in this experiment, many real-life circumstances require that we estimate probabilities without having direct access to the population that these probabilities describe. In such cases, we must rely on memory as the source for our estimates. The memory factors we studied in Chapters 6 and 7 serve to explain how such estimates can be biased. Under the reasonable assumption that words are more strongly associated to their first letter than their third letter, the bias exhibited in the experimental results can be explained in terms of the spreading-activation theory (Chapter 6). In the case of these gross overestimates of words beginning with particular letters, with the focus of attention on, say, *k*, activation will spread from that letter to words beginning with it. This process will tend to make words beginning with *k* more available than other words. Thus, these words will be overrepresented in the sample that subjects take from memory to estimate the true proportion in the population. The same overestimation does not occur for words with *k* in the third position, since words are unlikely to be directly associated to the letters that occur in their third position. Therefore, it is not possible to associatively prime these words and make them more available.

Similarity (The Gambler's Fallacy)

Other factors besides memory lead to biases in probability estimates. Consider another example from Tversky and Kahneman (1974). Which of the following sequences of six tosses from a fair coin is more likely (where H denotes *heads* and T *tails*): H T H T T H or H H H H H H? Many people think that the first sequence is more likely to occur, but the two sequences are actually equally probable. The probability of the first sequence is the probability of H on the first toss (which is .50) times the probability of T on the second toss (which is .50), times the probability of H on the third toss (which is .50), and so on. The probability of the whole sequence is .50 × .50 × .50 × .50 × .50 × .50 = .016. Similarly, the probability of the second sequence is the product of the probabilities of each coin toss and the probability of a head on each coin toss is .50. Thus, the final probability again is also .50 × .50 × .50 × .50 × .50 × .50 = .016. Why do some people have the illusion that the first sequence is more probable? It is because the first event seems similar to a lot of other events, for example, H T H T H T or H T T H T H. These similar events serve to bias upward a person's probability estimate of the target event. On the other hand, H H H H H H, straight heads, seems unlike any other event, and its probability will therefore not be biased upward by other similar sequences. In conclusion, a person's estimate of the probability of an event will be biased by other events that are similar to it.

Note that the effect of this fallacy is that subjects underestimate the frequency of runs of events, such as straight heads. This tendency to underestimate leads to a common phenomenon known as the *gambler's fallacy*. The fallacy is the belief that if an event has not occurred for a while, then it is more likely by the "law of averages" to occur in the near future. This phenomenon can be demonstrated in an experimental setting, for instance, where subjects see a sequence of coin tosses and must guess whether each toss will be a head or a tail. If they see a string of heads, they become more and more likely to guess that tails will come up on the next trial. Casino operators count on this fallacy to help them make money. Players who have had a string of losses at a table will keep playing, assuming that by the "law of averages" they will experience a compensating string of wins. However, the game is set in favor of the house. The dice do not know or care whether a gambler has had a string of losses. The consequence is that players tend to lose more as they try to recoup their losses. The "law of averages" is itself a fallacy.

The gambler's fallacy can be used to advantage in certain situations—for instance, at the racetrack. Most racetracks operate by a pari-mutuel system, in which the odds on a horse are determined by the number of people betting on the horse. By the end of the day, if favorites have won all the races, people tend to doubt that another favorite can win, and they switch their bets to the long shots. As a consequence, the betting odds on the favorite deviate from what they should be, and a person can sometimes make money by betting on the favorite.

Remarks and Suggested Readings

A good introduction to logic is Suppes (1957). A number of texts offer a more formal and technical development in logic, including Mendelson (1964), Church (1956), Kleene (1952), Schoenfield (1967), and Robbin (1969). Church's text is particularly significant as a standard in the field and provides discussions of many of the important conceptual issues. It is probably better to study mathematical logic as part of a formal course than just out of a textbook. Such courses are offered by many college departments, including philosophy, mathematics, and computer science.

A number of books and some edited collections of papers review research on deductive reasoning. Among these are Wason and Johnson-Laird (1972) and Falmagne (1975). Other important papers in the field are those of Erickson (1974), Johnson-Laird and Steedman (1978), Taplin (1971), Taplin and Staudenmayer (1973), and Rips and Marcus (1977). Among the important "classic" papers are those by Woodworth and Sells (1935), Chapman and Chapman (1959), and Henle (1962). The work of Newell and Simon provides a distinctive approach to logic and is extensively presented in their 1972 book. Newell (1980) has recently written a paper forcefully advancing the view that deductive reasoning is problem solving. Osherson, in a series of books and perhaps most clearly in his 1975 paper, has argued for a logiclike analysis of human deduction. Rips (in press) gives a more recent argument for this position, responding to some of the points by Newell.

A good introduction to the philosophy of inductive logic is the book by Skyrms (1966). A number of textbooks offer a thorough review of the concept-formation literature; these include Bourne (1966); Johnson (1972); Bourne, Ekstrand, and Dominowski (1971); and Kintsch (1970). Trabasso and Bower (1968) is an important book on concept formation. Levine (1975) provides a collection of papers spanning the history of research on concept formation. Bruner et al. (1956) remains a classic well worth reading. Simon and Lea (1974) provides a discussion of the similarity between inductive reasoning and problem solving. Tversky and Kahneman's (1974) *Science* article provides a good survey of their research on probabilistic judgment. The paper by

Slovic and Lichenstein (1971) contains an extensive review of psychological research on Bayes's theorem.

Appendix

A derivation of Bayes's theorem follows.

The posterior probability of a hypothesis if given evidence E is

$$P(H|E) = \frac{P(H \cap E)}{P(E)} \tag{1}$$

where $P(H \cap E)$ is the probability of both H and E being true and $P(E)$ is the probability of the evidence. We can express these as

$$P(H \cap E) = P(E|H)P(H) \tag{2}$$

and

$$P(E) = P(H \cap E) + P(\overline{H} \cap E) \tag{3}$$

where

$$P(\overline{H}) \cap E = P(E|\overline{H})P(\overline{H}). \tag{4}$$

In these equations, $P(\overline{H} \cap E)$ denotes the probability of both the hypothesis being false and the evidence still obtaining; $P(E|H)$ is the conditional probability of the evidence if the hypothesis is true; $P(E|\overline{H})$ is the conditional probability of the evidence if the hypothesis is false; $P(H)$ is the prior probability of the hypothesis; and $P(\overline{H}) = 1 - P(H)$. Substituting equations 2, 3 and 4 into equation 1, we get the form of Bayes's theorem that we have been using:

$$P(H|E) = \frac{P(E|H)P(H)}{P(E|H)P(H) + P(E|\overline{H})P(\overline{H})}.$$

Chapter 11

Language: An Overview

Summary

1. The linguist is concerned with characterizing our linguistic competence, which is our abstract knowledge about the structure of language. This concern contrasts with the psychologist's concern with language performance, which is how we actually use language.

2. The linguist wants to account for the productivity and regularity of language and the linguistic intuitions of language speakers. Productivity means that there are an infinite number of acceptable sentences. Regularity means that sentences have to satisfy a strict set of rules in order to be acceptable. Among the important linguistic intuitions are judgments of paraphrase and judgments of ambiguity.

3. The surface structure of a sentence is a hierarchical analysis of the sentence into phrases and subphrases.

4. Chomsky proposed transformational grammar to explain the regularities in the surface structures of different types of sentences. He proposed that similar deep structures underlie different sentences that have similar meanings, and that transformations are applied to these deep structures to produce the surface structures of these sentences.

5. There is little evidence for the psychological reality of transformations such as Chomsky has proposed. More recent linguistic theories have tried to account for syntactic regularities without reference to transformations.

6. It has long been debated whether language is dependent on thought, whether thought is dependent on language, or whether the two are independent of each other. The evidence is not decisive but favors the view that language is dependent on thought.

7. Human beings constitute the only species with a communication system that qualifies as a language. Recently, some efforts have been made to

teach languages to apes, but so far these efforts have failed in transmitting to the apes full language facility.

8. Chomsky and others have advanced the claim that language is a unique system within human cognition. They point to evidence from language acquisition. They claim there are linguistic universals that characterize all natural languages and that a child knows and uses to learn a language.

Of all the human beings' cognitive abilities, the use of language is the most impressive. The difference between human language and the natural communication systems of other species is enormous. More than anything else, language is responsible for the current advanced state of human civilization. It is the principal means by which knowledge is recorded and transmitted from one generation to the next. Without language there would be little technology. Language is the principal medium for establishing religions, laws, and moral conventions. Therefore, without language no means would exist for establishing rules to govern groups ranging in size from tennis partners to nations. Language also provides people with the principal means of assessing what another person knows. So, without language human beings would experience countless more misunderstandings than they currently do. Language provides an important medium for art, a means of getting to know people, and a valuable aid to courtship. Therefore, without language much of the joy of living would be lost. In its written form, language enables humans to communicate over spatial distance and through time, as this book demonstrates.

In this chapter, we will cover three general aspects of language. First, we will review the work in linguistics through which a characterization of the structure of language has been developing. Second, we will review the speculations and research about the possible relations between language and thought. Third, we will consider the issues surrounding the purported uniqueness of language to humans. With these general points as background, the following two chapters will explore in detail the two major aspects of language usage: comprehension and generation.

Throughout this chapter we will be discussing many ideas that were either proposed or strongly influenced by Noam Chomsky. Chomsky is an American linguist who began developing his theories in the 1950s at the University of Pennsylvania and then moved to the Massachusetts Institute of Technology, where he has been ever since. His work has had a revolutionary influence on linguistics, a powerful influence on cognitive psychology, and a lesser but important influence on other social sciences. His ideas are difficult to comprehend, and the psychological implications of his claims often seem obscure.

However, understanding his ideas is important not only because of their influence in cognitive psychology, but also because Chomsky is one of the major intellectual figures of our time.

The Structure of Language

Productivity and Regularity

The academic field of linguistics, which is distinct from psychology, attempts to characterize the nature of language. Although opinion and practice in linguistics vary widely, "average linguists" pursue their studies of language with little concern for how language is used. The fact that language is a functional human tool is largely irrelevant. Later in the chapter, we will discuss the competence–performance distinction, which linguists use to divorce their studies of the structure of language from the ways in which language is used. The linguist focuses on two aspects of language: its *productivity* and its *regularity*. The term productivity refers to the fact that an infinite number of utterances are possible in any language. Regularity refers to the fact that these utterances are systematic in many ways.

We need not seek far to convince ourselves of the highly productive and creative character of language. We have to only pick up a book and select a sentence from it at random. Suppose that, having chosen a sentence, an individual were instructed to go to the library and begin searching for a repetition of the sentence! Obviously, no sensible person would take up this challenge. But, were a person to try, it is very unlikely that he or she would find the sentence repeated among the billions of sentences in the library. Still, it is important to realize that the components that make up sentences are quite small in number: In English, only 26 letters, 40 phonemes (see the discussion in the "Speech Recognition" section of Chapter 3), and 100,000 words are used. Nevertheless, with these components we can and do generate trillions of novel sentences.

A look at the structure of sentences makes clear why this productivity is possible. Natural language has facilities for endlessly embedding structure within structure and coordinating structure with structure. A mildly amusing party game is to start with a simple sentence and require participants to keep adding to the sentence:

> The girl hit the boy.
>
> The girl hit the boy and he cried.
>
> The big girl hit the boy and he cried.

The big girl hit the boy and he cried loudly.

The big girl hit the boy who was misbehaving and he cried loudly.

The big girl with authoritarian instincts hit the boy who was misbehaving and he cried loudly.

The big girl with authoritarian instincts hit the boy who was misbehaving and he cried loudly and ran to his mother.

The big girl with authoritarian instincts hit the boy who was misbehaving and he cried loudly and ran to his mother who went to her husband.

The big girl with authoritarian instincts hit the boy who was misbehaving and he cried loudly and ran to his mother who went to her husband who called the police,

and so on until someone can no longer extend the sentence.

The fact that an infinite number of word strings can be generated would not be particularly interesting in itself. If we have 100,000 words for each position and if sentences can be of any length, it is not hard to see that a very large (in fact, an infinite) number of word strings is possible. However, if we just combine words at random we get "sentences" like this:

From runners physicians prescribing miss a states joy rests what thought most.

In fact, very few of the possible word combinations are acceptable sentences. The speculation is often jokingly made that, given enough monkeys working at typewriters during a long enough time, some monkey will type a best-selling book. It should be clear that it would take a lot of monkeys a long time to type just one acceptable *R@!#s.

So, balanced against the productivity of language is its highly regular character. One goal of linguistics is to discover a set of rules that will account for both the productivity and the regularity of natural language. Such a set of rules is referred to as a *grammar*. A grammar should be able to prescribe or generate all the acceptable sentences of a language and be able to reject all the unacceptable sentences in the language. Besides rejecting such obvious nonsentences as the one given above, grammar must be able to reject such near misses as

The girls hits the boys.

Did hit the girl the boys?

The girl hit a boys.

The boys were hit the girl.

The sentences above all contain *syntactic violations* (violations of sentence structure). That is, they are fairly meaningful but contain some mistakes in word combinations or word forms. Other nonsentences are possible in which the words are correct in form and syntactic position but their combination is nonsense. For instance:

> Colorless green ideas sleep furiously.

> Sincerity frightened the cat.

These constructions are called *anomalous sentences* and are said to contain *semantic violations* (violations of meaning). Still other sentences can be correct syntactically and semantically but be mispronounced. Such sentences are said to contain *phonological violations*. Consider this example:

> The Inspector opened his notebook.
> "Your name is Halcock, is't no?" he began.
> The butler corrected him.
> "H'alcock," he said, reprovingly.
> "H,a,double-l?" suggested the Inspector.
> "There is no h'aich in the name, young man. H'ay is the first letter,
> and there is h'only one h'ell." (Sayers, 1968, p. 73)

To account for the regularity of language, then, linguists need a grammar that will specify *phonology* (sound), *syntax* (structure), and *semantics* (meaning).

Linguistic Intuitions

Another feature that linguists want a grammar to explain is the *linguistic intuitions* of speakers of the language. Linguistic intuitions are judgments about the nature of linguistic utterances or about the relationships between linguistic utterances. Speakers of the language are often able to make these judgments without knowing how they do so. Among these linguistic intuitions are judgments about why sentences are ill formed. For instance, we can judge that some sentences are ill formed because they have bad syntactic structure, and that other sentences are ill formed because they lack meaning. Linguists require that a grammar capture this distinction and clearly express the reasons for it. Another kind of intuition is about *paraphrase*. A speaker of English will judge that the following two sentences are very similar in meaning, and hence are paraphrases:

> The girl hit the boy.

> The boy was hit by the girl.

Yet another kind of intuition is about *ambiguity*. The following sentence has two meanings:

> They are cooking apples.

This sentence can either mean that some people are cooking some apples or that the apples being referred to are for cooking. Moreover, speakers of the language can distinguish this type of ambiguity, which is called *structural ambiguity,* from *lexical ambiguity,* in

I am going to the bank,

where *bank* can refer either to a monetary institution or a river bank. Lexical ambiguities arise when a word has two or more distinct meanings; structural ambiguities arise when an entire phrase or sentence has two or more meanings.

So, in summary, linguists strive to create grammars that (1) specify the nature of the well-formed sentence in a language; (2) specify which utterances are ill formed and why; and (3) explain intuitions that speakers have about such things as paraphrase and ambiguity.

Competence versus Performance

Our everyday use of language does not always correspond to the prescriptions of linguistic theory. We generate sentences in conversation that, in a more reflective situation, we would judge to be ill formed and unacceptable. We hesitate, repeat ourselves, stutter, and make slips of the tongue. We misunderstand the meaning of sentences. We hear sentences that are ambiguous but do not note their ambiguity.

Another complication is that linguistic intuitions are not always clear cut. For instance, we find the linguist Lakoff (1971) telling us that the first sentence below is not acceptable but that the second is:

Tell John where the concert's this afternoon.

Tell John that the concert's this afternoon.

People are not always reliable in their judgments of such sentences and certainly do not always agree with Lakoff.

Considerations about the unreliability of human linguistic behavior and judgment led Noam Chomsky to make a distinction between *linguistic competence,* a person's abstract knowledge of the language, and *linguistic performance,* the actual application of that knowledge in speaking or listening. In Chomsky's view, the linguist's task is to develop a theory of competence; the psychologist's task is to develop a theory of performance.

The exact relationship between a theory of competence and a theory of performance is unclear and can be the subject of heated debates. Chomsky has argued that a theory of competence is central to performance—that our linguistic competence underlies our ability to use language, if indirectly. Others believe that the concept of linguistic competence is based on a rather unnatural activity (making linguistic judgments) and has very little to do with everyday language use. One reason that this issue is so unclear is that linguists differ as to what should be covered under the topic of competence. Some want to cover topics such as mispronunciations or rules of conversation, which certainly seem to be parts of a performance theory.

In the remainder of this section we will take a rather traditional view of the function of a competence grammar and focus on proposals, largely derived from Noam Chomsky's theory, for how to formulate such a grammar for a language. A competence grammar has the virtue of identifying and articulating much of the syntactic structure of language. This material will prove particularly important in later chapters.

Grammatical Formalisms

Surface Structure

One central linguistic concept is *surface structure*. Surface-structure analysis is not only significant in linguistics, but it is also very important to an understanding of the processes of comprehension and generation. Therefore, our coverage of this topic here is partially a preparation for material in subsequent chapters. Those of you who have had a certain kind of high school training in English will find the analysis of surface structure to be similar to parsing exercises. For the rest of you the analysis will be more novel.

The surface structure of a sentence is the hierarchical division of the sentence into units called phrases. Consider this sentence:

The brave dog saved the drowning child.

If asked to divide this sentence into two major parts in the most natural way, most people would provide the following division:

(The brave dog)(saved the drowning child),

where the parentheses distinguish the two separate parts. The two parts of the sentence correspond to what are traditionally called subject and predicate, or noun phrase and verb phrase. If asked to divide the second part, the verb phrase, further, most people would give

(The brave dog)(saved (the drowning child)).

Often analysis of a sentence is represented as an upside-down tree, as in Figure 11-1. In this surface-structure tree, *sentence* points to its subunits, *noun phrase* and *verb phrase,* and each of these units points to its subunits. Eventually, the branches of the tree terminate in the individual words. Such

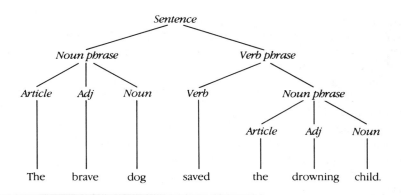

Figure 11-1 An example of the surface structure of a sentence. The tree structure illustrates the hierarchical division of the sentence into phrases.

tree-structure representations for surface structures are very common in linguistics. In fact, it is common to use the term surface structure to refer to such tree structures.

An analysis of surface structure can point up syntactic ambiguities. Consider again this sentence:

They are cooking apples.

Depending on the meaning, *cooking* is either part of the verb with *are* or part of the noun phrase with *apples*. Figure 11-2 illustrates the surface structure for these two interpretations. In part (a) *cooking* is part of the verb, while in part (b) it is part of the noun phrase.

Rewrite Rules

Note that the various nodes in the trees showing surface structure have meaningful labels, such as *sentence, noun phrase, verb phrase, verb, noun,* and *adj* (for *adjective*), which indicate the character of these sentence units or constituents. Such labels can serve to form *rewrite rules* for actually generating sentences. Linguists formulate grammars for languages in terms of such rewrite rules. Table 11-1 consists of a set of rewrite rules indicating ways of rewriting these labels, or symbols. The symbol on the left can be rewritten as the symbols on the right. Thus, rule 1 says that *sentence* may be rewritten as *noun phrase* plus *verb phrase*. Rule 2A indicates that a noun phrase can be rewritten as an optional article, an optional adjective, and a noun. The parentheses indicate that the article and adjective are optional. Rule 2B indicates that another way to rewrite a noun phrase is as a pronoun.

(a)

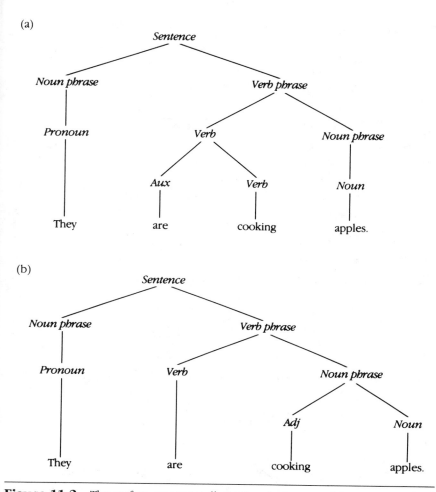

(b)

Figure 11-2 The surface structures illustrating the two possible meanings of the ambiguous sentence *They are cooking apples:* (a) that those people (they) are cooking apples; (b) that those apples are for cooking.

It is possible to derive a sentence through these rewrite rules. For instance, consider the following sequence:

$$Sentence \rightarrow noun\ phrase\ +\ verb\ phrase \qquad (1)$$
$$\rightarrow article\ +\ adj\ +\ noun\ +\ verb$$
$$+\ prep\ phrase \qquad (2)$$
$$\rightarrow article\ +\ adj\ +\ noun\ +\ verb$$
$$+\ preposition\ +\ noun\ phrase \qquad (3)$$
$$\rightarrow article\ +\ adj\ +\ noun\ +\ verb$$

Table 11-1   *Rewrite rules for generating a fragment of English*

Symbol	Rewrite as
1. Sentence	→noun phrase + verb phrase
2A. Noun phrase	→(article) + (adj) + noun
2B.	→pronoun
3A. Verb phrase	→verb + noun phrase
3B.	→verb + prep phrase
4. Prep phrase	→preposition + noun phrase
5A. Verb	→aux + verb
5B.	→hit, saved, cooking, danced
6. Noun	→dog, child, boy, girl, apples, river
7. Article	→the, a
8. Adj	→brave, drowning, cooking
9. Pronoun	→he, she, they
10. Preposition	→in, by
11. Aux	→was, were

$$+ \ preposition \ + \ article \ + \ noun \qquad (4)$$
$$\rightarrow the \ + \ brave \ + \ boy \ + \ danced$$
$$+ \ in \ + \ the \ + \ river \qquad (5)$$

In line 1, we rewrote *sentence* as *noun phrase* plus *verb phrase* according to rewrite rule 1. In line 2, we rewrote *noun phrase* into *article* plus *adj* plus *noun* (according to rewrite rule 2A) and *verb phrase* into *verb* plus *prep phrase* (according to rule 3B). In line 3, we rewrote *prep phrase* into *preposition* plus *noun phrase* (according to rule 4). In line 4, we rewrote the *noun phrase* from line 3 into *article* plus *noun* (rule 2A). Finally, in line 5, we replaced each of the symbols by words according to rules 5B, 6, 7, 8, and 10.

The tree representation of the surface structure of a sentence serves to illustrate derivation of the sentence through the rewrite rules. Figure 11-3 illustrates the surface structure of the sentence derived in Table 11-1. In such a tree structure, a symbol is connected below to the symbols that the rule rewrites into.

A set of rewrite rules is referred to as a grammar. Such rules constitute one way of specifying the acceptable sentences of the language. As such they provide a means of achieving one important goal of linguistics, which is to devise a grammar that (1) generates all the acceptable sentences of the language, and (2) does not generate any unacceptable sentences. Can you find ways in which the simple set of rewrite rules in Table 11-1 fail to achieve these two criteria? Although linguists have come up with grammars that are much more complex and comprehensive than the one in Table 11-1, they

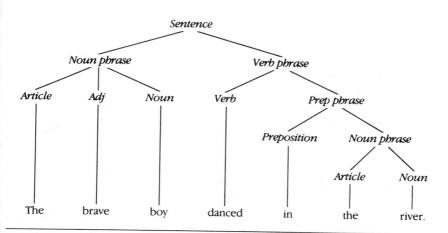

Figure 11-3 The surface structure of the sentence *The brave boy danced in the river.* The branches in this tree derive from the rewrite rules in Table 11-1.

have not yet come close to specifying a grammar that completely satisfies criteria 1 and 2 stated above. Many issues in the field remain unresolved, including whether these two goals are realistic.

Transformations

The rewrite rules in Table 11-1 are referred to as a *phrase-structure grammar,* because they define the phrases in a sentence, such as the noun phrases, verb phrases, and prepositional phrases. Chomsky has argued (1957) that such grammars are inadequate as complete descriptions of natural language, since they fail to capture certain generalities and intuitions about natural language. Consider another pair of sentences:

1. The cat chased the mouse.

2. The mouse was chased by the cat.

These sentences have very similar meanings, but their surface structures do not reflect this similarity. The only difference is that sentence 1 is in the active voice, whereas sentence 2 is in the passive voice.

That examples of synonymy like this exist but cannot be represented in the surface structure of a sentence indicates the need for making a distinction between the surface structure and the deep structure of a sentence. In contrast to surface structure, which refers to the phrases in the actual sentence, *deep structure* refers to the phrases in an underlying hypothetical word string, postulated by Chomsky to more directly reflect the meaning of the sentence. Consider sentences 1 and 2. Parts (a) and (b) of Figure 11-4 show the surface

(a)

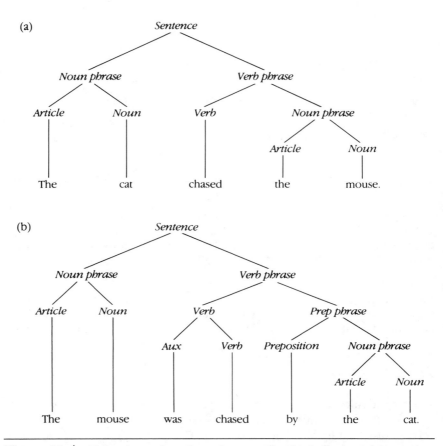

Figure 11-4 The active and passive voice conveying basically the same meaning. The deep structure in (a) is transformed into (b), which is the surface structure for the passive voice.

structures for these two sentences. Chomsky (1957) proposed that the deep structure underlying two such sentences was similar to the active surface structure, shown in part (a), but that the passive surface structure, shown in part (b), was derived from (a) by means of an optional passive transformation:[1]

> *noun phrase-1* + *verb* + *noun phrase-2*
>
> *noun phrase-2* + was + *verbed* + by + *noun phrase-1*

---

[1]In the active case, a distinction was made between its deep and surface structure, but this subtlety is not critical here.

A fair fraction of natural language appears to have such transformational regularities. Another classic example of transformational regularity is the relationship between the affirmative sentences and yes-no questions in the following pairs of sentences:

3a. The cat did chase the mouse.

3b. Did the cat chase the mouse?

4a. The cat is chasing the mouse.

4b. Is the cat chasing the mouse?

5a. The mouse could have been chased by the cat.

5b. Could the mouse have been chased by the cat?

In each case, the first verb auxiliary in the verb phrase *(did, is, could)* is moved to the front of the sentence to create the question form. This procedure can be formalized by the following transformational rule:

noun phrase + verb auxiliary + verb phrase

→ *verb auxiliary + noun phrase + verb phrase*

Transformational regularities refer to the fact that the syntax of one type of sentence is related to the syntax of another type of sentence by a rearrangement of surface structure. Chomsky proposed to capture such transformational regularities by deriving the different surface structures from similar deep structures.

Psychological Reality of Transformational Grammar

Under Chomsky's original analysis, much of the syntax of natural language was determined by such transformations. While Chomsky's primary motivation in proposing such transformations was to account for certain abstract facts about syntax, other researchers have inquired as to whether there is any psychological reality to such rules. For instance, in generating a passive, do we first generate an activelike deep structure, and then transform it into a passive sentence?

During the 1960s, many experiments were performed that looked for correlates of transformational distinctions in tasks involving paraphrase, memory, perception, and the like. A fair summary of this research is provided by Fodor, Bever, and Garrett (1974), who wrote,

> the experimental evidence for the psychological reality of deep and surface structure is considerably stronger than the experimental evidence for the psychological reality of transformations. (p. 274)

Given the close connection between deep structure and the meaning of a sentence, it is not surprising that there is considerable evidence for the existence of a deep structure. Indeed, much of the research in Chapter 5 on propositional codes can be construed as evidence for a deep structure. In Chapters 12 and 13 we will review some of the ample evidence that surface structure is intimately involved in sentence comprehension and generation. The fact that little evidence exists for transformations, which form the heart of the Chomsky proposal, is symptomatic of the weak connection between transformational grammar and performance.

Slobin (1966) performed a well-known experiment to test the psychological reality of transformations. He had subjects comprehend sentences like the following:

1. John smelled the cookies.

2. The cookies were smelled by John.

3. The cookies were smelled.

Because a passive transformation is involved in deriving sentence 2, it has one more transformation in its derivation than sentence 1. Sentence 3, called a *truncated passive,* involves a further transformation to delete the phrase *by John* from sentence 2, so transformational analysis would predict that sentence 1 is easiest to comprehend and sentence 3 most difficult. Slobin had subjects verify that the sentence correctly described the action depicted in a picture. A measure of the difficulty of comprehending the sentence was the time that it took subjects to make this judgment. Slobin found no difference in the time it took to verify sentence 1 and sentence 2, and both required more time to verify than sentence 3. Thus, processing time did not increase with number of transformations and indeed was fastest for the sentence (3) that involved the most transformations.

Lexicalist Grammar

Results like these have led a number of linguists (e.g., Bresnan, 1978) to propose that we have rules that directly map between passive structures and their meanings without intervening transformations. Different rules take meanings and map them into actives, passives, and truncated passives. If we represent the meaning of *John smelled the cookie* as the proposition (smell John cookies) then we have the following three rules that could apply to this proposition (in these rules NP_1 and NP_2 represent noun phrases):

1. (smell NP_1 NP_2) $\rightarrow$ NP_1 smelled NP_2

2. (smell NP_1 NP_2) $\rightarrow$ NP_2 was smelled by NP_1

3. (smell NP_1 NP_2) $\rightarrow$ NP_2 was smelled

These are rather like production rules—a point we will elaborate on in the next two chapters. In these rules NP$_1$ would match *John* and NP$_2$ would match *the cookie*. Rule 1 would generate *John smelled the cookie;* rule 2 would generate *The cookie was smelled by John;* and rule 3 would generate *The cookie was smelled.* Thus, in contrast to transformational grammer, these rules do not predict that passives are more difficult.

Bresnan's position is called the *lexicalist position* because it assumes that these rules are associated with particular lexical items like *smell* rather than general transformational rules. In this way, Bresnan can account for the fact that certain grammatical structures appear only with certain words. For instance, consider these four sentences:

1. Carter told his decision to Mondale.
2. Carter told Mondale his decision.
3. Carter announced his decision to Mondale.
4. Carter announced Mondale his decision.

Transformational linguists have proposed that sentence 2 is derived from sentence 1 by a transformation that is called a *dative movement* transformation. The problem, then, is to explain why sentence 4 does not similarly derive from sentence 3. The lexicalist linguist, however, proposes simply that the dative form exists for *told,* as in sentence 2, but not for *announced,* as in sentence 4.

The state of linguistic theory is very much in flux right now. However, the emergence of ideas such as lexicalist grammar, based in part on psychological data, shows that the field is reconsidering the sharp distinction that Chomsky made between competence and performance. The remainder of this chapter will focus on possible relationships between language and thought.

The Relationship between Language and Thought

The Behaviorist Proposal

A wide variety of proposals have been put forth as to the connection between language and thought. The strongest such proposal was advanced by John B. Watson, the father of behaviorism. It was one of the tenets of Watson's behaviorism (Watson, 1930) that no such thing as internal mental activity existed. All humans did, he argued, was to emit responses that had been conditioned to stimuli. This radical proposal, which, as noted in Chapter 1, held sway in America for some time, seemed to fly in the face of the abundant evidence that humans can engage in thinking behavior (e.g., do mental arithmetic) that involves no response emission. To deal with this obvious counter, Watson proposed that thinking was just subvocal speech, that when people were engaged in such "mental" activities they were really talking to themselves. Hence, Watson's proposal was that a very important component of thought was simply subvocal speech. (The philosopher Herbert Feigl once said that Watson "made up his windpipe that he had no mind.")

This proposal was a stimulus for a research program that engaged itself in taking recordings to see if evidence could be found for subvocal activity of the speech apparatus during thinking. Indeed, often when a subject is engaged in thought it is possible to get recordings of subvocal speech activity. However, the more important observation is that in some situations people engage in various silent thinking tasks with no detectable vocal activity. However, this finding did not upset Watson. He claimed that we think with our whole bodies—for instance, with our arms. He cited the fascinating evidence that deaf mutes actually make signs while asleep. (Speaking people who have done a lot of communication in sign language also sign while asleep.)

The decisive experiment addressing Watson's hypothesis was performed by Smith, Brown, Toman, and Goodman (1947). They used a curare derivative that paralyzed the human musculature. Smith was the subject for the experiment and had to be kept alive by means of an artificial respirator. Because his entire musculature was completely paralyzed, it was impossible for him to engage in subvocal speech or any other body movement. Nonetheless, under curare, Smith was able to observe what was going on around him, comprehend speech, remember these events, and think about them. Thus, it seems clear that thinking can proceed in the absence of any muscle activity. For current purpose, the relevant additional observation is that thought is not just implicit speech but is truly an internal, nonmotor activity.

Additional evidence that thought is not to be equated with language comes from the research on propositional memories that was reviewed in Chapter 5. There we discussed that people tend to retain not the exact words of a linguistic communication, but rather some more abstract representation of the meaning of the communication. Thought should be identified, at least in part, with this abstract, nonverbal propositional code.

Still more information comes from the occasional cases of individuals who have no apparent language at all but who certainly give evidence of being able to think. Also, it seems hard to claim that nonverbal animals such as apes are unable to think. Recall, for instance, the problem-solving exploits of Sultan in Chapter 8. It is always hard to determine the exact character of the "thought processes" of nonverbal subjects and how these differ from the thought processes of verbal subjects, since there is no language with which subjects can be interrogated. Thus, the apparent dependence of thought on language may be an illusion that derives from the fact that it is hard to obtain evidence about thought without using language.

The Whorfian Hypothesis of Linguistic Relativity

Linguistic relativity, or linguistic determinism, is the claim that language determines or strongly influences the way a person thinks or preceives the world. This proposal is much weaker than Watson's position, because it does not claim language and thought are identical. The hypothesis has been advanced by a good many linguists but has been most strongly associated with Benjamin Lee Whorf (1956). Whorf was quite an unusual character himself. He was trained as a chemical engineer at the Massachusetts Institute of Technology, spent his life working for the Hartford Fire Insurance Company, and studied North American Indian languages as a hobby. He was very impressed by the fact that different languages emphasize in their structure rather different aspects of the world. He believed that these emphases must have a great influence on the way language speakers think about the world. For instance, Eskimos have many different words for snow, each of which refers to snow in a different state (wind-driven, packed, slushy, and so on), whereas English speakers have only a single word for snow. Many other examples exist at the vocabulary level. The Hanunoo people in the Phillipines have 92 names for different varieties of rice. The Arabic language supposedly has many different ways of naming camels. Whorf felt that such a rich variety of terms would cause the speaker of the language to perceive the world differently from a person who had only a single word for a particular category.

Deciding how to evaluate the Whorfian hypothesis is very tricky. Nobody would be surprised to learn that Eskimos know more about snow than the average English speaker. After all, snow is a more important part of their life experience. The question is whether their language has any effect on the Eskimos' perception of snow over and above the effect of experience. If speakers of English went through the Eskimo life experience, would their perception of snow be any different than that of the Eskimo-language speakers? (Indeed, ski bums have a life experience that involves a great deal of exposure to snow and have a great deal of knowledge about snow.)

One fairly well researched test of the issue involves color words. English has 11 *basic color words*—black, white, red, green, yellow, blue, brown, purple, pink, orange, and gray—a relatively large number. These words are called basic color words because they are short and are used frequently, in contrast to such terms as saffron, turquoise, or magenta. At the other extreme is the language of the Dani, a Stone Age agricultural people of Indonesian New Guinea. This language has just two basic color terms: *mili* for dark, cold hues and *mola* for bright, warm hues. If the categories in language determine perception, the Dani should perceive color in a less refined manner than English speakers do. The relevant question is whether this speculation is true.

Speakers of English, at least, judge a certain color within the range referred to by each basic color term to be the best—for instance, the best red, the best blue, and so on (see Berlin and Kay, 1969). Each of the 11 basic color terms in English appears to have one generally agreed upon best color, called a *focal color.* English speakers find it easier to process and remember focal colors than nonfocal colors (e.g., Brown & Lenneberg, 1954). The interesting question is whether the special cognitive capacity for identifying focal colors evolved because English speakers have special words for these colors. If so, this would be a clear case of language influencing thought.

To test whether the special processing of focal colors was an instance of language influencing thought, Rosch (she has published some of this work under her former name, Heider) performed an important series of experiments on the Dani. The point was to see whether the Dani processed focal colors differently than English speakers. One experiment (Rosch, 1973) compared the ability of the Dani to learn nonsense names for focal versus nonfocal colors. English speakers find it easier to learn arbitrary names for focal colors. Dani subjects also found it easier to learn arbitrary names for focal colors than for nonfocal colors even though they have no names for these colors. In another experiment (see Heider, 1972), subjects were shown a color chip for 5 sec; 30 sec after the presentation ended they were required to select the color from among 160 color chips. English speakers perform better at this task when the chip they are to remember is a focal color rather than a nonfocal color. The Dani also perform better at this task for focal colors.

Thus, it appears that despite the differences in their linguistic terminology for colors, the Dani and English speakers see colors in much the same way. It appears that the 11 focal colors are processed specially by all people regardless of language. In fact, some facts about the physiology of color vision suggest that these focal colors are specially processed by the visual system (de Valois & Jacobs, 1968). The fact that many languages develop basic color terms for just these 11 colors can be seen as an instance of thought determining language.

Another test of the Whorfian hypothesis was performed by Carroll and Casagrande (1958). The Navaho language requires different verb forms depending on the nature of the thing being acted upon, particularly regarding its shape, rigidity, and material. Carroll and Casagrande presented Navaho-speaking children with three objects, such as a yellow stick, a piece of blue rope, and a yellow rope. The children had to say which of the two objects went with the third. Since Navaho requires that a different verb form be used for sticks (rigid) than ropes (flexible), the experimenters predicted that the Navaho-speaking subjects would tend to match the ropes and not match on color. They found that Navaho-speaking children preferred shape and that English-speaking Navaho children preferred color. However, in another study they found that English-speaking Boston children exhibited an even greater tendency to match on the basis of form. It seems that the Boston children's experience with toys (for which shape and rigidity are critical) was more important than the Navaho-language experience, although the language experience may have had some effect.

To conclude, the evidence tends not to support the hypothesis that language has any significant effect on the way we think or on the way we perceive the world. It is certainly true that language can influence us (or else there would be little point in writing this book), but its effect is to communicate ideas, not to determine the kinds of ideas we can think about.

Does Language Depend on Thought?

The alternative possibility is that the structure of language is influenced by thought. Aristotle argued 2500 years ago that the categories of thought determined the categories of language. There are some reasons for believing that he was correct, but most of these reasons were not available to Aristotle. So, although the hypothesis has been around for 2500 years, we have better reasons for holding it today.

There are numerous reasons to suppose that the human's ability to think (i.e., to engage in nonlinguistic cognitive activity such as remembering and problem solving) appeared earlier evolutionarily and occurs sooner developmentally than the ability to use language. Many species of animals without language appear to be capable of a complex cognition. Children, before they are effective at using their language, give clear evidence of relatively complex cognition. If we accept that thought occurred before language, it seems natural to suppose that language is a tool whose function is to communicate thought. It is generally true that tools are shaped to fit the objects on which they must operate. Analogously, it seems reasonable to suppose that language has been shaped to fit the thoughts it must communicate. In addition to general arguments for the view that language depends on thought, a number of pieces of evidence to support the notion have been generated in cognitive psychology and related fields. I will review a few of the lines of evidence.

We saw in Chapter 5 that propositional structures constituted a very important type of knowledge structure in representing information both derived from language and derived from pictures. Every language has a phrase structure. The basic phrase units of a language tend to convey propositions. For instance, *the tall boy* conveys the proposition that the boy is tall. Much of the discussion in the two chapters that follow will be concerned with how the phrase structure of language controls comprehension and generation. This phenomenon itself—the existence of a linguistic structure, the *phrase*, designed to accommodate a thought structure, the *proposition*—seems to be a clear example of the dependence of language on thought.

Another example of the way in which thought shapes language comes from Rosch's research on focal colors. As stated earlier, the human visual system is maximally sensitive to certain colors. As a consequence, languages have special, short, high-frequency words with which to designate these colors. We noted that in English these basic color words are black, white, red, yellow, green, blue, brown, purple, pink, orange, and gray. Thus, the visual system has determined how the English language divides up the color space.

A related piece of evidence suggesting that thought influences language is that we find highly differentiated terms for a category in a language only if instances of that category are relevant to the life experience of the language users. Thus, it is Eskimos who have many words for snow and Arabs who have many words for camels, not vice versa. Also, languages tend to evolve to encode differences important to the users. Thus, English-speaking skiers have developed their own dialect, which permits discriminations among many types of snow.

We find additional evidence for the influence of thought on language when we consider word order. Every language has a preferred word order for expressing subject (S), verb (V), and object (O). Consider this sentence, which exhibits the preferred word order in English:

Lynne petted the Labrador.

English is referred to as SVO language. In a study of a diverse sample of the world's languages, Greenberg (1963) found that only four of the six possible orders of S, V, and O are used in natural languages, and one of these four orders is rare. Below are the six possible word orders and the frequency with which each order occurs in the world's languages (the percentages are from Ultan, 1969):

SOV	44 percent	VOS	2 percent
SVO	35 precent	OVS	0 percent
VSO	19 percent	OSV	0 percent

The important feature is that the subject almost always precedes the object. This order makes good sense when we think about cognition. An action starts with the agent and then affects the object. Therefore, it is natural that the subject of a sentence, when it reflects its agency, occurs first. Also, as we will discuss more fully in the next chapter, sentences tend to be "about" their subject, and a speaker naturally wants to establish first what the sentence is about.

Thus it seems that, in an important sense, Whorf's hypothesis reversed the actual relation of language and thought. The shape of language is determined in part by thought—just what we would expect if language were a tool designed to permit the communication of thought. However, it is possible to argue that language is much more intimately connected to thought than is a tool to its medium. This argument claims that the mechanisms underlying language use are basically the same in kind as the mechanisms underlying other aspects of cognition. It will be implicitly assumed that this claim is true in subsequent chapters, where production systems for language comprehension and language generation will be presented. This point, however, is by no means universally accepted as true. Linguists and psychologists from the Chomsky camp have claimed that language is a unique system and that linguistic processes are quite different from general thought processes. Their position on the language-thought issue, then, would be that the two systems are in some senses independent. The remainder of this chapter will be devoted to assessing the claims about the uniqueness of language.

Those language theorists propounding Chomsky's position insist that language is a very special facility in three senses:

1. Unlike most cognitive facilities, it is unique to human beings. No other species possesses a true language.

2. Special learning mechanisms exist for acquiring language that are different from the mechanisms underlying acquisiton of any other cognitive skill.

3. The mechanisms for language comprehension and generation are unlike the mechanisms underlying the exercise of any other cognitive skill.

Most discussion in the field has concerned points 1 and 2, and these are the points that we will focus on.

The Uniqueness of Language to Humans

It is certainly not the case that humans have the only communication system. If you have had a dog or cat, you know all too well how much these creatures can communicate. Birds have songs to indicate sexual readiness and possession of territory. An interesting communication system is possessed by honeybees (von Frisch, 1967). A bee, upon finding some food, returns to the hive and performs a dance. The speed of the dance and the direction relative to the sun conveys information about the distance and direction of the food.

A Definition of Language

The question is whether any of these communicative systems qualify as language. To answer this question we must define when we mean by language. Hockett (1960) suggested some criteria for language that are worth reviewing and adding to:

1. *Semanticity and Arbitrariness of Units.* One feature of language is that its units (words) have meaning and the connection between the form or sound of the units and the meaning is arbitrary. There is no reason why a shoe should be called *shoe;* it just is. It appears that the warning calls of some monkeys (Marler, 1967) have this property of arbitrary meaning. The monkeys have different warning calls for different types of predators—a "chutter" for snakes; a "chirp" for leopards; and a "kraup" for eagles. The dance of the honeybee, described above, also exhibits this arbitrary feature. On the other hand, when dogs snarl and show their teeth to communicate hostility, they are not using an arbitrary communication system. Their teeth are very directly related to the message they are trying to communicate.

2. *Discreteness.* Language contains discrete units such as words. By this criterion, the bee dance system would be disqualified as a language because it does not contain any discrete units. On the other hand, the monkey warning system meets this criterion because each warning signal is a discrete unit.

3. *Displacement.* Language is generated in the absence of any direct controlling stimuli. Perhaps the bee dance meets this criterion in that the bee can communicate nonpresent food. But by this criterion, the monkey warning system cannot be considered a language because the monkeys give their warning calls only in the presence of danger.

4. *Productivity.* The productivity of language, discussed earlier in this chapter, is a very important feature. By using our verbal communication system, we can essentially produce an infinite number of novel expressions. This property distinguishes language from the monkey warning calls. Interestingly, it does not distinguish language from bee dances. In principle, honeybees should be able to convey an infinite variety of messages by slight changes in the speed and direction of the dance. Note, however, that "infinity" in this sytem is achieved because the dance is continuous and it is possible to make ever more refined discriminations in speed and direction. True languages achieve their infinity by means of the iteration and recursion of discrete symbols.

5. *Iteration and Recursion. Iteration* is the capacity for adding on to the ends of sentences or phrases to create new sentences. This iteration can go on without limit, as in the following sequence:

The child breathed the air.

The child breathed the air and coughed loudly.

The child breathed the air and coughed loudly and felt sick.

Recursion is the capacity to embed one structure within the same kind of structure. Again, recursion can go on without limit, as in this sequence:

The child whom the mother loved breathed the air.

The child whom the mother whom the man left loved breathed the air.

The child whom the mother whom the man whom the police wanted left loved breathed the air.

And so on.

The last two sentences in the sequence above are interesting in that they are very difficult to comprehend; nonetheless most linguists would judge them to be grammatical.

To the best of anyone's knowledge, no natural communication system of any other species possesses property 5, and none possesses all four of the other properties listed. These properties appear to be essential to the concept of a language. Thus, humans are unique in having created langauge, and so far they are the only species to have used it. The interesting question is whether this says anything about the uniqueness of human abilities with respect to language. Could other species acquire and use a language? The effort to answer this question is one of the motivations for the many projects in which researchers have tried to teach language to apes.

Linguistic Apes?

There are good reasons for choosing apes in the attempt to teach language to another species. Apes are very intelligent and are the animals most like humans. A number of early attempts to each chimpanzee to speak were total failures (Hayes, 1951; Kellogg & Kellogg, 1933). However, it is now clear (Lenneberg, 1967) that the human's vocal apparatus is specially designed to permit speech whereas the ape's is not. Thus, these early studies only provided information relevant to the physiology and musculature of apes, not to their cognitive capabilities.

While their vocal abilities are limited, their manual dexterity is considerable. Therefore, a number of recent attempts have been made to teach apes

Figure 11-5 The chimp Peony (a successor to Sarah in Premack's lab) creates sentences by attaching plastic shapes to a magnetic board (Courtesy of David Premack.)

languages using a manual system. Some studies have used American Sign Language (Ameslan), which is used by many deaf people. It is clear that Ameslan is a language by the criteria set forth earlier. Therefore, if apes could become proficient in Ameslan, their capacity for acquiring a language would be firmly established.

One of the best-known research efforts inside and outside of psychology was started by Beatrice and Allen Gardner (Gardner & Gardner, 1969) in 1966 on a 1-year-old female chimpanzee named Washoe. Washoe was raised somewhat as a human child would be, following regimens of play, bathing, eating, and toilet training, all of which provided ample opportunity for sign learning. After 4 years, she had learned a vocabulary of 132 signs, was able to generate novel strings up to 5 signs in length, and was able to initiate conversation. She used order of sign in such utterances as *You tickle me* and *I tickle you* to distinguish subject from object. (See Figure 11-6 for other Gardner and Gardner subjects.)

David Premack (1971, 1976; Premack & Premack, 1983) developed an artificial language in which the "words" were colored plastic shapes that could be attached to a magnetic board. A chimp named Sarah was raised in a laboratory situation and was trained to use the symbols to make up "sen-

Figure 11-6 Tatu, one of the new subjects of Gardner and Gardner, signing *drink* to her friend Moja. (Courtesy of B. T. Gardner.)

tences" (see Figure 11-5). Because the chimp was raised in a laboratory situation, she never used her language in spontaneous, social situations as Washoe did. Sarah displayed considerable understanding of the significance of word order as well as control of a great many different constructions: yes-no interrogatives; negatives; class concepts of color, size, and shape; compound and coordinate sentences; quantifiers (all, none, one, several); logical connectives (if . . . then); the copula (is); metalinguistic utterances (e.g., name of); and wh— interrogatives (what, where, when, etc.)

A great many experiments are presently being conducted on chimp language, and some of the more recent chimp studies have produced even more impressive results than the Washoe and Sarah studies. It is unclear just how far chimps will advance. Differences in brain capacity will probably mean that chimps will never match humans. One of the interesting questions is whether these chimps will ever start teaching Ameslan to other chimps. B. T. Gardner (personal communication) reports some success in this direction (see Figure 11-6).

Limitations of Ape Language

Terrace, Petitto, Sanders, and Bever (1979) came up with relatively negative conclusions about the ability of chimpanzees to learn a true language. Their subject was nicknamed Nim (true name Neam Chimpsky) and was taught American Sign Language. They noted that unlike human children acquiring either spoken or signed language, Nim did not show an increase in the length of its utterances with development in the language. Also, unlike human children, Nim had a strong tendency to repeat words in its utterances, producing sequences like "grape eat Nim eat." Nim also did a great deal more imitation of its teachers than do human children. Another difference was that Nim showed much less variety in its generations. For instance, 99 percent of the objects of verbs like *give* or *tickle* were *Nim* or *me*—that is, Nim would sign *tickle me* or *give Nim*. It is hard to judge whether these differences disqualify Nim's accomplishment as a natural language. We know chimps are different from and less intelligent than humans, and therefore their generations are bound to show some differences. The critical question is which differences are significant. This brings us back to the issue of what we mean by a true language.

Probably the right criteria to apply to chimps like Nim are the features we listed earlier as being essential properties of a true language. If we apply the criteria of productivity, recursion, and iteration, it seems clear that chimps are not using a full-fledged language. They do not have productive control of the iterative and recursive features of language the way humans do. This is clear simply because their utterances are short and because they have not spontaneously generated new phrase structures that rely on iteration and recursion. For instance, they could not play the party game described earlier in which each participant built on a sentence. However, this interpretation may be unfair. Human children probably do not acquire full productive control of these properties of their language until after as much as 10 years of language training. No ape has had this much training. One constraint is that chimps become dangerous as they mature. Also, it is difficult to provide learning situations that are interesting to older chimps. A related problem is that the concentration of linguistic exposure and practice during the chimps' years of linguistic training is not as intensive as that for a normal human during its years of linguistic learning.

Efforts to teach apes languages have come under serious criticism from various public and governmental sources. These projects are supported by government research grants, and critics characterize these experiments as the wasting of public tax dollars to develop circus acts. But these projects are important scientific research efforts. They are shedding light on questions such as the nature of language, its relation to thought, and what it means to be human. There is no doubt that these questions are abstract, but they are no more abstract and no less important than the questions regarding the nature of the universe investigated in the space program at much greater expense. It is important to be frugal in spending public money, and the scientific programs funded publicly should be carefully evaluated, but these considerations themselves suggest that we should be all the more careful not to fall victim to simplistic mischaracterizations of scientific research.

The Uniqueness of Language within Humans

Another question, related to but independent of whether language is unique to humans, is whether language is unique among the human mental capacities—that is, whether special psychological principles are required to explain the acquisition and use of language. As we have noted, Chomsky and his associates take the position that language is different from other cognitive faculties. The analogy is made to various body systems. We have one system for digestion, another for breathing, and another for circulation. While these systems have to interact, it is clear that the principles governing one are not the same as the principles that govern another. Similarly, it is argued that the human has separate systems for language, problem solving, reasoning, and so on. On the other hand, it can be argued that the analogy between language and physical body systems is poor, that it is hard to draw boundaries around language the way we can around the digestive system. Thus, the argument by analogy does little to help the uniqueness-of-language position.

The arguments cited earlier for the species specificity of language can be used to bolster the view that language is a unique system within human beings. Consider the argument that chimpanzees do not differ from humans qualitatively in their general intellectual abilities, only quantitatively. For instance, Fodor, Bever, and Garrett (1974) argue that an adult chimpanzee has the same mental age as a 3-year-old child. However, the argument goes, 3-year-old children are highly verbal and adult chimpanzees are not. The research on ape languages is beginning to challenge the assumption that chimps cannot achieve the proficiency of a human 3-year-old language. Further evidence that general intelligence and language development are correlated is the fact that retarded children have retarded language development (Lenneberg, Nichols, & Rosenberger, 1969; Lackner, 1968) and the fact that precocious children whose general intellectual development is accelerated also display accelerated language development (Luchsinger & Arnold, 1965). Thus, language appears to be highly dependent on, not independent of, general intellectual facility.

Like the chimpanzee case, most of the other arguments for the uniqueness of language rest on various observations regarding language acquisition. We will review some of these arguments in the following subsection.

A Critical Period for Language Acquisition

A related argument for the uniqueness of language has to do with the claim that young children appear to acquire a second language much faster than older children or adults. It is claimed that there is a certain critical period, from 2 to about 11 years of age, when it is easiest to learn a language. If this claim were true, humans would be best able to learn a language when their intellectual faculties were least fully developed, which would mean that language ability and intelligence are not correlated. However, the claim that young children learn second languages more readily is just folk wisdom. It is based on informal observations of children of various ages and adults in new linguistic communities, for example, when families are moved to a foreign country in response to a corporate assignment or when immigrants come to a country permanently. Young children are said to acquire a facility to get along in the new language more quickly than older children or adults. However, there are a great many differences among adults versus the older children versus younger children in terms of amount of linguistic exposure, type of exposure (e.g., whether stocks, history, or marbles are being discussed), and willingness to try to learn (McLaughlin, 1978; Nida, 1971). In careful studies in which situations have been selected that controlled for these factors, a positive relationship is exhibited between children's ages and language development (Ervin-Tripp, 1974). That is, the older children (greater than 11 years) learn faster than younger children (the possible exception is phonology—younger children may learn to speak with less of an accent.)

While the argument from second-language acquisition is weak, Lenneberg's (1967) observations about recovery from traumatic aphasias (aphasia is a loss of language function) are somewhat more convincing evidence that an early critical period does exist for language acquisition. Damage to the left hemisphere of the brain often results in aphasia. Children who suffer such damage before the age of 11 appear to have a 100 percent chance of recovering language function. For older asphasics recovery is 60 percent at best.

Considerable evidence (e.g., Gazzaniga, 1967) is converging to suggest that the left hemisphere is specialized in the adult for language function and other symbolic, analytic functions, while the right hemisphere is specialized for nonanalytic, wholistic functions such as art appreciation. This process of the specialization of the hemispheres is referred to as *lateralization*. Lenneberg argued for a causal connection between lateralization and loss of ability to recover from aphasias. He claimed that this lateralization was complete by about puberty. Thus, he argued, before puberty the brain had not specialized, and in aphasics the right hemisphere could take over the language functions of the left hemisphere. After puberty and lateralization it was much harder for the now specialized right hemisphere to take over language function. This line of evidence appeared to indicate that the ability to acquire language is especially programmed as a phase of our neural development, a suggestion that is certainly consistent with the view that language is a unique cognitive ability.

It appears, however, that Lenneberg considerably overestimated the period during which lateralization of the brain takes place. More recent evidence (e.g., Kinsbourne & Smith, 1974; Krashen & Harshman, 1972) has indicated that lateralization is complete somewhere between ages 2 and 5. Children show 100 percent recovery from aphasias after age 5. Thus, loss of ability to recover from aphasias does not seem to be related to lateralization. While loss of such ability undoubtedly has a physiological basis, it may not be part of a preprogrammed developmental sequence for the brain.

Reynolds and Flagg (1977) have argued that the critical factor in success of recovery from aphasias is how well language is encoded. The brain of a post-11-year-old, having already acquired a language, may have restructured itself to the point at which recovering after damage would be difficult. So, in the view promoted by Reynolds and Flagg, it is experience and not age per se that is critical for relearning language. It follows that loss of ability to recover from aphasias is not part of a language-specific fixed sequence of neural development; rather, it is a consequence of the neural restructuring required to encode a very complex skill. In this view, a child who did not start learning a language until age 10 would probably recover completely from an aphasia after 15 or older. Similarly, losses of other highly learned complex skills sustained through brain damage would be permanent. For instance, the abilities of a chess master, which take at least 10 years to develop, might be lost permanently due to neural damage.

The case study of Genie (Fromkin, Krashen, Curtiss, Rigler, & Rigler, 1974) provides an important test case for the hypothesis of Reynolds and Flagg. Genie had been locked in a tiny room until she was discovered and released at age 13 years, 9 months. She had had virtually no social contact. Her blind mother would hurriedly feed her. She was punished if she made any sound. Her father and older brother never spoke to her. Not surprisingly, she possessed no language.

While there are many sad aspects to Genie's history and many heartwarming aspects to the recovery attempts, the critical fact is that she had no opportunity to acquire a language until after the purported critical period. Fromkin et al. reported that in the two years after her discovery Genie showed considerable language-learning abilities. She was learning vocabulary more rapidly than a comparable child (i.e., a child of 3) but was learning syntax more slowly. In an updated report on Genie's development (1977), Curtiss noted that by age 18 Genie was able to speak in short sentences, to use a minimum of grammar, to understand English word order, and to use some prepositions. However, Genie has no generative control over many aspects of English syntax, even though her comprehension seems quite advanced. It is clear from her report that Curtiss believes that Genie will never gain full adult facility in the syntax of language.

To summarize the available evidence, the argument that a biologically determined critical period for language acquisition exists is only partially supported. Consequently, this argument provides only modest support for claims as to the uniqueness of language.

Language Universals

Chomsky has argued that special mechanisms underlie the acquisition of language. Specifically, his claim is that the number of formal possibilities for a natural language is so great that learning the language would simply be impossible unless we possessed some innate information about the possible forms of natural human languages. It is possible to prove formally that Chomsky is correct in his claim. While the formal analysis is beyond the scope of this book, an analogy might help. In Chomsky's view, the problem that child-learners face is to discover the grammar of their language when given instances of utterances of the language. The task can be compared to trying to find a book in a library by using sentences from the book. If the library contains enough books on similar topics, the task could prove impossible. Likewise, enough formally possible grammars are similar enough to each other to make language learning impossible. Thus, since language learning obviously occurs, according to Chomsky we must have special, innate knowledge that allows us to powerfully restrict the number of possible grammars that we have to consider. In the library analogy, the effect would be knowing ahead of time which shelf the book was on.

Chomsky proposes that *language universals* exist that limit the possible characteristics of a natural language and a natural grammar. He assumes that children can learn a natural language because they possess innate knowledge of these language universals. A language that violated these universals would simply be unlearnable. This means that there are hypothetical languages that no humans could learn. Languages that humans can learn are referred to as *natural languages*.

As noted above, we can prove formally that Chomsky's assertion is correct—that is, that constraints on the possible form of a natural language exist. However, the critical issue is whether these constraints reflect any linguistic-specific knowledge on children's part, or whether they simply reflect general cognitive constraints on learning mechanisms. Chomsky would argue that the constraints are language specific. It is this claim of Chomsky's that is open to serious question. Stated as a question the issue is, Are the constraints on the form of natural languages universals of language or universals of cognition?

In speaking of language universals, Chomsky is concerned with a competence grammar. Recall that a competence analysis is concerned with an abstract specification of what a speaker knows about a language; in contrast, a performance analysis is concerned with the way a speaker uses language. Thus, Chomsky is claiming that children possess innate constraints about the types of phrase structures and transformations that might be found in a natural language. Because of the abstract, non-performance-based-character of these purported universals, evaluating Chomsky's claims about their existence has proven very difficult.

Although languages can be quite different from one another, some clear uniformities, or near-uniformities, exist among languages. For instance, as we saw earlier, virtually no language favors the word order subject-after-object. However, as we noted, this constraint (and many other limits on language form) appears to have a cognitive explanation. The literature is very thin on universal features of language that do not have general cognitive explanations.

Often, the uniformities among languages seem so natural that we do not realize that other possibilities might exist. One such language universal is that adjectives occur near the nouns they modify. Thus, we translate *The brave woman hit the cruel man* into French as

La femme brave a frappé l'homme cruel,

and not as,

La femme cruel a frappé l'homme brave,

although a language in which the adjective beside the subject noun modified the object noun and vice versa would be logically possible. However, it is clear that such a language design would be absurd in terms of its cognitive demands. It would require that listeners hold the adjectives from the beginning of the sentence until the noun at the end. No natural language has this perverse structure. If it really needed showing, I have shown with artificial languages that adult subjects were unable to learn such a language (Anderson, 1978b).

The A-over-A *Constraint*

There are a set of peculiar constraints on transformations that have been used to argue for the existence of linguistic universals. One of the more extensively discussed of these is what is called the *A-over-A constraint*. Compare sentence 1 with sentence 2:

1. Which woman did John meet who knows the senator?
2. Which senator did John meet the woman who knows?

Linguists would consider the first to be acceptable but not the second. Sentence 1 can be derived by a transformation from sentence 3. This transformation moves *woman* forward and tags it with *which*.

3. John did meet the woman who knows the senator.

Sentence 2 could be derived by a similar transformation operating on *the senator* in sentence 3, but apparently such a transformation cannot apply. The *A-over-A* constraint states that a transformation cannot move a noun like *senator* if it is embedded within a clause modifying another noun, like *woman*. Transformations can move deeply embedded nouns if these nouns are not in clauses modifying other nouns. So for instance, sentence 4 is derived transformationally from sentence 5:

4. Which senator does Mary believe that Bill said that John likes?
5. Mary believes that Bill said that John likes the senator.

Thus we see that there is a very arbitrary constraint on the transformation that forms which-questions. It can apply to any embedded noun unless that noun is part of a clause modifying another noun. The arbitrariness of this constraint makes it hard to imagine how a child would ever figure it out—unless the child already knew it as a universal of language.

The existence of such constraints on the form of language certainly offers a challenge to any theory of language acquisition. They are so peculiar that it is hard to imagine how they could be learned unless the child were especially prepared to deal with them. To show that these constraints are examples of true linguistic universals, it is also necessary to show that similar constraints appear in all languages where they would be applicable. This issue of whether these constraints apply across languages has yet to be systematically investigated.

The Uniqueness of Language: A Summary

Little direct evidence exists to support the view that language is a unique system. There is only a little more direct evidence that language obeys general cognitive laws. In my opinion, the status of language is shaping up to be a major issue for cognitive psychology. The issue will be resolved by empirical and theoretical efforts more detailed than those reviewed in this chapter. The ideas here have served to define the context for the investigation of the issue. The next two chapters will review the current state of our knowledge about the details of comprehension and generation. Experimental research on all of these topics will finally resolve the issues about the uniqueness of language.

Remarks and Suggested Readings

A number of introductions to linguistics are available. These include Bolinger (1975), Culicover (1976), Fromkin and Rodman (1978), and Sampson (1975). Perhaps the best introduction to Chomsky's ideas is a book by Lyons (1970). You should not get the impression that anything like unanimity exists in linguistics regarding Chomsky's ideas, or even that Chomsky still propounds all the details of the theory sketched in this chapter (which he developed between 1957 and 1965). However, that theory is essential to the understanding of many other developments in linguistics. Certain of the ideas comprised by the theory (transformations, distinctions between deep and surface structure) are important in their own right. The book edited by Bresnan (1981) contains a series of papers putting forth the lexicalist position.

Of interest are a number of fairly recent textbooks on the psychology of language, sometimes called psycholinguistics. These include Cairns and Cairns (1976); Clark and Clark (1977); Fodor et al. (1974); Foss and Hakes (1978); and Glucksberg and Danks (1975). A great deal of research on language has been performed in artificial intelligence. The book by Charniak and Wilks (1976) provides an introduction to some of this work.

Fodor et al. (1974) provide a strong argument for the uniqueness of language. Reynolds and Flagg (1977) provide arguments for the opposite position. Gardner (1975) discusses the effects of brain injuries on language and other facilities. Gazzaniga (1970) describes research on patients whose interhemispheric connections have been severed to arrest epileptic symptoms. This work is an important source of evidence for brain specialization. Roger Brown has done a great deal of research on child language acquisition; much of the research is reviewed in his 1973 book. Other reviews of first-language acquisition include those of Dale (1976) and deVilliers and deVilliers

(1978). McLaughlin (1978) provides a review of research on second-language acquisition.

The book by Wexler and Culicover (1980) is one effort to develop a theory of language acquisition that depends on a set of language-specific assumptions. The recent book by Fodor (1983) also argues for this position. Anderson (1983) develops the opposite position. Chomsky (1980) argues that not only language, but many other activities like language, depend on specific cognitive faculties.

Chapter 12

Language Comprehension

Summary

1. Comprehension can be analyzed into three stages: perception, parsing, and utilization. Perception concerns translation from sound to a word representation. Parsing concerns translation from the word representation to a meaning representation. Utilization concerns the use to which the comprehender puts the meaning of the message.

2. The comprehender parses a sentence by analyzing it into phrases, or constituents, and interpreting the meaning of each constituent. This process can be modeled by productions whose conditions describe constituent patterns and whose actions place meaning interpretations in memory.

3. Language comprehenders sometimes parse sentences by considering the meaning of the words alone and not the syntactic information conveyed by the sentence.

4. Comprehenders tend to choose just one meaning for ambiguous clauses. Consequently, they have to reanalyze the clause if later information indicates that the original choice was wrong.

5. Comprehenders combine both syntactic and semantic cues in order to interpret a sentence.

6. Part of the utilization process involves relating the information in the sentence to information already in memory. Languages have various syntactic devices for signaling supposed as opposed to asserted information. Supposed information is material the speaker supposes to be already in the listener's memory. Asserted information is new information that the speaker wants to relate to the supposed information.

7. Linguistic units larger than sentences, such as paragraphs and texts, are structured hierarchically according to certain relations. Information higher in a text structure tends to be better recalled than that lower in the struc-

ture. Comprehension of a text depends critically on the perceiver's ability to identify the higher order structures that organize it.

8. Adults tend not to be limited in their reading ability by physiological or perceptual factors. Rather, they are limited by the extent of their general language-comprehension abilities and by their ability to adaptively control their reading rate.

A favorite device in science fiction is the computer or robot that can understand and speak langauge—whether evil, like HAL in *2001,* or beneficial, like C3PO in *Star Wars.* Workers in artificial intelligence have been trying to develop computers that understand and generate language. Some progress is being made, but it is clear from current research on language that actually inventing a language-processing machine will be a monumental achievement. An enormous amount of knowledge and intelligence underlies the successful use of language. In this chapter and in the next we will consider what is known about the human ability to understand and generate language. We start with comprehension because this aspect of language processing has been studied most thoroughly.

Language comprehenders unavoidably play a passive role. They must respond to what is said to them. In contrast, language generators play a correspondingly active role, in that they basically control the conversation. (Of course, in a typical conversation participants regularly switch roles according to prevailing rules of etiquette.) This asymmetry explains why we know more about the comprehension process than about language generation. Experimenters can exercise control over the material a subject is asked to comprehend, but gaining control over that which the subject generates is very difficult.

In discussing language comprehension, we will be treating comprehension as it is involved in both listening and reading. It is often thought that of the two, the listening process is the more basic. Comprehension in reading involves the listening factors, but it is thought to involve other factors as well. Therefore, researchers give a primary emphasis to understanding the comprehension processes that are common to listening and reading. Research on basic comprehension processes can involve either written or spoken material. Researchers' choice of whether to use written or spoken material is determined by considerations of experimental tractibility. We will review in this chapter what is known about the general language processes, and will close with a section on the factors that are unique to reading.

Comprehension can be analyzed into three stages. The first stage comprises the *perceptual processes* by which the acoustic or written message is originally encoded. The second stage is termed the parsing stage. *Parsing* is the process by which the words in the message are transformed into a mental representation of the combined meaning of the words. The third stage is the *utilization* stage, in which comprehenders actually use the mental representation of the sentence's meaning. If the sentence is an assertion, the listeners may simply store the meaning in memory; if it is a question, they may answer; if it is an instruction, they may obey. However, listeners are not always so compliant. They may use an assertion about the weather to make an inference about the speaker's personality, they may answer a question with a question, or they may do just the opposite of what the speaker asks. These three stages— perception, parsing, and utilization—are by necessity partially ordered in time; however, they also partly overlap. Listeners can be making inferences from the first part of a sentence while they are perceiving a later part.

This chapter will focus on the two higher level processes—parsing and utilization. The perceptual stage was already discussed in Chapter 3.

Parsing

Sentence Patterns

Language is structured according to a set of rules that tells us how to go from a particular string of words to an interpretation of that string's meaning. For instance, in English we know that if we hear a sequence of the form *A noun verb a noun,* the speaker means that an instance of the first noun has the specified relation (verb) to an instance of the second noun. In contrast, if the sentence is of the form *A noun was verbed by a noun,* the speaker means that an instance of the second noun has the specified relation to the first noun. Thus, our knowledge of the structure of English allows us to appreciate the difference between *A doctor shot a lawyer* and *A doctor was shot by a lawyer.* One way to represent our knowledge of such rules is as a series of productions, in which the condition of each production specifies the word pattern and the action builds into memory the meaning conveyed by that pattern. Such constructs are called *parsing productions.* We might represent our knowledge of the two English structures cited above with the following pair of productions:

IF the sentence is of the form *A noun-1 verb a noun-2*
THEN the meaning is that an instance of *noun-1*
has the relation *verb* to an instance of *noun-2*

IF the sentence is of the form *A noun-1 was verbed by a noun-2*
THEN the meaning is that an instance of *noun-2* had the relation *verbed* to an instance of *noun-1*

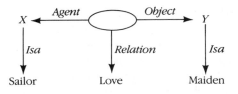

Figure 12-1 The network representation of the meaning corresponding to the sentence *A sailor loved a maiden.* The letter *X* represents an instance of a sailor and *Y* an instance of a maiden.

In these productions, *noun-1, verb,* and *noun-2* serve to indicate whether the words should be nouns or verbs. The first production would apply if the sentence was *A sailor loved a maiden,* and its action would be to build a representation of the sentence's meaning: that an instance of *sailor* had the relation of *loving* to an instance of *maiden.* (For simplicity we are ignoring the distinction between words and the concepts they refer to.) The effect of these productions can be represented as building propositional networks in active memory (see Chapter 5). So, for instance, the first production above applied to the sentence *A sailor loved a maiden* would build the network illustrated in Figure 12-1.

In learning to comprehend a language we acquire a great many rules that encode the various linguistic patterns in the language and relate these patterns to meaning interpretations. However, pattern rules that process whole sentences are not always possible because of the productivity of language discussed in the last chapter. Sentences can be very long and complex. A very large (probably infinite) number of patterns would be required to encode all possible sentence forms. Consider this example:

> There is a tendency in the average citizen, even if he has a high standing in his profession, to consider the decisions relating to the life of the society to which he belongs as matters of fate on which he has no influence.

A single pattern constructed to process this sentence might take the following form:

> There is a *noun preposition* the *adjective noun,* even if *pronoun verb* a *adjective noun preposition adjective noun,* to *verb* the *noun participle preposition* the *noun preposition* the *noun preposition relative-pronoun pronoun verb* as *noun preposition noun preposition relative-pronoun pronoun verb adjective noun.*

Note that most words in the sentence are replaced by classes such as noun, verb, and preposition. Thus, this pattern could characterize a large number of sentences, for instance.

> There is an inclination in the adult female, even if she practices a great deal of personal independence, to regard the officials participating in the government of the community in which she lives as men of character to whom she owes absolute allegiance.

While many potential sentences would satisfy this pattern, it is unlikely that we have encountered any of them. To see that this is so, let us calculate the number of different patterns 43 words long. We can do this by considering how many variations there are on the pattern above. At almost any point, this pattern could be continued in a variety of ways. For instance, consider the possible ways of continuing the sentence after the first three words, *There is a:*

1. with a noun, as in the original examples;
2. with an adjective, as in *There is a funny story. . . ;*
3. with an adverb, as in *There is a very funny story. . . .*

Having chosen a noun for this position, consider the number of options we have for continuing *There is a noun:*

1. with a preposition, as in the original examples;
2. with the infinitive *to,* as in *There is a tendency to believe. . . ;*
3. with a relative pronoun, as in *There is a tendency that is hard to resist. . . ;*
4. with an article, as in *There is a tendency, a desire, and a compulsion. . . ;*
5. with a participle, as in *There is a tendency growing in our society. . . ;*
6. with an adverb, as in *There is a tendency, unfortunately, to construct. . . .*

A conservative assumption might be that each fragment can be continued in three possible ways. Since there are 43 positions in the sentence, this assumption would mean that $3^{43} \cong 328,260,000,000,000,000,000$ different 43-word patterns are possible in the English language. This number, a great deal larger than the number of seconds in an average human life, is another testament to the productivity of natural language. It is by this reasoning that we can be certain that learned patterns do not exist in any language for every possible sentence structure within that language.

The Concatenation of Constituents

Although we have not learned to process full sentence patterns such as the one above, we have learned to process subpatterns, or phrases, of these sentences and to combine, or *concatenate,* these subpatterns. These subpatterns correspond to basic phrases, or units, in a sentence's surface structure. These units are referred to as *constituents.*

Table 12-1 displays three productions capable of analyzing a variety of sentences by concatenating analyses of the sentence constituents. This production set uses the term *string* to refer to sequences of words that occur in the sentence. The productions look for various string patterns. Production NP will recognize some simple noun phrases; RELATIVE will recognize some relative clause patterns (i.e., noun-modifying clauses such as *who ate the cheese, who loved a sailor*); and MAIN will recognize some simple subject-verb-object sentences. This set of productions can handle sentences composed from indefinite articles, nouns, verbs, and relative clauses. An example of such a sentence is

A princess, who loved a sailor, bought a ship.

The whole sentence can be regarded as a string of words; the productions in Table 12-1 enable the perceiver to pick out various constituents in the string. Figure 12-2 illustrates the application of these productions to the analysis of this sentence. Part (a) shows the range over which each production would apply, and part (b) shows the resulting meaning representation.

It is worthwhile to emphasize the important features of this example:

1. Language-processing productions look for typically occurring sentence patterns or constituents, such as *a noun* or *person verb object.*

2. The productions build in memory the semantic interpretation of these patterns.

Table 12-1 *Production for parsing various sentence constituents*

Name of production		Form of production
NP	IF	the string is of the form *A noun*
	THEN	the meaning is an instance of *noun*
RELATIVE	IF	the string is of the form *person who verb object*
	THEN	the meaning is that *person* has the relation *verb* to *object*
MAIN	IF	the string is of the form *person verb object*
	THEN	the meaning is that *person* has the relation *verb* to *object*

(a)

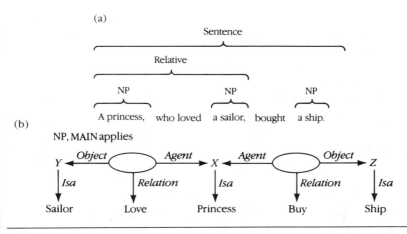

(b) NP, MAIN applies

Figure 12-2 (a) Range of the example sentence over which the productions in Table 12-1 apply; (b) meaning representation built as a result of their application.

3. A total sentence is processed through the concatenation of a number of pattern-recognizing productions.

Pattern-recognizing production systems are a means of implementing the idea that people have a set of strategies and rules for dividing a sentence up into constituents, identifying the character of each constituent, and applying a semantic interpretation to each constituent. Each production embodies one such rule. The productions rely for their success on the fact that sentences contain various clues (word order; key words, such as *who*; inflections) that allow the constituents to be identified. This conception of parsing has been proposed by many researchers (e.g., Bever, 1970; Fodor & Garrett, 1967; Kimball, 1973; Watt, 1970). It is also similar to proposals (Kaplan & Bresnan, 1981) for parsing the lexicalist grammer that we discussed in Chapter 11.

A similarity exists between pattern-recognizing productions and the rewrite rules that generate the surface structure of a sentence, discussed in Chapter 11. The three rewrite rules that correspond to the productions in Table 12-1 are

SENTENCE →NP verb NP	(MAIN)
NP →NP who verb NP	(RELATIVE)
NP →a noun	(NP)

In applying these rewrite rules,[1] we would generate the example sentence— *A princess, who loved a sailor, bought a ship*—in the following steps:

---

[1]In Chapter 11 we followed the traditional linguistic practice of analyzing SENTENCE into subject + predicate, subject into NP, and predicate into verb + NP. The subject-predicate distinction has been glossed over here for the sake of simplicity.

SENTENCE → NP *bought* NP	(apply MAIN)
SENTENCE → NP *bought a ship*	(apply NP)
SENTENCE → NP, *who loved* NP, *bought a ship*	(apply RELATIVE)
SENTENCE → *A princess, who loved a sailor, bought a ship.*	(apply NP twice)

Thus, parsing productions analyze a sentence by reversing the process of deriving a sentence through rewrite rules, interpreting the meaning of each phrase as they do so.

The Psychological Reality of Constituent Structure

The production systems examined in the preceding subsection process a sentence in terms of constituents, or phrases. If this analysis accurately models language comprehension, we would expect that the more clearly identifiable the constituent structure of a sentence is, the more easily understandable the sentence would be. Graf and Torrey (1966) presented sentences to subjects a line at a time. The passages could be presented in form A, in which each line corresponded with a major constituent boundary, or in form B, in which this was not the case. Examples of the two types of passages follow:

Form A	*Form B*
During World War II,	During World War
even fantastic schemes	II, even fantastic
received consideration	schemes received
if they gave promise	consideration if they gave
of shortening the conflict.	promise of shortening the conflict.

Subjects showed better comprehension of passages in form A. This finding demonstrates that the identification of constituent structure is important to the parsing of a sentence.

Another feature of the parsing process is that after a production has applied to interpret a constituent, the exact words in the constituent are no longer needed. Thus, we would predict that subjects will show poorer memory for the exact wording of a constituent after it has been parsed and parsing on another constituent has begun. An experiment by Jarvella (1971) confirms this prediction. He read subjects passages that were interrupted at various points. At the points of interruption, subjects were instructed to write down as much of the passage as they could remember. Of interest were passages that ended with 20 words, such as the following:

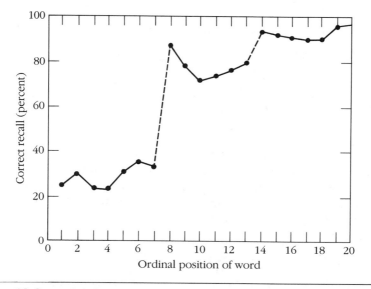

Figure 12-3 Probability of recalling a word as a function of its position in the last 20 words in a passage. The broken lines show jumps in recall at constituent boundaries. (Adapted from Jarvella, 1971.)

```
     1    2   3   4      5      6        7
    The tone of the document was threatening.
        8     9    10   11    12     13
    Having failed to disprove the charges,
       14    15   16   17   18  19      20
    Taylor was later fired by the president.
```

Subjects were prompted, after hearing the last word, to recall the entire passage. Each passage ended with a seven-word sentence followed by a sentence composed of a six-word subordinate clause followed by a seven-word main clause. The two clauses are the two major constituents of the second sentence. Because the production-system model outlined earlier retains a verbatim representation of only the last constituent in the sentence it is currently processing, that model would predict that a subject would have better memory for the second constituent of the second sentence than for its first constituent.

Figure 12-3 plots probability of recall for each of the 20 words in a passage of the form shown above. Note that sharp rises in the function occur at two points—once at word 8, the beginning of the second sentence, and once at word 14, the beginning of the main clause. The graph indicates that subjects have the poorest memory for the first sentence, that a jump occurs to better memory for the first clause of the second sentence, and that another jump occurs to best memory for the most recent clause. Thus, these data reflect two effects. First, as expected, subjects show best memory for the last major constituent, a result consistent with the hypothesis that they retain a verbatim representation of the last constituent only. The second effect, the sharp drop-off at the sentence boundary, requires a different explanation. It may occur because subjects work on a different meaning structure for each sentence. After finishing a sentence, they lose their access to that sentence's meaning representation. This effect would make reconstruction of the previous sentence quite difficult.

An experiment by Caplan (1972) also presents evidence for use of constituent structure, but this study uses a reaction-time methodology. Subjects were presented aurally first with a sentence and then with a probe word; they then had to indicate as quickly as possible whether the probe word was in the sentence. Caplan contrasted pairs of sentences such as the following:

1. Now that artists are working fewer hours oil prints are rare.

2. Now that artists are working in oil prints are rare.

Interest focused on how quickly subjects would recognize *oil* in these two sentences when probed at the ends of the sentences. The sentences were cleverly constructed so that in both sentences the word *oil* was fourth from the end and was followed by the same words. In fact, by splicing tape, Caplan arranged the presentation so that subjects heard the same recording of these last four words whichever full sentence they heard. However, in sentence 1 *oil* is part of the last constituent, *oil prints are rare,* whereas, in sentence 2 it is part of the first constituent, *now that artists are working in oil*. Caplan predicted that subjects would recognize *oil* more quickly in sentence 1 because they would still have active in memory a representation of this constituent. As he predicted, the probe word was recognized more rapidly if it occurred in the last constituent.

The Use of Syntactic Cues

Consider again the patterns in the conditions of the productions in Table 12-1. Note that function words, such as *a* and *who,* are very important to correct pattern recognition. Consider the following set of sentences:

1. The boy whom the girl liked was sick.

2. The boy the girl liked was sick.

3. The boy the girl and the dog were sick.

Sentences 1 and 2 are equivalent except that in 2 *whom* is deleted. Sentence 2 is a shorter sentence, but the cost of shortening is the loss of a cue as to how the sentence should be analyzed. At the point of *The boy the girl* it is ambiguous whether we have a relative clause, as in sentence 2, or a conjunction, as in sentence 3. If it is true that function words such as *whom* are used to indicate which parsing patterns are relevant, then constructions such as sentence 2 should be more difficult to parse than those similar to sentence 1.

Hakes and Foss (1970; Hakes, 1972) tested this prediction using what has been called the *phoneme-monitoring task*. They used double embedded sentences such as the following:

1. The zebra which the lion that the gorilla chased killed was running.

2. The zebra the lion the gorilla chased killed was running.

Sentence 2 lacks relative pronouns and so is easily confused with sentences having a noun-conjunction structure. Subjects were required to perform two simultaneous tasks. One task was to comprehend and paraphrase the sentence. The second task was to listen for a particular phoneme—in this case a [g] (in gorilla). Hakes and Foss predicted that the more difficult a sentence was to comprehend, the more time subjects would take to detect the target phoneme, since they would have less attention left over from the comprehension task with which to perform the monitoring. In fact, the prediction was borne out; subjects did take longer to indicate hearing [g] when presented with sentences such as sentence 2, which lacked relative pronouns.

Semantic Considerations

Semantic Patterns

While it is clear that people use syntactic patterns, such as those illustrated above, for understanding sentences, they can also make use of the meanings of the words involved. An individual can determine the meaning of a string of words simply by considering how they can be put together in order to make sense. Thus, when Tarzan says, "Jane fruit eat," we know what he means even though this sentence does not correspond to the syntax of English. We realize that a relationship is being asserted between something edible and someone capable of eating. Thus, the listener uses a semantic pattern to comprehend a sentence. This semantic pattern could be embodied by the following production:

EATING   IF   the speaker says *eat*
                       and the speaker says the name of a food
                       and the speaker says the name of a person
         THEN   the speaker is asserting that the person
                       eats the food

Translated, production EATING assumes that if the speaker mentions eating, an edible food, and a person, then the speaker means that the person ate (or should eat) the food.

Considerable evidence suggests that people use such strategies in language comprehension. Strohner and Nelson (1974) had 2- and 3-year old children act out with animal dolls the following two sentences:

The cat chased the mouse.

The mouse chased the cat.

In both cases, the children interpreted the sentence as indicating that the cat chased the mouse, a meaning that corresponded to their prior knowledge about cats and mice. Thus, these young children were relying more heavily on semantic patterns than on syntactic patterns.

Fillenbaum (1971, 1974) had adults paraphrase sentences among which were "perverse" items such as

John was buried and died.

More than 60 percent of the subjects paraphrased the sentences in a way that gave them a more conventional meaning, for example, here indicating that John died first and then was buried. However, the normal syntactic interpretation of such constructions would be that the first activity occurred before the second, as in

John had a drink and went to the party.

as opposed to

John went to the party and had a drink.

So it seems that when a semantic principle is placed in conflict with a syntactic principle the semantic principle sometimes (but not always) will determine the interpretation of the sentence.

Integration of Syntax and Semantics

It appears that a listener combines both syntactic and semantic information in comprehending a sentence. Tyler and Marslen-Wilson (1977) had subjects try to continue fragments like

(a) If you walk too near the runway, landing planes are

(b) If you've been trained as a pilot, landing planes are

The phrase *landing planes,* by itself, is ambiguous. It can mean either "planes that are landing" or "to land planes." Followed by the plural verb *are,* however, it must have the first meaning. Thus, the syntactic constraints determine a meaning for the ambiguous phrase. The prior context in (a) is consistent with this meaning, whereas the prior context in (b) is not. Subjects took longer to continue (b), which suggests that they were using both the semantics of the prior context and the syntax of the current phrase to disambiguate *landing planes.* When these factors are in conflict, the subject's comprehension is hurt.

Bates, McNew, MacWhinney, Devesocvi, and Smith (1982) looked at the issue of combining syntax and semantics in a different paradigm. They had subjects interpret word strings like

Chased the eraser the dog

If you were forced to, what meaning would you assign to this word string? The syntactic fact that agents precede objects seems to imply that it was the eraser that did the chasing and the dog who was being chased. The semantics, however, suggest the opposite. In fact, American speakers prefer to go with the syntax, but sometimes will adopt the semantic interpretation—that is, most say *The eraser chased the dog,* but some say *The dog chased the eraser.* On the other hand, if the word string is:

Chased the dog the eraser

listeners all agree on the interpretation—that is that the dog chased the eraser.

Another interesting part of the Bates et al. study concerned comparing Americans with Italians. When syntactic cues were put in conflict with semantic cues, Italians tended to go with the semantic cues, whereas Americans preferred the syntax. The most critical case concerned sentences like

The eraser bites the dog

or its Italian translation:

La gomma morde il cane

Americans almost always followed the syntax and interpreted this sentence to mean that the eraser is doing the biting. In contrast, Italians preferred to use the semantics and interpret that the dog is doing the biting. Like English, however, Italian, has a subject-verb-object syntax. Thus, we see that listeners combine both syntactic and semantic cues in interpreting the sentence. Moreover, the weighting of these two types of cues can vary from language to language. This and other evidence indicates that speakers of Italian weight semantic cues more heavily than do speakers of English.

Ambiguity

One of the problems a language comprehender must deal with is ambiguity. There are sentences that are capable of two or more interpretations, either because of ambiguous words or ambiguous syntactic interpretations. Examples of such sentences are the following:

John went to the bank.

Flying planes can be dangerous.

It is also useful to distinguish between *transient ambiguity* and *permanent ambiguity*. The examples above are of permanent ambiguity. That is, the ambiguity remains to the end of the sentence. Transient ambiguity refers to sentences that are temporarily ambiguous but that are no longer ambiguous by the end of the sentence. An instance is

The old train the young.

Following the word *train,* it is unclear whether *old* is a noun or an adjective. The sentence could have continued to yield a sentence in which *train* was a noun:

The old train left the station.

This ambiguity is resolved by the end of the sentence.

Transient ambiguity is quite prevalent in language. Consider this sentence:

The model snapped the picture.

After *The model,* it is ambiguous whether the sentence refers to a person or an inanimate object, or an adjective, or a theory. After *snapped,* a great many interpretations are still possible. Consider the following alternative continuations:

The model snapped at the photographer.

The model snapped at by the photographer cried.

The model snapped on a dress.

The model snapped open and the parts spewed over the table.

Each of these continuations represents a different interpretation of the phrase *The model snapped.* Partly because of the ambiguity of natural language, efforts to develop computer programs that will understand natural languages have not yet been fully successful. Because a sentence can be interpreted in many ways at many points, it is difficult to program a computer to choose the intended meaning for a whole sentence. Often, programs must compute a large number of different meanings for sentences. As this number of meanings grows, so does the cost of computation time.

We do not fully understand how humans deal with ambiguity in order to comprehend natural language. However, some of the mechanisms are clear. Humans make heavy use of contextual constraints in their efforts to select a single meaning for each pattern to be interpreted. However, it appears that they select only one interpretation (their best guess) for a pattern and carry it through to the end of the sentence. If the best guess turns out to be wrong, their comprehension suffers and they have to backtrack and try another interpretation. Consider this example:

I know more beautiful women than Miss America

although she knows quite a few.

Such instances indicate that we can be misled in our initial interpretation of a sentence. It is sometimes said that the listener has been "led down a garden path." For this reason, the theory that we consider only a single meaning at a time is referred to as the *garden-path theory* of ambiguity.

Apparently, humans are affected by ambiguity while they are trying to interpret a sentence constituent, but once they have interpreted the constituent, ambiguity has no further effect. Bever, Garrett, and Hurtig (1973) had subjects complete the following four types of fragments:

1. Although flying airplanes can

2. Although flying airplanes can be dangerous, he

3. Although some airplanes can

4. Although some airplanes can be dangerous, he

Note that fragments 1 and 2 are ambiguous whereas 3 and 4 are not. Fragments 1 and 3 are very similar in structure, but only sentence 1 is ambiguous. That is, in fragment 1 we can either be referring to airplanes that are flying or to the act of flying planes. If ambiguous constituents are harder to process because multiple meanings must be considered, subjects should take longer to continue fragment 1 than 3. This prediction was confirmed. Fragments 2 and 4 are also very similar except for the ambiguity of 2. However, in fragment 2, unlike 1, the ambiguity occurs in a constituent that has been completed. If subjects settle on a meaning after a constituent is complete, there should be no difference in continuation time between ambiguous fragment 2 and unambiguous fragment 4. Again, this prediction was confirmed. Thus, it appears that we do consider the ambiguity of a constituent while processing it, but once we have finished with the constituent we settle on a particular interpretation. As long as we do not have to change our interpretation, the ambiguity has no further effect on sentence processing.

Lexical Ambiguity

A series of experiments by Swinney (e.g., Swinney, 1979) have been useful in revealing how ambiguous words are disambiguated. He had subjects listen to sentences like the following:

> Rumor had it that, for years, the government building had been plagued with problems. The man was not surprised when he found several spiders, roaches, and other bugs in the corner of the room.

Swinney was concerned with the ambiguous word *bugs*. Just after hearing the word, subjects would be presented with a string of letters on the screen, and their task was to judge whether that string made a correct word or not. Thus, if they saw *sew* they would say *yes*; but if they saw *siw*, they would say *no*, it was not a word. This is the lexical decision task that we described earlier in Chapter 6 in discussing the mechanisms of spreading activation.

The critical contrasts involved having subjects judge words like *spy, ant,* or *sew,* following *bugs.* The word *ant* is related to the primed meaning of *bugs,* while *spy* is related to the unprimed meaning. The word *sew* defines a neutral control condition. If the to-be-judged word is presented within 400 msec of the prime, *bugs,* Swinney found that recognition of both *spy* and *ant* was speeded. Thus, the presentation of *bugs* immediately activates both of its meanings and their associations. If Swinney waited over 700 msec, however, there was facilitation only for the related word *ant.* It appears that a correct meaning is selected in this time and the other meaning is deactivated. Thus, two meanings of an ambiguous word are momentarily active, but context operates very rapidly to indicate the appropriate meaning.

Utilization

Once a sentence has been parsed and mapped into a meaning representation, what then? A listener seldom simply passively records the meaning. If the sentence is a question or imperative, the speaker expects the listener to take some action in response. However, even for declarative sentences there is usually more to be done than simply to register the sentence. Consider this sentence:

> The General Assembly condemned Israeli occupation of Arab lands.

Figure 12-4A illustrates the propositional-network representation that might be assigned to this sentence by a set of parsing productions. However, a

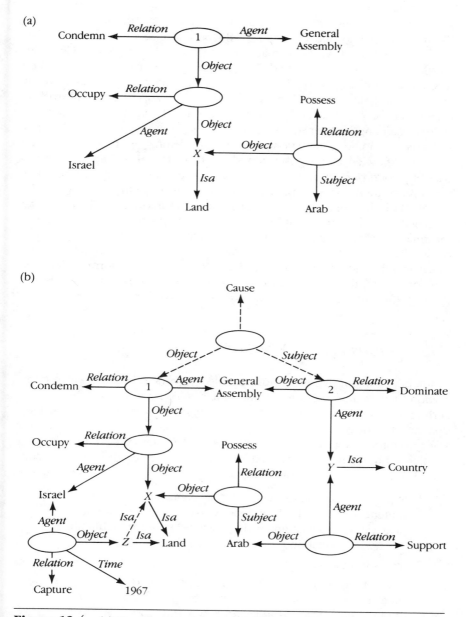

Figure 12-4 (a) Construction of the meaning representation for the sentence. *The General Assembly condemned Israeli occupation of Arab lands.* (b) Integration of this structure with past knowledge. The dotted lines indicate new links added in order to achieve this integration.

number of connections are necessary in order to relate this sentence to the listener's other knowledge. Figure 12-4b shows the memory structure after these connections have been made to integrate this new knowledge with existing knowledge. The dotted lines indicate additional connections. The listener will probably recognize the lands in the sentence as an entity already known—the lands captured by Israel in the 1967 war. Thus, a link will be established between the node *X* which stands for the land mentioned in the sentence, and node *Z,* representing the concept of the captured land, already in memory. Another connection relates the condemnation (proposition node 1) to the knowledge (proposition node 2) that the United Nations is dominated by countries supportive of the Arabs. Thus, at the very least, listeners try to relate the information in sentences to knowledge they have about the world. Basically, this task involves relating new information to old. Most sentences in a comprehensible communication contain both new and old information. This is because the speaker, in trying to assert new information, must relate it to old information that the listener knows. The speaker is said to *suppose* the old information in order to *assert* the new information. In the example given, the old information is that Israel occupied Arab lands and the new information is that the United Nations voted to condemn this.

Suppositions versus Assertions

A number of linguistic conventions enable speakers to indicate which information they assume the listener knows and which information they are asserting as new. In this context, the term *supposition* refers to information assumed by speakers to be already known by listeners; the term *assertion* refers to information the speakers consider either new or warranting special emphasis. Among the devices used for signaling whether information is supposed or asserted are the following:

1. Supposed information tends to be contained in subjects of sentences; asserted information tends to occur in predicates. Also, various special linguistic structures exist for highlighting asserted information by emphasizing its predicate position.
2. Stress indicates asserted information.
3. The definite article *the* before a noun phrase indicates that the speaker assumes that the referent of the noun phrase is known; the indefinite article *a* indicates a new referent.

The devices for indicating whether supposed or asserted information is being expressed can be complex in their interactions, but generally their functions are clear.

Consider the following sentences, in which words in all capitals are stressed:

1. John hit BILL.

2. What happened to Bill was that JOHN HIT him.

3. The pilot caused an accident.

4. The pilot caused the accident.

5. The breed Bob likes is LABRADOR.

6. The one who likes Labradors is BOB.

7. The lawyer SHOT the sailor.

8. As for the shooting, it was the lawyer who did it to the sailor.

9. A lawyer shot a sailor.

10. I am HONEST.

11. I am NOT a crook.

In sentence 1, *Bill* is stressed and occurs in the predicate. Thus, this sentence would probably be used when the listeners knew that John hit somebody and the speaker wanted to tell them whom. In sentence 2, a circumlocution is used to put *John hit* into the predicate position, where it is stressed. Thus, the sentence structure indicates the supposition that something happened to BILL and the assertion that what happened was that John hit him. In sentences 3 and 4 no stress is used, but in sentence 3 the indefinite article *an* occurs in the predicate position, whereas in sentence 4 the definite article *the* occurs. In both cases a definite article is used with the subject *pilot*. Thus, sentence 3 assumes that the listeners know of the pilot and asserts that an accident took place that the pilot caused. In contrast, sentence 4 assumes that listeners know of both the pilot and the accident and asserts that the first caused the second. Sentences 5 and 6 also illustrate redundant linguistic devices of stress and position for signaling supposed versus asserted information. Sentence 5 supposes that the listeners know Bob likes a breed and asserts that this breed is the Labrador. In contrast, sentence 6 supposes that someone likes Labradors and asserts that this person is Bob. Sentence 7 assumes that the listeners know both the lawyer and the sailor and asserts that one shot the other. Sentence 8, in addition to assuming that the lawyer and the sailor are known, also supposes that the listeners know of the shooting. Sentence 8 asserts information only about who was involved in the shooting. Sentence 9 is interesting in that it signals that the listeners should expect to know nothing— not who the lawyer is, who the sailor is, or that a shooting occurred. We might expect to find this kind of sentence at the beginning of a story.[2]

---

[2]However, in the modern literary style called *in media res* ("in the middle of things"), such openings, which clearly acknowledge that the reader does not yet know anything about what is going on, are in disfavor. Rather, modern stories tend to open in the midst of things.

Sentences 10 and 11 provide an interesting sociopolitical contrast. Sentence 10 simply asserts that I am honest. However, sentence 11 has a more complex structure, although it conveys the same meaning. As we will discuss further shortly, sentence 11 supposes that it is reasonable to suppose that I am a crook, but asserts that this is not true.

Evidence for the Supposition-Assertion Distinction

This supposition-assertion contrast constitutes part of what is called the *pragmatics* of language—that is, information conveyed by the sentence about how the sentence is to be used once its meaning has been extracted. One thing listeners must do with supposed information is to search for it in their memories, because the information should provide a connection between the sentence and past knowledge. Thus, we would expect a subject to be slow to comprehend a sentence when information was signaled as being supposed but the subject was unable to find a referent in memory for the supposed information. Haviland and Clark (1974) report an experiment directed at this issue. They compared subjects' comprehension time for two sentence pairs such as the following:

1. Ed was given an alligator for his birthday. The alligator was his favorite present.

2. Ed wanted an alligator for his birthday. The alligator was his favorite present.

Both pairs have the same second sentence. Pair 1 introduces in its first sentence a specific antecedent for the *alligator*. On the other hand, although in pair 2 *alligator* is mentioned in the first sentence, a specific alligator is not posited. Thus, no antecedent occurs in the first sentence of pair 2 for *the alligator*. The definite article *the* in the second sentence of the pair supposes a specific antecedent. Therefore, we would expect that subjects would have difficulty with the second sentence in pair 2 but not in pair 1. In the Haviland and Clark experiment subjects saw pairs of such sentences one at a time. After they comprehended each sentence they pressed a button. The time was measured from the presentation of the second sentence until subjects pressed a button indicating that they understood that sentence. Subjects took an average of 1031 msec to comprehend the second sentence in pairs such as 1 above, in which an antecedent was given, but they took an average of 1168 msec to comprehend the second sentence in pairs such as 2 above, in which no antecedent for the definite noun phrase occurred. Thus, comprehension took over a tenth of a second longer when no antecedent occurred. This result confirms the hypothesis that comprehension is impaired if the supposed information is not available to the comprehender.

Figure 12-5 Examples of pictures presented to subjects by Hornby to determine the effect of the supposition-assertion distinction on question answering. Subjects make more errors processing sentences about the pictures that contain an error in supposition rather than assertion. (From *Psychology and Language* by Herbert H. Clark and Eve V. Clark. Copyright 1977 by Harcourt Brace Jovanovich, Inc. Reproduced by permission of the publisher.)

Another interesting aspect of the supposition-assertion distinction is that it implies that listeners should assume they know the supposed information and apply their critical attention to that which is asserted. An experiment by Loftus and Zanni (1975) illustrates the power of suppositions in this regard. These experimenters showed subjects a film of an automobile accident and asked them a series of questions. Some subjects were asked,

1. Did you see a broken headlight?

Other subjects were asked,

2. Did you see the broken headlight?

In fact, there was no broken headlight in the film, but question 2 uses a definite article, which supposes the existence of a broken headlight. Subjects were more likely to respond *yes* when asked the question in form 2. As Loftus notes, this finding has important implications for the interrogation of eyewitnesses.

An experiment by Hornby (1974) also illustrates the importance of the supposition-assertion distinction. He showed subjects one of a pair of pictures such as those in Figure 12-5 and asked subjects to verify whether a sentence was true of it. The picture was shown for only 50 msec and the subjects therefore made many errors. Of interest were their error rates in responding to the following false sentences:

1. It is the BOY who is petting the cat.
2. It is the CAT which the boy is petting.
3. The one who is petting the cat is the BOY.
4. What the boy is petting is the CAT.

Sentence 1 supposes that someone is petting the cat and asserts that the someone is a boy; the same is true for sentence 3. In contrast, sentences 2 and 4 suppose that the boy is petting something and assert that the something is the cat. Each sentence matches one picture on its supposed information and contradicts it on its asserted information; the match is reversed for the other picture in the pair. Subjects made more errors when the sentence contradicted the picture on its supposed rather than its asserted information. That is, for sentence 1 they made more errors on picture b than a; for sentence 2, more errors on picture a than b; for sentence 3, more errors on picture b than a; and for sentence 4, more errors on picture a than b. It seems that subjects often did not bother to check the supposed information but only considered the asserted information. Overall, 72 percent errors were recorded when the supposed information was wrong, but only 39 percent when the asserted information was wrong.

Negatives

Negative sentences appear to suppose a positive sentence and then assert the opposite. For instance, the sentence *John is not a crook* supposes that it is reasonable to assume *John is a crook* but asserts that this is false. As another example, imagine the following four replies from a normally healthy friend to the question *How are you feeling?*

1. I am well.
2. I am sick.
3. I am not well.
4. I am not sick.

Replies 1 through 3 would not be regarded as unusual linguistically, but reply 4 does seem peculiar. By using the negative it is supposing that thinking of our friend as sick is reasonable. In contrast, the negative in reply 3 is quite acceptable, since supposing that the friend is normally well is reasonable.

Clark and Chase (e.g., Chase & Clark, 1972; Clark & Chase, 1972; Clark,

Figure 12-6 A card such as that presented to subjects in sentence-verification experiments of Clark and Chase. Subjects were to say whether simple positive and negative sentences correctly described these pictures.

1974) have been involved in a series of experiments on the verification of negatives (see also Trabasso, Rollins, & Shaughnessy, 1971; Carpenter & Just, 1975). In a typical experiment, they presented subjects with a card like that shown in Figure 12-6 and asked them to verify one of four sentences about this card:

1. The star is above the plus—true affirmative.
2. The plus is above the star—false affirmative.
3. The plus is not above the star—true negative.
4. The star is not above the plus—false negative.

The terms *true* and *false* refer to whether the sentence is true of the picture; the terms *affirmative* and *negative* refer to whether the sentence structure has a negative element. Sentences 1 and 2 involve a simple assertion, but sentences 3 and 4 involve a supposition plus an assertion. Sentence 3 supposes that the plus is above the star and asserts that this supposition is false; sentence 4 supposes that the star is above the plus and asserts that this supposition is false. Clark assumes that subjects will check the supposition first and the assertion next. In sentence 3, the supposition does not match the picture, but in sentence 4 the supposition does match the picture. Assuming that mismatches will take longer to process, Clark and Chase predict that subjects will take longer to respond to sentence 3, a true negative, than to sentence 4, a false negative. In contrast, subjects should take longer to process sentence 2, the false affirmative, than sentence 1, the true affirmative, because sentence 2's assertion mismatches the picture. In fact, the difference between sentences

Table 12-2 *Observed and predicted reaction times in experiment verification*

Condition	Observed time	Equation	Predicted time
True affirmative	1463 msec	T	1469 msec
False affirmative	1722 msec	$T + M$	1715 msec
True negative	2028 msec	$T + M + N$	2035 msec
False negative	1796 msec	$T + N$	1789 msec

2 and 1 should be identical to the difference between sentences 3 and 4 because both differences reflect the extra time due to a mismatch to the picture.

Clark and Chase developed a simple and elegant mathematical model for such data. They assumed that processing sentences 3 and 4 took N time units longer than processing 1 and 2 because of the more complex supposition-plus-negation structure of 3 and 4. They also assumed that processing sentence 2 took M time units longer than processing 1 because of the mismatch between picture and assertion, and similarly that processing 3 took M time units longer than processing 4 because of the mismatch between picture and supposition. Finally, they assumed that processing a true affirmative such as sentence 1 took T time units. The time T reflects the time used in processes not involving the negation-and-supposition mismatch. Let us consider the total time subjects should spend processing a sentence such as 3. This sentence has a complex supposition-and-negation structure, which costs N time units, and a supposition mismatch, which costs M time units. Therefore, total processing time should be $T + M + N$. Table 12-2 shows both the observed data and the reaction-time predictions that can be derived for the Clark and Chase experiment. The best predicting values for T, M, and N for this experiment can be estimated from the data as $T = 1469$ msec, $M = 246$ msec, and $N = 320$ msec. As you and confirm, the predictions match the observed time remarkably well. In particular, the difference between true negatives and false negatives is close to the difference between false affirmatives and true affirmatives. This finding supports the hypothesis that subjects do extract the suppositions of negative sentences and match these to the picture.

Problem Solving and Reasoning

Our discussion to this point seems to have implied that utilization involves only processes specific to analyzing language structure. However, much of the utilization process involves more general cognitive abilities. Consider the following passage:

Mira was hiding in the ladies' room. She called it that even though someone had scratched out the word *ladies'* in the sign on the door, and written *women's* underneath. She called it that out of thirty-eight years habit, and until she saw the cross-out on the door, had never thought about it. "Ladies' room" was a euphemism, she supposed, and she disliked euphemisms on principle. (French, 1978, p. 7)

Language comprehenders might ask themselves the following questions in attempting to understand the passage:

1. What is Mira doing in the ladies' room?

2. Why was *ladies'* scratched off the door?

3. How old is Mira?

4. How could *ladies'* be considered a euphemism?

5. How does Mira respond to feminist issues?

Clearly, none of these questions are answered through processes specific to language. Rather the questions require a certain amount of world knowledge (in this case, about women's rooms and feminist issues) and an ability to solve problems and reason with this knowledge. Previous chapters were concerned with how knowledge is used and how we solve problems and reason. It is important to realize that language comprehension rests in part on nonlinguistic abilities and knowledge. Thus, a person can be quite fluent linguistically and still fail to comprehend. For instance, it is hard to comprehend a text on a topic with which we have little familiarity even if it is well written.

Text Structure

So far we have focused on the comprehension of single sentences in isolation. Sentences are more frequently processed in larger contexts, for example, in the reading of a textbook. We consider now the effects on the utilization process of the structure of larger portions of text.

Text, like sentences, are structured according to certain patterns, although these patterns are perhaps more flexible than those associated with sentences. Much research has been conducted on the ways in which texts tend to be structured (e.g., Grimes, 1975; Kintsch, 1977; Kintsch & van Dijk, 1976; Mandler and Johnson, 1977; Meyer, 1974; Rumelhart, 1975; Thorndyke, 1977; van Dijk, 1977; van Dijk & Kintsch, 1976). Researchers have noted that a number of recurring relationships serve to organize sentences into larger portions of a text. Some of the relations that have been identified are listed in Table 12-3. These structural relations provide cues as to how a sentence should be

Table 12-3 *Some possible types of relationships among sentences in a text*

Type of relationship	Description
1. Response	A question is presented and an answer follows, or a problem is presented and a solution follows.
2. Specific	Some specific information is given following a more general point.
3. Explanation	An explanation is given for a point.
4. Evidence	Evidence is given to support a point.
5. Sequence	Points are presented in their temporal sequence as a set.
6. Cause	An event is presented as the cause of another event.
7. Goal	An event is presented as the goal of another event.
8. Collection	A loose structure of points is presented. (This is perhaps a case where there is no real organizing relation.)

utilized. For instance, the first text structure (response) in Table 12-3 directs the reader to relate one set of sentences as part of the solution to problems posed by other sentences. These relations can occur at any level of a text. That is, the main relation organizing a paragraph might be any of the eight in the table. Subpoints in a paragraph may also be organized according to any of these relations.

To see how the relations in Table 12-3 might be used, consider Meyer's (1974) analysis of the following paragraph:

Parakeet Paragraph

The wide variety in color of parakeets that are available on the market today resulted from careful breeding of the color mutant offspring of green-bodied and yellow-faced parakeets. The light green body and yellow face color combination is the color of the parakeets in their natural habitat, Australia. The first living parakeets were brought to Europe from Australia by John Gould, a naturalist, in 1840. The first color mutation appeared in 1872 in Belgium; these birds were completely yellow. The most popular color of parakeets in the United States is sky-blue. These birds have sky-blue bodies and white faces; this color mutation occurred in 1878 in Europe. There are over 66 different colors of parakeets listed by the Color and Technical Committee of the Budgerigar Society. In addition to the original green-bodied and yellow-faced birds, colors of parakeets include varying shades of violets, blues, grays, greens, yellows, and whites. (p. 61)

Her analysis of this paragraph is approximately reproduced in Table 12-4. Note that this analysis tends to organize various facts as more or less major points. The highest level organizing relationship in this paragraph is explanation (see item 3, Table 12-3). Specifically, the major points in this explanation are that (A) there has been careful breeding of color mutants and (B) there is a wide variety of parakeet color, and point A is given as an explanation

Table 12-4 *Analysis of the Parakeet Paragraph*

I. A explains B.
  A. There was careful breeding of color mutants of green-bodied and yellow-faced parakeets. The historical sequence is
    1. Their natural habitat was Australia. Specific detail:
      a. Their color here is light-green body and yellow-face combination.
    2. The first living parakeets were brought to Europe from Australia by John Gould in 1840. Specific detail:
      a. John Gould was a naturalist.
    3. The first color mutation appeared in 1877 in Belgium. Specific detail:
      a. These birds were completely yellow.
    4. The sky-blue mutation occurred in 1878 in Europe. Specific details:
      a. These birds have sky-blue bodies and white faces.
      b. This is the most popular color in America.
  B. There is a wide variety in color of parakeets that are on the market today. Evidence for this is
    1. There are over 66 different colors of parakeets listed by the Color and Technical Committee of the Budgerigar Society.
    2. There are many available colors. A collection of these is
      a. The original green-bodied and yellow-faced birds
      b. Violets
      c. Blues
      d. Grays
      e. Greens
      f. Yellows
      g. Whites

of point B. Organized under A are some events from the history of parakeet breeding. This organization is an example of a sequence relationship. Organized under these events are specific details. So, for instance, organized under A2 is the fact that John Gould was a naturalist. Organized under point B is evidence supporting the assertion about the wide variety and some details about the variation in color available.

Text Structure and Memory

A great deal of research has demonstrated the psychological significance of text structure. Considerable disagreement prevails in the field as to exactly what system of relations should be used in the analysis of texts, and uncertainty exists as to how such systems should be applied to a text. However, memory experiments have yielded evidence that subjects do, to some degree, respond to the structure of a text.

The kind of hierarchical structure exemplified in Meyer's analysis is reminiscent of the hierarchical structures we studied in Chapter 7 on memory. From the data cited in that chapter we would expect such hierarchies to have large effects on memory—if the subjects use these hierarchies in comprehension. Meyer has shown that subjects do display better memory for the major points in such a structure. For instance, subjects are more likely to remember that there was careful breeding of color mutants (point A) than that John Gould was a naturalist (point A2a).

Thorndyke (1977) has also shown that memory for text is poorer if the organization of the text conflicts with what would be considered its "natural" structure. This is clearly what we would expect given the results of Chapter 7 (consider, for instance, the experiment of Bower et al., 1969, in that chapter). Thorndyke used a story that had a strong causal structure (relation 6 in Table 12-3). Some subjects studied the original story while other subjects studied the story with its sentences presented in a scrambled order. Subjects were able to recall 85 percent of the facts in the original story but only 32 percent of the facts in the scrambled story.

Such results are suggestive, but they tell us little about how often subjects perceive structure in text or how consistent their perceptions of text structure are with those of other subjects. If students often fail to correctly perceive the hierarchical structure of a text, then it would be quite helpful to train students to develop a structure based on relationships such as those in Table 12-3. Indeed, students are often urged to develop such a hierarchical structure in their note taking. One reason for encouraging this practice is to make students aware of the hierarchical structure in the material they are taking notes on.

Mandler and Johnson (1977) showed that children are much poorer than adults at recalling the causal structure of a story. Adults recall events and the outcomes of those events together, whereas children recall the outcomes but tend to forget how they were achieved. For instance, children might recall from a particular story that the butter melted but forget that this occurred because the butter was out in the sun. Adults do not have trouble with such simple causal structures, but they may have difficulty perceiving the more complex relationships connecting portions of a text. For instance, how easy is it for you to specify the relationship that connects this paragraph to the preceding text?

Meyer, Brandt, and Bluth (1978) studied students' perception of the high-level structure of a text—that is, the structural relations at the higher levels of hierarchies like that in Table 12-4. They found considerable variation in subjects' ability to recognize the high-level structure that organized a text. Moreover, they found that subjects' ability to identify the top-level structure of a text was an important predictor of their memory for the text. In another study, on ninth graders, Bartlett (1978) found that only 11 percent of the subjects consciously identified and used high-level structure to remember text material. This select group did twice as well as other students on their recall scores. Bartlett also showed that training students to identify and use top-level structure more than doubled recall performance.

Applications to Reading

Reading is one form of language comprehension. One of the major goals of society is to raise the reading abilities of its citizenry. Thus, it seems apt to close this chapter with a discussion of the implications of language-comprehension research for the reading process.

During reading, the eye engages in *saccadic movements*. In this mode, the eye jumps approximately every 200 msec from one position to the next. This jump is called a *saccade*. The saccade has been termed a *ballistic movement* because the time to change position is very brief (only about 5–10 msec) and because it is not possible to change the direction of the saccade once it has started. Thus, in reading the pattern is jump, pause, jump, pause, and so on. It is generally believed that information is extracted from the text only when the eye is at rest. The pause while the eye is at rest and collecting information is called a *fixation*.

Readers of English normally proceed along one line at a time, fixating at various points on a line in a left-to-right fashion. In reading fairly difficult text carefully, many readers tend to fixate on almost each word once and often twice (Just & Carpenter, 1980). Such readers are making almost 20 fixations on an average line of text. However there is no really "typical" reading rate. Depending on the reader, the material, and the purpose in reading, number of fixations per line can range from a couple to more than 20. Both the number of fixations and the time per fixation tend to increase with the difficulty of the material. In contrast, the time for the saccades from fixation to fixation does not change. Occasionally, regressions occur in reading, in which the reader moves back to an earlier part of the line or an earlier line. Frequency of regressions also varies with difficulty of text. Thus, three eye measures vary with text difficulty: number of fixations per line, duration of fixation, and number of regressions. Of course, increases in all these activities slow reading speed. There is evidence to show that slow readers differ from fast readers on all three dimensions.

It is interesting to ask what the maximum possible reading speed is. An important issue in deciding the limits of reading has to do with the number of characters that we are capable of processing during any one fixation. Experiments by McConkie and Rayner (1974) and Rayner (1975) are particularly important in assessing this issue. McConkie and Rayner, using a computer-controlled system, manipulated the amount of text that the subject could see around a fixation point. The text around the fixation area was always well composed and understandable, but the text in the periphery was mutilated (i.e., a meaningless jumble of letters). The computer monitored the fixation point of the eye by taking a reflection off the cornea. The computer controlled what text was presented to the subject on a screen. Every time the subjects changed their fixation points, the computer advanced the readable portion of the text. McConkie and Rayner were interested in measuring the area around the fixation point that subjects could use. They reasoned that if mutilated information entered this area, reading rate would drop. They found that subjects used information within an arc only about 5° around the fixation point (this area represents the fovea and the immediately surrounding retina), or no more than 10 characters to the right or left of the fixation point. Mutilation of text beyond this range had no effect on reading rate. These findings imply that subjects can process only a relatively small portion (20 characters, 10 on each side of the fixation point) of the text at any one time.

Foss and Hakes (1978) offer a rather convincing demonstration of the limitations of a single fixation. When you finish reading this paragraph, turn to page 366 and look at Figure 12-7. The figure consists of a series of words in a line with a circled X in the middle. You are to fix your vision on the X, the fixation point; when you turn to this figure (not yet), go directly to the X. As you fixate on the X, without moving your eyes, try to take in as much information to the left as possible. Then try to take in as much information to the right as possible. Remember: Do not move your eyes. OK, try it.

You should have been able to make out about two words on either side of the fixation point. The third word to either side exceeds 10 characters (blanks count) and is therefore outside the boundary of perception. This exercise is an informal demonstration of McConkie and Rayner's more precise findings.

Determinants of Reading Skill

If we are able to process 10 characters on either side of a fixation point, then we can process about 20 characters a fixation, or about three words. Assuming four fixations a second, these figures imply a maximum reading rate of approximately 750 words a minute.[3] The average adult, in fact, reads at the rate of 200–400 words per minute (usually closer to 200 words). Therefore, it seems clear that our normal reading limit is not being imposed upon us by physiological factors. Our reading speed is limited by the rate at which we

---

[3]Hakes and Foss, using estimates they admit are very optimistic, came up with a maximum of 1200 words.

can process information cognitively. This observation is important: The limits on adult reading speed tend to be *cognitive,* not motor or sensory. This conclusion is also implied by the results showing that duration of fixation, number of fixations per line, and number of regressions increase with the complexity of the text.

If the limits on reading are cognitive, are they related to speed of pattern recognition or to higher order language-comprehension factors such as parsing and utilization? There is no doubt that young children in the first years of reading are limited by their facility at the new perceptual skill. There is also no doubt that for some proportion of the population these perceptual problems remain in effect in adult life. However, general language-comprehension abilities are now believed to be the most important factors controlling reading rate in most adults and children beyond elementary school (Lesgold, Resnick, & Beck, 1978; Miller et al., 1974). The Lesgold et al. (1978) study showed that in early grades (1 through 3) the most important determinant of reading skills is perceptual ability. At this stage, students are just learning to recognize letters. The experimenters found that in later grades, as letter recognition becomes more and more automatic, the important factor is general language ability. It is particularly likely that people with reading difficulties in a college context are experiencing the effects of language-comprehension factors and not perceptual factors. It is often very hard to follow a complex conversation, and speech is usually under 200 words per minute, which would be a slow reading rate. Therefore, it should come as no surprise that general language-comprehension factors prove to be the most important limits on reading skill.

Also relevant to this issue is the series of experiments by Sticht (1972), who compared learning by reading with learning by listening in adults (Army recruits). He found a high correlation between the two types of learning. People who were poor learners by reading were poor learners by listening. This result has been replicated a number of times (e.g., Jackson & McClelland, 1979). Again the implication is that most reading difficulties are comprehension difficulties, and that the most effective way to improve reading skill is to improve language comprehension.

It is interesting to consider what the implications of knowledge about language comprehension might be for reading improvement. To start, let us review the various factors entailed in comprehension. First, we use our knowledge of the general syntactic and semantic patterns of the language to translate from words to meaning. Second, our general knowledge of the supposition-assertion distinction helps us to relate new information to old. Relevant also are such general cognitive skills as reasoning and problem solving plus general world knowledge. Finally, our knowledge of typical text structure helps us to perceive the relations between relatively large portions of linguistic input.

ONE   HOP   SILK   BUT   EYE   NOW   (X)   How   far   away   can   you   see?

Figure 12-7   Fixate on the X and see how far you can read on the periphery. (From Foss & Hakes, 1978.)

The extent to which adults use text structure in comprehension is unclear. As noted earlier, Bartlett (1978) was able to double the recall scores of ninth graders by instructing them for just 5 hours about the relations used in text structure. It is possible that a relatively small investment in remedial training on text structure might also improve adult text comprehension considerably. It should be noted, however, that Bartlett's effect was on retention, not reading rate. With respect to the other knowledge and skill components involved in reading, it seems clear that any improvement will be slow indeed. These other components are already acquired and in some cases are fairly well learned. However, as we discussed in Chapter 9, the speed with which a cognitive skill can be performed will continue to increase with practice. So, to the extent that our reading comprehension is limited by slow linguistic procedures, this constraint is reducible by general linguistic practice. Chapter 9 also provided evidence for the diminishing returns of practice. Therefore, significant effects on reading rate may occur only after years of practice.

The Importance of Childhood Practice

The importance to reading of the practice of general comprehension skills implies that childhood experience is critical to the development of reading skills. Children who have done a lot of reading, who have listened to a lot of verbal communication similar to that in text (e.g., who have had many stories read to them), and who have had the kind of upper middle-class experiences assumed in most texts have had a good preparation (i.e., a lot of practice) for reading typical high school and college texts. Durkin (1966) studied children who learned to read prior to entering school. She found that these children started with a large advantage over comparable students and maintained this advantage for the six years in which she followed them. In interviewing parents of these children, she found a higher tendency to encourage reading and to read to the children. The single most important environmental factor affecting reading skills is the amount of literacy in the home. Parents who read a lot and who buy lots of magazines, newspapers, and books tend to have children who read well (Thorndike, 1973).

From this point of view, another conclusion seems unavoidable: that television, if it replaces reading and being read to, is harmful to the development of reading skills. Television is a relatively nonlinguistic medium. To the extent that linguistic communication is involved in television, it is communication of a simple dialogue structure—not particularly apt preparation for typical text structures. Speculation as to the relationship between television and the recent drop in verbal Scholastic Aptitude Test scores has been common. (Of course, the precise amount of reading and book listening that occurred before television appeared is unknown.) Research has shown a negative correlation between the watching of almost all television shows and reading performance (the only exceptions were news programs and M*A*S*H).

The Effects of Culture and Dialect

If we accept the premises that language-comprehension factors have the greatest influence on reading performance and that practice and experience are critical to language comprehension, then it would be expected that children who come from cultures outside the mainstream or who speak dialects other than standard English are at a disadvantage with respect to the reading of textbooks written in standard American English. Much research and speculation has been concerned with possible effects of black English, an English dialect spoken by 80 percent of the black population in America (Dillard, 1972), on the reading performance of its speakers. A host of factors distinguish standard[4] and black American English. For example, at a phonological level, [i] and [e] may show no difference in black English; thus, *pin* and *pen* may be pronounced identically. At a slightly higher level, a copula like *is* may be deleted from sentences, resulting in such constructions as *He sick*. Consider another example, which would be incomprehensible to most speakers of standard American English, *You makin' sense but you don't be makin' sense*. This sentence might be liberally translated (Dillard, 1972) as *For once you've said something intelligent*. Obviously, such observable *differences* in black English are just that—differences, not instances of inferiority. However, these differences can create problems for comprehension of standard English. A speaker of standard English has difficulty in understanding black English; conversely, speakers of black English find standard English hard.

It is not the case that black-English speakers do not know standard English. In fact, many have fair ability to switch speech styles depending on context. So, in this sense black-English speakers are more capable and flexible than

---

[4]It should also be noted that "standard American English," like all other dialects, is gradually changing. One of the ways it is changing is through the importation of black-English style and vocabulary.

speakers of standard American English who do not know the dialect. The problem is that they have had much less practice on standard English and lag behind when they have to comprehend standard English. In addition, the content of their life experiences tends to differ more from the content of standard reading material than does that of standard-English speakers.

Black students, on the average, score lower on standard reading achievement tests than their white counterparts. However, the degree to which this difference is due to dialect variation is unclear. The fact that the gap increases in later school years, when general comprehension factors are more important, is consistent with the hypothesis that reading difficulty in those years is attributable to comprehension factors. However, other factors could be more important. Two major problems might be social conflict and a lack of understanding of black students by the typical school personnel. Piestrup (1973) studied the reading scores of black students whose teachers were more aware of and more supportive of cultural and linguistic characteristics of black students. Their reading scores did not lag behind the national average.

Some efforts have been made to create reading texts that reflect black culture and dialect. However, such texts might even accentuate the problem by giving black students still less practice in the standard English that typifies much of the important reading they will have to do in later years. Indeed, some black parents have complained about attempts to use such texts in schools, whereas other black parents have supported the use of such texts. Considerable controversy prevails as to the best course of action. It is not the role of cognitive psychology to make this decision, but research in the field should eventually be able to determine the consequences of the different courses of action. With all the data in, society would be able to make an informed choice.

Adaptive Control of Reading Rate

To this point, we have stressed the importance of language comprehension for reading ability, but other factors contribute significantly. One important factor is the voluntary, adaptive control of reading rate, that is, the ability to adjust the reading rate to the particular type of material being read.

Adaptive reading involves changing reading speed throughout a text in response to both the difficulty of the material and your purpose in reading it. Learning how to monitor and adjust reading style is a skill that requires a good deal of practice.

Many people, even college students, are unaware that they can learn to control their reading speed. However, this factor can be greatly improved with a few hundred hours of work, as opposed to the thousands of hours needed to significantly affect language comprehension. Many college reading-skills programs include a training procedure aimed at improving students' adaptive control of reading speed (e.g., Robinson, 1961; Thomas & Robinson, 1972). However, a number of problems are involved in successfully implementing such a program. The first problem is to convince students that they should adjust their reading rates. Many students regard skimming as a sin and read everything in a slow methodical manner. On the other hand, some students believe that everything, including difficult mathematics texts, can be read at the rate appropriate for a light novel. There seems to be evidence that people normally read more slowly than necessary. A number of studies on college students (e.g., Kieras, 1974; Kintsch, 1974) have found that when the students are forced to read faster than their self-imposed rate, there is no loss in retention of information typically regarded as important.

The second problem involved in teaching adaptive control lies in convincing students of the need to be aware of their purposes in reading. The point of adjusting reading rates is to serve particular purposes. Students who are unaware of what they want to get out of a reading assignment will find it difficult to adjust their rates appropriately. This point is related to the motivation for advance questions in the PQ4R method discussed in Chapter 7: The formation of advance questions helps the reader to identify study purposes. You should read more slowly those parts of the text that are related to the advance questions.

Once these problems of attitude are overcome, a reading-skills course can concentrate on teaching students the techniques for reading at various rates. Since most students have had little practice at rapid reading, most such instruction focuses on how to read rapidly. *Scanning* is a rapid-reading technique appropriate for searching out a piece of information embedded in a much larger text—for example, a student might scan this chapter for the effects of ambiguity on language comprehension. A skilled scanner can process 10,000 or more words a minute. Obviously, at this rate scanners pick up only bits and pieces of information, and skip whole paragraphs. It is easy for scanners to miss target information entirely, and they often have to rescan the text. Making quick decisions as to what should be ignored and what looked at takes much practice. However, the benefit is enormous. I would not be able to function as an academic without that skill because I would not be able to keep up with all the information that is generated in my field.

Skimming is the processing of about 800–1500 words a minute—a rate at which identifying every word is probably impossible. Skimming is used for extracting the gist of the text. This skill is useful when the skimmer is deciding whether to read a text, is implementing the preview phase in the PQ4R method, or is going over material that is mostly already known. In some applications, the reader must slow down when new important information is encountered.

Both scanning and skimming are aided by an appreciation of where the main points tend to be found in a text. A reader who knows where an author tends to put the main points can read selectively. Authors vary in their construction style, and the reader has to adjust to author differences, but some general rules usually apply. Section headings, first and last paragraphs in a section, first and last sentences in a paragraph, and highlighted material all tend to convey the main points.

In certain circumstances, we are able to deduce information that we have not read. For instance, in skimming or scanning experimental articles in fields with which I am familiar, I am able to know what methodology was used and what hypotheses were being tested just from reading the results sections, which do not contain this information. I am sufficiently familiar with the field that I can predict what I have not read. This ability is not just confined to academics. Suppose you are reading a popular novel and on one page you find this sentence:

> He asked her whether she would come up to his apartment
> for a nightcap.

Then you skip five pages and read this line:

> They left together for work the next morning.

You would probably have a fair idea of what went on in the intervening five pages. Basically, when the material we are reading conforms to our schemas, we are able to use this schematic knowledge in making predictions about the material rather than reading it fully. Thus, schematic knowledge (Chapter 5) proves to be important in yet another way.

Students in reading-skills programs often complain that rapid reading techniques require hard work and that they tend to regress toward less efficient reading habits after the end of the program. It should be emphasized that the adaptive control of reading rate is hard work because it is a novel skill. Older reading habits seem easy because they have been practiced for longer. As students become more practiced in adjusting reading rate, they find it easier. I can report that after practicing variable reading rates for more than 15 years, I find it easier to read a text at an adjustable rate than to read at a slow, methodical, word-by-word rate. This is something of a problem for me because part of my professional duties is to edit papers that I would normally not process word by word. I now find it very painful to have to read at this rate.

Speed Reading

As a final point, we come to the claims that have been made for speed reading by various commercial firms. In contrast to the responsible and modest claims of study-skills programs offered in colleges, commercial programs claim that with the investment of well under a 100 hours, students will be able to read at rates of 1500 words or more per minute and process every word. Our analyses of the facts about eye movement and amount taken in during a fixation suggest an upper limit of about 750 words per minute. The eye movements of graduates from such courses are of the basic saccadic variety, although they are often quite unorthodox (for instance, going straight down one page and up the other).

The most well known of the commercial courses teaches students to read straight down pages using the hand as a pacer. It is claimed that students see large portions of the page, and that they read thought patterns and ideas rather than single words at a time. This course promises that students will be able to at least triple their reading rates, often to well over 1500 words a minute, with no loss in comprehension score. This claim probably indicates more about the nature of the comprehension test than anything else. The techniques taught appear to be appropriate for scanning or skimming. As long as the comprehension tests tap the kind of information that people extract when scanning or skimming (i.e., the main points) no comprehension loss will be detected.

It seems very unlikely that speed reading involves anything more than skimming and scanning. These are valuable skills, but it is dangerous to overrate them. It is important to recognize that slow reading is called for by certain purposes and certain kinds of text. The consequences of speed reading a sales contract, for example, could be disastrous.

Remarks and Suggested Readings

The research on language comprehension is extensively reviewed in a text by Clark & Clark (1977). They make three independent distinctions that are similar to, but different than, the supposition-assertion distinction used here. Their distinctions are new-given, subject-predicate, and frame-insert. Their text is a good source for students interested in a more detailed discussion of language comprehension than that provided here. Just and Carpenter (1977) edited a series of research papers on the comprehension process.

This chapter strongly emphasizes the connection between language and memory. This "memory-connection perspective" on language is found in my work (e.g., Anderson, 1976; Anderson & Bower, 1973) and in the work of others in the field (Collins & Quillian, 1972; Kintsch, 1974; Norman & Rumelhart, 1975). A number of schemes have been developed in artificial intelligence for parsing sentences besides the production-system proposal set forth here (e.g., Kaplan, 1973; Marcus, 1978; Riesbeck, 1974; Schank, 1975; Winograd, 1972; Woods, 1973).

Black (1984) provides a review of research on story comprehension. Kintsch and van Dijk (1978) describe an extremely elaborate application of a theory of text structure to predicting memory for text material. Recently, applications of such text structures have been criticized (Black & Wilensky, 1979) for being too syntactic, formally ill defined, and not incorporating enough world knowledge. The book edited by Spiro, Bruce, and Brewer (1980) contains recent articles on text processing.

Gibson and Levin (1975) and Just and Carpenter (1984) offer extensive reviews of research on reading. Several papers are contained in Reber and Scarborough (1977). Just and Carpenter (1980) describe a detailed theory of reading based on the monitoring of eye movements. Thibadeau, Just, and Carpenter (1982) describe a production system model of reading that relates eye movements to the process of text comprehension.

The books by Robinson (1961) and Thomas and Robinson (1972) both describe numerous study-skills techniques. As these writers emphasize, it is not enough just to read about the techniques—the techniques require *practice*. A word of warning: Although such study-skill programs seem for the most part to be well founded, some aspects seem to be without good support. These texts lack much self-criticism, so the user is advised to take their recommendations with a grain of salt.

Chapter 13

Language Generation

Summary

1. Language generation can be analyzed into three stages: construction, transformation, and execution. Construction is the process of deciding on the meaning to be communicated. Transformation is the process of transforming the meaning into a linguistic message. Execution is the process of realizing the message in spoken or written form.

2. Construction can be divided into two stages: the planning of what is to be said and the planning of how it is to be said. An important component in deciding what to say is deciding in what order to communicate the information.

3. In planning how to say a message, speakers must decide what they can suppose of their listeners so that they can assert their intended messages. Successful communication also requires that speakers observe conversational maxims and the listeners understand these maxims.

4. In the transformation stage, sentences are generated in phrase-structure units. This generation process can be modeled by productions whose conditions specify pieces of meaning structure and whose actions create linguistic structures.

5. The writing process can be divided into three stages: idea generation, composition, and rewriting. A major problem in writing is the coordination of multiple information-processing demands.

6. The writing stage of idea generation can be analyzed as a type of problem solving. This stage can be divided into the actual generation of ideas and the subsequent evaluation of the ideas.

The Stages of Language Generation

"Then you should say what you mean," the March Hare went on.
"I do," Alice hastily replied; "at least—at least I mean what I say—
that's the same thing, you know."
"Not the same thing a bit!" said the Hatter.
"Why, you might just as well say that 'I see what I eat' is the same
thing as 'I eat what I see'!" (Carroll, 1866, p. 80)

Alice is not the only one who has faced the frustration of intending to say one thing but of being misinterpreted. The path from thought to word can be tortuous and full of pitfalls. We will analyze this process of language generation by dividing it into three stages:

1. *Construction.* Building the meaning to be communicated in accordance with your goals.

2. *Transformation.* Applying syntactic rules to transform the meaning into a linguistic message.

3. *Execution.* Realizing the message in some physical form (e.g., speech or writing).

While the earlier stages must start before the later stages can begin, it is not necessary for one step to be completed before another begins. We all have had the experience of starting sentences before knowing how they would end.

It is interesting to compare the stages of generation with the stages of comprehension. In Chapter 12 comprehension was also broken down into three stages:

1. *Perception.* Analyzing the linguistic message and identifying its units (e.g., words).

2. *Parsing.* Applying syntactic and semantic rules to extract a representation of the meaning of the analyzed message.

3. *Utilization.* Processing the meaning representation in accordance with your goals.

Stage 1 of comprehension is analogous to stage 3 of generation, stage 2 of comprehension to stage 2 of generation, and stage 3 of comprehension to stage 1 of generation. While thinking of comprehension as simply language generation in reverse proves wrong, and while none of the comprehension stages is simply the corresponding generation stage in reverse, the kinds of knowledge required in the corresponding stages do overlap considerably. Perception, involving the eyes and the ears, obviously has to be somewhat different from execution, which involves the mouth and the hands. However, we have already seen that, at least with respect to speech perception (Chapter 3), the system seems geared to identifying sounds with respect to their articulatory significance. That is, we seem to perceive speech by perceiving the way in which speech is articulated.

This chapter will concentrate on the first two stages of language generation, construction and transformation, which involve high-level mental processes. We will show that the syntactic patterns used in transformation during generation are similar to those used in parsing during comprehension. However, parsing and transformation are not identical. For instance, the patterns apply in different orders.

Again, similarities and differences exist between the processes of construction and utilization. As an example of a similarity, both speakers and listeners must consider the supposition-assertion distinction. Speakers must decide what listeners do not know and what needs to be asserted. Correspondingly, listeners must decide how the information they know relates to that which they are hearing. On the other hand, little overlap exists between the motives and goals that lead speakers to generate a sentence and the motives and goals that govern the processing of the sentence by listeners. The distinction between constructing and utilizing questions serves as an example. Question construction involves deciding that you need to know an answer and ascertaining that the listener might be able to provide the answer. The utilization stage in question comprehension involves deciding that you are willing and able to provide an answer and then making the mental or physical search for an answer.

While comprehension and generation exhibit some strong similarities, a significant unanswered question concerns whether the two activities use some of the same knowledge and processes. This chapter will treat the knowledge and processes involved in language generation as similar to but separate from those involved in comprehension. However, the two phenomena have not been shown to be entirely separate. To date, no incisive research has been addressed to the issue of whether comprehension and generation are distinct processes. The common wisdom seems to be that the two systems overlap a great deal, that training in one leads to improvement in the other, and that good readers are good writers. However, no hard evidence on the issue exists.

This chapter has three main sections. The first two review what is known about the construction and transformation stages of generation. The third covers the process of language generation during writing. Here we will be concerned with applying our knowledge of the process to the improvement of writing skills.

Construction

Deciding What to Say

Language generation is fundamentally a goal-oriented activity. People speak and write for reasons: to obtain information, to answer questions, to break the ice, to impress others with their linguistic virtuosity, to give orders, to be polite, to keep from being bored, to record information, to earn royalties, and so on. Sometimes people can easily see how to achieve their linguistic goals (as when they are deciding how to respond to the question "What time is it?"); at other times, they have difficulty in seeing how to achieve their goals (say, in deciding what to write to win the Nobel Prize in literature). To the extent that achieving such goals is difficult, problem-solving and reasoning processes will be important to the construction process. Therefore, much of the problem-solving analysis in Chapter 8 is relevant to language generation. We will return to this goal-seeking aspect of generation in more detail in considering the writing process.

Construction can often be divided into two substages: deciding which basic facts should be expressed and deciding how these facts should be structured and embellished. The former substage is the more complex and the less well understood. To illustrate what is involved in this stage, suppose a friend asks you, "What did you do today?" How would you go about deciding what to answer? (First, of course, you would want to decide what your friend really meant by this question—is the question well meant, ironic, demanding? This interpretation of the question is really part of language comprehension, not language generation. But suppose you decide that there is no hidden meaning in the question and that you will try to be cooperative and provide an answer.) To begin the process of generating an answer, you might decide on a plan for searching memory. The obvious one is to start with the morning and trace your activities until the current point in time. For each activity you would have to decide whether you should report it. Would your friend want to hear such predictable facts as that you got out of bed, or is the question intended to elicit only nonpredictable facts—such as when you got to school, what classes you took, whom you talked to? Next you would have to resolve the question of detail: Would it be enough to say that you went to math class or would you have to describe what was taught? In sum, to generate an answer, you would have to search through your day's activities, editing them for inclusion according to your goals and the listener's goals as you perceive them.

Linearization of Thought

Speech is linear, while the ideas communicated in speech are not always linearly structured. In speaking, we must decide to say one thing before another. How do people typically decide to order their thoughts in speech? In describing events, people choose to order their description by time. So, in describing a baseball game, we would describe the first inning before the second. But what if we are trying to describe something that does not have a linear temporal structure? For instance, how would you describe your apartment or your home? Linde and Labov (1975) found that subjects would describe their apartment by taking the listener on a tour through the apartment, describing the rooms as they were encountered. Thus, they converted a spatial structure into a linear structure for the purpose of description.

Levelt (1982) investigated what subjects would do when asked to describe arbitrary networks like part (a) in Figure 13-1, where each node is a different color and the description must start at the node with the arrow. A typical description was

> We begin at gray. From gray one can go up to red. From red, one can go right to yellow and still further right to green. From red, one can also go left, then you first reach pink and still farther left, then you come to blue. (p. 207)

The arrows in Figure 13-1 illustrate the path of the description. As this protocol illustrates, speakers tended to describe a tour through the network just as the subjects of Linde and Labov did when describing an apartment. An interesting case concerns what subjects will do when they encounter loops, as in part (b). As illustrated there, subjects tend to go around the loop first and in this way preserve the linear structure of their description. These examples testify to the powerful influence linearization has on speech plans, and how people will strive to linearize nonlinear structures for purposes of description.

Suppositions versus Assertions

Assuming that a speaker has decided what to say, how does he or she go about structuring a set of facts for communication? Suppose the speaker wants to assert the proposition, represented in Figure 13-2, that *X bought Y*. The speaker may believe that the listener does not know this and may want to convey the fact. Or the speaker may think that the listener knows it but may want to draw the listener's attention to the fact. Whatever the motive, the speaker cannot simply assert *X bought Y*. She or he must make contact with

(a)

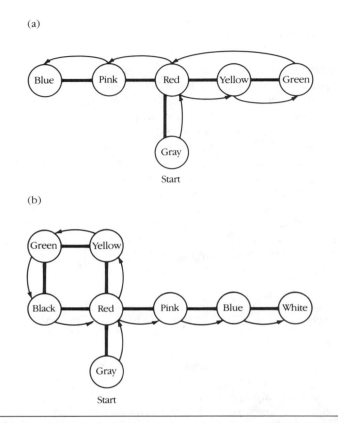

(b)

Figure 13-1 Networks that subjects were asked to describe in the experiments by Levelt (1982).

concepts *X* and *Y* in the listener's memory. This task involves diagnosing what the listener knows and making word choices accordingly. Suppose the speaker judges that this listener knows *X*'s name is Bill and that *Y* is Fred's old Chevy. Then the spoken form chosen might be *Bill bought Fred's old Chevy.* To another listener the speaker might have communicated the same proposition in this form. *Professor Jones bought the car that you saw parked in front of the office.* Thus, the speaker must decide what needs to be supposed about the listener in order to assert the desired proposition. This dual task, first to make contact with concepts in the listener's memory and then to structure the message around these concepts, is the origin of the supposition-assertion distinction, discussed from the listener's perspective in the preceding chapter. For another illustration of the supposition-assertion distinction see Figure 13-3.

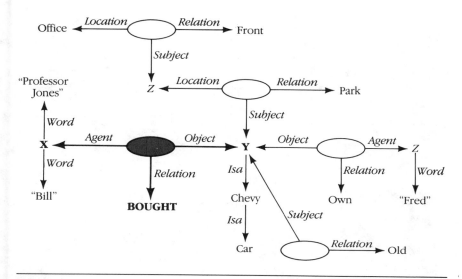

Figure 13-2 A propositional-network representation of *Bill bought Fred's old Chevy.* A speaker saying this sentence is asserting *X bought Y* in this network, but is supposing additional information from the network to make contact with the right nodes in the listener's network.

Conversational Maxims

A number of principles control conversation. Consider the following conversation:

1. *Dumb:* I saw you sleeping during the lecture. I guess you thought it was pretty boring too.

2. *Weird:* No, it was a really exciting lecture.

3. *Dumb:* Why would you fall asleep during an exciting lecture? Didn't you get any sleep last night?

4. *Weird:* Can you tell me what time it is?

5. *Dumb:* I don't have a watch.

6. *Weird:* But you can read mine—the Seiko watch with a gold wristband on my left arm just above the hand.

7. *Dumb:* It's 12 o'clock.

8. *Weird:* Actually the watch is broken.

9. *Dumb:* Then why did you ask me to read it?

Figure 13-3 Illustration in terms of semantic networks of the importance of the distinction between supposition and assertion. The speaker's communication should add new structure (assertion) to knowledge that the listener already had (supposition). (From Lindsay & Norman, 1977, p. 466.)

10. *Weird:* Actually, if you appreciated Grice's maxim of quality, you would have understood why I said the lecture was exciting.

This conversation between Dumb and Weird is clearly bizarre. The reason is that Weird is constantly violating what Grice (1975) called the *cooperativeness principle,* which states that speakers and listeners have to cooperate to succeed in communication. Grice suggests that, to satisfy the cooperativeness principle, the speaker has to satisfy at least four *conversational maxims*:

1. *The maxim of quantity.* Be as informative as is required, but not more informative than is required. Weird violated this rule twice in line 6. He implied that his watch was working, which it wasn't (not informative enough), and he gave an overly long description of the watch (too informative).

2. *The maxim of quality.* Be truthful. Weird violated this maxim in line 2 to create sarcasm. When an utterance is obviously false to both speaker and listener it is often intended for sarcastic effect. An obvious violation of truth can be acceptable in conversation, and would have been successful in this conversation had Dumb not been so obtuse. For instance, consider *The problem with Nixon was that he could never tell a lie.*

3. *The maxim of relation.* Say things relevant to the conversation. Weird violates this rule twice, in lines 4 and 10, where he introduces huge shifts in the conversation.

4. *The maxim of manner.* Be clear. Assuming that Dumb did not know Grice's maxim of quality, Weird was being unnecessarily obscure in line 10.

Of these four maxims, the maxim of quantity seems to be the most powerful in shaping conversation. Most sentences generated seem to be relatively bare-bones attempts to perform the two functions of supposition and assertion—making contact with concepts in the listener's memory and changing the state of the structure around these concepts. Speakers often choose the simplest sentence that serves these functions. They try to avoid being overly informative. Of course, speech can also be quite flowery when the goal of a speaker is more complicated than the simple communication of facts. However, more commonly, it seems, speech is not flowered with irrelevant information. Consider, for instance, the following sentence:

> Ronald Reagan, who is 74 years old and hails from a small town in Illinois, invited Edward Kennedy, brother of the late John Kennedy, to Camp David, which is a presidential retreat.

In a newscast this sentence would strike us as odd, since the same assertion could be made this way:

> Reagan invited Ted Kennedy to Camp David.

Olson (1970) brings out these ideas in his analysis of the use of adjective phrases. He invites us to consider how we would refer to the same object in the three sets in Figure 13-4. For set A we would use the phrase *the white one,* for set B, *the round one,* and for set C, *the round, white one.* Using both

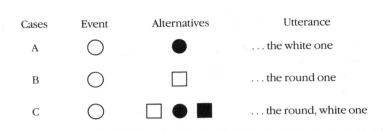

Figure 13-4 Three arrays of figures and the noun phrases that are chosen to describe the left-hand circle in each. The chosen phrases suggest that simplicity guides speech. (From Olson, 1970. Copyright 1970 by the American Psychological Association. Reprinted by permission.)

adjectives seems appropriate only for set C, where both are needed to identify the object. Thus, a principle governing speech appears to be simplicity: Say only what needs to be said to achieve a communicative intention.

Transformation

Constituent Structure in Generation

Once language speakers have decided what they want to assert and what they should suppose about their listeners' knowledge, they must translate these assertions and suppositions into sentential form. Recall that listeners seem to parse sentences in terms of multiword patterns such as noun phrases and prepositional phrases. The corresponding question naturally arises, How do speakers generate sentences? Do they generate them a word at a time or in clumps that constitute phrases? The evidence suggests that speakers generate language in phrases or constituents, just as listeners comprehend in constituents. For instance, Boomer (1965) analyzed examples of spontaneous speech and found that pauses did occur more frequently at grammatical junctures, and that these pauses were longer than pauses at other locations. The average pause time at a grammatical juncture was 1.03 sec, while the average within grammatical clauses was .75 sec. This finding suggests that speakers tend to generate sentences a clause at a time and often need to pause after one clause to plan the next. Other research has also found that speakers tend to pause between constituents (e.g., Cooper & Paccia-Cooper, 1980; Grosjean, Grosjean, & Lane, 1979).

A Production System for Generation

The data cited above as well as other evidence reviewed later point to the conclusion that language is generated in terms of constituents, or phrases. The theoretical question raised by this conclusion is, What kind of system would generate language in phrase units? A production system for generation that would complement the production system described in the previous chapter for comprehension would be interesting to consider. Table 13-1 gives a production set for generation that is analogous to Table 12-1, in which productions for comprehension were given. Like the production set in Chapter 12, this set has productions for generating main-clause constituents (MAIN), noun phrase constituents (NP), and relative-clause constituents (RELATIVE). This production set assumes that representations such as the one in Figure 13-5, are active in the speaker's memory, setting forth what he or she wants to communicate. The production system in Table 13-1 has a goal-structured character, like the production systems we saw in the problem-solving chapters. It starts with the goal of generating the major assertion and breaks this down into subgoals until it comes to the words of the sentence.

Consider how the production system in Table 13-1 would apply to the

Table 13-1 *Productions for generating sentence constituents*

Name of production	Form of production
MAIN	IF the goal is to assert that a person performed an action on an object THEN set as subgoals to describe the person, then the action, and then the object.
RELATIVE	IF the goal is to describe a person and it is supposed the person performed an action on an object THEN set as subgoals after describing the person to say *who*, to describe the action and then to describe the object.
NP	IF the goal is to describe a person and the person is in a noun category THEN set as subgoals to say *the* and then the *noun*.
VERB	IF the goal is to describe an action and the action occurred in the past THEN set as subgoals to say the *action* with a past tense inflection.

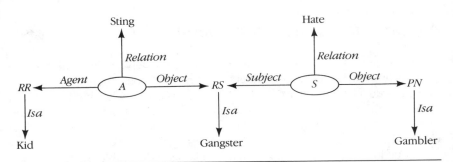

Figure 13-5 The productions in Table 13-1 applied to this network representation would generate the sentence *The kid stung the gangster who hated the gambler.*

network representation in Figure 13-5. The nodes labeled *RR, RS,* and *PN* refer to individuals. The speaker has decided that the following proposition represented is to be asserted.

    1. *RR* stung *RS.*

This proposition is denoted by the *A* proposition node. The following information is supposed:

    2. *RR* is a kid.

    3. *RS* is a gangster.

    4. *RS* hates *PN.*

    5. *PN* is a gambler.

    Figure 13-6 illustrates the goal and subgoals involved in the generation of the sentence. For instance, production MAIN decomposes the goal of describing the main assertion into the goals of describing *RR,* then the stinging, and then *RS.* This goal decomposition continues until specific words, like *the gangster,* are reached. Note that such a goal structure corresponds to the surface structure of a sentence that we discussed in Chapter 11. Thus, as in the case of comprehension, processes involved in generation are defined in terms of a sentence's surface structure.

More Evidence for Constituent Structure

The example presented in the preceding subsection illustrates that generation productions build a sentence in a manner analogous to that in which comprehension productions analyze a sentence—that is, a constituent at a time.

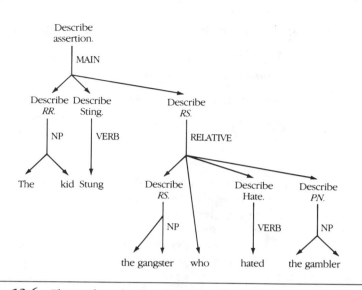

Figure 13-6 The goals and subgoals set by the production set in Table 13-1 in order to communicate the meaning structure in Figure 13-6.

Comprehension productions map constituent patterns into meaning representations, whereas generation productions do just the reverse.[1] If we accept that the system presented in Table 13-1 models language generation, we would predict that longer pauses would occur at constituent breaks than occur at other points in a sentence. Before a speaker could actually generate the words in a constituent, extra productions would have to apply to set forth the structure of the constituent. We reviewed earlier data that confirmed this prediction (e.g., Boomer, 1965).

Other research efforts have tested this constituent-generation theory. For example, Maclay and Osgood (1959) analyzed spontaneous recordings of speech to determine whether speech is generated in constituent units. They found a number of speech errors that suggested that constituents do have a psychological reality. They found that when speakers repeated themselves or corrected themselves they tended to repeat or correct a whole constituent.

---

[1]Clearly, production MAIN here corresponds to MAIN in Table 12-1. Similarly, the productions RELATIVE and NP in the two tables correspond. Note, however, that the productions apply in different order. If the comprehension productions in Table 12-1 were to parse this sentence, they would apply in the order NP, NP, NP, RELATIVE, MAIN, whereas the generation productions apply in the order MAIN, NP, RELATIVE, NP, NP. This difference in order illustrates the general point that comprehension is not simply generation in reverse.

For instance, the following is the kind of repeat that is found:

Turn on the heater/the heater switch.

And the pair below constitutes a common type of correction:

Turn on the stove/the heater switch.

In the preceding example, the noun phrasé is repeated. In contrast, speakers do not provide repetitions such as

Turn on the stove/on the heater switch,

in which the noun phrase and part of the verb phrase are repeated.

Other kinds of speech errors also provide evidence for the psychological reality of constituents as major units of speech generation. For instance, some research has analyzed slips of the tongue in speech (Fromkin, 1971, 1973; Garrett, 1975). Such errors are called *spoonerisms,* after the English clergyman William A. Spooner to whom are attributed some colossal and clever errors of speech. The following are among the errors of speech attributed to Spooner:

You have hissed all my mystery lectures.

I saw you fight a liar in the back quad; in fact, you have tasted the whole worm.

I assure you the insanitary spectre has seen all the bathrooms.

Easier for a camel to go through the knee of an idol.

The Lord is a shoving leopard to his flock.

Take the flea of my cat and heave it at the louse of my mother-in-law.

There is every reason to suspect that these errors were deliberate attempts at humor by Spooner. However, people do generate genuine spoonerisms, although they are seldom so funny.

By patient collecting, researchers have gathered a large set of errors made by friends and colleagues. Some of these involve simple sound anticipations or sound exchanges:

Take my bike → bake my bike [an anticipation].

night life → nife lite [an exchange]

beast of burden → burst of beadan [an exchange]

One that gives me particular difficulty is

coin toss → toin coss

The first error listed above is an example of an anticipation, where an early phoneme is changed to a later phoneme. The others are examples of exchanges in which two phonemes switch. The interesting feature about these kinds of errors is that they tend to occur within a single constitutent rather than across constituents. So, we are unlikely to find the following anticipation:

1. The dancer took my bike. → The bancer took my bike.

where an anticipation occurs between subject and object noun phrases. Also unlikely are sound exchanges where an exchange occurs between the initial prepositional phrase and the final noun phrase, as in

2. At night John lost his life. → At nife John lost his lite.

Note that a production system such as that in Table 13-1, which generates language by constituents, plans only the words it will generate for the immediate constituent. Thus, sound-exchange errors cannot occur across the relatively large distance exhibited in example 2. For instance, such a system would have already generated *night* before planning *life. Life* would be decided upon after an exchange could occur. On the other hand, such a system might plan to say two words in a constituent, such as *night life,* before actually generating either word. Thus, an opportunity for the exchange *nife lite* would exist.

Another kind of speech error consistent with the constituent model is called the *stranded morpheme.* (A morpheme is a minimum unit of meaning, such as *trunk,* which indicates an object, or —*ed,* which indicates past tense.) Some examples are

I'm not in the read for mooding.

She's already trunked two packs.

Fancy getting your model renosed.

This type of error exhibits two interesting features. First, like the other errors, this type tends to occur within a constituent boundary. Second, the content morphemes, such as *trunk* and *pack,* are always the ones that are switched. The functional morphemes, such as *ing, ed,* and *s,* stay put. Thus, we do not find such errors as

I'm not in the mooding for read.

The phenomenon of the stranded morpheme seems to suggest that speakers first decide on the pattern they want to generate, for example, a phrase such as

noun for verb + ing.

In the process of filling in the specific words of the pattern, however, the speaker switches the noun and verb.

The Relationship between Construction and Transformation

We have been describing language generation as if the speaker first planned the meaning completely and then transformed that meaning into linguistic form. However, speakers usually plan their meanings as they generate their sentences. Many of the awkward or grammatically deviant sentences that occur in discourse reflect the conflicting demands of these two ongoing processes of construction and transformation. Deese (1978) compared spontaneous speech, such as answers to unexpected questions, with prepared speech in which content (but not wording) was planned, such as seminar presentations. The latter, where content was planned, was much freer of grammatical and stylistic problems. A similar result is reported by Levin, Silverman, and Ford (1967), who found that children who are asked to generate simple descriptions of events exhibit fewer grammatical errors than children who are asked to give explanations of the events. Explanations are more demanding cognitively. Such research implies that processing capacity is limited and must be divided between construction and transformation. When the demands for construction (planning) increase, the quality of linguistic transformation suffers.

The Writing Process

Just as the research on language comprehension can be applied most naturally to reading, so the research on generation can be most naturally applied to writing. However, research on writing is more than just an applied arm of language-generation research. Writing appears to provide an important independent opportunity for the basic study of language generation. In this section, in the course of examining some recommendations for improving writing, we will develop some additional ideas about the nature of language generation.

The discussion in this section is based on two principles. The first is that the same basic processes involved in speech are involved in writing. Gould (Gould, 1978; Gould & Boies, 1977), in a comparative study of writing, dictating, and speaking, found a fairly high correlation among these three modes with respect to quality of composition. That is, people who were good speakers tended to be good writers.

The second principle is that the basic problem in writing is the coordination of the multiple, independent information-processing demands involved in creating good prose (this idea has been emphasized by Bruce,

Collins, Rubin, & Gentner, 1979). In this discussion, the term *coordination problem* refers to this difficulty. A problem of coordination also arises in speech, but it is clearer when we consider writing.

Students were being taught to write long before cognitive psychology existed as a field of study. The suggestions in the following pages will draw heavily from the concepts developed in this pedagogical tradition. These concepts have been edited to reflect the general insights of cognitive psychology and elaborated with relevant findings in cognitive psychology research. Currently, a surge of research is being experienced in America to further validate these ideas and to extract more ideas from cognitive psychology with respect to writing. I believe that these efforts will prove to be a notably fruitful application of cognitive psychology. The ideas of the field seem to be particularly relevant to writing, and people generally need to improve their writing skill, as this example, taken from an Internal Revenue Service tax form, suggests:

> Under the nonfarm optional method, you as a regularly self-employed individual may report two-thirds of your gross nonfarm profits (but not more than $1,600) as your net earnings from self-employment if your net earnings from such self-employment are less than $1,600 and less than two-thirds of your gross nonfarm profits from such self-employment. However, unlike the farm optional method, the nonfarm optional method precludes you from reporting less than your actual net earnings from nonfarm self-employment.

Some experimental data on writing exist, and it is to be hoped that a good deal more will soon be generated. Currently, however, much psychological information about writing comes from self-observation and informal reports. Written communication is an important part of science, and it is not unusual to find psychologists spending hours comparing and analyzing their writing experiences.

Stages of Writing

In a typical model of writing, the process is divided into three phases. First is an *idea generation,* or *prewriting,* phase, in which the writer decides on what he or she wants to say. Next is the actual *composition,* or *writing,* phase, in which the text is generated. The final stage is the *rewriting,* or *editing,* phase, in which the writer reworks the text to make it a more effective communicative device.

Recall the construction, transformation, and execution stages of language generation described at the beginning of this chapter. Clearly, the prewriting phase corresponds to construction, and both writing and rewriting are aspects of the transformation process. The aspect corresponding to execution would be the physical process by which the text is created—longhand writing, typing, dictating, and the like. This aspect is not trivial, and a whole technology has developed around manuscript preparation. With the continued elaboration of computer-based editing systems, this technology is becoming quite complex. However, it is typically ignored in analysis of writing because the major roadblocks to successful writing lie elsewhere.

In the following subsections, we will consider recommendations for the development of writing skills and the psychological bases for these recommendations with respect to each stage of the process. Although the discussion treats each stage independently, these phases are not necessarily discrete in the actual activity of writing. That is, prewriting is not necessarily completed before writing begins, and writing is not necessarily finished when editing begins. It is sometimes appropriate and even necessary to alternate among the phases. Properly relating these three stages is a major aspect of the coordination problem.

Prewriting: Idea Generation

Of the three, the prewriting phase involves creativity most. This phase tends to be shrouded with mystery and teachers tend to refrain from analyzing it in standard efforts at teaching English. A superstition has long prevailed that analyzing the creative act destroys it. Related to this mystique is a certain disastrous style of writing, practiced by some otherwise capable students, whereby they simply wait to be inspired by the gods. One healthy result of analyzing writing psychologically is the destruction of this aspect of the mystique of creativity. Generating ideas for writing is simply (or not so simply) the process of problem solving to achieve a goal. The problem-solving nature of the activity was emphasized by Flower and Hayes (1977). If you conceive of writing as problem solving, then it is natural to try to bring the various problem-solving techniques to bear. All such techniques require that you start with a definiton of the goal. You could hardly hope to succeed in a problem-solving task without clearly defining the goal state that the problem solving is trying to achieve. Unfortunately, the goals of college students are often not well articulated—for instance, the goal of achieving an A in a course. The goals of more advanced writers are often ill-specified as well—for instance, the goal of writing a paper that can be published in a prestigious journal.

Let us consider some of the problem-solving techniques as they would apply to the writing process. For instance, recall the method of working backward (see Chapter 8). Suppose you start with the goal of getting an A on an essay about language generation. This goal requires choosing an innovative theme. Such a theme might be to argue that more is involved in creative writing than "just problem solving." The topic would be a subgoal in service of the main goal, getting an A. Thus, you have worked backward from the main goal to a subgoal. You might work backward again from this subgoal. For instance, you might decide upon a line of argument that would establish the point. One such line of argument would be to present evidence that successful writers have experiences of "true inspiration." Thus, from the general subgoal of presenting a convincing argument, you would have worked backward to the additional subgoal of collecting testimonials for this point. A means-ends analysis might suggest that you go to the library to find books reporting the experiences of successful writers. And so you could go on, setting subgoals and solving them until the essay was written.

Another method of problem solving discussed in Chapter 8 involves the use of analogy. This method seems to be the basis of the synectics techniques (a variety of brainstorming) advocated by Gordon (1961) and Prince (1970). A great many creative solutions result from the use of analogy. For instance, the Wright brothers based their work on the turning and stabilizing of an airplane on observations of how buzzards keep their balance in flight. Flower and Hayes (1977) suggest the following example of using analogy in writing:

> Suppose, for example, you are analyzing the operation of a university. It occurs to you that universities have much in common with big businesses. The potential connections between the two are numerous: the analogy could suggest that both need professional management, or that both would benefit from healthy competition, or perhaps that both turn out a product but seem to spend most of their advertising budget marketing a self-image. (p. 455)

Studies of Idea Generation

As noted earlier, the prewriting stage is the most creative phase of the writing process. We turn now to a review of the research on the creativity involved in writing. The typical creativity experiment poses to subjects a rather open-ended problem. For instance, subjects might be given the plot of a story or movie and asked to write alternative titles for it. The titles would then be rated by independent judges who had been carefully trained and were in close agreement. This paradigm addresses the creativity involved in a much simpler task than the writing of an essay, but the results of such studies are nevertheless instructive.

One reasonable analysis of such tasks is what I refer to as the *generate-and-judge model*. In this model, the problem solving underlying the creative thinking required by the tasks is seen as a process of generating and judging possible solutions. In this view, the central issue is the relationship between quantity (how many ideas can be generated) and quality (how good the ideas are). That is, can we generate better ideas by trying to generate many or by inhibiting most and concentrating on trying to come up with one good idea?

Brainstorming, a creativity technique that has been advocated by some (e.g., Osborn, 1953), emphasizes the uninhibited generation of ideas. The goal of this technique is to postpone judgment, so that your attention is free for idea generation. The experiment of Johnson, Parrott, and Stratton (1968) is typical of the research into brainstorming techniques. It compared the effect of instructions that encouraged subjects to keep the quality of their ideas high with the effect of instructions that encouraged a lack of inhibition and the generation of many ideas. One group of subjects (group 1) was instructed to generate one best solution to creativity problems such as generating plot titles. The other group (group 2) was asked to write as many solutions as possible. Figure 13-7 illustrates the data from the quality group, group 1, and the quantity group, group 2. Two judges rated the quality of the solutions on a 1–7 scale with 7 indicating best. On the abscissa of the figure we have plotted the quality (the sums of two judges' ratings) and on the ordinate the number of solutions with each quality rating generated in each group. Since the sum of two ratings are given, the range is 2–14 rather than 1–7.

A number of conclusions are evident from Figure 13-7. First, the quantity instructions certainly generated more solutions. Second, the mean quality of the solutions in the quantity group went down; that is, a majority of the solutions from that group got low ratings. Most important, however, was that the quantity group showed a greater number of superior solutions. So, *proportionally* the quantity group generated fewer good solutions but *absolutely* they generated more good solutions. Thus, in one sense, brainstorming does work in generating more good solutions.

It is interesting to ask whether the subjects in the brainstorming condition were able to judge which of their solutions were best. When asked, they tended to pick out better than average solutions, but not always the best. A comparision of the self-judged solutions in the brainstorming condition with the single solutions generated in group 1 yielded no difference in ratings (Johnson, et al., 1968). It appears that subjects instructed to give just one best solution may implicitly generate many solutions and edit them, just as the brainstorming subjects are required to do overtly.

The analysis of these data confirms the idea that productive thinking has two major components: the generation of ideas and the judgment of the quality of the ideas. Thus, a researcher should be able to improve the quality of the idea chosen as best both by training subjects to generate more ideas and by training subjects to judge their ideas. This prediction was borne out in a study by Stratton and Brown (1972). They compared training techniques that emphasized quantity, quality, and both. The combined technique produced the most superior solutions to the plot-title problem.

Standard recommendations for idea generation in writing involve a variant

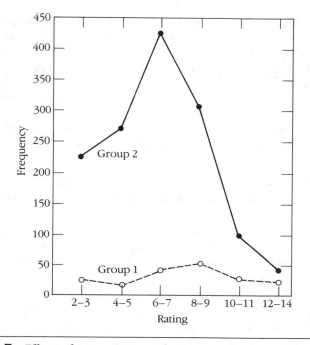

Figure 13-7 Effects of instructions emphasizing quality (group 1) and quantity (group 2) on the frequency of solutions of varying qualities. (Data are from Johnson et al., 1968.)

of this first-brainstorm-then-judge model. Students are encouraged to concentrate on generating ideas, reserving judgment for later. True, we naturally edit ideas as we generate them, choosing to set forth only those that seem good. However, students are encouraged not to concentrate on judgment in the initial stage, postponing it to the rewriting stage. Thus, under this recommendation, students are to write their papers from beginning to end, following their trains of thought and spurring themselves on whenever they hit a roadblock with problem-solving techniques designed to promote the generation of ideas. However, it should be emphasized that random association is not being recommended. All the ideas generated should be organized as solutions to explicit goals and subgoals generated in the writing process.

Composition

As Wason (1978) notes, in pedagogy we can find two rather contradictory models for relations between idea generation and composition. Under the first model, the writer generates ideas first, creating an outline of the paper to be written, and then translating this outline into a first draft. Under the second model, the writer composes the first draft as he or she generates ideas. In the extreme case under model 1, no further ideas are generated once the outline is created. In the extreme case under model 2, no outline is made at all. It appears that good writers can be found who practice each of the extremes. However, most good writers represent some compromise between the two extremes. It is worthwhile reviewing the advantages for each model. Let us turn first to the advantages of the model utilizing an outline, model 1.

1. Under this model, the writer can avoid wasting the effort of preparing a draft that might later be judged unfit with respect to the overall structure.

2. Ideas are often generated more quickly than they can be expressed coherently. Keeping up with the flow of ideas is easier if we need only jot down notes about our ideas rather than write complete prose.

3. Attention to matters of writing style is not required. Such attention would detract from that given to the ideas. Again, this point relates to the coordination problem, identified earlier.

Now consider the advantages of the first-draft model, model 2:

1. Writers often do not know what certain points in their own outline really mean until they write the paper out. Thus, writers often complain that they cannot follow their outlines because the points, when expanded, do not fit together as they had intended them to.

2. The process of expanding a point often stimulates new ideas and new modes of organization. Thus, writers often claim that they do their thinking in the act of writing.

The arguments for both models are valid. Optimal writing requires free alternation between the two models. Achieving flexibility in alternating between idea generation and composition is important to solving the coordination problem. Having an outline—if only mentally—is always useful to writers in helping them to focus on their goals and to prevent them from going off on tangents. However, at the same time, writers need to be flexible regarding the outline and be able to reorganize it when necessary. They should never feel compelled to stick to the initial organization.

Thus, the composition process is inevitably intertwined with idea generation. This fact has an important practical implication: Writers should not labor over the style and syntax of their writing in composing the first draft.

The important task initially is to get ideas onto the paper. Content should be the focus of the first draft. The time to worry about style is during the rewriting phase.

Of course, the more poorly written the first draft, the more time rewriting will require. In fact, most writers spend much more time on rewriting than they do in creating the first draft. The ability to write a final-draft-quality paper the first time through is an enviable skill, but few have it. A few of my colleagues claim that they write only one draft. Without exception, these are people whose spontaneous speech is of final-draft quality. This observation suggests that the quality of a writer's first-draft writing reflects his or her general linguistic skill at transforming ideas into words. Indeed, these colleagues' papers sound very much like their spontaneous speech.

It is usually true that content is more important than style. Of course, in some situations the reverse is the case, and a writer should be flexible and willing to sacrifice content for style. This consideration returns us to the principal moral of this section: Always be aware of your goals in writing and of the means of achieving them.

Since many writers do emphasize content over style in first drafts, they tend not to practice the kinds of linguistic skills that lead to a high-quality first draft. Thus, the stylistic quality of first drafts probably does not improve as quickly as it could. (Of course, by focusing on idea generation, writers improve the content of their first drafts.) Some veteran writers report that the stylistic quality of their first drafts does not improve much over the years, although the quality of their final drafts does improve.

Rewriting or Editing

The first two phases of writing are intended to be relatively uninhibited. Their function is to get good ideas onto paper. It is in the third phase, *rewriting,* that the misjudgments made in the first two phases are corrected or edited. It is a maxim that subsequent drafts should be shorter than the first draft; a major goal at this stage is to cut out the poor ideas that got in because of the writer's low threshold for acceptance in the first two stages. In the framework of the generate-and-judge model of creativity discussed earlier, this is the stage in which judgment should be brought to bear. However, again flexibility needs to be emphasized. A writer should not fail to pursue a good idea just because it originates during rewriting—and good ideas do originate at this stage.

It is useful to review some of the major factors that usually need editing.

1. *Ideas.* Some of the ideas that seemed strong initially might really be weak or in conflict with other ideas. This problem

gives writers particular difficulty. They find it hard to convince themselves that ideas should be thrown out after such a great effort was spent in generating them.

2. *Structure.* Since the structure of the text can change in the writing, the organization of the first draft is often mangled and in need of major restructuring. It is often necessary to rearrange sections in order to obtain a coherent structure. A useful technique is to develop a hierarchical outline of the paper after it is written, enabling the writer to inspect the structure. The structure should be clearly signaled so that it is apparent to the reader. Beginning paragraphs with main points, underlining, and using headings are all ways of highlighting the structure of a piece. A writer who is uncertain whether the structure is clear might begin with a paragraph explaining the text's structure.

3. *Connective tissue.* Although the writer may see clearly how the ideas in a piece are related, a reader may not. It is sometimes necessary to write into subsequent drafts sentences or phrases (e.g., "On the other hand,") that indicate the relationship among ideas.

4. *Style.* Many problems arise regarding style in first drafts. In scientific writing, for instance, first drafts tend to be too verbose. Sentences are too long, too many abstract nouns occur where concrete verbs would do, and so on. Consider the following sentence, taken from a scientific paper: *In studies pertaining to the identification of phenolic derivations, drying of the paper gives less satisfactory visualization.* This sentence should have been edited to read *Phenolic derivations are more easily seen and identified if the paper is left wet.*

5. *Grammar and spelling.* These errors occur with relatively high frequency in many first drafts (e.g., my own). Besides creating a poor "public relations" image for the writer, such errors distract readers' attention from the content of the passage.

Clearly, these errors are listed in order of decreasing complexity. The simplest errors are easiest to detect and correct but they are also the least important. Particularly with respect to the more complex errors, writers suffer from problems of incorrect set (see Chapter 8). Their ideas and structure may seem excellent to them, the connections among their ideas obvious, and their style beautiful. The trick is to escape this egocentric perspective and perceive the prose as another reader would. A number of solid recommendations can be made about rewriting.

1. Again, as always, practice makes perfect. Earlier we noted that judgment training improves the mean quality of ideas. Analogously, training in editing improves rewriting. A particularly beneficial practice technique is rewriting someone else's prose. Editing someone else's material makes it easier to practice reading objectively and critically, finding problems, and deciding on solutions. A real advantage in multiple-author papers is that one person can edit another's writing.

2. If possible, writers should put their first drafts away for a while before rewriting. This time lapse allows all the little biases and self-understandings to dissipate. With a long enough lag between first draft and rewriting, rewriting your own text will become like rewriting someone else's. The effect of this technique is similar to an incubation effect (discussed in Chapter 8).

3. Writers do well to try their work out on someone else. It is amazing how rapidly their golden prose crumbles before their eyes when they watch someone try to make sense of it. A person who cannot find a friend to suffer through first-draft scribble might imagine speaking the text to a friend. This practice alone often enables a writer to achieve objectivity.

4. Writers need to be their own critics, trying to poke holes in their own arguments, to make fun of their own styles, and so on. If your ego is up to it, taking this perspective can also serve as a profitable way to troubleshoot prose.

5. Committing to memory the basic rules of style, grammar, and text structure is a necessity. Many texts on writing can serve as reference sources (e.g., Strunk & White, 1972; Woodward, 1968). These works also document the most common errors. For many points of style and grammar, writers can make accurate judgments when forced to, but fail to recall these points unless specifically prompted. By committing these points to memory so they can be freely recalled, writers strengthen the representation of these points in memory and increase the probability that they will be activated when relevant in the rewriting process.

6. Another good technique is to practice speaking about complex topics. When we consider the nature of the writing difficulties discussed here, it becomes clear that many involve fundamental weaknesses in language-generation abilities. The inability to properly appreciate the reader's perspective reflects a weak-

ness in developing suppositions and assertions. Some stylistic problems also reflect a lack of control over the necessary syntactic patterns. These language-generation deficits do not often show up in ordinary speech, since ordinary speech is not nearly so demanding as the typical essay topic. Typical discussions about movies, football, or the weather require a much less developed command of the language than an essay on the evidence for short-term memory. However, in certain circumstances oral discussion can be as demanding as in essay topic— for instance, in some college seminars. Clearly, entering into such discussions will help writers develop their language-generation skills.

7. Reading is thought to be good practice for writing (e.g., Haynes, 1978). As we mentioned earlier in this chapter, virtually nothing is known about the connection between language comprehension and language generation. However, it is generally believed that some connection exists between the two and that positive transfer should occur between one and the other.

8. The low-level skills, such as typing, spelling, and composing grammatical sentences, should be practiced until they become automatic. In Chapter 3, we saw how a task ceases to interfere with other ongoing tasks when it becomes automatic. Thus, it is wise to practice the low-level skills in preparation for the more difficult phases of composition. We might take the view that this function is served (or should be served) by the teaching of writing in grade school.

A number of researchers (e.g., Bruce et al., 1979) have remarked that the central difficulty in performing, learning, or teaching writing is the coordination problem—the problem of integrating many levels at once. A common variation of the coordination problem is what Bruce et al. called *downsliding,* the tendency of writers to focus on the lower levels (e.g., spelling and grammar) to the neglect of the higher (e.g., idea generation and organization). Another phenomenon, which should perhaps be called *upsliding,* is the focusing on higher levels to the exclusion of lower. Many of my papers are living proof of this. The researchers named above suggest training procedures in which students learn to do each level separately. This suggestion echoes the issue of part-to-whole training discussed in Chapter 9. To the extent that editing can be performed at various levels independently, it is efficient to learn to perform each level separately and then to integrate them rather than learning to perform all levels at once.

Remarks and Suggested Readings

There have been a number of recent theoretical efforts to come to a deeper understanding of the processes involved in speech. Cooper and Paccia-Cooper (1980) have developed a systematic account of pausing and other prosodic features in speech. Stemberger (1982) has developed a activation-based model speech errors.

As you may have noted, most of the recommendations on writing were based on general knowledge of cognitive psychology and not on specific knowledge about language generation. In fact, this knowledge is quite sparse. If cognitive psychology could come to a better understanding of language generation, much more could be said about improving writing skills. Perhaps, in this context, studying effective writing would be a good way to study language generation.

For more reading on creativity and writing, see the texts by Johnson (1972) and by Hayes (1978) and the papers by Flower and Hayes (1977) and by Hayes and Flower (1980). A recent collection of papers on writing education was edited by Frederiksen, Whiteman, and Dominic (1979). Another was edited by Gregg and Steinberg (1980). The two-volume series by Stein (1975–1976) provides a survey of the many popular, but largely unproven, techniques for stimulating creativity.

Chapter 14

Cognitive Development

Summary

1. According to Piaget, an infant enters the world lacking most basic cognitive competencies and passes through a series of stages in which the child develops more and more adequate bases for representing the world and reasoning about it.

2. Piaget's preoperational period extends from age 2 to age 7. At the end of this period the child has schemes for accurately thinking about the physical world.

3. Cognitive development after the age of 2 largely depends on acquiring needed knowledge and not on improvement of the basic mental abilities of the child.

4. Children improve their memory by developing better encoding and rehearsal strategies. They also acquire more knowledge relevant to elaborating and chunking the to-be-remembered information.

5. Cognitive development often depends on children's learning to represent knowledge in such a way that efficient and effective mental processes can apply to that knowledge.

6. Young children have difficulty, particularly in unfamiliar domains, with setting and remembering the subgoals involved in solving a problem.

7. Children's development in many tasks can be modeled by the addition of more adequate production rules for performing the task.

8. Certain developmental improvements can be explained by assuming an increase in the child's ability to keep relevant information in working memory.

In Chapter 1 we noted that intelligence was the defining trait of the human species. To enable our species to achieve such intelligence, evolution has produced some features of human development that contrast with those of other mammalian species. Humans have very large brains in relation to their body size, which eventuated in a major evolutionary problem: How was the birth of such large-brained babies to be effected? One way was through progressive enlargement of the birth canal, which is now as large as is considered possible given the constraints of mammalian skeletons (Geschwind, 1980.) In addition, children are born with a skull that is sufficiently pliable for it to be compressed into a cone shape in order to fit through the birth canal. Still, the human birth process is particularly difficult compared to that of most other mammals.

Not even the evolutionary modifications just mentioned would suffice, however, if humans were born with fully developed brains. Compared with many other mammals, human infants are born with particularly immature brains. At birth a human brain occupies a volume of about 350 cm³. During the first year it doubles to 700 cm³; and before a human being reaches puberty, the size of its brain doubles again. Most other mammals do not have as much growth in brain size after birth (Gould, 1977). Since the human birth canal has been expanded to its limits, much of our neural development has been postponed until after birth.

Even though they spend nine months developing in the womb, human infants are quite helpless at birth and spend an extraordinarily long time growing to adult stature—around 15 years; which is about a fifth of their lifetime. Contrast this with a puppy: After a gestation period of just nine weeks, it is born more capable than an infant. In less than a year, less than a tenth of its life-span, it has reached full size and reproductive capability. Childhood is prolonged more than would be needed to develop large brains. Indeed, most neural development is complete by age 5. Humans are kept children by the slowness of their physical development. It has been speculated (de Beer, 1959) that the function of this slow physical development has been to keep children in a dependency relationship to adults. There is much that has to be learned in order to become a competent adult, and staying a child so long gives the human time enough to acquire that learning. Childhood is an apprenticeship for adulthood.

Modern society is so complex that we cannot learn all that is needed by simply associating with our parents for 15 years. To provide the needed training, society has created social institutions such as high schools, colleges, and post-college professional schools. It is not unusual for people to spend over 25 years, almost as long as their professional life, preparing for their role in society.

Viewed from this perspective, we should expect a study of cognitive development to provide major insights into the nature of human intelligence. However, the study of child cognition is more difficult than the study of adult cognition. It is very hard to get children to follow instructions before the age of 3, and children younger than 6 months are capable of only a few motor movements, such as sucking, swinging their hands, and kicking. However, many of the most interesting cognitive changes are occurring in these early years. Developmental psychologists have had to be very clever in finding methodologies to determine what children know.

In their research, development psychologists have been strongly influenced by the Swiss psychologist Jean Piaget, who studied and theorized about child development for over half a century. Recent information-processing work in cognitive development has largely been concerned with correcting and restructuring Piaget's theory of cognitive development. Despite these revisions, his research has organized a large set of qualitative observations about cognitive development spanning the period from birth to adulthood. Modern cognitive-psychology research has been concerned with identifying the mechanisms that account for these developments. Thus, in this chapter, we will first describe Piaget's view of cognitive development and then turn to the more recent research.

Piaget's Stages of Development

According to Piaget, a child enters the world lacking virtually all the basic cognitive competencies of the adult, and gradually develops these competencies by passing through a series of *stages* of development. Piaget distinguishes four major stages: The *sensory-motor stage* occupies the first two years. During this stage, children develop schemes for thinking about the physical world—for instance, they develop the notion of an object as a permanent thing in the world. The second stage is the *preoperational stage,* which is characterized as spanning the period from 2 to 7 years. Unlike the younger child, a child in this period can engage in internal thought about the world, but these mental processes are intuitive and lack systematicity. For instance, a 4-year-old asked to describe his painting of a farm and some animals said, "First over here is a house where the animals live. I live in a house. So do my mommy and daddy. This is a horse. I saw horses on TV. Do you have a TV?"

The next stage is the *concrete-operational period*, which spans the period from 7 to 11 years. In this period children develop a set of mental operations that allow them to treat the physical world in a systematic way. However, children still have major limitations on their capacity for abstract thought.

The capacity for abstract thought emerges during Piaget's fourth period, the *formal-operational period*, spanning the years from 11 to 15. After emerging from this period, the child has become an adult conceptually and is capable of scientific reasoning—which Piaget takes as the paradigm case of mature intellectual functioning.

Piaget's concept of a stage has always been a sore point in developmental psychology. Obviously a child does not suddenly change on an 11th birthday from the stage of concrete operations to the stage of formal operations. There are large differences among children and cultures, and the ages given are just rough figures. However, careful analysis of the development within a single child also fails to find abrupt changes at any age. One response to this gradualness has been to break down the stages into smaller substages. Another response has been to interpret stages as simply ways of characterizing what is inherently a gradual and continuous process.

Just as important as Piaget's stage analysis is his analysis of children's performance in specific tasks within these stages. These task analyses provide the empirical substance to back up his broad and abstract characterization of the stages. They have also provided the focus for a great deal of developmental research. Therefore I will describe his results on a few of these tasks. Later in the chapter I will consider the newer analyses of these tasks that have come out of information-processing research.

Hidden Objects

As adults we would be surprised if objects started to magically appear and disappear in our environment. A question that interested Piaget is whether newborn children would be similarly surprised. That is, do children come into the world thinking of objects as having separate existences that continue over transformations in time and space? Piaget concluded from his experiments that a child does not, and that children develop a concept of object permanence over the first year. If a cloth is placed over a toy that a 6-month-old is reaching for, the infant stops reaching and appears to lose interest in the toy (see Figure 14-1). It is as if the object ceases to exist for the child when no longer in view.

The concept of object permanence develops slowly. An older infant will search for an object that has been hidden, but more demanding tests reveal failings in the older infant's understanding of a permanent object. In one experiment, an object is put under cover A and then, in front of the child, is removed and put under cover B. The child will often look for the object under cover A. It is only after the age of 12 months that the child can succeed consistently at this task.

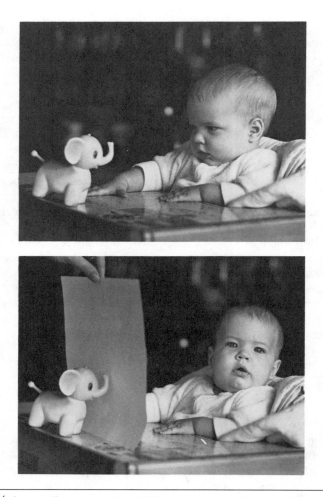

Figure 14-1 An illustration of a child's apparent inability to understand the permanence of an object.

Conservation

As adults we can almost instantaneously recognize that there are four apples in a bag and can confidently know that these apples will remain four when dumped into a bowl. Piaget was interested in how a child develops the concept of quantity and learns that quantity is something that is preserved under

Figure 14-2 A typical experimental situation to test for conservation of number.

various transformations. His research on this topic is referred to as research on *conservation* because he was interested in how children come to know that quantity is conserved under various transformations.

Figure 14-2 illustrates a typical conservation problem that has been posed by psychologists in many variations to countless preschool children. A child is presented with two rows of objects, such as checkers. The two rows contain the same number of objects and have been lined up so as to correspond.

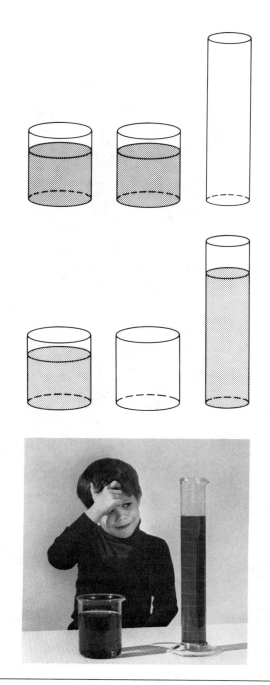

Figure 14-3 A typical experimental situation to test for conservation of liquid.

The child is asked whether the two rows have the same amount, and says that they do. The child can be asked to count the objects in the two rows to confirm that conclusion. Now, before the child's eyes, one row is compressed so that it is shorter than the other row, but the number is not changed. Again asked which row has more objects, the child now says the longer row has. The child appears not to know that quantity is something that is preserved under transformations such as compression of space. If asked to count the two rows, the child expresses great surprise that they have the same number.

The general feature of lack of conservation is that children are distracted by irrelevant physical features of a display. Figure 14-3 illustrates the liquid conservation task. A child is shown two identical beakers containing identical amounts of water, and an empty, tall, thin beaker. He is asked whether the two identical beakers hold the same amount of water, and agrees that they do. Now the water from one beaker is poured into the tall, thin beaker, and when asked whether the amount of water in the two containers is the same, the child now says that the tall beaker holds more. Children are distracted by physical appearance and do not relate their having seen the water go from one beaker into the other to the quantity of liquid. Bruner (1964) demonstrated that children will not make this error if the tall beaker is hidden from sight while it is filled so that the children cannot see the physical appearance. So, it is a case of being overwhelmed by physical appearance, not that the child does not know that water preserves its quantity after being poured.

Failure of conservation has also been shown with weight and volume of solid objects (for a discussion of studies of conservation see Brainerd, 1978; Flavell, 1977; Ginsburg & Opper, 1980). It was once thought that failure of conservation was a more or less unitary problem. Now, however, it is clear that successful conservation appears earlier on some tasks than on others. For instance, conservation of number usually appears before conservation of liquid. Also, children in transition will show conservation of number in one experimental situation but not another.

Transitive Inference

If we are told that *Fred is taller than Bill* and *George is taller than Fred,* we have no difficulty in concluding that *George is tallest.* In contrast, children have great difficulty in ordering objects serially. Given the problem just stated, they will often conclude that *Fred is tallest.* As another example, a child given a set of wooden sticks and asked to order them will produce an order like the one in Figure 14-4a rather than the correct order (Figure 14-4b). Piaget felt that these problems in seriation were important because they reflected fundamental problems in logical reasoning.

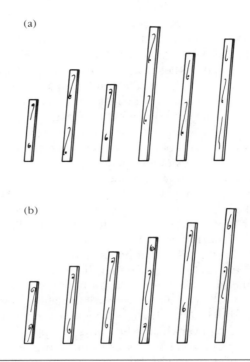

Figure 14-4 A preoperational child will produce an ordering of sticks like that in (a) rather than the correct ordering in (b).

Balance-Scale Task

Inhelder and Piaget (1958) have also looked at children's reasoning on a wide variety of elementary physics tasks: balance scales, projections of shadows, pendulums, falling bodies, and the like. On all these tasks they tend to find the same development trends: 5-year-olds (preoperational) have little or no systematic understanding; 10-year-olds (concrete operations) understand the qualitative but not the quantitative relations; 15-year-olds (formal operations) understand both the qualitative and quantitative relations and have some understanding of the relevant theoretical constructs.

Figure 14-5 illustrates the balance-scale task. Piaget collected protocols of children solving various problems involving the balance scale. The problems involved two sets of various weights placed at various distances from the fulcrum. Children around the age of 5 predict that the side with more weights will be down; they do not consider distance from the fulcrum. Children

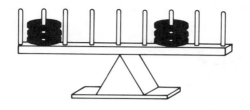

Figure 14-5   The balance-scale problem used by Inhelder and Piaget.

around the age of 10 engage in crude attempts to trade off distance and weight. Children at 15 reason quite accurately about the problems, often bringing to bear the correct mathematical formula.

What Develops?

Clearly, as Piaget has documented, major intellectual changes occur during childhood. However, there are serious questions concerning what underlies these changes. There are two basic classes of explanation for why children perform better on various intellectual tasks as they get older: One is that they think better and the other is that they know better. The *think-better* option holds that children's basic cognitive processes are better. Perhaps they can hold more information in working memory, retrieve information faster, apply productions faster. The *know-better* option holds that children have learned more and more facts and methods as they get older. Perhaps this greater knowledge enables them to perform the tasks more efficiently. Once again, the computer metaphor is apt. A computer system (e.g., for doing deduction) can be made to perform better by running the same program on a faster machine that has more memory or by running a better program on the same machine. Which is it in the child's case—better machine or better program?

Of course this is not an either-or situation. The child's improvement is due to both factors, but this leaves open the relative contributions of the two. It is tempting to emphasize the improvement in processing capacity. After all, consider the physical difference between a 2-year-old and an adult. When my son was 2, he had difficulty mastering the unsnapping of his pajama buttons. If his muscles and coordination had so much maturation ahead, why not his brain? This analogy, however, does not hold: A 2-year-old has reached only 20 percent of his adult body weight, whereas the brain has already reached 80 percent of its final size. We might argue that cognitive development after age 2 will, to an approximation, depend on the knowledge an individual

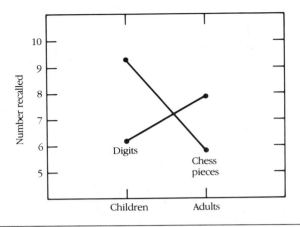

Figure 14-6 Number of chess pieces and number of digits recalled by children versus adults. From Chi (1978).

puts in the brain rather than on physical improvement in the capacities of the brain.

Chi (1978) has demonstrated that developmental differences may be knowledge related. Her domain of demonstration was memory. Not surprisingly, children do worse than adults on almost every memory task. Is this because their memories have less capacity, or is it because they know less about what they are being asked to remember? To address this question, she compared memory performance of 10-year-old children to that of adults on two tasks—a standard digit-span task and a chess memory task (see the discussion of these tasks in Chapters 6 and 9). The 10-year-olds were skilled chess players, whereas the adults were novices at chess. The chess task was the one illustrated earlier in Figure 9-5—a chessboard was presented for 10 sec and then withdrawn, and the subjects were asked to reproduce the chess pattern.

Figure 14-6 illustrates the number of chess pieces recalled by children and adults. The figure also contrasts these results with the number of digits recalled in the digit-span task. As Chi predicted, the adults were better on the digit-span task but the children were better on the chess task. The children's superior chess performance was attributed to their greater knowledge of chess. The adults' superior digit performance was due to their greater familiarity with digits—the dramatic digit-span performance of SF in Chapter 1 shows just how much digit knowledge can lead to improved memory performance.

Recall the novice-expert contrast from Chapter 9. We saw there that a great deal of experience in a domain is required if a person is to become an expert.

Chi's argument is that children, because of their lack of knowledge, are universal novices and can become as expert as adults only through experience.

In the next part of the chapter we will review developmental changes in the basic aspects of cognition studied in previous chapters—memory, representation, and problem solving.[1] We will constantly be asking the thinking-better versus knowing-better question. With this as background, we will return to the Piagetian tasks considered earlier and try to understand the nature of the developmental changes displayed on these tasks.

Memory

Despite Chi's demonstration, adults and older children typically outperform younger children on memory tasks. One point of view is that this is not due to greater capacity but rather to the use of better strategies for encoding and retrieving information. When we look at recognition memory, something that typically does not involve an important strategic component, there is little change through the span of childhood (Brown, 1975; Perlmutter, 1980).

Young children appear to lack some of the most basic strategies of memory performance. The clearest case concerns rote rehearsal. If you were asked to dial a novel seven-digit number, I would hope you would rehearse it to yourself until you were confident you had it memorized or until you had dialed the number. It would never occur to a young child that they should rehearse the number. In one study comparing 5-year-olds with 10-year-olds, Keeney, Cannizzo, and Flavell (1967) found that 10-year-olds almost always verbally rehearsed a set of objects to be remembered, whereas the 5-year-olds seldom did. Young children's performance often improves if they are instructed to follow a verbal rehearsal strategy, although very young children are simply unable to execute such a strategy.

Part of the reason children do not spontaneously use verbal rehearsal may be their inaccurate knowledge about how their memories work. Flavell, Friedrichs, and Hoyt (1970) presented children with 10 pictures and asked them how many they could remember. Most nursery-schoolers and kindergartners thought they could remember all 10. Older children had more realistic estimates. In another study, Kreutzer, Leonard, & Flavell (1975) asked children what they would do in order to remember a telephone number. Almost all (95 percent) of the third and fifth graders said they would phone first before getting a drink of water, but only 40 percent of the kindergartners thought that to be a wise strategy. In addition, almost all of the older children thought they would adopt some measure like writing the number down or rehearsing

---

[1]We considered developmental changes in language in Chapter 11.

it. In contrast, only 60 percent of the kindergartners thought that any special measures were required. It would be interesting to know what role schooling plays in the acquisition by the older children of better memory strategies.

Chapter 7 emphasized the importance of elaborative strategies for good memory performance. Particularly for long-term retention, elaboration appears to be much more effective than rote rehearsal. There also appear to be sharp developmental trends with respect to the use of elaborative encoding strategies. For instance, Paris and Lindauer (1976) looked at the elaborations that children use to relate two paired-associate nouns like *lady* and *broom*. Older children are more likely to generate interactive sentences like *The lady flew on the broom* than static sentences like *The lady had a broom*. Such interactive sentences will lead to better memory performance. Children are also poorer at drawing the inferences that improve memory for a story (Stein & Trabasso, 1981).

In summary, memory improves as children get older for the following reasons:

1. Children learn the proper strategies for memorization and practice these strategies until they become effective at applying them.

2. Children acquire more knowledge that is relevant to elaborating and chunking the to-be-remembered information.

Knowledge Representation

A frequent key to developmental improvement is the representation of knowledge in such a way that efficient and effective mental processes can apply to that knowledge. Earlier in the book we contrasted perceptually based representations with meaning-based representations. There we noted that meaning-based representations were often more effective. A recurring hypothesis in developmental psychology is that young children rely on the more perceptually based representations, whereas adults depend on the meaning-based representations (Bruner, Oliver, & Greenfield, 1966; Kosslyn, 1980; Piaget & Inhelder, 1971). Although this conjecture is appealing, it has proven remarkably resistant to experimental exploration.

An experiment reported by Kosslyn (1980) represents one attempt to get at this issue. He had first-graders and adults verify statements like *A cat has claws*. He reasoned that for adults, the efficient way to verify this assertion was to retrieve an abstract proposition. In contrast, he thought children would have to inspect an image of a cat and notice the claws. This was a less efficient strategy but the only one the children had, given their representational abilities. Of course, he found adults faster to respond. However, he also manip-

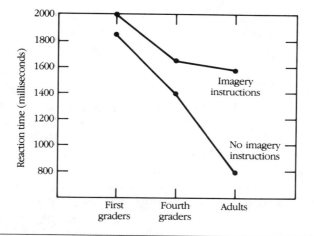

Figure 14-7   Time to verify a statement for adults and for children. Subjects were instructed to verify the assertion by imagery or were given no instruction as to method of verification. From Kosslyn (1980).

ulated how the adults decided on their responses. Some he explicitly asked to inspect an image, whereas others were free to respond as fast as they could. He used a similar instructional manipulation with children. Figure 14-7 presents his results. Adults are very much slower with the imagery strategy, suggesting that it is more efficient to inspect abstract propositions. In contrast, first-graders are almost as slow given no instructions as they are given imagery instructions, suggesting that the imagery strategy is their default strategy even when they are not instructed to use it.

Although the results of this study support the hypothesis that children are more inclined to use imagery representations than abstract representations, the study leaves open the cause of their different representational usage. Is it that children are unable to form abstract representations? Or, given their young ages, do they just have less information encoded abstractly? Perhaps it is not that they are unable to encode a propositional representation of the fact that *A cat has claws,* but that they simply have not yet had the opportunity to do so.

It is also the case that some developments do not involve going from abstract representations to concrete representations, but rather from less adequate to more adequate abstract representations. For instance, in solving problems like the balance-scale problem, it is important that the child be able to think in terms of ratios rather than differences. Both ratios and differences are abstract concepts; however, ratios are a more complex abstract concept that takes more experience (schooling) to acquire. Whatever the source of these representational changes, we will see again and again that improvement in representation seems to be key to cognitive development.

Problem Solving

A series of studies by Klahr (Klahr, 1978; Klahr & Robinson, 1981) provides an interesting vantage point on the problem-solving abilities of children. He looked at the ability of children to solve the tower of Hanoi problem (discussed earlier in Chapter 8). However, to make the problem more sensible to young children, he used the setup illustrated in Figure 14-8. The three cans were colored and described as monkeys—a big yellow daddy, a medium-sized blue mommy, and a little red baby. These monkeys jumped from tree to tree with the constraint that big cans (monkeys) could fit only on little cans. Children were shown one configuration of cans (monkeys) and were asked to arrange a second configuration of copycat monkeys (cans) into the same configuration.

The child's task was to make a tower, as in the regular tower of Hanoi task, but the problem was started at varying numbers of moves from the goal, or final tower state. Problems were classified according to the number of moves required for successful solution. The original three-disk problem in Chapter 8 involved seven moves. Figure 14-9 illustrates configurations that require (a) two moves, (b) three moves, and (c) six moves, from the goal state in order to have all the cans on peg 3. On average, 4-year-olds were able to solve problems requiring 2.5 moves; 5-year-olds, 3.8 moves; and 6-year-olds, 5.6 moves. There is clearly a very strong developmental progression with age. It is interesting, however, that only one 6-year-old was able to solve the full seven-move tower of Hanoi problem.

What underlies the developmental improvement in problem-solving ability? Klahr and Robinson note that children gradually pick up the strategic features needed to solve the problem. Critical to solving the problem is the ability to move an obstructing can out of the way. The youngest children do not have this ability, and can solve only problems like Figure 14.9a, where there are no obstructing cans. Next, if an obstructing can is to be moved, as in Figure 14-9b, it is important to choose the right peg to move it to. In Figure 14.9b, we would not want to move the can from peg 2 to peg 3 because this would obstruct the move of the bottom can on peg 2 to peg 3. Children who are capable of solving such a problem are capable of solving a subgoal. They set the subgoal of moving one can out of the way so that they can correctly place another can. Klahr and Robinson found that children are reliably able to achieve such subgoals only after the age of 5. The next level of problem solving involves handling more than one level of subgoals, as required in

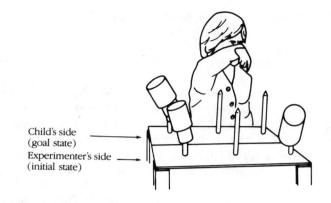

Child's side
(goal state)

Experimenter's side
(initial state)

Figure 14-8 Children's version of the tower of Hanoi problem.

(a)

(b)

(c)

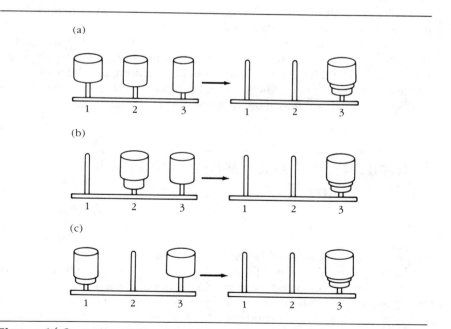

Figure 14-9 Tower of Hanoi problems that are (a) two, (b) three, and (c) six moves from the goal state.

Figure 14.9c. The evidence from Klahr's work is that children are only beginning to handle this level of complexity by age 6.

The simple conclusion might be that over this period children are developing a general ability to handle subgoals. However, Klahr and Robinson note that even at 18 months a child can set the subgoal of removing one object to get at another. When my son was 3, he was capable of getting a parent so that the parent would open a door so that he could go upstairs so he could play with Daddy's computer terminal. Thus it seems that children have the ability to deal with subgoals at a very early age. Klahr and Robinson suggest that young children fail to represent the problem in such a way that they can apply their subgoaling ability. For instance, children may perceive one can as simply on top of another can rather than more abstractly as blocking the move of the can. Thus, the major developmental trend may not be in problem-solving ability per se, but rather in representational ability.

Development of Basic Cognitive Abilities: A Summary

In general, it seems that the improvement in children's intellectual abilities depends on increased knowledge of what to do rather than increased ability to do it. Development of memory and development of problem solving seem related to appropriate encoding strategies. Also, children seem to develop more effective representational abilities over time. With this perspective on the nature of the difference between younger children and older ones, we can go back and consider whether these differences might help explain the development that children show in some of the Piagetian tasks.

Information-Processing Analyses of Piagetian Tasks

Hidden Objects

Recall Piaget's discussion of the problems young children have in searching for hidden objects and his inference that these difficulties reflect a lack of adequate concept of object permanence. A popular paradigm was one in which an object was hidden in location A, then moved before the child to location B, after which the child continued to look for the object in location A. Recently, researchers (Bjork & Cummings, 1984; Sophian, 1984a), have suggested that this finding may really reflect a memory or encoding failure: Perhaps the infant simply forgets the move from A to B.

Sophian has produced evidence for this conclusion in two ways. First she showed that if infants were practiced on the move from A to B, they were much more likely to correctly look under B. Thus, by increasing the probability that the child would remember the A-to-B move, Sophian increased the probability of correct performance on the task.

The second paradigm involved three locations—A, B, and C—for hidden objects. As before, the object would be moved from A to B, but now it was possible to determine how often children made incorrect searches at C as well as at A. If the infant simply forgot everything, it would be just as likely to search at A as C. In fact, this is just what was found.

Thus, much of what Piaget thought of as fundamental conceptual changes in understanding the nature of the world are just improvements in memory. Of course, this leaves open the cause of these memory improvements. We reviewed earlier the evidence that children increase their memory by better encoding strategies. However, this was at considerably older ages. It may well be that the 9-month-olds in Sophian's task have not yet fully developed their memory capacities.

Transitive Inference

Recall the earlier evidence that preoperational children have great difficulty in performing transitive inference (e.g., when given *A is longer than B* and *B is longer than C*, to conclude that *A is longer than C*). Trabasso and his co-workers speculated that childrens' difficulty stemmed from not memorizing and properly representing the pairwise relationships (e.g., *A>B*). Bryant and Trabasso (1971) taught preschoolers the pairwise orderings among five colored sticks (e.g., the red stick is longer than the blue stick). Unlike the typical procedure, they drilled the children on the four pairwise relations *A>B, B>C, C>D, D>E* until the children were able to recall with a high level of accuracy. Having been forced to achieve this memory criterion, the children were able to make the transitive inferences (e.g., *B>D*), with a high degree of accuracy. Thus, it appears that part of the children's difficulty was their failure to keep the pairwise relations in mind.

Riley and Trabasso (1974) compared two training procedures for getting children to memorize the pairwise relations. In one condition they had subjects answer questions of both the form *Which is shorter, A or B?* and the form *Which is longer, A or B?* In the other condition they had children answer questions of just one form or the other. Of the 4-year-olds trained with both forms, 87 percent were able to learn the relations, whereas only 35 percent were successful when trained with just one form. Riley & Trabasso (1974) propose that children trained just that *Stick A is longer than B* simply encoded *Stick A is long* and *Stick B is long*. Such absolute encoding did not enable them to answer the questions. The effect of using both *long* and *short*, Trabasso and Riley claimed, was to force the children to encode the sticks in a relative form such that they could answer the transitive questions. Thus, once again we find that a major factor in children's success on a problem is the way that they represent the information in the task.

Conservation

Klahr and Wallace (1973, 1976) have shown that children's performance on conservation tasks can be understood in terms of the production rules the children possess. They assume that children start with an initial ability to quantify arrays consisting of small numbers of objects—that is, assign a number to an array. According to Klahr and Wallace, development of the concept of number and development of the ability to quantify are prerequisites to conservation. They contend that the child's development of conservation depends on observation of what happens to the number of single arrays of objects after various transformations. For instance, the child observes that the number of cookies stays the same after physical rearrangement, decreases after eating, and increases when more cookies are added from the cookie jar. The child learns the class (Class 1) of operations that preserve the number of an object—adding space between objects, piling objects on each other, holding them in hand, and the like. Similarly, the child learns the class of operations that increase (Class 2) and decrease (Class 3) number. Then the child can form generative production rules like the following:

> IF a set of objects undergoes a transformation in Class 1
> THEN the number of objects does not change.

> IF a set of objects undergoes a transformation in Class 2
> THEN the number of objects increases.

> IF a set of objects undergoes a transformation in Class 3
> THEN the number of objects decreases.

Children's ability to make the judgments modeled by these rules emerges before their ability to perform in the traditional conservation task, which requires judging the quantity of two arrays. According to Klahr and Wallace, this ability to deal with single arrays is prerequisite because it involves learning the classes of operations that preserve, increase, and decrease quantity. Knowing these classes of operations, a child is ready to deal with what happens in the traditional task—when two arrays, originally judged to be equal, are present, and then one undergoes a transformation. The child notes that if the array undergoes a transformation in Class 1, the two arrays are equal; if it undergoes a transformation in Class 2, the transformed array has more;

and if it undergoes a transformation in Class 3, the transformed array has less. Thus, the following three rules are formed:

> IF   two arrays have equal number
> and array 1 undergoes a transformation in Class 1
> THEN the two arrays still have equal number.

> IF   two arrays have equal number
> and array 1 undergoes a transformation in Class 2
> THEN array 1 has more than array 2.

> IF   two arrays have equal number
> and array 1 undergoes a transformation in Class 3
> THEN array 1 has less than array 2.

Klahr and Wallace (1976) can be consulted for a detailed production-system model that actually simulates the behavior of children at various stages of development. There are still important questions about how the children actually acquire such production rules from experience. However, the important feature about the Klahr and Wallace demonstration is that cognitive development can be simulated basically by adding new productions to an existing system of rules.

Analysis of the Balance-Scale Problem

Siegler (1980) gives a similar rule-based analysis of the balance-scale problems.[2] He proposes that children operate according to one of the four rule sets in Table 14-1 when working with the balance scales.

Rule set 1 represents a child completely dominated by the dimension of weight. If the weights are different, the child chooses the greater weight *(rule A)*; otherwise the child believes the scale will balance *(rule B)*. Siegler found that this rule set characterized 5-year-olds. As children get older, *rule B* is replaced by *rules C and D*, which enable the child to respond to the distance from the fulcrum if the weights are equal. This defines *rule set 2*. Rule set 2 still has rule A, and so the child erroneously decides that the side with more weights will go down even when distance from the fulcrum invalidates this decision. *Rule set 3* is derived by replacing rule A by rule E, which decides that the side with more weights will go down only if the distances from the fulcrum are equal. Siegler found that children in the 8- to 12-year range could be characterized as following either rule set 2 or rule set 3. Rule set 2 has

---

[2]Siegler presents his rule analysis in terms of decision trees, but these decision trees and Klahr's production systems are largely equivalent (see Klahr & Siegler, 1978).

Table 14-1 *Siegler's four rule sets*

Rule set 1:

A   IF   the number of weights is greater on side 1
                   THEN   side 1 will go down.

B   IF   the number of weights on the two sides are equal
                   THEN   the two sides will stay in balance.

Rule set 2:   Rule A from rule set 1 plus

C   IF   the number of weights on the two sides are equal
                         and the weights are farther from the fulcrum on side 1
                   THEN   side 1 will go down.

D   IF   the number of weights on both sides are equal
                         and the distances from the fulcrum are equal
                   THEN   the weights will balance.

Rule set 3:   Rules C and D from rule set 2 plus

E   IF   the number of weights is greater on side 1
                         and the weights are as far or farther from the fulcrum
                         on side 1
                   THEN   side 1 will go down.

Rule set 4:   Rules C, D, and E from rule set 3 plus

F   IF   the number of weights on side 1 is greater
                         and the weights are as far or farther from the fulcrum
                         on side 2
                   THEN   multiply weight and distance for each side and compare
                             the products.

Adapted from Siegler, 1980.

children incorrectly responding when a distance difference compensates a weight difference. Rule set 3 does not provide the child with a basis for deciding when weight and distance are in conflict, and children using this rule set respond randomly. Only rule set 4 precribes the correct multiplicative combination of weight and distance. Siegler found a few 12-year-olds who used the multiplicative rule and a few more college students. However, even a majority of the college students did not know the multiplicative rule.

Siegler (1976) shows that these rule sets are very accurate in modeling the behavior of individual children. Siegler (1976) has argued that development can be modeled by adding better production rules and deleting poorer ones. Klahr and Siegler also showed that very young children do not even notice the differences in distance. If these children are instructed to attend to these differences in distance and encode them, they will benefit from experience with the balance scale. So 5-year-olds behaving according to rule set 1 can be trained to behave according to rule set 3 if they attend to the distance dimension. Thus, once again we see that adopting the correct representation is critical to cognitive development.

Piagetian Tasks: A Summary

At the beginning of this chapter we reviewed some of the classical tasks used by Piaget to illustrate the intellectual development of children. Now we have looked at some attempts to explain these tasks in modern information-processing terms. We have seen that developments in memory and knowledge representation seem to be important to many of the developmental trends observed in children. We have also seen that accumulation of knowledge is important.

The evidence we have reviewed from the information-processing approach tends to favor the view that increased knowledge, not increased cognitive ability, underlies children's cognitive development. Earlier we reviewed the evidence that better memory performance depended more on better use of memory than on increased memory capacity. Also, improved representational ability may really depend on simply experiencing information presented in new representational codes. Although there is evidence of this sort that greater knowledge is the key to cognitive development, there are information-processing analyses that argue for the importance of increased cognitive capacity. We will now review one of these analyses.

Memory Space Approaches

There have been a number of efforts to build information-processing accounts of cognitive development that attribute developmental improvements to increased capacity. For instance, Case and Pascual-Leone (Case, 1978; Pascual-Leone, 1980) have developed "neo-Piagetian" models of development that propose that a growing working-memory capacity is the key to the developmental sequence. The basic idea is that more advanced cognitive performance requires that more information be held in working memory.

As an example of this analysis, consider Case's (1978) description of how children solve Noelting's (1975) juice problem. The child is given two empty pitchers, *A* and *B*, and is told that several tumblers of orange juice and water will be poured into each. The child's task is to predict which pitcher will taste most strongly of orange juice. Figure 14-10 illustrates the problems that children can solve at various ages. At the youngest age, children can reliably solve only problems where all orange juice goes into one pitcher and all water into another. At ages 4–5 they can count the number of tumblers of orange juice going into a pitcher and choose the pitcher with the larger number—not considering the number of tumblers of water. At age 7–8, they notice whether there is more orange juice or more water going into a pitcher.

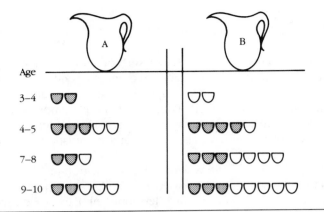

Figure 14-10 The Noelting juice problems that children can solve at various ages. The problem is to tell which pitcher will taste more strongly of orange juice after observing the tumblers of water and juice that will be poured into each.

If pitcher *A* has more orange juice than water and pitcher *B* has more water than orange juice, they will choose pitcher *A* even if the absolute number of orange juice glasses is less. Finally, at age 9–10, children compute the difference between the amount of orange juice and the amount of water (still not a perfect solution).

Case argues that the working-memory requirements differ for the various types of problems represented in Figure 14-10. For the simplest problems the child has to keep only one fact in memory—which set of tumblers has the orange juice. Children at ages 3–4 can keep only one such fact in mind. If both sets of tumblers have orange juice, the child cannot solve the problem. For the second type of problem the child needs to keep two things in memory— the number of orange juice tumblers in each array. In the third type of problem the child needs to keep additional partial products in mind to determine which side has more orange juice. To solve the fourth type of problem, the child needs four facts to make a judgment:

1. the absolute difference in tumblers going into pitcher A;
2. the sign of the difference for pitcher A (i.e., whether there is more water or more orange juice going into pitcher A);
3. the absolute difference in tumblers going into pitcher B;
4. the sign of the difference for pitcher B.

Case argues that children's developmental sequences are controlled by their working-memory capacity for the problem. Only when they can keep four facts in memory will they achieve the fourth stage in the developmental sequence.

Case's theory has been criticized (e.g., Flavell, 1978) because it is hard to decide how to count the working-memory requirements. We noted earlier, in discussing short-term memory, that memory span is a slippery concept and depends in large part on the chunks with which information is represented. Recently Case (personal communication) has argued that a major factor in determining developmental sequence may be the representation that the child chooses for encoding the information. Thus, again we see that representational changes may be an important factor determining cognitive development.

Development of Subtraction Skills

The understanding of mathematics is subject to a developmental progression that starts with the preverbal child and continues well into college. It is perhaps the most sustained developmental process that members of our society engage in. It is also characterized by a considerable range in the end points reached—some can barely count reliably, whereas others become professional mathematicians. Therefore, understanding the development of mathematical knowledge has enormous potential benefits to society. Whereas Piaget was interested in characterizing the full span of this development of mathematical understanding, modern information-processing psychologists have focused only on aspects. We will discuss one of these aspects—the development of subtraction skills. The work of John Seely Brown and his colleagues on this topic provides us with an excellent example of the potential applications of cognitive science research.

Like other educational researchers before them, Brown and Burton (1978) observed the curious error patterns generated by some middle-school children in solving subtraction problems. For instance, one student produced the following two errors:

$$\begin{array}{r} 500 \\ -\ 65 \\ \hline 565 \end{array} \qquad \begin{array}{r} {}^{0} \\ 3\mathbf{1}^{1}2 \\ -24\ 3 \\ \hline 14\ 9 \end{array}$$

The response of most people, including some schoolteachers, to such errors is to conclude that the child is extremely careless, is responding randomly, or knows nothing. It turns out that this child is following faithfully a procedure for subtraction that has only one error, or "bug," as Brown and Burton called it. The child believes that $0 - N = N$; that is, the student thinks that if a digit is subtracted from 0, the result is that digit.

Brown and Burton found no less than 110 such bugs that can adversely affect the subtraction procedures of young children. Although children are sometimes careless or respond randomly, the important discovery is that the majority of their mistakes are caused by systematic errors in the subtraction procedures they are using. Thus, the appropriate remedial action is not just drill and practice, which will only ingrain these errors, but specific instruction to correct the errors. One of the important contributions of Brown and Burton and Burton (1982) is that they have produced a diagnostic computer program that can look at a child's behavior and identify the bug(s) that child has. This can be a considerable aid to the mathematics teacher.

Thus, students' development of subtraction skills is much like their development of conservation or their development on the balance-scale problem. They have procedures for solving these problems that can be more or less accurate. Indeed, Brown and Van Lehn have shown that, as in other domains, subtraction skills can be modeled by production systems, and improvement or development can occur by replacing less adequate productions by more adequate productions. Young and O'Shea (1981) have argued for a similar conclusion.

Origins of Subtraction Bugs

How are these bugs in the subtraction skill generated in the first place? Certainly, the teacher did not tell the student that when subtracting N from 0 to write N. Brown and Van Lehn (1980) have addressed this issue, and their answer may indicate how erroneous procedures arise in other domains, like conservation. They suppose that children sometimes fail to learn the complete procedure, and consequently that certain critical production rules are missing. This means that, when solving a problem, they will reach an impasse when they come to the point where a missing rule should be applied. Brown and Van Lehn assume that the child creates a solution to bridge this impasse, and that this solution becomes encoded as a new rule. If the rule is incorrect, the child has, in effect, taught himself or herself a bug.

Let us consider an example: One rule of subtraction is that if the digit in the upper row is smaller than the digit in the bottom row, the student should borrow from the preceding digit in the upper row. Suppose the student has not learned that rule and comes upon the following problem:

$$413$$
$$-242$$

When it comes to subtracting 4 from 1, the child hits an impasse. What is the child to do? One thing might be to simply leave the 10's column of the answer blank, but the child knows answers don't have holes in them and therefore this repair is rejected. Another possibility is to subtract the 1 from the 4. This leaves an answer that looks right even if it is nonsense. Some children do this and develop this as a systematic bug. Another possibility is to write 0, the smallest digit available. Other children do this and develop that as a systematic bug.

Thus, errors in procedures occur as a result of the child's attempt to fill in the missing steps of a procedure. Note that the child is not totally uncritical in producing repairs. For instance, repairs are not generated that leave holes in the answer. Van Lehn and Brown (1981) have argued that mathematics education would be improved if children were given a deeper understanding of domains like subtraction so that they would be able to recognize the nonsense in other repairs that they make.

This is an appropriate topic on which to close a book on cognitive psychology. I predict that cognitive science is going to make major contributions to mathematics education and related domains of science and technology education. There is a national (indeed international) crisis in the teaching of these domains as technology assumes dominance in our society. As illustrated in the work of Brown and his colleagues, the field of cognitive science has the concepts for making penetrating analyses of these skills. These analyses can be converted into practical tools. The computer techniques are available for automating the diagnosis of student problems and for automating instruction.

Remarks and Suggested Readings

Piaget and his co-authors have written a great many books on child development that have been translated from the original French. These include his *The Origins of Intelligence* (1952a), *The Child's Conception of Number* (1952b), and by Inhelder and Piaget, *The Growth of Logical Thinking from Childhood to Adolescence* (1958). Brainerd (1978) and Gruber and Voneche (1977) are secondary books written about Piaget's theory. More general texts on cognitive development include those by Flavell (1977) and Siegler (in press). Gelman (1978) offers a review of the field of cognitive development. Mussen's (1983) handbook contains a thorough overview of the whole field of developmental psychology. Two recent Carnegie Symposia on Cognition (Siegler, 1978; Sophian, 1984b) contain a large number of papers presenting information-processing approaches to cognition. Klahr and Wallace (1976) present a theory of development heavily influenced by production systems. Gelman & Gallistel (1978) present a modern analysis of what is developing in children's understanding of numbers.

A recent trend in cognitive psychology is to study what is happening in children's understanding of school topics. Siegler and Shrager (1984) discuss early development of addition and subtraction. Brown and Burton's (1978) analysis of children's understanding of subtraction is already a classic. Sleeman and Brown (1982) contains a set of papers describing the state of the art in producing intelligent computer systems for tutoring students in such domains as subtraction, algebra, and computer programming.

References

Abelson, R. P. (1981). Psychological status of the script concept. *American Psychologist, 36,* 715–729.

Alba, J. W., & Hasher, L. (1983). Is memory schematic? *Psychological Bulletin, 93,* 203–231.

Anderson, J. A. (1973). A theory for the recognition of items from short memorized lists. *Psychological Review, 80,* 417–438.

Anderson, J. R. (1972). Recognition confusions in sentence memory. Unpublished manuscript. (1974a).

Anderson, J. R. (1974a). Retrieval of propositional information from long-term memory. *Cognitive Psychology, 6,* 451–474.

Anderson, J. R. (1974b). Verbatim and propositional representation of sentences in immediate and long-term memory. *Journal of Verbal Learning and Verbal Behavior, 13,* 149–162.

Anderson, J. R. (1976) *Language, Memory, and Thought.* Hillsdale, NJ: Lawrence Erlbaum Associates.

Anderson, J. R. (1978a). Arguments concerning representations for mental imagery. *Psychological Review, 85,* 249–277.

Anderson, J. R. (1978b). Computer simulation of a language acquisition system: A second report. In D. LaBerge & S. J. Samuels (Eds.), *Perception and Comprehension.* Hillsdale, NJ: Lawrence Erlbaum Associates.

Anderson, J. R. (1981a). *Cognitive Skills and Their Acquisition.* Hillsdale, NJ: Lawrence Erlbaum Associates.

Anderson, J. R. (1981b). Tuning of search of the problem space for geometry proofs. *Proceedings of IJCAI-81,* 165–170.

Anderson, J. R. (1982). Acquisition of cognitive skill. *Psychological Review, 89,* 369–406.

Anderson, J. R. (1983). *The Architecture of Cognition.* Cambridge, MA: Harvard University Press.

Anderson, J. R. (1984). Spreading activation. In J. R. Anderson & S. M. Kosslyn (Eds.), *Essays in Learning and Memory.* New York: W. H. Freeman and Company.

Anderson, J. R., & Bower, G. H. (1972). Configural properties in sentence memory. *Journal of Verbal Learning and Verbal Behavior, 11,* 595–605.

Anderson, J. R., & Bower, G. H. (1973). *Human Associative Memory.* Washington, DC: Winston.

Anderson, J. R., Boyle, C. F., Farrell, R., & Reiser, B. (1984). Cognitive principles in the design of computer tutors. *Proceedings of the Cognitive Science Program,* 2–11.

Anderson, J. R., Farrell, R., & Sauers, R. (1984). Learning to program in LISP. *Cognitive Science, 8,* 87–129.

Anderson, J. R., & Kosslyn, S. M. (Eds.) (1984). *Tutorials in Learning and Memory.* New York: W. H. Freeman and Company.

Anderson, J. R., & Paulson, R. (1977). Representation and retention of verbatim information. *Journal of Verbal Learning and Verbal Behavior, 16,* 439–451.

Anderson, J. R., & Reder, L. M. (1979). An elaborative processing explanation of depth of processing. In L. S. Cermak and F. I. M. Craik (Eds.), *Levels of Processing in Human Memory.* Hillsdale, NJ: Lawrence Erlbaum Associates.

Anderson, R. C., & Biddle, W. B. (1975). On asking people questions about what they are reading. In G. H. Bower (Ed.), *The Psychology of Learning and Motivation,* Vol. 9, New York: Academic Press.

Anderson, T. H. (1978). Another look at the self-questioning study technique. Technical Education Report No. 6. Champaign: University of Illinois, Center for the Study of Reading.

Angiolillo-Bent, J. S., & Rips, L. J. (1982). Order information in multiple element comparison. *Journal of Experimental Psychology: Human Perception and Performance, 8,* 392–406.

Atkinson, R. C., & Raugh, M. R. (1975). An application of the mnemonic keyword method to the acquisition of Russian vocabulary. *Journal of Experimental Psychology: Human Learning and Memory, 104,* 126–133.

Atkinson, R. C., & Shiffrin, R. M., (1968). Human memory: A proposed system and its control processes. In K. Spence & J. Spence (Eds.), *The Psychology of Learning and Motivation,* Vol. 2. New York: Academic Press.

Atwood, M. E., & Polson, P. G. (1976). A process model for water jug problems. *Cognitive Psychology, 8,* 191–216.

Ausubel, D. P. (1968). *Educational Psychology: A Cognitive View.* New York: Holt, Rinehart, & Winston.

Baddeley, A. D. (1976). *The Psychology of Memory.* New York: Basic Books.

Baddeley, A. D., & Ecob, J. R. (1973). Reaction-time and short-term memory: Implications of repetition for the high-speed exhaustive scan hypothesis. *Quarterly Journal of Experimental Psychology, 25,* 229–240.

Banks, W. P., & Flora, J. (1977). Semantic and perceptual processes in symbolic comparisons. *Journal of Experimental Psychology: Human Perception and Performance, 3,* 278–290.

Barnes, C. A., & McNaughton, B. L. (1980). Spatial memory and hippocampal synaptic plasticity in middle-aged and senescent rats. In D. Stein (Ed.), *The Psychobiology of Aging: Problems and Perspectives.* Amsterdam: Elsevier.

Bartlett, B. J. (1978). Top-level structure as an organizational strategy for recall of classroom text. Unpublished doctoral dissertation, Arizona State University.

Bartlett, F. C. (1932). *Remembering: A Study in Experimental and Social Psychology.* New York & London: Cambridge University Press.

Bates, A., McNew, S., MacWhinney, B., Devesocvi, A., & Smith, S. (1982). Functional constraints on sentence processing: A cross-linguistic study. *Cognition, 11,* 245–299.

Battig, W. F., & Montague, W. E. (1969). Category norms for verbal items in 56 categories: A replication and extension of the Connecticut category norms. *Journal of Experimental Psychology Monograph.*

Bennett, T. L. (1977). *Brain and Behavior.* Monterey, CA: Brooks Cole.

Benson, D. F., & Greenberg, J. P. (1969). Visual form agnosia. *Archives of Neurology, 20,* 82–89.

Berlin, B., & Kay, P. (1969). *Basic Color Terms: Their Universality and Evolution.* Berkeley, CA: University of California Press.

Bever, T. G. (1970). The cognitive basis for linguistic structures. In J. R. Hayes (Ed.), *Cognition and the Development of Language.* New York: Wiley.

Bever, T. G., Garrett, M. F., & Hurtig, R. (1973). The interaction of perceptual processes and ambiguous sentences. *Memory and Cognition, 1,* 277–286.

Biederman, I., Glass, A. L., & Stacy, E. W. (1973). Searching for objects in real world scenes. *Journal of Experimental Psychology, 97,* 22–27.

Biederman, I., Mezzanotte, R. J., & Rabinowitz, J. C. (1982). Scene perception: Detecting and judging objects undergoing relational violations. *Cognitive Psychology, 14,* 143–177.

Bilodeau, I. McD. (1969). Information feedback. In E. A. Bilodeau (Ed.), *Principles of Skill Acquisition.* New York: Academic Press.

Bjork, R. A. (1975). Short-term storage: The ordered output of a central processor. In F. Restle, R. M. Shiffrin, N. J. Castellan, H. R. Lindman, & D. B. Pisoni (Eds.), *Cognitive Theory,* Vol. 1. Hillsdale, NJ: Lawrence Erlbaum Associates.

Bjork, R. A. (1979). Information-processing analysis of college teaching. *Educational Psychologist, 14,* 15–23.

Bjork, E. L., & Cummings, E. M. (1984). Infant search errors: Stage of concept development or stage of memory development. *Memory & Cognition, 12,* 1–19.

Black, J. B. (1984). Understanding and remembering stories. In J. R. Anderson & S. M. Kosslyn (Eds.), *Tutorials in Learning and Memory.* New York: W. H. Freeman and Company.

Black, J., & Wilensky, R. (1979). An evaluation of story grammars. *Cognitive Science, 3,* 213–230.

Blackburn, J. M. (1936). Acquisition of skill: An analysis of learning curves. IHRB Report No. 73.

Bobrow, D. G., & Winograd, T. (1977). An overview of KRL, a knowledge representation language. *Cognitive Science, 1,* 3–46.

Bobrow, S., & Bower, G. H., (1969). Comprehension and recall of sentences. *Journal of Experimental Psychology, 80,* 455–461.

Bolinger, D. L. (1975). *Aspects of Language.* New York: Harcourt Brace Jovanovich.

Boole, G. (1854). *An Investigation of the Laws of Thought.* London: Walton and Maberly.

Boomer, D. S. (1965). Hesitation and grammatical encoding. *Language and Speech, 8,* 148–158.

Boring, E. G. (1950). *A History of Experimental Psychology.* New York: Appleton Century.

Bourne, L. E. (1963). Some factors affecting strategies used in problems of concept formation. *American Journal of Psychology, 75,* 229–238.

Bourne, L. E. (1966). *Human Conceptual Behavior.* Boston: Allyn & Bacon.

Bourne, L. E., Ekstrand, B. R., Dominowski, R. L. (1971). *The Psychology of Thinking.* Englewood Cliffs, NJ: Prentice-Hall.

Bower, G. H. (1970a). Analysis of a mnemonic device. *American Scientist, 58,* 496–510.

Bower, G. H. (1970b). Imagery as a relational organizer in associative learning. *Journal of Verbal Learning and Verbal Behavior, 9,* 529–533.

Bower, G. H. (1970c). Organizational factors in memory. *Cognitive Psychology, 1,* 18–46.

Bower, G. H. (1972). Mental imagery and associative learning. In L. Gregg (Ed.), *Cognition in Learning and Memory.* New York: Wiley.

Bower, G. H., Black, J. B., & Turner, T. J. (1979). Scripts in memory for text. *Cognitive Psychology, 11,* 177–220.

Bower, G. H., & Clark, M. C. (1969). Narrative stories as mediators for serial learning. *Psychonomic Science, 14,* 181–182.

Bower, G. H., Clark, M. C., Lesgold, A. M., & Winzenz, D. (1969). Hierarchical retrieval schemes in recall of categorical word lists. *Journal of Verbal Learning and Verbal Behavior, 8,* 323–343.

Bower, G. H., Karlin, M. B., & Dueck, A. (1975). Comprehension and memory for pictures. *Memory & Cognition, 3,* 216–220.

Bower, G. H., Monteiro, K. P., & Gilligan, S. G. (1978). Emotional mood as a context for learning and recall. *Journal of Verbal Learning and Verbal Behavior, 17,* 573–587.

Brainerd, C. J. (1978). *Piaget's Theory of Intelligence.* Englewood Cliffs, NJ: Prentice-Hall.

Bransford, J. D., Barclay, J. R., & Franks, J. J. (1972). Sentence memory: A constructive versus interpretive approach. *Cognitive Psychology, 3,* 193–209.

Bray, C. W. (1948). *Psychology and Military Proficiency.* Princeton: Princeton University Press.

Bresnan, J. W. (1978). A realistic tranformational grammar. In M. Halle, J. Bresnan, & G. Miller (Eds.), *Linguistic Theory and Psychological Reality.* Cambridge, MA: MIT Press.

Bresnan, J. (Ed.) (1981). *The Mental Representation of Grammatical Relations.* Cambridge, MA: MIT Press.

Brewer, W. F., & Treyens, J. C. (1981). Role of schemata in memory for places. *Cognitive Psychology, 13,* 207–230.

Broadbent, D. E. (1975). The magic number after fifteen years. In R. A. Kennedy & A. Wilkes (Eds.), *Studies in Long-Term Memory.* New York: Wiley.

Brooks, L. R. (1968). Spatial and verbal components of the act of recall. *Canadian Journal of Psychology, 22,* 349–368.

Brown, A. L. (1975). The development of memory: Knowing, knowing about knowing, and knowing how to know. In H. W. Reese (Ed.), *Advances in Child Development and Behavior,* Vol. 10. New York: Academic Press.

Brown, A. L. (1979). Theories of memory and the problems of development: Activity, growth, and knowledge. In L. S. Cermak & F. I. M. Craik (Eds.), *Levels of Processing in Human Memory.* Hillsdale, NJ: Lawrence Erlbaum Associates.

Brown, J. (1958). Some tests of decay theory of immediate memory. *Quarterly Journal of Experimental Psychology, 10,* 12–21.

Brown, J. S., & Burton, R. R. (1978). Diagnostic models for procedural bugs in basic mathematical skills. *Cognitive Science, 2,* 155–192.

Brown, J. S., & Van Lehn, K. (1980). Repair theory: A generative theory of bugs in procedural skills. *Cognitive Science, 4,* 397–426.

Brown, R. (1973). *A First Language.* Cambridge, MA: Harvard University Press.

Brown, R., & Lenneberg, E. H. (1954). A study in language and cognition. *Journal of Abnormal and Social Psychology, 49,* 454–462.

Brown, T. S., & Wallace, P. M. (1980). *Physiological Psychology.* New York: Academic Press.

Bruce, B., Collins, A. M., Rubin, A. D., & Gentner, D. (1979). A cognitive science approach to writing. In C. H. Fredericksen, M. F. Whiteman, & J. D. Dominic (Eds.), *Writing: The Nature, Development and Teaching of Written Communication.* Hillsdale, NJ: Lawrence Erlbaum Associates.

Bruner, J. S. (1964). The course of cognitive growth. *American Psychologist, 19,* 1–15.

Bruner, J. S., Goodnow, J., & Austin, G. A. (1956). *A Study of Thinking.* New York: Wiley.

Bruner, J. S., Oliver, R. R., & Greenfield, P. M. (Eds.) (1966). *Studies in Cognitive Growth.* New York: Wiley.

Bryant, P. E., & Trabasso, T. (1971). Transitive inferences and memory in young children. *Nature, 232,* 457–459.

Buckley, P. B., & Gillman, C. B. (1974). Comparison of digits and dot patterns. *Journal of Experimental Psychology, 103,* 1131–1136.

Burton, R. R. (1982). Diagnosing bugs in a simple procedural skill. In D. Sleeman & J. S. Brown (Eds.), *Intelligent Tutoring Systems.* New York: Academic Press.

Cairns, H. S., & Cairns, C. E. (1976). *Psycholinguistics: A Cognitive View of Language.* New York: Holt, Rinehart & Winston.

Caplan, D. (1972). Clause boundaries and recognition latencies for words in sentences. *Perception and Psychophysics, 12,* 73–76.

Carbonell, J. G. (1983). Learning by analogy: Formulating and generalizing plans from past experience. In R. S. Michalski, J. G. Carbonell, & T. M. Mitchell, (Eds.), *Machine Learning.* Palo Alto, CA: Tioga.

Card, S. K., Moran, T. P., & Newell, A. (1983). *The Psychology of Human-Computer Interaction.* Hillsdale, NJ: Lawrence Erlbaum Associates, 1983.

Carmichael, L., Hogan, H. P., & Walter, A. (1932). An experimental study of the effect of language on the reproduction of visually perceived form. *Journal of Experimental Psychology, 15,* 73–86.

Carpenter, P. A., & Just, M. A. (1975). Sentence comprehension; A psycholinguistic processing model of verification. *Psychological Review, 82,* 45–73.

Carroll, J. B., & Casagrande, J. B. (1958). The function of language classifications in behavior. In E. E. Maccoby, T. M. Newcomb, & E. L. Hartley (Eds.), *Readings in Social Psychology,* (3rd Ed.) New York: Holt, Rinehart, & Winston.

Carroll, Lewis. (1927). *Alice's Adventures in Wonderland.* New York: Appleton. Originally published 1866.

Case, R. (1978). Intellectual development from birth to adulthood: A neo-Piagetian approach. In R. S. Siegler (Ed.), *Children's Thinking: What Develops?* Hillsdale, NJ: Lawrence Erlbaum Associates.

Ceraso, J., & Provitera, A. (1971). Sources of error in syllogistic reasoning. *Cognitive Psychology, 2,* 400–410.

Cermak, L. S., & Craik, F. I. M. (1979). *Levels of Processing in Human Memory.* Hillsdale, NJ: Lawrence Erlbaum Associates.

Chapman, L. J., & Chapman, J. P. (1959). Atmosphere effect reexamined. *Journal of Experimental Psychology, 58,* 220–226.

Charness, N. (1976). Memory for chess positions: Resistence to interference. *Journal of Experimental Psychology: Human Learning and Memory, 2,* 641–653.

Charniak, E., & Wilks, Y. (1976). *Computational Semantics.* Amsterdam: North-Holland.

Chase, W. G., & Clark, H. H. (1972). Mental operations in the comparisons of sentences and pictures. In L. W. Gregg (Ed.), *Cognition in Learning and Memory.* New York: Wiley.

Chase, W. G., & Ericsson, K. A. (1982). Skill and working memory. In G. H. Bower (Ed.) *The Psychology of Learning and Motivation,* Vol. 16. New York: Academic Press.

Chase, W. G., & Simon, H. A. (1973). The mind's eye in chess. In W. G. Chase (Ed.), *Visual Information Processing*. New York: Academic Press.

Cherry, E. C. (1953). Some experiments on the recognition of speech with one and with two ears. *Journal of the Acoustical Society of America, 25,* 975–979.

Chi, M. T. H. (1978). Knowledge structures and memory development. In R. S. Siegler (Ed.), *Children's Thinking: What Develops?* Hillsdale, NJ: Lawrence Erlbaum Associates.

Chi, M. T. H., Feltovich, P. J., & Glaser, R. (1981). Categorization and representation of physics problems by experts and novices. *Cognitive Science, 5,* 121–152.

Chi, M. T. H., Glaser, R., & Farr, M. (Eds.) (In preparation). *The Nature of Expertise.*

Chomsky, N. (1951). *Syntactic Structures.* The Hague: Mouton.

Chomsky, N. (1965). *Aspects of the Theory of Syntax.* Cambridge, MA: MIT Press.

Chomsky, N. (1975). *Reflections on Language.* New York: Pantheon Books.

Chomsky, N., & Halle, M. (1968). *The Sound Pattern of English.* New York: Harper.

Christen, F., & Bjork, R. A. (1976). On updating the loci in the method of loci. Paper presented at the seventeenth annual meeting of the Psychonomic Society, St. Louis, MO.

Church, A. (1956). *Introduction to Mathematical Logic.* Princeton: Princeton University Press.

Clark, H. H. (1974). Semantics and comprehension. In R. A. Sebeok (Ed.), *Current Trends in Linguistics,* Vol. 12. The Hague: Mouton.

Clark, H. H., & Chase, W. G. (1972). On the process of comparing sentences against pictures. *Cognitive Psychology, 3,* 472–517.

Clark, H. H., & Clark, E. V. (1977). *Psychology and Language.* New York: Harcourt Brace Jovanovich.

Cohen, M. R., & Nagel, E. (1934). *An Introduction to Logic and Scientific Method.* New York: Harcourt, Brace.

Collins, A. M., & Loftus, E. F. (1975). A spreading-activation theory of semantic processing. *Psychological Review, 82,* 407–428.

Collins, A. M., & Quillian, M. R. (1969). Retrieval time from semantic memory. *Journal of Verbal Learning and Verbal Behavior, 8,* 240–247.

Collins, A. M., & Quillian, M. R. (1972). Experiments on semantic memory and language comprehension. In L. W. Gregg (Ed.), *Cognition and Learning.* New York: Wiley.

Conrad, C. (1972). Cognitive economy in semantic memory. *Journal of Experimental Psychology, 92,* 149–154.

Conrad, R., & Hull, A. J. (1968). The preferred layout for numerical data entry sets. *Ergonomics, 11,* 165–173.

Cooper, L. A., & Shephard, R. N. (1973). Chronometric studies of the rotation of mental images. In Chase, W. G. (Ed.), *Visual Information Processing.* New York: Academic Press.

Cooper, W. E., & Paccia-Cooper, J. (1980). *Syntax and Speech*. Cambridge, MA: Harvard University Press.

Craik, F. I. M., & Jacoby, L. L. (1975). A process view of short-term retention. In F. Restle, R. M. Shiffrin, N. J. Castellan, H. R. Lindman, & D. B. Pisoni (Eds.), *Cognitive Theory*, Vol. 1. Hillsdale, NJ: Lawrence Erlbaum Associates.

Craik, F. I. M., & Lockhart, R. S. (1972). Levels of processing: A framework for memory research. *Journal of Verbal Learning and Verbal Behavior, 11,* 671–684.

Crossman, E. R. F. W. (1959). A theory of the acquisition of speed-skill. *Ergonomics, 2,* 153–166.

Crowder, R. G. (1976). *Principles of Learning and Memory*. Hillsdale, NJ: Lawrence Erlbaum Associates.

Crowder, R. G. (1982). The demise of short-term memory. *Acta Psychologica, 50,* 291–323.

Culicover, P. W. (1976). *Syntax*. New York: Academic Press.

Curtiss, S. (1977). *Genie: A Psycholinguistic Study of a Modern Day "Wild Child."* New York: Academic Press.

Dale, P. S. (1976). *Language Development: Structure and Function*. New York: Holt, Rinehart, & Winston.

Darwin, C. J., Turvey, M. T., & Crowder, R. G. (1972). The auditory analogue of the Sperling partial report procedure: Evidence for brief auditory storage. *Cognitive Psychology, 3,* 255–267.

de Beer, G. R. (1959). Paedomorphesis. *Proceedings of the 15th International Congress of Zoology,* 927–930.

Deese, J. (1978). Thought into speech. *American Scientist, 66,* 314–321.

de Groot, A. D. (1965). *Thought and Choice in Chess*. The Hague: Mouton.

de Groot, A. D. (1966). Perception and memory versus thought. In B. Kleinmuntz (Ed.), *Problem-Solving*. New York: Wiley.

de Valois, R. L., & Jacobs, G. H. (1968). Primate color vision. *Science, 162,* 533–540.

deVilliers, J. G., & deVilliers, P. A. (1978). *Language Acquisition*. Cambridge, MA: Harvard University Press.

Dickstein, L. S. (1978). The effect of figure on syllogistic reasoning. *Memory & Cognition, 6,* 76–83.

Dillard, J. L. (1972). *Black English: Its History and Usage in the United States*. New York: Random House.

Dominowski, R. L. (1977). Reasoning. *Interamerican Journal of Psychology, 1,* 68–77.

Dominowski, R. L., & Jenrick, R. (1972). Effects of hints and interpolated activity on solution of an insight problem. *Psychonomic Science, 26,* 335–338.

Dooling, D. J., & Christiaansen, R. E. (1977). Episodic and semantic aspects of memory for prose. *Journal of Experimental Psychology: Human Learning and Memory, 3,* 428–436.

Downs, R. M., & Stea, M. (1977). *Maps in Minds: Reflections in Cognitive Mapping.* New York: Harper & Row.

Duncker, K. (1945). On problem-solving (translated by L. S. Lees). *Psychological Monographs, 58,* No. 270.

Durkin, D. (1966). *Children Who Read Early.* New York: Teachers College Press.

Ebbinghaus, H. (1885). Memory: A Contribution to Experimental Psychology (translated by H. A. Ruger, & C. E. Bussenues, 1913). New York: Teachers College, Columbia University.

Eccles, J. C. (1979). Synaptic plasticity. *Naturwissenchaften, 66,* 147–153.

Edwards, W. (1968). Conservatism in human information processing. In B. Kleinmuntz (Ed.), *Formal Representations of Human Judgment.* New York: Wiley.

Eich, J., Weingartner, H., Stillman, R. C., & Gillin, J. C. (1975). State-dependent accessibility of retrieval cues in the retention of a categorized list. *Journal of Verbal Learning and Verbal Behavior, 14,* 408–417.

Eimas, P. D., & Corbit, J. (1973). Selective adaptation of linguistic feature detectors. *Cognitive Psychology, 4,* 99–109.

Erickson, J. R. A. (1974). A set analysis theory of behavior in formal syllogistic reasoning tasks. In R. L. Solso (Ed.), *Theories in Cognitive Psychology: The Loyola Symposium.* Hillsdale, NJ: Lawrence Erlbaum Associates.

Ernst, G., & Newell, A. (1969). *GPS: A Case Study in Generality and Problem Solving.* New York: Academic Press.

Ervin-Tripp, S. M.(1974). Is second language learning like the first? *TESOL Quarterly, 8,* 111–127.

Estes, W. K. (1975–1979). *Handbook of Learning and Cognitive Processes,* Vols. 1–6. Hillsdale, NJ: Lawrence Erlbaum Associates.

Falmagne, R. J. (1975). *Reasoning: Representation and Process.* Hillsdale, NJ: Lawrence Erlbaum Associates.

Fillenbaum, S. (1971). On coping with ordered and unordered conjunctive sentences. *Journal of Experimental Psychology, 87,* 93–98.

Fillenbaum, S. (1974). Pragmatic normalization: Further results for some conjunctive and disjunctive sentences. *Journal of Experimental Psychology, 103,* 913–921.

Fitts, P. M., & Posner, M. I. (1967). *Human Performance.* Belmont, CA: Brooks Cole.

Flavell, J. H. (1977). *Cognitive Development.* Englewood Cliffs, NJ: Prentice-Hall.

Flavell, J. H. (1978). Comment. In R. S. Siegler (Ed.), *Children's Thinking: What Develops?* Hillsdale, NJ: Lawrence Erlbaum Associates.

Flavell, J. H., Friedrichs, A. G., & Hoyt, J. D. (1970). Developmental changes in memorization processes. *Cognitive Psychology, 1,* 324–340.

Flexser, A. J., & Tulving, E. (1978). Retrieval independence in recognition and recall *Psychological Review, 85,* 153–172.

Flower, L. S., & Hayes, J. R. (1977). Problem-solving strategies and the writing process. *College English, 39,* 449–461.

Fodor, J. A. (1975). *The Language of Thought.* New York: Thomas Y. Crowell.

Fodor, J. A., (1983). *The Modularity of Mind.* Cambridge, MA: MIT/Bradford Books.

Fodor, J. A., Bever, T. G., & Garrett, M. F. (1974). *The Psychology of Language.* New York: McGraw-Hill.

Fodor, J. A., & Garrett, M. F. (1967). Some syntactic determinants of sentential complexity. *Perception and Psychophysics, 2,* 289–296.

Foss, D. J., & Hakes, D. T. (1978). *Psycholinguistics.* Englewood Cliffs, NJ: Prentice-Hall.

Frase, L. T. (1975). Prose processing. In G. H. Bower (Ed.), *The Psychology of Learning and Motivation,* Vol. 9. New York: Academic Press.

Frederiksen, C. H. (1975). Representing logical and semantic structure of knowledge acquired from discourse. *Cognitive Psychology, 7,* 371–458.

Frederiksen, C. H., Whiteman, M. F., & Dominic, J. D. (1979). *Writing: The Nature, Development, and Teaching of Written Communications.* Hillsdale, NJ: Lawrence Erlbaum Associates.

French, M. (1978). *The Women's Room.* New York: Jove.

Fromkin, V. (1971). The non-anomalous nature of anomalous utterances. *Languages, 47,* 27–52.

Fromkin, V. (1973). *Speech Errors as Linguistic Evidence.* The Hague: Mouton.

Fromkin, V., Krashen, S., Curtiss, S., Rigler, D., & Rigler, M. (1974). The development of language in Genie: A case of language acquisition beyond the "critical period." *Brain and Language, 1,* 81–107.

Fromkin, V., & Rodman, R. (1978). *An Introduction to Language.* New York: Holt, Rinehart, & Winston.

Gagne, R. M. (1973). Learning and instructional sequence. *Review of Research in Education, 1,* 3–33.

Gardner, E. (1968). *Fundamentals of Neurology.* Philadelphia, PA: W. B. Saunders.

Gardner, H. (1975). *The Shattered Mind.* New York: Alfred A. Knopf.

Gardner, R. A., & Gardner, B. T. (1969). Teaching sign language to a chimpanzee. *Science, 165,* 664–672.

Garrett, M. F. (1975). The analysis of sentence production. In G. H. Bower (Ed.), *The Psychology of Learning and Motivation,* Vol. 9. New York: Academic Press.

Gay, I. R. (1973). Temporal position of reviews and its effect on the retention of mathematical rules. *Journal of Educational Psychology, 64,* 171–182.

Gazzaniga, M. S. (1967). The split brain in man. *Scientific American, 217,* 24–29.

Gazzaniga, M. S. (1970). *The Bisected Brain.* New York: Appleton-Century-Crofts.

Gazzaniga, M. S. (1983). Right hemisphere language following brain bisection: A 20-year perspective. *American Psychologist, 38,* 525–537.

Gazzaniga, M. S., Steen D., & Volpe, B. T. (1979). *Functional Neuroscience.* New York: Harper & Row.

Gelman, R. (1978). Cognitive development. *Annual Review of Psychology, 29,* 297–332.

Gelman, R., & Gallistel, C. R. (1978). *The Child's Understanding of Numbers.* Cambridge, MA: Harvard University Press.

Geschwind, N. (1980). Neurological knowledge and complex behaviors. *Cognitive Science, 4,* 185–194.

Gibson, E. J., & Levin, H. (1975). *The Psychology of Reading.* Cambridge, MA: MIT Press.

Gibson, J. J. (1950). *Perception of the Visual World.* Boston: Houghton.

Gibson, J. J. (1966). *The Senses Considered as Perceptual Systems.* Boston: Houghton.

Gibson, J. J. (1979). *The Ecological Approach to Visual Perception.* Boston: Houghton Mifflin.

Gick, M. L., & Holyoak, K. J. (1980). Analogical problem solving. *Cognitive Psychology, 12,* 306–355.

Gick, M. L., & Holyoak, K. J. (1983). Schema induction and analogical transfer. *Cognitive Psychology, 15,* 1–38.

Ginsburg, H. J., & Opper, S. (1980). *Piaget's Theory of Intellectual Development.* Englewood Cliffs, NJ: Prentice-Hall.

Glucksberg, S., & Danks, J. H. (1968). Effects of discriminative labels and of nonsense labels upon availability of novel function. *Journal of Verbal Learning and Verbal Behavior, 7,* 72–76.

Glucksberg, S., & Danks, J. H. (1975). *Experimental Psycholinguistics.* New York: Halsted Press.

Glucksberg, S., & Weisberg, R. W. (1966). Verbal behavior and problem solving: Some effects of labeling in a functional fixedness problem. *Journal of Experimental Psychology, 71,* 659–664.

Godden, D. R., & Baddeley, A. D. (1975). Context-dependent memory in two natural environments: On land and under water. *British Journal of Psychology, 66,* 325–331.

Gordon, W. J. J. (1961). *Synectics: The Development of Creative Capacity.* New York: Harper & Row.

Gould, J. D. (1978). An experimental study of writing, dictating, and speaking. In R. Requin (Ed.), *Attention and Performance,* Vol. 7. Hillsdale, NJ: Lawrence Erlbaum Associates.

Gould, J. D., & Boies, S. J. (1977). Writing, dictating, and speaking letters. IBM Research Report RC 6683 (No. 28698).

Gould S. J. (1977). *Ontogeny and Phylogeny.* Cambridge, MA: Belknap.

Graesser, A. C. (1981). *Prose Comprehension Beyond the Word.* New York: Springer-Verlag.

Graf, P., & Torrey, J. W. (1966). Perception of phrase structure in written language. *American Psychological Association Convention Proceedings,* 83–88.

Gray, G. W. (1948). The great ravelled knot. *Scientific American, 179,* 26–38.

Gray, J. A., & Wedderburn, A. A. I. (1960). Grouping strategies with simultaneous stimuli. *Quarterly Journal of Experimental Psychology, 12,* 180–184.

Greenberg, J. H. (1963). Some universals of grammar with particular reference to the order of meaningful elements. In J. H. Greenberg (Ed.), *Universals of Language.* Cambridge, MA: MIT Press.

Greeno, J. G. (1974). Hobbits and orcs: Acquisition of a sequential concept. *Cognitive Psychology, 6,* 270–292.

Greeno, J. G. (1976). Cognitive objectives of instruction: Theory of knowledge for solving problems and answering questions. In D. Klahr (Ed.), *Cognition and Instruction.* Hillsdale, NJ: Lawrence Erlbaum Associates.

Greeno, J. G. (1978). Notes on problem-solving abilities. In W. K. Estes (Ed.), *Handbook of Learning and Cognitive Processes.* Hillsdale, NJ: Lawrence Erlbaum Associates.

Greeno, J. G. (1983). Forms of understanding in mathematical problem-solving. In S. Paris, G. M. Olson, & H. W. Stevenson (Eds.), *Learning and Motivation in the Classroom.* Hillsdale, NJ: Lawrence Erlbaum Associates.

Greeno, J. G., Magone, M. E., & Chaiklin, S. (1979). Theory of constructions and set in problem solving. *Memory & Cognition, 7,* 445–461.

Gregg, L. W. (1974). *Knowledge and Cognition.* Hillsdale, NJ: Lawrence Erlbaum Associates.

Gregg, L. W., & Steinberg, E. (1980). *Cognitive Processes in Writing.* Hillsdale, NJ: Lawrence Erlbaum Associates.

Grice, H. P. (1975). Logic and conversation. In P. Cole and J. L. Morgan (Eds.), *Syntax and Semantics,* Vol. 3: *Speech Acts.* New York: Seminar Press.

Grimes, L. (1975). *The Thread of Discourse.* The Hague: Mouton.

Grosjean, F., Grosjean, L., & Lane, H. (1979). The patterns of silence: Performance structures in sentence production. *Cognitive Psychology, 11,* 58–81.

Gruber, H. E., & Voneche, J. J. (Eds.) (1977). *The Essential Piaget: An Interpretative Reference and Guide.* London: Routledge & Kegan Paul.

Guyote, M. J., & Sternberg, R. S. (1981). A transitive-chain theory of syllogistic reasoning. *Cognitive Psychology, 13,* 461–525.

Hakes, D. T. (1972). Effects of reducing complement constructions on sentence comprehension. *Journal of Verbal Learning and Verbal Behavior, 11,* 278–286.

Hakes, D. T., & Foss, D. J. (1970). Decision processes during sentence comprehension: Effects of surface structure reconsidered. *Perception and Psychophysics, 8,* 413–416.

Hammerton, M. (1973). A case of radical probability estimation. *Journal of Experimental Psychology, 101,* 252–254.

Harris, R. J. (1977), Comprehension of pragmatic implications in advertising. *Journal of Applied Psychology, 62,* 603–608.

Haviland, S. E., & Clark, H. H. (1974). What's new? Acquiring new information as a process in comprehension. *Journal of Verbal Learning and Verbal Behavior, 13,* 512–521.

Hayes, C. (1951). *The Ape in Our House.* New York: Harper.

Hayes, J. R. (1978). *Cognitive Psychology.* Homewood, IL: Dorsey Press.

Hayes, J. R. (1984). *Problem Solving Techniques.* Philadelphia: Franklin Institute Press.

Hayes, J. R. (In press). Three problems in teaching general skills. In J. Segal, S. Chipman, & R. Glaser (Eds.), *Thinking and Learning,* Vol. 2. Hillsdale, NJ: Lawrence Erlbaum Associates.

Hayes, J. R., & Flower, L. S. (1980). Identifying the organization of writing processes. In L. W. Gregg & I. Steinberg (Eds.), *Cognitive Processes in Writing.* Hillsdale, NJ: Lawrence Erlbaum Associates.

Haygood, R. C., & Bourne, L. E. (1965). Attribute- and rule-learning aspects of conceptual behavior. *Psychological Review, 72,* 175–195.

Haynes, E. (1978). Using research in preparing to teach writing. *English Journal, 67,* 82–88.

Heider, E. (1972). Universals of color naming and memory. *Journal of Experimental Psychology, 93,* 10–20.

Henle, M. (1962). On the relation between logic and thinking. *Psychological Review, 69,* 366–378.

Hilgard, E. R. (1968). *The Experience of Hypnosis.* New York: Harcourt Brace Jovanovich.

Hinton, G. E., & Anderson, J. A. (1981). *Parallel Models of Associative Memory.* Hillsdale, NJ: Lawrence Erlbaum Associates.

Hintzman, D. L. (1974). Theoretical implications of the spacing effect. In R. L. Solso (Ed.), *Theories in Cognitive Psychology: The Loyola Symposium.* Potomac, MD: Lawrence Erlbaum Associates.

Hintzman, D. L., O'Dell, C. S., & Arndt, D. R. (1981). Orientation in cognitive maps. *Cognitive Psychology, 13,* 149–206.

Hockett, C. F. (1960). The origin of speech. *Scientific American, 203,* 89–96.

Holyoak, K. J., & Walker, J. H. (1976). Subjective magnitude information in semantic orderings. *Journal of Verbal Learning and Verbal Behavior, 15,* 287–299.

Hornby, P. A. (1974). Surface structure and presupposition. *Journal of Verbal Learning and Verbal Behavior, 13,* 530–538.

Hovland, C. I., & Weiss, W. (1953). Transmission of information concerning concepts through positive and negative instances. *Journal of Experimental Psychology, 45,* 175–182.

Hubel, D. H., & Wiesel, T. N. (1962). Receptive fields, binocular interaction, and functional architecture in the cat's visual cortex. *Journal of Physiology, 166,* 106–154.

Hunt, E. B. (1975). *Artificial Intelligence.* New York: Academic Press.

Hunt, M. (1982). *The Universe Within.* New York: Simon & Schuster.

Hyde, T. S., & Jenkins, J. J. (1973). Recall for words as a function of semantic, graphic, and syntactic orienting tasks. *Journal of Verbal Learning and Verbal Behavior, 12,* 471–480.

Inhelder, B., & Piaget, J. (1958). *The Growth of Logical Thinking from Childhood to Adolescence.* New York: Basic Books.

Jackson, M. D., & McClelland, J. L. (1979). Processing determinants of reading speed. *Journal of Experimental Psychology: General, 108,* 151–181.

Jacoby, L. L. (1978). On interpreting the effects of repetition: Solving a problem versus remembering a solution. *Journal of Verbal Learning and Verbal Behavior, 17,* 649–667.

James, W. (1890). *The Principles of Psychology,* Vols. 1 and 2. New York: Holt.

Jarvella, R. J. (1971). Syntactic processing of connected speech. *Journal of Verbal Learning and Verbal Behavior, 10,* 409–416.

Jeffries, R., Turner, A. A., Polson, P. G., & Atwood, M. E. (1981). The processes involved in designing software. In J. R. Anderson (Ed.), *Cognitive Skills and Their Acquisition.* Hillsdale, NJ: Lawrence Erlbaum Associates.

Jeffries, R. P., Polson, P. G., Razran, L., & Atwood, M. (1977). A process model for missionaries-cannibals and other river-crossing problems. *Cognitive Psychology, 9,* 412–440.

Johnson, D. M. (1939). Confidence and speed in the two-category judgment. *Archives of Psychology,* No. 241, 1–52.

Johnson, D. M. (1972). *A Systematic Introduction to the Psychology of Thinking.* New York: Harper & Row.

Johnson, D. M., Parrott, G. L., & Stratton, R. P. (1968). Production and judgment of solutions to five problems. *Journal of Educational Psychology, 59,* Monograph Supplement No. 6.

Johnson, M. K., & Raye, C. L. (1981). Reality monitoring. *Psychological Review, 88,* 67–85.

Johnson, N. F. (1970). The role of chunking and organization in process of recall. In G. H. Bower (Ed.), *Psychology of Language and Motivation,* Vol. 4.

Johnson-Laird, P. N., Legrenzi, P., & Legrenzi, M. S. (1972). Reasoning and a sense of reality. *British Journal of Psychology, 63,* 305–400.

Johnson-Laird, P. N., & Steedman, M. (1978). The psychology of syllogisms. *Cognitive Psychology, 10,* 64–99.

Just, M. A., & Carpenter, P. A. (1980). A theory of reading: From eye fixations to comprehension. *Psychological Review, 87,* 329–354.

Just, M. A., & Carpenter, P. A. (Eds.) (1977). *Cognitive Processes in Comprehension.* Hillsdale, NJ: Lawrence Erlbaum Associates.

Just, M. A., & Carpenter, P. (In preparation). The psychology of reading: Cognition and instruction.

Kahneman, D. (1973). *Attention and Effort.* Englewood Cliffs, NJ: Prentice-Hall.

Kahneman, D., & Tversky, A. (1972). Subjective probability: A judgment of representiveness. *Cognitive Psychology, 3,* 430–454.

Kahneman, D., & Tversky, A. (1973). On the psychology of prediction. *Psychological Review, 80,* 237–251.

Kaplan, R. (1973). A general syntactic processor. In R. Rustin (Ed.), *Natural Language Processing.* Englewood Cliffs, NJ: Prentice-Hall.

Kaplan, R. M., & Bresnan, J. W. (1982). Lexical-functional grammar: A formal system for grammatical representation. In J. W. Bresnan (Ed.), *The Mental Representation of Grammatical Relations.* Cambridge, MA: MIT Press.

Katz, B. (1952). The nerve impulse. *Scientific American, 187,* 55–64.

Kaufman, L. (1974). *Sight and Mind: An Introduction to Visual Perception.* New York: Oxford University Press.

Keele, S. W. (1973). *Attention and Human Performance.* Pacific Palisades, CA: Goodyear.

Keeney, T. J., Cannizzo, S. R., & Flavell, J. H. (1967). Spontaneous and induced verbal rehearsal in a recall task. *Child Development, 38,* 953–966.

Keeton, W. T. (1980). *Biological Science.* New York: Norton.

Kellogg, W. N., & Kellogg, L. A. (1933). *The Ape and the Child.* New York: McGraw-Hill.

Kelso, J. A. S. (Ed.) (1982). *Human Motor Behavior: An Introduction.* Hillsdale, NJ: Lawrence Erlbaum Associates.

Keppel, G., & Underwood, B. J. (1962). Proactive inhibition in short-term retention of single items. *Journal of Verbal Learning and Verbal Behavior, 1,* 153–161.

Kerst, S. M., & Howard, J. H., Jr. (1977). Mental comparisons for ordered information in abstract and concrete dimensions. *Memory & Cognition, 5,* 227–234.

Kieras, D. E. (1974). Analysis of the effects of word properties and limited reading time in a reading comprehension and verification task. Unpublished doctoral dissertation, University of Michigan.

Kimball, J. P. (1973). Seven principles of surface structure parsing in natural language. *Cognition, 2,* 15–47.

Kinney, G. C., Marsetta, M., & Showman, D. J. (1966). Studies in display symbol legibility, part XXI. The legibility of alphanumeric symbols for digitized television (ESD-TR-66-117). Bedford, MA: The Mitre Corporation.

Kinsbourne, M., & Smith, W. L. (1974). *Hemispheric Disconnection and Cerebral Function.* Springfield, IL: Charles C Thomas.

Kintsch, W. (1970). *Learning Memory and Conceptual Processes.* New York: Wiley.

Kintsch, W. (1974). *The Representation of Meaning in Memory*. Hillsdale, NJ: Lawrence Erlbaum Associates.

Kintsch, W. (1977). On comprehending stories. In M. A. Just & P. A. Carpenter (Eds.), *Cognitive Processes in Comprehension*. Hillsdale, NJ: Lawrence Erlbaum Associates.

Kintsch, W., & van Dijk, T. A. (1976). Recalling and summarizing stories *(Comment on se rappelle et on résume des histoires)*. *Languages, 40*, 98–116.

Kintsch, W., & van Dijk, T. A. (1978). Toward a model of text comprehension and reproduction. *Psychological Review, 85*, 363–394.

Klahr, D., & Siegler, R. S. (1978). The representations of children's knowledge. In H. Reese & L. P. Lipsitt (Eds.), *Advances in Child Development*, Vol. 12. New York: Academic Press.

Klahr, D., & Wallace, J. G. (1973). The role of quantification operators in the development of conservation of quantity. *Cognitive Psychology, 4*, 301–327.

Klahr, D., & Wallace, J. G. (1976). *Cognitive Development: An Information Processing View*. Hillsdale, NJ: Lawrence Erlbaum Associates.

Klahr, D., & Robinson, M. (1981). Formal assessment of problem-solving and planning processes in preschool children. *Cognitive Psychology, 13*, 113–148.

Klahr, D., Chase, W. G., & Lovelace, E. A. (1983). Structure and process in alphabetic retrieval. *Journal of Experimental Psychology: Learning, Memory, and Cognition, 9*, 462–477.

Klatzky, R. L. (1975). *Human Memory*, 1st ed. New York: W. H. Freeman and Company.

Klatzky, R. L. (1979). *Human Memory*. New York: W. H. Freeman and Company.

Kleene, S. C. (1952). *Introduction to Mathematics*. Princeton, NJ: Van Nostrand.

Koch, H. L. (1923). A neglected phase of a part/whole problem. *Journal of Experimental Psychology, 6*, 366–376.

Köhler, W. (1927). *The Mentality of Apes*. New York: Harcourt, Brace.

Köhler, W. (1956). *The Mentality of Apes*. London: Routledge & Kegan Paul.

Kolers, P. A. (1976). Reading a year later. *Journal of Experimental Psychology: Human Learning and Memory, 2*, 554–565.

Kolers, P. A. (1979). A pattern analyzing basis of recognition. In L. S. Cermak & F. I. M. Craik (Eds.), *Levels of Processing in Human Memory*. Hillsdale, NJ: Lawrence Erlbaum Associates.

Kolers, P. A., & Perkins, P. N. (1975). Spatial and ordinal components of form perception and literacy. *Cognitive Psychology, 7*, 228–267.

Kosslyn, S. M. (1980). *Image and Mind*. Cambridge, MA: Harvard University Press.

Kosslyn, S. M., Ball, T. M., & Reiser, B. J. (1978). Visual images preserve metric spatial information: Evidence from studies of image scanning. *Journal of Experimental Psychology: Human Perception and Performance, 4*, 47–60.

Kosslyn, S. M., & Pomerantz, J. P. (1977). Imagery, propositions, and the form of internal representations. *Cognitive Psychology, 9*, 52–76.

Kosslyn, S. M., & Shwartz, S. P. (1977). A simulation of visual imagery. *Cognitive Science, 1,* 265–298.

Krashen, S., & Harshman, R. (1972). Lateralization and the critical period. *Working Papers in Phonetics, 23,* 13–21.

Kreutzer, M. A., Leonard, C., & Flavell, J. H. (1975). An interview study of children's knowledge about memory. *Monographs of the Society for Research in Child Development, 40,* 1, Series No. 159.

Kuffler, S. W. (1953). Discharge pattern and functional organization of mamalian retina. *Journal of Neurophysiology, 16,* 37–68.

Kuffler, S. W., & Nichols, J. G. (1976). *From Neuron to Brain.* Sunderland, MA: Sinauer Associates.

LaBerge, D. (1973). Attention and the measurement of perceptual learning. *Memory & Cognition, 1,* 268–276.

LaBerge, D., & Samuels, S. J. (1974). Toward a theory of automatic information processing in reading. *Cognitive Psychology, 6,* 293–323.

Labov, W. (1973). The boundaries of words and their meanings. In C.-J. N. Bailey & R. W. Shuy (Eds.), *New Ways of Analyzing Variations in English,* Washington, DC: Georgetown University Press.

Lackner, J. A. (1968). A developmental study of language behavior in retarded children. *Neuropsychologica, 6,* 301–320.

Lakoff, G. (1971). On generative semantics. In D. Steinberg & L. Jakobovits (Eds.), *Semantics—An Interdisciplinary Reader in Philosophy, Linguistics, Anthropology, and Psychology.* London: Cambridge University Press.

Larkin, J. (1981). Enriching formal knowledge: A model for learning to solve textbook physics problems. In J. R. Anderson (Ed.), *Cognitive Skills and Their Acquisition.* Hillsdale, NJ: Lawrence Erlbaum Associates.

Larkin, J. H., McDermott, J., Simon, D. P., & Simon, H. A. (1980). Expert and novice performance in solving physics problems. *Science, 208,* 1335–1342.

Lee, C. L., & Estes, W. K. (1981). Item and order information in short-term memory: Evidence for multilevel perturbation processes. *Journal of Experimental Psychology: Human Learning and Memory, 7,* 149–169.

Lenneberg, E. H. (1967). *Biological Foundations of Language.* New York: Wiley.

Lenneberg, E. H., Nichols, I. A., & Rosenberger, E. F. (1969). Primitive stages of language development in mongolism. *Disorders of Communication,* Vol. 42. Baltimore, MD: Williams & Wilkins.

Lesgold, A. M. (1984). Acquiring expertise. In J. R. Anderson & S. M. Kosslyn (Eds.), *Tutorials in Learning and Memory.* New York: W. H. Freeman and Company.

Lesgold, A. M., Resnick, L. B., & Beck, I. C. (1978). Preliminary results of a longitudinal study of reading acquisition. Paper presented at the meeting of the Psychonomic Society, San Antonio.

Levelt, W. J. M. (1982). Linearization in describing spatial networks. In S. Peter & E. Saarinen (Eds.), *Processes, Beliefs, and Questions*. Utrecht: D. Reidel.

Levin, H., Silverman, I., & Ford, B. (1967). Hesitations in children's speech during explanations and description. *Journal of Verbal Learning and Verbal Behavior, 6*, 560–564.

Levine, M. (1975). *A Cognitive Theory of Learning*. Hillsdale, NJ: Lawrence Erlbaum Associates.

Lewis, C. H., & Anderson, J. R. (1976). Interference with real world knowledge. *Cognitive Psychology, 7*, 311–335.

Lewis, D., McAllister, D. E., & Adams, J. A. (1951). Facilitation and interference in performance on the modified Mashburn apparatus: I. The effects of varying the amount of original learning. *Journal of Experimental Psychology, 41*, 247–260.

Lewis, M., & Anderson, J. R. (In press). The role of feedback in discriminating problem-solving operators. *Cognitive Psychology*.

Linde, C., & Labov, W. (1975). Spatial structures as a site for the study of langauge and thought. *Language, 51*, 924–939.

Lindsay, P. H., & Norman, D. A. (1977). *Human Information Processing*. New York: Academic Press.

Lisker, L., & Abramson, A. (1970). The voicing dimension: Some experiments in comparative phonetics. *Proceedings of Sixth International Congress of Phonetic Sciences, Prague, 1967*. Prague: Academia.

Loftus, E. F. (1974). Activation of semantic memory. *American Journal of Psychology, 86*, 331–337.

Loftus, E. F., & Zanni, G. (1975). Eyewitness testimony: The influence of the wording of a question. *Bulletin of the Psychonomic Society, 5*, 86–88.

Loftus, G. R., & Loftus, E. F. (1976). *Human Memory*. Hillsdale, NJ: Lawrence Erlbaum Associates.

Lorayne, H., & Lucas, J. (1974). *The Memory Book*. New York: Stein & Day.

Luchins, A. S. (1942). Mechanization in problem solving. *Psychological Monographs, 54*, No. 248.

Luchins, A. S., & Luchins, E. H. (1959). *Rigidity of Behavior: A Variational Approach to the Effects of Einstellung*. Eugene, OR: University of Oregon Books.

Luchsinger, R., & Arnold, G. (1965). *Voice, Speech, Language: Clinical Communicology: Its Physiology and Pathology*. Belmont, CA: Wadsworth.

Lyons, J. (1970). *Noam Chomsky*. New York: Viking Press.

Maclay, H., & Osgood, C. E. (1959). Hesitation phenomena in spontaneous speech. *Word, 15*, 19–44.

Madigan, S. A. (1969). Intraserial repetition and coding processes in free recall. *Journal of Verbal Learning and Verbal Behavior, 8*, 828–835.

Maier, N. R. F. (1931). Reasoning in humans: II. The solution of a problem and its appearance in consciousness. *Journal of Comparative Psychology, 12,* 181–194.

Mandler, G. (1967). Organization and memory. In K. W. Spence & J. A. Spence (Eds.). *The Psychology of Learning and Motivation,* Vol. 1. New York: Academic Press.

Mandler, G. (1972). Organization and recognition. In E. Tulving & W. Donaldson (Eds.), *Organization and Memory.* New York: Academic Press.

Mandler, J. M., & Johnson, N. S. (1977). Remembrance of things parsed: Story structure and recall. *Cognitive Psychology, 9,* 111–151.

Mandler, J. M., & Ritchey, G. H. (1977). Long-term memory for pictures. *Journal of Experimental Psychology: Human Learning and Memory, 3,* 386–396.

Marcus, M. (1978). A computational account of some constraints on language. *Proceedings of TINLAP-2,* 236–246.

Marcus, S. L., & Rips, L. J. (1979). Conditional reasoning. *Journal of Verbal Learning and Verbal Behavior, 18,* 199–223.

Marler, P. (1967). Animal communication signals. *Science, 157,* 764–774.

Marr, D. (1976). Early processing of visual information. *Philosophical Transactions of the Royal Society, London, Series B, 275,* 483–524.

Marr, D. (1982). *Vision.* San Francisco: W. H. Freeman and Company.

Marr, D., & Hildreth, E. (1980). Theory of edge detection. *Proceedings of the Royal Society, London, Series B, 207,* 187–217.

Massaro, D. W. (1975). *Experimental Psychology and Information Processing.* Chicago: Rand McNally.

Mayer, A., & Orth, I. (1901). Zur qualitativen utersuchung der Association. *Zeitschaft für Psychologie, 26,* 1–13.

McClelland, J. L., & Rumelhart, D. E. (1981). An interactive model of context effects in letter perception: I. An account of basic findings. *Psychological Review, 88,* 375–407.

McCloskey, M. E., & Glucksberg, S. (1978). Natural categories. Well-defined or fuzzy sets? *Memory & Cognition, 6,* 462–472.

McConkie, G. W., & Rayner, K. (1974). Identifying the span of the effective stimulus in reading. Final Report OEG 2-71-0531, U.S. Office of Education.

McKeithen, K. B., Reitman, J. S., Rueter, H. H., & Hirtle, S. C. (1981). Knowledge organization and skill differences in computer programmers. *Cognitive Psychology, 13,* 307–325.

McLaughlin, B. (1978). *Second-Language Acquisition in Childhood.* Hillsdale, NJ: Lawrence Erlbaum Associates.

Melton, A. W. (1963). Implications of short-term memory for a general theory of memory. *Journal of Verbal Learning and Verbal. Behavior, 2,* 1–21.

Melton, A. W., & Martin, E. (1972). *Coding Processes in Memory.* Washington, DC: Winston.

Mendelson, E. (1964). *Introduction to Mathematical Logic.* New York: Van Nostrand.

Metzler, J., & Shepard, R. N. (1974). Transformational studies of the internal representations of three dimensional objects. In R. L. Solso (Ed.), *Theories of Cognitive Psychology: The Loyola Symposium.* Hillsdale, NJ: Lawrence Erlbaum Associates.

Meyer, B. J. F. (1974). The organization of prose and its effect on recall. Unpublished doctoral dissertation, Cornell University.

Meyer, B. J. F., Brandt, D. M., & Bluth, G. J. (1978). Use of author's textual schema: Key for ninth-grader's comprehension. Paper presented at the annual conference of the American Educational Research Association, Toronto.

Meyer, D. E., & Schvaneveldt, R. W. (1971). Facilitation in recognizing pairs of words: Evidence of a dependence between retrieval operations. *Journal of Experimental Psychology, 90,* 227–234.

Miller, G. A. (1956). The magical number seven, plus or minus two: Some limits on our capacity for processing information. *Psychological Review, 63,* 81–97.

Miller, G. A. et al. (1974). Report of the study group on linguistic communication to the National Institute of Education.

Miller, G. A., & Isard, S. (1963). Some perceptual consequences of linguistic rules. *Journal of Verbal Learning and Verbal Behavior, 2,* 217–228.

Miller, G. A., & Nicely, P. (1955). An analysis of perceptual confusions among some English consonants. *Journal of the Acoustical Society of America, 27,* 338–352.

Minsky, M. (1975). A framework for representing knowledge. In P. H. Winston (Ed.), *The Psychology of Computer Vision.* New York: McGraw-Hill.

Moray, N. (1959). Attention in dichotic listening: Affective cues and the influence of instruction. *Quarterly Journal of Experimental Psychology, 11,* 56–60.

Moray, N., Bates, A., & Barnett, T. (1965). Experiments on the four-eared man. *Journal of the Acoustical Society of America, 38,* 196–201.

Moyer, R. S. (1973). Comparing objects in memory: Evidence suggesting an internal psychophysics. *Perception and Psychophysics, 13,* 180–184.

Moyer, R. S., & Landauer, T. K. (1967). Time required for judgments of numerical inequality. *Nature, 215,* 1519–1520.

Murdock, B. B., Jr. (1961). The retention of individual items. *Journal of Experimental Psychology, 62,* 618–625.

Murray, H. G., & Denny, J. P. (1969). Interaction of ability level and interpolated activity (opportunity for incubation) in human problem solving. *Psychological Reports, 24,* 271–276.

Mussen, P. H. (Ed.) (1983). *Handbook of Child Psychology.* New York: Wiley.

Neisser, U. (1967). *Cognitive Psychology.* New York: Appleton.

Neisser, U. (1976). *Cognition and Reality: Principles and Implications of Cognitive Psychology.* New York: W. H. Freeman and Company.

Nelson, D. L. (1979). Remembering pictures and words: Appearance, significance, and name. In L. S. Cermak & F. I. M. Craik (Eds.), *Levels of Processing in Human Memory*. Hillsdale, NJ: Lawrence Erlbaum Associates.

Nelson, T. O. (1971). Savings and forgetting from long-term memory. *Journal of Verbal Learning and Verbal Behavior, 10,* 568–576.

Nelson, T. O. (1976). Reinforcement and human memory. In W. K. Estes (Ed.), *Handbook of Learning and Cognitive Processes,* Vol. 3. Hillsdale, NJ: Lawrence Erlbaum Associates.

Nelson, T. O. (1978). Detecting small amounts of information in memory: Savings for nonrecognized items. *Journal of Experimental Psychology: Human Learning and Memory, 4,* 453–468.

Neves, D. M., & Anderson, J. R. (1981). Knowledge compilation: Mechanisms for the automatization of cognitive skills. In J. R. Anderson (Ed.), *Cognitive Skills and Their Acquisition*. Hillsdale, NJ: Lawrence Erlbaum Associates.

Newell, A. (1980). Reasoning, problem-solving, and decision processes: The problem space as a fundamental category. In R. Nickerson (Ed.), *Attention and Performance,* Vol. 8. Hillsdale, NJ: Lawrence Erlbaum Associates.

Newell, A., & Simon, H. (1972). *Human Problem Solving*. Englewood Cliffs, NJ: Prentice-Hall.

Nida, E. A. (1971). Sociopsychological problems in language mastery and retention. In P. Pimsleur & T. Quinn (Eds.), *The Psychology of Second Language Acquisition*. London: Cambridge University Press.

Nilsson, N. J. (1971). *Problem-Solving Methods in Artificial Intelligence*. New York: McGraw-Hill.

Nilsson, N. J. (1980). *Principles of Artificial Intelligence*. Palo Alto, CA: Tioga.

Noelting, G. (1975). Stages and mechanisms in the development of the concept of proportion in the child and adolescent. Paper presented at the Fifth Interdisciplinary Seminar on Piagetian Theory and Its Implications for the Helping Professions, University of Southern California, Los Angeles.

Norman, D. A. (1973). Memory, knowledge, and the answering of questions. In R. L. Solso (Ed.), *Contemporary Issues in Cognitive Psychology*. Washington, DC: Winston.

Norman, D. A. (1976). *Memory and Attention: An Introduction to Human Information Processing,* 2nd ed. New York: Wiley.

Norman, D. A., & Bobrow, D. G. (1975). On data-limited and resource-limited processes. *Cognitive Psychology, 7,* 44–64.

Norman, D. A., & Rumelhart, D. E. (1975). *Explorations in Cognition*. New York: W. H. Freeman and Company.

Olson, D. R. (1970). Language and thought: Aspects of a cognitive theory of semantics. *Psychological Review, 77,* 257–273.

Osborn, A. F. (1953). *Applied Imagination*. New York: Scribners.

Osherson, D. (1975). Logic and models of logical thinking. In R. J. Falmagne (Ed.), *Reasoning: Representation and Process.* Hillsdale, NJ: Lawrence Erlbaum Associates.

Owens, J., Bower, G. H., & Black, J. B. (1979). The "soap opera" effect in story recall. *Memory & Cognition, 7,* 185–191.

Paivio, A. (1971). *Imagery and Verbal Processes.* New York: Holt, Rinehart, & Winston.

Paivio, A. (1975). Perceptual comparisons through the mind's eye. *Memory & Cognition, 3,* 635–647.

Paivio, A. (1978). Mental comparisons involving abstract attributes. *Memory & Cognition, 6,* 199–208.

Palmer, S. E. (1975). The effects of contextual scenes on the identification of objects. *Memory & Cognition, 3,* 519–526.

Palmer, S. E. (1977). Hierarchical structure in perceptual representation. *Cognitive Psychology, 9,* 441–474.

Palmer, S. E. (1978). Fundamental aspects of cognitive representation. In E. Rosch & B. Lloyd (Eds.), *Cognition and Categorization.* Hillsdale, NJ: Lawrence Erlbaum Associates.

Paris, S. C., & Lindauer, B. K. (1976). The role of inference in children's comprehension and memory for sentences. *Cognitive Psychology, 8,* 217–227.

Parker, E. S., Birnbaum, I. M., & Noble, E. P. (1976). Alcohol and memory: Storage and state dependency. *Journal of Verbal Language and Verbal Behavior, 15,* 691–702.

Pascual-Leone, J. (1980). Constructive problems for constructive theories: The current relevance of Piaget's work and a critique of information-processing psychology. In R. H. Kluwe & H. Spada (Eds.), *Developmental Models of Thinking.* New York: Academic Press.

Penfield, W. (1959). The interpretive cortex. *Science, 129,* 1719–1725.

Perky, C. W. (1910). An experimental study of imagination. *American Journal of Psychology, 21,* 422–452.

Perlmutter, M. (1980). Development of memory in the preschool years. In R. Green & T. D. Yawkey (Eds.), *Early and Middle Childhood: Growth, Abuse, and Delinquency and Its Effects on Individual, Family, and Community.* Westport, CT: Technomic.

Peterson, L. R., & Peterson, M. (1959). Short-term retention of individual items. *Journal of Experimental Psychology, 58,* 193–198.

Peterson, S. B., & Potts, G. R. (1982). Global and specific components of information integration. *Journal of Verbal Learning and Verbal Behavior, 21,* 403–420.

Piaget, J. (1952a). *The Child's Conception of Number.* New York: Humanities Press.

Piaget, J. (1952b). *The Origins of Intelligence in Children.* New York: International Universities Press.

Piaget, J., & Inhelder, B. (1971). *Mental Imagery in the Child.* New York: Basic Books.

Piestrup, A. (1973). Black dialect interference and accommodation of reading instruction in first grade. *Monographs of the Language-Behavior Research Laboratory, 4.*

Poincaré, H. (1929). *The Foundations of Science.* New York: Science House.

Pomerantz, J. P., Sager, L. C., & Stoever, R. J. (1977). Perception of wholes and their component parts: Some configural superiority effects. *Journal of Experimental Psychology: Human Perception and Performance, 3,* 422–435.

Posner, M. I. (1969). Abstraction and the process of recognition. In G. H. Bower (Ed.), *The Psychology of Learning and Motivation,* Vol. 3. New York: Academic Press.

Posner, M. I., & Snyder, C. R. R. (1975). Attention and cognitive control. In R. L. Solso (Ed.), *Information Processing and Cognition.* Hillsdale, NJ: Lawrence Erlbaum Associates.

Postman, L. (1964). Short-term memory and incidental learning. In A. W. Melton (Ed.), *Categories of Human Learning.* New York: Academic Press.

Postman, L. (1971). Transfer, interference, and forgetting. In L. W. Kling & L. A. Riggs (Eds.), *Experimental Psychology.* New York: Holt, Rinehart, & Winston.

Postman, L., & Underwood, B. J. (1973). Critical issues in interference theory. *Memory & Cognition, 1,* 19–40.

Potts, G. R. (1972). Information-processing strategies used in the encoding of linear orderings. *Journal of Verbal Learning and Verbal Behavior, 11,* 727–740.

Potts, G. R. (1975). Bringing order to cognitive structures. In F. Restle, R. M. Shiffrin, N. J. Castellan, H. R. Lindman, & D. B. Pisoni (Eds.), *Cognitive Theory,* Vol. 1. Hillsdale, NJ: Lawrence-Erlbaum Associates.

Premack, D. (1971). Language in chimpanzee? *Science, 172,* 808–822.

Premack, D. (1976). Language and intelligence in ape and man. *American Scientist, 64,* 674–683.

Premack, D., & Premack, A. J. (1983). *The Mind of an Ape.* New York: Norton.

Prince, G. M. (1970). *The Practice of Creativity.* New York: Harper & Row.

Pylyshyn, Z. (1973). What the mind's eye tells the mind's brain: A critique of mental imagery. *Psychological Bulletin, 80,* 1–24.

Pylyshyn, Z. W. (1981). The imagery debate: Analogue media versus tacit knowledge. *Psychological Review, 88,* 16–45.

Quillian, M. R. (1966). *Semantic Memory.* Cambridge, MA: Bolt, Beranak and Newman.

Quillian, M. R. (1969). The teachable language comprehender. *Communications of the Association for Computing Machinery, 12,* 459–476.

Quine, W. V. O. (1950). *Methods of Logic.* New York: Holt.

Ratcliff, R. A. (1981). A theory of order relations in perceptual matching. *Psychological Review, 88,* 552–572.

Ratcliff, R., & McKoon, G. (1978). Priming in item recognition: Evidence for the propositional structure of sentences. *Journal of Verbal Learning and Verbal Behavior, 17,* 403–417.

Ratcliff, R., & McKoon, G. (1981). Does activation really spread? *Psychological Review, 88,* 454–462.

Rayner, K. (1975). The perceptual span and peripheral cues in reading. *Cognitive Psychology, 7,* 65–81.

Reber, A. S., & Scarborough, D. L. (1977). *Toward a Psychology of Reading: The Proceedings of the CUNY Conference.* Hillsdale, NJ: Lawrence Erlbaum Associates.

Reddy, D. R. (1978). Machine models of speech perception. In R. A. Cole (Ed.), *Perception and Production of Fluent Speech.* Hillsdale, NJ: Lawrence Erlbaum Associates.

Reder, L. M., (1979). The role of elaborations in memory for prose. *Cognitive Psychology, 11,* 221–234.

Reder, L. M. (1982). Plausibility judgment versus fact retrieval: Alternative strategies for sentence verification. *Psychological Review, 89,* 250–280.

Reder, L. M., & Anderson, J. R. (1980). A comparison of texts and their summaries: Memorial consequences. *Journal of Verbal Learning and Verbal Behavior, 19,* 12–34.

Reder, L. M., & Ross B. H. (1983). Integrated knowledge in different tasks: Positive and negative fan effects. *Journal of Experimental Psychology: Human Learning and Memory, 8,* 55–72.

Reed, S. K. (1974). Structural descriptions and the limitations of visual images, *Memory & Cognition, 2,* 329–336.

Reed, S. K., & Johnsen, J. A. (1975). Detection of parts in patterns and images. *Memory & Cognition, 3,* 569–575.

Reicher, G. (1969). Perceptual recognition as a function of meaningfulness of stimulus material. *Journal of Experimental Psychology, 81,* 275–280.

Reitman, W. (1965). *Cognition and Thought.* New York: Wiley.

Reynolds, A. G., & Flagg, P. W. (1977). *Cognitive Psychology.* Cambridge, MA: Winthrop.

Reynolds, J. H., & Glaser, R. (1964). Effects of repetition and spaced review upon retention of a complex learning task. *Journal of Educational Psychology, 55,* 297–308.

Rickards, J. P. (1976). Interaction of position and conceptual level of adjunct questions in immediate and delayed retention of text. *Journal of Educational Psychology, 68,* 210–217.

Riesbeck, C. K. (1974). Computational understanding: Analysis of sentences and context. Stanford Artificial Intelligence Laboratory Memo AIM-238.

Riley, C. A., & Trabasso, T. (1974). Comparatives, logical structures, and encoding in a transitive inference task. *Journal of Experimental Child Psychology, 45,* 972–977.

Rips, L. J. (1984). Reasoning as a central intellectual ability. In R. J. Sternberg (Ed.), *Advances in the Study of Human Intelligence*, Vol. 2. Hillsdale, NJ: Lawrence Erlbaum Associates.

Rips, L. J., & Marcus, S. L. (1977). Supposition and the analysis of conditional sentences. In M. A. Just & P. A. Carpenter (Eds.), *Cognitive Processes in Comprehension*. Hillsdale, NJ: Lawrence Erlbaum Associates.

Robbin, J. W. (1969). *Mathematical Logic—A First Course*. New York: Benjamin.

Robinson, F. P. (1961). *Effective Study*. New York: Harper & Row.

Robinson, G. H. (1964). Continuous estimation of a time-varying probability. *Ergonomics, 7,* 7–21.

Rock, I. (1975). *An Introduction to Perception*. New York: Macmillan.

Rosch, E. (1973). On the internal structure of perceptual and semantic categories. In T. E. Moore (Ed.), *Cognitive Development and the Acquisition of Language*. New York: Academic Press.

Rosch, E. (1975). Cognitive representations of semantic categories. *Journal of Experimental Psychology: General, 104,* 192–223.

Rosch, E. (1977). Human categorization. In N. Warren (Ed.), *Advances in Cross-Cultural Psychology*, Vol. 1. London: Academic Press.

Rosenbloom, P. S., & Newell, A. (1983). The chunking of goal hierarchies: A generalized model of practice. *Proceedings of the International Machine Learning Workshop*.

Ross, J., & Lawrence, K. A. (1968). Some observations on memory artifice. *Psychonomic Science, 13,* 107–108.

Rothkopf, E. Z. (1966). Learning from written instruction materials: An explanation of the control of inspection behavior by test-like events. *American Educational Research Journal, 3,* 241–249.

Rothkopf, E. Z. (1972). Structural text features and the control of processes in learning from written materials. In R. O. Freedle & J. B. Carroll (Eds.), *Language Comprehension and the Acquisition of Knowledge*. Washington, DC: Winston.

Rothkopf, E. Z., & Coke, E. V. (1963). Repetition interval and rehearsal method in learning equivalences from written sentences. *Journal of Verbal Learning and Verbal Behavior, 2,* 406–416.

Rothkopf, E. Z., & Coke, E. V. (1966). Variations in phrasing, repetition intervals, and the recall of sentence material. *Journal of Verbal Learning and Verbal Behavior, 5,* 86–91.

Rumelhart, D. E. (1975). Notes on a schema for stories. In D. G. Bobrow & A. M. Collins (Eds.), *Representation and Understanding*. New York: Academic Press.

Rumelhart, D. E. (1977). *An Introduction to Human Information Processing*. New York: Wiley.

Rumelhart, D. E., Lindsay, P., & Norman D. A. (1972). A process model for long-term memory. In E. Tulving & W. Donaldson (Eds.), *Organization of memory*. New York: Academic Press.

Rumelhart, D. E., & Norman, D. A. (1978). Accretion, tuning, and restructuring: Three modes of learning. In J. W. Cotton & R. Klatzky (Eds.), *Semantic Factors in Cognition.* Hillsdale, NJ: Lawrence Erlbaum Associates.

Rumelhart, D. E., & Norman, D. A. (1981). Analogical processes in learning. In J. R. Anderson (Ed.), *Cognitive Skills and Their Acquisition.* Hillsdale, NJ: Lawrence Erlbaum Associates.

Rumelhart, D. E., & Ortony, A. (1977). The representation of knowledge in memory: In R. C. Anderson, R. J. Spiro, & W. E. Montague (Eds.), *Schooling and the Acquisition of Knowledge.* Hillsdale, NJ: Lawrence Erlbaum Associates.

Rumehlart, D. E., & Siple, P. (1974). Process of recognizing tachistoscopically presented words. *Psychological Review, 81,* 99–118.

Rundus, D. (1971). Analysis of rehearsal processes in free recall. *Journal of Experimental Psychology, 89,* 63–77.

Sacerdoti, E. D. (1977). A structure for plans and behavior. New York: Elsevier North-Holland.

Safren, M. A. (1962). Associations, set, and the solution of word problems. *Journal of Experimental Psychology, 64,* 40–45.

Sampson, G. (1975). *The Form of Language.* London: George Weidenfeld and Nicolson.

Santa, J. L. (1977). Spatial transformations of words and pictures. *Journal of Experimental Psychology: Human Learning and Memory, 3,* 418–427.

Sayers, D. L. (1968). *Five Red Herrings.* New York: Avon.

Schank, R. C. (1975). *Conceptual Information Processing.* Amsterdam: North-Holland.

Schank, R. C. (1982). *Dynamic Memory: A Theory of Reminding and Learning in Computers and People.* New York: Cambridge University Press.

Schank, R. C., & Abelson, R. (1977). *Scripts, Plans, Goals, and Understanding.* Hillsdale, NJ: Lawrence Erlbaum Associates.

Schmidt, R. A. (1982). Motor control and learning. Champaign, IL: Human Kinetics.

Schneider, W., & Fisk, A. D. (1982). Degree of consistent training: Improvements in search performance and automatic process development. *Perception & Psychophysics, 31,* 160–168.

Schneider, W., & Shiffrin, R. M. (1977). Controlled and automatic human information processing: I. Detection, search, and attention. *Psychological Review, 84,* 1–66.

Schoenfield, J. R. (1967). *Mathematical Logic.* Reading, MA: Addison-Wesley.

Schonberg, H. C. (1970). *The Lives of the Great Composers.* New York: W. W. Norton.

Selfridge, O. G. (1955). Pattern recognition and modern computers. *Proceedings of the Western Joint Computer Conference.* New York: Institute of Electrical and Electronics Engineers.

Shaw, R., & Bransford, J. D. (1977). *Perceiving, Acting, and Knowing: Toward an Ecological Psychology.* Hillsdale, NJ: Lawrence Erlbaum Associates.

Shepard, R. N. (1967). Recognition memory for words, sentences, and pictures. *Journal of Verbal Learning and Verbal Behavior, 6,* 156–163.

Shepard, R. N., & Cooper, L. A. (1983). *Mental Images and Their Transformations.* Cambridge, MA: MIT Press.

Shepard, R. N., & Feng, C. (1972). A chronometric study of mental paper folding. *Cognitive Psychology, 3,* 228–243.

Shepard, R. N., & Metzler, J. (1971). Mental rotation of three-dimensional objects. *Science, 171,* 701–703.

Shepard, R. N., & Podgorny, P. (1978). Cognitive processes that resemble perceptual processes. In W. K. Estes (Ed.), *Handbook of Learning and Cognitive Processes.* Hillsdale, NJ: Lawrence Erlbaum Associates.

Shiffrin, R. M. (1975). Short-term store: The basis for a memory system. In F. Restle, R. M. Shiffrin, N. J. Castellan, H. R. Lindman, & D. B. Pisoni (Eds.), *Cognitive Theory,* Vol. 1. Hillsdale, NJ: Lawrence Erlbaum Associates.

Shiffrin, R. M., & Dumais, S. T. (1981). The development of automatism. In J. R. Anderson (Ed.), *Cognitive Skills and Their Acquisition.* Hillsdale, NJ: Lawrence Erlbaum Associates.

Shiffrin, R. M., & Schneider, W. (1977). Controlled and automatic human information processing: II. Perceptual learning, automatic attending, and a general theory. *Psychological Review, 84,* 127–190.

Shneiderman, B. (1976). Exploratory experiments in programmer behavior. *International Journal of Computer and Information Services, 5,* 123–143.

Shneiderman, B. (1980). *Software Psychology.* Cambridge, MA: Winthrop.

Shuford, E. H. (1961). Percentage estimation of proportion as a function of element type, exposure time, and task. *Journal of Experimental Psychology, 61,* 430–436.

Siegler, R. S. (1976). Three aspects of cognitive development. *Cognitive Psychology,* 481–520.

Siegler, R. S. (Ed.) (1978). *Children's Thinking: What Develops?* Hillsdale, NJ: Lawrence Erlbaum Associates.

Siegler, R. S. (1980). Developmental sequences within and between concepts. *Monographs of the Society for Research in Child Development.*

Siegler, R. S. (In press). *Children's Thinking: An Information Processing Approach.* Englewood Cliffs, NJ: Prentice-Hall.

Siegler, R. S., & Shrager, J. (1984). Strategy choices in addition: How do children know what to do? In C. Sophian (Ed.), *Origins of Cognitive Skills.* Hillsdale, NJ: Lawrence Erlbaum Associates.

Silveira, J. (1971). Incubation: The effect of interruption timing and length on problem solution and quality of problem processing. Unpublished doctoral dissertation, University of Oregon.

Simon, H. A. (1974). How big is a chunk? *Science, 183,* 482–488.

Simon, H. A. (1975). The functional equivalence of problem solving skills. *Cognitive Psychology, 7,* 268–288.

Simon, H. A. (1978a). Information-processing theory of human problem solving. In W. K. Estes (Ed.), *Handbook of Learning and Cognitive Processes.* Hillsdale, NJ: Lawrence Erlbaum Associates.

Simon, H. A. (1978b). On forms of mental representation. In C. Wade Savage (Ed.), *Perception and Cognition: Issues in the Foundation of Psychology,* Vol. 9, Minnesota Studies on The Philosophy of Science, Minneapolis: University of Minnesota Press.

Simon, H. A., & Gilmartin, K. (1973). A simulation of memory for chess positions. *Cognitive Psychology, 5,* 29–46.

Simon, H. A., & Lea, G. (1974). Problem solving and rule induction: A unified view. In L. W. Gregg (Ed), *Knowledge and Cognition.* Hillsdale, NJ: Lawrence Erlbaum Associates.

Singley, K., & Anderson, J. R. (In press). The transfer of text-editing skill. *International Journal of Man-Machine Studies.*

Skyrms, B. (1966). *Choice and Chance: An Introduction to Inductive Logic.* Belmont, CA: Dickenson.

Slamecka, N. J., & Graf, P. (1978). The generation effect: Delineation of a phenomenon. *Journal of Experimental Psychology: Human Learning and Memory, 4,* 592–604.

Sleeman, D., & Brown, J. S. (Eds.) (1982). *Intelligent Tutoring Systems.* New York: Academic Press.

Slobin, D. I. (1966). Grammatical transformations and sentence comprehension in childhood and adulthood. *Journal of Verbal Learning and Verbal Behavior, 5,* 219–227.

Slovic, P., & Lichtenstein, S. (1971). Comparison of Bayesian and regression approaches to the study of information processing in judgment. *Organizational Behavior and Human Performance, 6,* 649–744.

Smith, M. (1982). Hypnotic memory enhancement of witnesses: Does it work? Paper presented at the meeting of the Psychonomic Society, Minneapolis.

Smith, S. M., Brown, H. O., Toman, J. E. P., & Goodman, L. S. (1947). The lack of cerebral effects of d-Tubercurarine. *Anesthesiology, 8,* 1–14.

Smith, S. M., Glenberg, A., & Bjork, R. A. (1978). Environmental context and human memory. *Memory & Cognition, 6,* 342–353.

Soloway, E. M. (1980). From problems to programs via plans: The context and structure of knowledge for introductory LISP programming. COINS Technical Report 80-19, University of Massachusetts at Amherst.

Soloway, E., Bonar, J., & Ehrlich, K. (1983). Cognitive strategies and looping constructs: An empirical study. *Communications of the ACM, 26,* 853–860.

Soloway, E., Ehrlich, K., & Gold, E. (1983). Reading a program is like reading a story (well, almost). *Proceedings of the Fifth Annual Conference of the Cognitive Science Society.*

Solso, R. L. (Ed.) (1973). *Contemporary Issues in Cognitive Psychology: The Loyola Symposium*. Washington, DC: Winston.

Solso, R. L. (Ed.). (1975). *Information Processing and Cognition: The Loyola Symposium*. Hillsdale, NJ: Lawrence Erlbaum Associates.

Sophian, C. (1984a). Developing search skills in infancy and early childhood. In C. Sophian (Ed.), *Origins of Cognitive Skills*. Hillsdale, NJ: Lawrence Erlbaum Associates.

Sophian, C. (1984b). *Origins of Cognitive Skills*. Hillsdale, NJ: Lawrence Erlbaum Associates.

Sperling, G. A. (1960). The information available in brief visual presentation. *Psychological Monographs, 74,* Whole No. 498.

Sperling, G. A. (1967). Successive approximations to a model for short-term memory. *Acta Psychologica, 27,* 285–292.

Spiro, R. J. (1977). Constructing a theory of reconstructive memory: The state of the schema approach. In R. C. Anderson, R. J. Spiro, & W. E. Montague (Eds.), *Schooling and the Acquisition of Knowledge*. Hillsdale, NJ: Lawrence Erlbaum Associates.

Spiro, R. J., Bruce, B. C., & Brewer, W. F. (1980). *Theoretical Issues in Reading Comprehension: Perspectives from Cognitive Psychology, Linguistics, and Education*. Hillsdale, NJ: Lawrence Erlbaum Associates.

Spoehr, K. T., & Lehmkuhle, S. W. (1982). *Visual Information Processing*. New York: W. H. Freeman and Company.

Standing, L. (1973). Learning 10,000 pictures. *Quarterly Journal of Experimental Psychology, 25,* 207–222.

Staudenmayer, H. (1975). Understanding conditional reasoning with meaningful propositions. In R. J. Falmagne (Ed.), *Reasoning: Representation and Process in Children and Adults*. Hillsdale, NJ: Lawrence Erlbaum Associates.

Stein, B. S., & Bransford, J. D. (1979). Constraints on effective elaboration: Effects of precision and subject generation. *Journal of Verbal Learning and Verbal Behavior, 18,* 769–777.

Stein, M. I. (1975–1976). *Stimulating Creativity,* Vols. 1 and 2. New York: Academic Press.

Stein, N. L., & Trabasso, T. (1981). What's in a story? Critical issues in comprehension and instruction. In R. Glaser (Ed.), *Advances in the Psychology of Instruction,* Vol. 2. Hillsdale, NJ: Lawrence Erlbaum Associates.

Stelmach, G. E., & Requin, J. (Eds.) (1980). *Tutorials in Motor Behavior*. Amsterdam: North-Holland.

Stemberger, J. P. (1982). Syntactic errors in speech. *Journal of Psycholinguistic Research, 11,* 313–345.

Sternberg, S. (1969). Memory scanning: Mental processes revealed by reaction time experiments. *American Scientist, 57,* 421–457.

Stevens, A., & Coupe, P. (1978). Distortions in judged spatial relations. *Cognitive Psychology, 10,* 422–437.

Sticht, T. G. (1972). Learning by listening. In R. O. Freedle & J. B. Carroll (Eds.), *Language Comprehension and the Acquisition of Knowledge.* Washington, DC: Winston.

Stratton, R. P., & Brown, R. (1972). Improving creative thinking by training in the production and judgment of solutions on a verbal problem. *Journal of Educational Psychology, 63,* 390–397.

Strohner, H., & Nelson, K. E. (1974). The young child's development of sentence comprehension: Influence of event probability, nonverbal context, syntactic form, and strategies. *Child Development, 45,* 567–576.

Strunk, W., Jr., & White, E. B. (1974). *The Elements of Style,* rev. ed. New York: Macmillan.

Studdert-Kennedy, M. (1976). Speech perception. In N. J. Lass (Ed.), *Contemporary Issues in Experimental Phonetics.* Springfield, IL: Charles C Thomas.

Sulin, R. A., & Dooling, D. J. (1974). Intrusion of a thematic idea in retention of prose. *Journal of Experimental Psychology, 103,* 255–262.

Suppes, P. (1957). *Introduction to Logic.* Princeton, NJ: Van Nostrand.

Swinney, D. A. (1979). Lexical access during sentence comprehension: (Re)consideration of context effects. *Journal of Verbal Learning and Verbal Behavior, 18,* 645–659.

Taplin, J. E. (1971). Reasoning with conditional sentences. *Journal of Verbal Learning and Verbal Behavior, 10,* 218–225.

Taplin, J. E., & Staudenmayer, H. (1973). Interpretation of abstract conditional sentences in deductive reasoning. *Journal of Verbal Learning and Verbal Behavior, 12,* 530–542.

Teborg, R. H. (1968). Dissipation of functional fixedness by means of conceptual grouping tasks. Unpublished doctoral dissertation, Michigan State University.

Terrace, H. S., Pettito, L. A., Sanders, R. J., & Bever, T. G. (1979). Can an ape create a sentence? *Science, 206,* 891–902.

Thibadeau, R., Just, M. A., & Carpenter, P. A. (1982). A model of the time course and content of reading. *Cognitive Science, 6,* 157–203.

Thomas, E. L., & Robinson, H. A. (1972). *Improving Reading in Every Class: A Sourcebook for Teachers.* Boston: Allyn & Bacon.

Thompson, R. F. (1967). *Foundations of Physiological Psychology.* New York: Harper.

Thompson, R. F. (1972). *Physiological Psychology: Readings from Scientific American.* New York: W. H. Freeman and Company.

Thompson, R. F. (1976). *Progress in Psychobiology. Readings from Scientific American.* New York: W. H. Freeman and Company.

Thomson, D. M. (1972). Context effects on recognition memory. *Journal of Verbal Learning and Verbal Behavior, 11,* 497–511.

Thorndike, R. L. (1973). *Reading Comprehension: Education in Fifteen Countries.* New York: Wiley.

Thorndyke, P. W. (1977). Cognitive structures in comprehension and memory in narrative discourse. *Cognitive Psychology, 9,* 77–110.

Thorndyke, P. W., & Stasz, C. (1980). Individual differences in procedures for knowledge acquisition from maps. *Cognitive Psychology, 12,* 137–175.

Tolman, E. C. (1932). *Purposive Behavior in Animals and Men.* New York: Appleton-Century-Crofts.

Trabasso, T. R., & Bower, G. H. (1968). *Attention in Learning.* New York: Wiley.

Trabasso, T. R., & Riley, C. A. (1975). The construction and use of representations involving linear order. In R. L. Solso (Ed.), *Information Processing and Cognition.* Hillsdale, NJ: Lawrence Erlbaum Associates.

Trabasso, T., Rollins, H., & Shaughnessy, E. (1971). Storage and verification stages in processing concepts. *Cognitive Psychology, 2,* 239–289.

Treisman, A. M., (1960). Verbal cues, language, and meaning in selective attention. *Quarterly Journal of Experimental Psychology, 12,* 242–248.

Treisman, A. M., & Gelade, G. (1980). A feature-integration theory of attention. *Cognitive Psychology, 12,* 97–136.

Tulving, E. (1983). *Elements of Episodic Memory.* London: Oxford University Press.

Tulving, E., Mandler, G., & Baumal, R. (1964). Interaction of two sources of information in tachistoscopic word recognition. *Canadian Journal of Psychology, 18,* 62–71.

Tulving, E., & Thomson, D. M. (1973). Encoding specificity and retrieval processes in episodic memory. *Psychological Review, 80,* 352–373.

Turvey, M. T., & Shaw, R. E. (1977). Memory (or knowing) as a matter of specification not representation: Notes toward a different class of machines. Paper presented at the conference on Levels of Processing, Rockport, Massachusetts.

Tversky, A., & Kahneman, D. (1974). Judgments under uncertainty: Heuristics and biases. *Science, 185,* 1124–1131.

Tyler, R., & Marslen-Wilson, W. (1977). The on-line effects of semantic context on syntactic processing. *Journal of Verbal Learning and Verbal Behavior, 16,* 683–692.

Ultan, R. (1969). Some general characteristics of interrogative systems. *Working Papers in Language Universals* (Stanford University), *1,* 41–63.

Underwood, G. (1974). Moray vs. the rest: The effect of extended shadowing practice. *Quarterly Journal of Experimental Psychology, 26,* 368–372.

Underwood, B. J. (1983). *Attributes of Memory.* Glenview, IL: Scott, Foresman.

van Dijk, T. A. (1977). Semantic macro-structures and knowledge frames in discourse comprehension. In M. A. Just & P. A. Carpenter (Eds.), *Cognitive Processes in Comprehension.* Hillsdale, NJ: Lawrence Erlbaum Associates.

van Dijk, T. A., & Kintsch, W. (1976). Cognitive psychology and discourse. In W. U. Dressler (Ed.). *Trends in Text Linguistics.* Berlin & New York: DeGruyter.

Van Lehn, K., & Brown, J. S. (1981). Planning nets: A representation for formalizing analogies and semantic models of procedural skills. In R. E. Snow, P. Federico, & W. E. Montague (Eds.), *Aptitude, Learning, and Instruction,* Vol. 2. Hillsdale, NJ: Lawrence Erlbaum Associates.

Vinacke, W. E. (1974). *The Psychology of Thinking.* New York: McGraw-Hill.

von Frisch, K. (1967). *The Dance Language and Orientation of Bees* (translated by C. E. Chadwick). Cambridge, MA: Belknap Press.

Wanner, H. E. (1968). On remembering, forgetting, and understanding sentences. A study of the deep structure hypothesis. Unpublished doctoral dissertation, Harvard University.

Warren, R. M. (1970). Perceptual restorations of missing speech sounds. *Science, 167,* 392–393.

Warren, R. M., & Warren, R. P. (1970). Auditory illusions and confusions. *Scientific American, 223,* 30–36.

Wason, P. C. (1960). On the failure to eliminate hypotheses in a conceptual task. *Quarterly Journal of Experimental Psychology, 12,* 129–140.

Wason, P. C. (1968). On the failure to eliminate hypotheses in a conceptual task: A second look. In P. C. Wason & P. N. Johnson-Laird (Eds.), *Thinking and Reasoning.* Middlesex, England: Penguin Books.

Wason, P. C. (1978). Specific thoughts on the writing process. Presented at the Cognitive Processes in Writing—Interdisciplinary Symposium on Cognition, Carnegie-Mellon University.

Wason, P. C., & Johnson-Laird, P. N. (1972). *Psychology of Reasoning: Structure and Content.* Cambridge, MA: Harvard University Press.

Watkins, M. J., & Tulving, E. (1975). Episodic memory: When recognition fails. *Journal of Experimental Psychology: General, 104,* 5–29.

Watson, J. (1930). *Behaviorism.* New York: Norton.

Watt, W. C. (1970). On two hypotheses concerning psycholinguistics. In J. R. Hayes (Ed.), *Cognition and the Development of Language.* New York: Wiley.

Weisberg, R. W. (1969). Sentence processing assessed through intrasentence word associations. *Journal of Experimental Psychology, 82,* 332–338.

Welford, A. T. (1968). *Fundamentals of Skill.* London: Methuen.

Wexler, K., & Culicover, P. (1980). *Formal Principles of Language Acquisition.* Cambridge, MA: MIT Press.

Wheeler, D. D. (1970). Processes in word recognition. *Cognitive Psychology, 1,* 59–85.

Whorf, B. L. (1956). *Language, Thought, and Reality.* Cambridge, MA: MIT Press.

Wickelgren, W. A. (1973). The long and the short of memory. *Psychological Bulletin, 80,* 425–438.

Wickelgren, W. A. (1974a). Single-trace fragility theory of memory dynamics. *Memory & Cognition, 2,* 775–780.

Wickelgren, W. A. (1974b). *How to Solve Problems.* New York: W. H. Freeman and Company.

Wickelgren, W. A. (1976). Memory storage dynamics. In W. K. Estes (Ed.), *Handbook of Learning and Cognitive Processes,* Vol. 4. Hillsdale, NJ: Lawrence Erlbaum Associates.

Wickelgren, W. A. (1979). *Cognitive Psychology.* Englewood Cliffs, NJ: Prentice-Hall.

Wickelgren, W. A. (1967). Rehearsal grouping and hierarchical organization of serial position cues in immediate memory. *Quarterly Journal of Experimental Psychology, 19,* 97–102.

Wickelgren, W. A. (1975). Alcoholic intoxication and memory storage dynamics. *Memory & Cognition, 3,* 385–389.

Winograd, T. (1972). Understanding language. *Cognitive Psychology, 3,* 1–191.

Winston, P. H. (Ed.). (1975). *The Psychology of Computer Vision.* New York: McGraw-Hill.

Winston, P. H. (1977). *Artificial Intelligence.* Reading, MA: Addison-Wesley.

Winston, P. H., & Brown, R. H. (Eds.) (1980). *Artificial Intelligence: An MIT Perspective,* Vol. 2. Cambridge, MA: MIT Press.

Wiseman, S., & Neisser, U. (1974). Perceptual organization as a determinant of visual recognition memory. *American Journal of Psychology, 87,* 675–681.

Wolford, G. (1971). Function of distinct associations for paired-associate performance. *Psychological Review, 73,* 303–313.

Woocher, F. D., Glass, A. L., & Holyoak, K. J. (1978). Positional discriminability in linear orderings. *Memory & Cognition, 6,* 165–175.

Woods, W. A. (1973). Progress in natural language and understanding: An application to lunar geology. *AFIPS Proceedings,* 1973 National Computer Conference and Exposition.

Woodword, F. B. (1968). *Scientific Writing for Graduate Students.* New York: The Rockefeller Press.

Woodworth, R. S., & Sells, S. B. (1935). An atmospheric effect in formal syllogistic reasoning. *Journal of Experimental Psychology, 18,* 451–460.

Yates, F. A. (1966). *The Art of Memory.* Chicago: University of Chicago Press.

Young, R., & O'Shea, T. (1981). Errors in children's subtraction. *Cognitive Science, 5,* 153–177.

Yuille, J. C. (1983). *Imagery, Memory, and Cognition: Essays in Honor of Allan Paivio.* Hillsdale, NJ: Lawrence Erlbaum Associates.

Name Index

Subject Index